SEA LANES IN WARTIME

SEA LANES IN WARTIME

The American Experience

1775-1945

by

ROBERT GREENHALGH ALBION
and JENNIE BARNES POPE

SECOND EDITION, ENLARGED

Archon Books, 1968

TO

PORTLAND HARBOR

OUR HOME PORT—STURDY VETERAN
OF ALL THESE WARS

Contents

Foreword to the Second Edition

THIS BOOK WAS WRITTEN IN MID-1942 WITH THE NATION'S major sea lanes in grave jeopardy from enemy attacks. We pushed the story right up to the time of going to press that autumn, some eight months before the Americans and their Allies finally gained the upper hand. To be sure, these World War II developments, because of security and other reasons, had to be based upon less solid historical foundations than the accounts of the earlier wars.

Now, a quarter century later, the time seems to have come to bring out a reissue. In addition to general use, the book is being sought for maritime history courses. It has seemed appropriate to take advantage of the opportunity to carry the account through to the close of World War II in 1945 with an extra chapter, "Towards Victory on the Sea Lanes." The earlier chapters are reproduced in their original form, but the bibliography has been updated.

R. G. A.

South Portland, Maine   J. B. P.

Foreword

THREE A DAY IN LATE SPRING, TWO A DAY IN EARLY SUMMER, AND one a day as autumn approached, has been the record of ships shattered by torpedo or gunfire in our waters in 1942. For months, ship after ship has been sinking into the Western Atlantic, from the world of cold fogs off Canada to the old pirate haunts of the Caribbean and points south. Some, for a while, were even going down within sight of our very beaches. Distant seas, in the meantime, have been yielding a still further toll. Three new vessels a day are at last being launched by shipyards from Portland around to another Portland and beyond. So have gone the first months of that grim race in our second World War, with the tonnage gained thus far barely equal to the tonnage lost.

Such a balance is not enough. If our war effort is to count for victory, the rate must speedily be many more new ships a day and far fewer lost. Freighters cannot win a war, but their lack perhaps can lose one. "We must regard this struggle at sea," so Churchill has said, "as the foundation of all the efforts of the United Nations. If we lose that, all else is denied us."

The seas which have long served as protective moats to keep Britain and America secure from armed invasion have lost that power in this age of mighty aircraft. And those same seas on their own part impose grave shipping demands when those nations try to meet the enemy overseas on his own ground. The sea lanes to be traveled are not simply the three thousand miles of the normal Atlantic crossing as in the last war. Instead, they stretch in ship-consuming distances through dreary Arctic wastes, across the wide Pacific to lands down under, or halfway round the world to the cradles of civilization. The sinews of war in this mechanized age bulk larger than ever before in the far too

9

scanty holds of ships. Even if the builders keep pace with the submarines, the United Nations are desperately hard-pressed to move men and munitions beyond the seas, while their strategists are sadly handicapped as they must perforce cut their plans to fit the meager tonnage. And as yet cargo planes are not available in sufficient numbers to bring relief.

Dark as the picture has been, one comforting fact remains as this book goes to press: our nation has been through black days before on the sea lanes and has won through them to victory. In war after war, from its very earliest days, the United States has had to fight its way by sea. Things could not have looked much worse than they did after Bunker Hill, when Washington found he had almost no gunpowder. Plenty was to be had in France or Holland; and although the mighty Royal Navy stood between, it was brought across the sea in ample quantity. Forty years later, the situation in our coastal waters was far worse than it is today. British warships blockaded our ports so closely that we were almost completely cut off from access to the sea. Pirates have threatened butchery or slavery; Confederate raiders have sallied into our very harbors and have made bonfires of our square-riggers from Sandy Hook to the Straits of Sunda; U-boats have shown their deadly effectiveness off our coasts a quarter of a century ago, as well as today. All those past perils placed our sea lanes in jeopardy for months on end; yet every time our seafaring nation fought its way through to make true its pledge of freedom of the seas to American vessels.

The origin of this volume goes back to the finding of a little manuscript notebook in which a New York merchant jotted down the insurance rates paid on voyages during the Revolution. That aroused curiosity in the subject and suggested a study of similar war-risk fluctuations in other conflicts as a barometer of sea power. Our particular gratitude goes to the publishers for recommending the wider scope of this volume. In the collaboration, all the research and much of the original draft was the work of the first author.

The book falls into two parts, one dealing with the "old wars" between 1775 and 1865, and the other with the two World Wars of this century. Each section starts with a general description of shipping conditions. The first part then proceeds chronologically from the Revolution through the Civil War. In the second part, however, it has seemed preferable to use a topical arrangement instead, in order to compare more clearly the fairly similar situations in each war. Consequently, the final chapters will treat in succession America's offerings of strategic cargoes, shipping conditions on the North Atlantic, conditions on the more distant sea lanes, and, finally, the efforts to secure adequate tonnage. This account has been carried into the summer of 1942. With the concentration upon merchantmen and cargoes, there has been no room to follow the intricacies of naval strategy or the fine points of neutrality and international relations.

It is a novel and nerve-racking experience to leave a story in mid-flight and to know that as the galleys come from the press the story will continue to be unfolded in the daily newspapers. Obviously the full story of present happenings is not yet available, nor have we been free to relate at this time much that has come to our notice, although some of it would add materially to the story. Remembering how suddenly the seemingly well-controlled situation on the seas went bad in two brief months last winter, we know that the picture may change again in the few weeks before this book is launched. Yet whatever happens, the American experience of the past on our dangerous sea lanes will throw light on the darkened situation brought about through current happenings.

So many have been helpful in the preparation of this work that only a few can be mentioned here, though our gratitude goes out to all. The staffs of Princeton University Library, Harvard College Library, the National Archives, New York Public Library, New York Historical Society, Massachusetts Historical Society, and the Historical Society of Pennsylvania have all given generous assistance. The other members of Dr. Edward Mead Earle's Military Studies Group of the Institute of Advanced Study and Princeton University spent two sessions discussing the projected outline of the book, offering helpful suggestions; Professor Harold Sprout gave additional advice; as did another Princeton colleague, Dr. Douglas Adair. Several Princeton seniors unearthed valuable material in the preparation of their theses supervised in this field; they are mentioned specifically in the bibliography. Mr. Mark O'Dea of the Maritime Commission furnished his frequent press releases and answered numerous questions, as did the Department of Commerce. Assistance also came from Hon. James C. Oliver, Mr. Percy Craig, Mr. Hendon Chubb, Mr. Percy Chubb, Mrs. Norton Q. Pope, Mr. George C. Randall, and Mr. Clifford N. Carver.

R. G. A.

Princeton, N. J.   J. B. P.
South Portland, Me.

Part I

THE OLD WARS

Chapter I

The Old Order

WARTIME SHIPPING ADVENTURES ARE NO NOVELTY TO THE UNITED States. Keeping the sea lanes open has always been one of the main concerns of American foreign policy. One might think from the daily grist of news about convoys, sinkings, and seizures that American vessels were venturing upon new and untried courses. Whenever war has struck the main shipping lanes, however, the United States has been on the scene sooner or later.

Threats to our sea-borne commerce, whether from submarine and airplane in this century or from privateer and frigate in the days of sail, have led us into war more often than any other single cause. The United States has had to protect its shipping in five major wars, and against pirates as well. Three times its role has been that of the outraged neutral demanding freedom of the seas for its lucrative trade; but on one occasion it was the belligerent blockader scoffing at that very same freedom it has so often sought to uphold. From colonial times, when the protection of the British Navy made the problem less acute for Americans, to the present, when our air force and our navy are dominant factors in world politics, this vital issue has affected our actions; and it will probably continue to do so as long as we have cargoes to send overseas.

From the very first days of the infant colonies, America was virtually driven to the seas in order to maintain contact with Europe. Normal commerce caused its merchant marine to grow and thrive in peacetime. The recurring strains of war made it doubly important, not only from trade considerations, but also because of the need of an eastbound, and once of a westbound, supply of vital war materials.

To a large extent because of its maritime interests, the United

States was unable to remain neutral throughout three great European conflicts. Its neutrality lasted almost twenty years during the French Revolutionary and Napoleonic contests; but in the first World War, only thirty-two months; and in the second, twenty-seven months. The American Revolution ran an opposite course. France and other European nations, after a period of neutral trading, were drawn into an American war. During the Civil War, Europe remained technically neutral, but our commerce suffered from England's unneutral conduct. Neither the Mexican nor the Spanish-American Wars, nor the relatively brief conflicts of the European powers between 1815 and 1914 had any particular effect upon our shipping; of more concern were several crops of pirate attacks.

Our attitude toward "freedom of the seas" has shifted along with the changing conditions in the different wars, as we shall see. In the earlier years, our desire was to make the most of neutral profits by trading with both sides; and, with both belligerents seizing our ships, we argued loudly that free ships made free goods and that neutral vessels should be immune from capture. During the Civil War, when we were playing England's old game of seizure and blockade, "freedom of the seas" was conspicuously absent from our state papers. Its scope was more or less one-sided in the World Wars, when our protests to England were in a different vein from the vigor and bluntness of those sent to Germany. One cynic has gone so far as to say that "freedom of the seas" merely implies the right of Americans to make money under any war conditions.

Our interest and our wartime worries have centered in outgoing rather than incoming cargoes. Except in the Revolution, American cargoes have been of greater importance, from the strategic standpoint, to Europe than its cargoes have been to us. This has become even more true in the twentieth century—when our gigantic American industry has produced the military supplies vitally needed overseas—than it was in the simpler and more self-sufficient days. In the two World Wars, our munitions and also our food supplies were indispensable to Britain and its

allies. At times between 1793 and 1813, our grain was important
to France and to England also, but not in the same degree. In
1812 and in the Civil War, the American industrial development
was sufficient to sustain military operations without munitions
from overseas.

With exports the major interest, the emphasis changed with
the years from centering upon the vessels that transported the
cargoes to the cargoes themselves, even when those cargoes were
carried in foreign ships. In the earlier period, however, the neutral status of the merchant shipping was of more importance both
to the United States and the current belligerents than were their
occasional cargoes of American produce. Shipowning was one of
the chief forms of early American capital investment, and Ameri-
ican vessels as neutrals were at a premium for trading where
belligerents dared not send their own. A century of economic
development in America made shipowning relatively far less important, for capital had shifted its attention from ships to factories. By 1914, our merchant marine was meager and our industry tremendous. Consequently, our concern was with the
cargoes of manufactures going overseas, whatever the flag that
might fly over the vessels that carried them.

The merchant marine has been violently affected by the various major wars. It was depressed by the Revolution and flourished vigorously in the years of neutral trading that followed.
To be sure, its later heyday around 1850 was not a product of
war, unless one wants to argue that the spoils of the Mexican
War made possible the clipper trade to California. The psychological effects of the Confederate raiding accelerated a long decline. World War I found us with almost no ocean shipping at
all and left us with a huge merchant fleet, not all of which was
of profitable use. World War II called for all that reserve, but
in its turn stimulated an enormous building program, which,
along with developments overseas, promised good postwar opportunities.

In the early years, in sharp contrast to the present, warships as
well as merchantmen remained indefinitely in style. Had a sea-

going Rip van Winkle fallen asleep in 1707 during Queen Anne's War and awakened a century later in the midst of the Napoleonic struggle, he would still have been in perfectly familiar surroundings, and might have gone efficiently about his work. The intervening years had seen little change either in the warships, in the merchantmen they chased or guarded, or in general wartime shipping practices. A description of cargoes, convoys, and condemnations, or of the vessels themselves, fits any of America's early troubles at sea. A wooden vessel was not likely to be outmoded. Nelson's flagship at Trafalgar was forty years old; the *Royal William* in the American Revolution was sixty-one. It was the same in the merchant marine, where vessels sometimes carried on for similar long periods if they escaped the ravages of dry rot or wracking by the seas. Not only was there little change from decade to decade, but by and large shipyards in the different countries turned out fairly similar products. A region might develop a few distinctive types, such as the American schooner, but, generally, captured warships or merchantmen were easily absorbed into a fleet with a minimum of adjustment.

As those familiar with shipping already know, the cargo carriers of that day fell into four main categories. These ranged in size from ships down through brigs and schooners to the small sloops. Technically, the distinction was one of rig, not size. The ship had three masts; the brig and (at that time) the schooner, two; and the sloop, one. The ships and brigs were square-rigged, with several sails at right angles on each mast; a feature which made a ship in full sail beautiful and unforgettable. The schooners and sloops were distinguished by the fore-and-aft rig, with a single large sail in place of the several smaller ones. At times they might carry, too, a single square topsail on the foremast. Various minor types do not concern us here—such as snows, hermaphrodite or half brigs, ketches, cutters, galliots, and the rest.

The full-rigged ship was the aristocrat of the merchant marine. Like most vessels of that time, her oaken hull was designed for cargo capacity in preference to speed. Her beam was often fully a third of her length. Her hull bulged outward at many points, in contrast to the concave streamlining of the later clippers. With this stocky build, her apple-cheeked bows tended to butt, rather than to cleave, the waves. But this very breadth gave her a hold, ample enough for a maximum load of bales, barrels, or boxes. Except in wartime, the average shipowner of the day preferred a vessel roomy enough to carry three hundred tons in three weeks to one of similar length and cost, but with the speed, to make the same voyage in two weeks, developed at the expense of some hundred tons of capacity. Full-rigged ships were generally employed on the long hauls, such as to England, western Europe, and the Orient; for the shorter runs, smaller vessels were more profitable.

The average ship of the late eighteenth century was nearly a hundred feet in length and thirty feet or so in beam, with a hold fifteen or twenty feet deep. She measured about 250 tons, indicating by the crude formula of that time a capacity of about 25,000 cubic feet, or the equivalent of some eight modern railway box cars. Occasional ships in the China trade ran to four hundred tons or more, but not until after 1850 were many ships much larger. By 1851, the *Flying Cloud* reached 1,782 tons, and the largest of the clippers was almost double that size. A few attempts to build bigger ships in the early days proved generally unprofitable; a ship of 250 tons was about what the traffic demanded. Such a vessel cost, when new, $15,000 to $20,000, and could normally be depended upon for some twenty years of service. The square-rigger required a considerable number in the crew to go aloft on the yards to loosen or shorten sail. Usually some twenty men, besides the captain and two mates, made up an average crew.

The two-masted, square-rigged brig was simply a smaller edition of the ship with a few special features. Her tonnage and her crew were usually about half as large. The Americans used brigs largely in the Baltic and Mediterranean, where cargoes were not apt to be big enough to fill a ship's hold. Brigs were the right size, too, for part of the Caribbean voyages and for the longer coasting ones.

The schooner was specially developed in America. Economically, its main advantage lay in its small crew. Fewer men were needed than on a brig of the same size, since the big sails could be hoisted or lowered from the deck without the necessity of men going aloft. From the standpoint of navigation, too, this fore-and-aft rig made a vessel easier to maneuver quickly and was better for clawing off a lee shore on a coastal run. Schooners varied considerably in size; probably ninety to a hundred tons would be a fair average. They were most important on the Caribbean routes and in much of the coasting trade.

Although many schooners were capacious and tubby in the current style, most of the fastest vessels of those days belonged to this class. Baltimore played a distinctive role in the development of these speedier vessels. At those all too frequent times when Yankee commerce had to operate under uncertain conditions, the sacrifice of a little cargo space in the interests of speed was deemed desirable. It was obviously more profitable to sneak eighty tons of cargo past an enemy blockade than to risk the loss of a hundred tons in a slower vessel. Their speed also made schooners valuable for conversion into privateers, as well as for smuggling or slaving. In fact, when a yard turned out a long, low, black schooner with raking masts, law-abiding citizens were wont to murmur suspiciously that she was intended for no honest purpose.

The sloop, with its single mast, varied in design according to its use. If intended for shallow waters, where deep square-riggers could not clear, it would be likely to have a centerboard. For deep-sea purposes an adequate keel would be built into it. Two or three men, even only one or two, could handle a sloop in local waters; for longer coasting voyages or a trip to the West Indies, a few more might be required. One sloop, the 84-ton *Experiment,* actually went from New York around the Cape of Good Hope to Canton in 1784 and returned safely with a valuable cargo. Normally the single-stickers averaged perhaps about

fifty tons and confined themselves to the short hauls and hum-
bler ladings of American commerce.

Warships likewise fell into several well-defined classifications.
While foreign merchantmen concern us little in this study of
American merchantmen, the reverse is true of naval craft. The
enemy warships were the ones that affected our shipping in more
ways than one. The types, however, were fairly well standardized
among the various nations. Functionally the warships of oak,
pine, and canvas fell into the same three main categories which
still divide their modern counterparts of steel hulls and mechani-
cal propulsion. Capital ships represent maximum strength, or did
at least before 1941, and ordinarily operate in fleets or squadrons;
cruisers have versatile adaptability to numerous useful purposes;
and the "hit-and-run" commerce raiders prey on weaker vessels
and try to avoid stronger adversaries.

The capital ship of the old days was the huge ship of the line
or line-of-battle ship, carrying 64 to 120 guns on the two or three
fighting decks of her massive hull. A navy might have a few
lofty, cumbersome, three-decked first- or second-rates, with ninety
guns or more, to serve as flagships, but the favorite type was the
two-decked third-rate seventy-four. She was about the largest
ship which could sail well and fight well under all conditions.
Such a vessel measured somewhat more than two thousand tons,
which was about as much as eight merchant ships, and carried
a crew of six hundred men crowded between her decks. A full-
dress naval battle of the eighteenth century was generally fought
according to the static tactics of the day. The rival fleets approached, with the vessels strung out in a line-ahead formation,
one after the other. Eventually, they would form into parallel
lines, each ship blasting away at a partner from the enemy line.
The naval guns mounted on wooden carriages were seldom effective at more than half a mile. At times the rivals lay almost
muzzle to muzzle, and boarding parties would swarm over the
enemy decks. American merchantmen were rarely directly concerned with ships of the line except as their battles or blockades
affected general conditions on the seas; the Yankee trader had a

much closer acquaintance with the smaller, faster cruisers which operated singly. The United States Navy did not have a single ship of the line in commission before 1815.

Cruisers, then and now, perform many duties. On the defensive side, they can convoy their own merchant shipping, or patrol the chief sea lanes to drive off enemy raiders. On the offensive, they can be effective raiders on their own, or they can control enemy and neutral shipping, or they can blockade ports. Tactically, their relative speed made them useful as the "eyes of the fleet" and as carriers of dispatches, in the days of slow communications and no airplanes. They can show the flag on distant stations, transport treasure, and, in fact, can do almost anything except stand up under the guns of capital ships and, in present warfare, under air attack without air support. But as far as the heavy "battle wagons" are concerned, cruisers usually have speed enough to escape unwelcome contact with them.

Frigates, in the sailing ship era, were counterparts of the modern heavy cruiser. The standard types carried from twenty-eight to thirty-eight guns on a single gun deck. The *Constitution* and her two companions with their forty-four guns were super-cruisers, stronger than any frigates in the British or other European navies. Next to the frigate in size came the sloop of war, which might be called a light cruiser. She had nothing but the name in common with the humble one-masted sloop of the merchant marine, for like the ship of the line and the frigate, she was a square-rigged ship of considerable size. Somewhat smaller, with two masts instead of three, was the gun brig, which had some of the functions of the modern destroyer, though that comparison cannot be pushed too close. All of these cruiser types were far more heavily manned than merchantmen, since crews had, in addition to the usual standing of watch and going aloft, the duties of gunners, powder passers, marines, and so on. Two hundred was perhaps the average crew.

Whereas the functions of the old regular naval cruisers have come on down to the present, privateering has been dead for about a century. Tactically, the privateer had something in common with the modern submarine and auxiliary cruiser in that she made a habit of picking weaker victims and tried to avoid serious combat. Structurally, the privateer did not have a distinct type. A privateer might be almost anything from a small open boat to a converted schooner, brig, or ship of the merchant marine; it might be a powerful vessel built for the purpose and comparable in gun power and personnel with regular naval cruisers. The significant feature of the privateer was her status. Unlike the naval vessel, she was privately owned, manned, and operated. On the other hand, she was not a pirate; that technical difference lay in her letters of marque and reprisal from the government, which gave her its official blessing to prey upon enemy commerce.

The privateer was generally the property of a small group of merchants or shipowners. Sometimes, to be sure, there was but a single owner, and at others the shares were widely distributed. By the usual procedure, a merchantman would be taken over; the necessary guns, munitions, and stores purchased; officers appointed; and advertisements placed for a crew to "cruize against the enemy." The crew were given food but no wages; they, like the owners, were in the venture for the prize money from the vessels which they hoped to seize. A certain specified proportion of this went to the owners as a return on their capital investment, while the remainder was divided among the officers and crew according to a prearranged schedule.

From the government's standpoint, the privateer was a helpful supplement to the cruisers in the work of damaging enemy commerce, including that part of it carried under neutral flags. On the defensive front, however, the privateer was of much less assistance in the protection of a nation's own trade, except for an occasional recapture of a merchantman from the enemy prize crew. They were not dependable at all for convoy duty and were usually under orders from their owners to avoid fighting enemy warships. Such activity was both risky and far less profitable than chasing fat merchantmen—and profits were the *raison d'être* of privateers. If, for instance, a naval gun brig cruising in the Windward Passage sighted an enemy warship of about equal strength, the naval commander would feel in duty bound to attack her and remove that threat to merchantmen. No such considerations would worry the privateer captain. Gold, not glory, being his primary interest, he would generally withdraw as quickly and prudently as possible. Another point against the privateers was the embarrassment caused to their government by their frequent improper conduct in the pursuit of rich prizes.

Altogether, the privateers were unpopular with both the navy and the merchant marine. The gambling instinct lured seamen to privateering from both. Wages aboard a freighter seemed very prosaic in contrast to the chances of rich seizures. The navy, too, seemed less attractive than the shorter enlistments, the more generous sharing of prize money, and the less chance of getting hurt aboard a privateer. The occasional tremendous profits of a few lucky privateers blinded men's eyes to the many that returned empty-handed. Owners and crew were ready to take a chance for the grand prize.

The War of 1812 was the final climax of privateering. It soon degenerated into piracy in the wars of Latin-American independence. Europe banned it in 1856, but a few Confederate vessels, licensed in the Civil War were the last "private men of war." Most honest merchants and mariners heaved a deep sigh of relief. From the nature of the system, a study of our merchant marine is little concerned with American privateers, but those that flew the British ensign were a different matter. Whether they hailed from Bristol, Liverpool, Tory New York, or the Maritime Provinces, they made themselves all too familiar to the Yankee skippers—and so, too, did those of French and Spanish origin.

Whereas the American privateers lie outside the story, our so-called "letters of marque" are an integral part of it. They were armed merchantmen, licensed by the government to pick up prizes only as by-products of normal trading voyages. These merchantmen were equipped for protection against enemy raiders, with fairly strong armament and with perhaps a few extra men in the crew. If in the course of a voyage such a vessel happened to capture a small raider or a weaker enemy merchant ship, her letter of marque (and reprisal) entitled her to the prize money. She would not, however, be supposed to search for prizes or go out of her way for them, as trade was her main objective. Hundreds of American merchantmen were so armed and licensed during the Revolution, the undeclared war with France, and the War of 1812. The arrival of such a vessel would be reported in the marine news as "Letter of Marque *Charming Polly*, Brown, 42 days from Lisbon, with salt & c."—in contrast to "Privateer *Harpy*, Smith, from a cruize." The letter of marque occupied an intermediate position between the ordinary armed merchantman and the auxiliary cruiser of the present day.

Those three—merchantmen, warships, and privateers—were the chief factors in the struggle for sea power in the days of sail. The relative strength of the belligerents, especially in the matter of capital ships, decided the nature of a particular conflict. Where Britain was involved, enemy traders were extremely vulnerable because of the preponderance of the Royal Navy. Ordinarily, if European, they scarcely dared venture on the seas and had to depend upon neutrals for most of their overseas trade. On the few occasions when the enemy fleets were fairly equal to the Royal Navy, it was a different story, because under those circumstances the merchant shipping of both sides continued on the high seas with an even chance of safety. At all times, the Americans, being more distantly located from the centers of British strength, were ready to take a chance with their shipping. With their superiority in capital ships, the British usually had little to fear from the danger of enemy fleets at large. They consequently were free to convoy their own merchantmen with moderate forces, and to use their cruisers, aided by privateers, to blockade enemy ports, patrol the sea lanes, and regulate neutral traffic. Weaker powers were forced for their offensive role, such as it was, to the so-called *guerre de course* or cruiser warfare. By this, their raiders would prey upon British commerce and were usually able to inflict considerable damage. Modern submarine and plane tactics against merchant shipping are of the same nature. The hope of the *guerre de course* has ever been to weary the enemy merchants and shipping interests with the increased insurance rates, losses, and consequent high prices; and eventually to induce them to bring pressure for peace upon their government. This objective has, however, never been fully attained.

The most effective protection against such raiders was the time-honored convoy system, by which one or more warships escort a large assemblage of, merchantmen either for the whole voyage or at least through the danger zones. This was in common use by the British and French until 1815 and was revived again in 1917 and in 1939. Convoying gave reasonable security, but at the expense of speed. In recent times, the United States frequently has had to guard its commerce against the *guerre de course;* but before 1815, it was waging such a war itself. In that day, we had few, if any, warships to spare for convoy service, and Yankee merchantmen usually had to trust to their own speed, guns, and luck.

Our commerce was more affected by the British methods of exercising control over hostile or neutral shipping, either through the close blockade of ports, patrolling of congested areas, or general cruising. The British purpose, of course, was to spread a net so fine that it could exercise restrictions over a considerable part of the world's shipping—and their supply of cruisers and privateers was ample for the work.

At first glance, the seas seem too tremendous to make this a possible task. Shipping, however, tended to follow certain well-defined sea lanes, dictated by consideration of the cargoes to be found at each end. Only the far-flung whaling fleets usually prowled over the vast extent of the oceans, as fancy took them. America at the outset concentrated its energies upon the transatlantic and the Caribbean routes.

From the days of the first settlements down to the present, the stormy three thousand mile run across the Atlantic to England has been the most important American route. It passed through the thick fogs on the Grand Banks south of Newfoundland, and then followed the warm current of the Gulf Stream eastward. The British west coast might be approached around the northern end of Ireland, but even for that destination most vessels aimed for the southern Irish coast. Strange as it sounds, sailing vessels bound from England to America traveled nearly five hundred miles farther than those going from America to England. The extra distance came from constant beating against the prevailing westerly winds. The sailors described the eastward passage as going downhill all the way, and the westbound trip as all uphill. For that reason, sailing vessels could frequently accomplish the eastbound trip in three or four weeks, whereas their westbound passages might vary anywhere from five to twelve weeks. It was regarded as a miracle of swift sailing during the Revolution when General Howe's private secretary went to England and back in just three months. Even today, the speed records established by the *Queen Mary* in 1938 show a difference of sixty-six minutes in favor of the eastbound crossings; and planes find the eastbound course beset by fewer difficulties than the westbound. The traffic of this "main line" has always loomed large in American commerce because of the value of the cargoes carried in the teeth of the westerlies. These came mainly from England at first, but as time went on, the Continental trade developed.

However valuable transatlantic cargoes might be, a much greater number of American vessels were engaged in the West Indian trade in the earlier days. It was a much shorter run. Havana, for instance, one of the nearest of the Caribbean ports, is 1,456 miles from Portland, 1,227 from New York, and only 606 from Savannah. That short route, coupled with the nature of the trade, made it available for little vessels barely averaging a third the size of those trading with England. Vessels from the northern ports generally followed the coast down to New Jersey and then headed out, to clear the treacherous Carolina sands off stormy Hatteras. Then they set their course for the particular passage where they desired to pierce the great semicircle of the Antilles in order to get to their destination.

Until after 1815, these two main sea lanes held most of America's shipping activity. Occasional valuable cargoes took the long route around the Cape of Good Hope to the Far East, and a few small vessels visited Africa—not always for honest purposes. Only gradually did Yankee vessels push down to Brazil, the Argentine, and around Cape Horn to the Pacific, while the route across that ocean developed still more slowly. Anyone bent on harassing American commerce in those early days, however, would have spent his time in the Caribbean or along the coast.

And the British were fully aware of this. They knew well every focal point where patrolling would pay the highest dividends. Luckily for the Yankees, geography often plays favorites. The northern coast was dotted with good harbors of refuge every few miles; even from New York southward where ports were fewer and farther between, our coast suffered from few bottlenecks—such as the narrow entrances to the Baltic or the Mediterranean, where a single squadron might stop all shipping from entering or leaving. In 1814, to be sure, the British did plug up all our major seaports, but it took a good many cruisers. Normally they contented themselves with general patrolling off the coast, which gave a merchantman at least a sporting chance. The favorite lurking place for cruisers and privateers—whether British, American, or other—were the few passages through the semicircle of islands between the Caribbean and the Atlantic. As for transatlantic trade, it had to go warily near the British Isles and around Gibraltar. The later happy hunting ground of Confederate cruisers and German raiders, off the coast of Brazil, would have yielded poor pickings at that early period.

The actual circumstances of capture followed a general pattern, which involves a tedious amount of repetition in the stories of privateering. Now and then it was exciting, with a lively chase and a brisk fight, but normally a regular ritual ensued. Thousands of times it was the same: a shot would crash across the bow of the luckless merchantman; she would back her top-sails and lay to, while a boat's crew came over; the boarding officer would examine her papers; a prize crew would then be put aboard the seized vessel to sail her to the nearest port where her case could be properly tried. Hope was not entirely gone yet, for the possibility still remained for her own crew to rise and take control, or for a chance rescue by a friendly cruiser or privateer, which would receive salvage money for the pains.

There was, however, a basic difference between seizing belligerent and neutral merchantmen. The former were certain to be fair game if caught; the best they could do was to run like hell, and, if there was any likelihood of success, use their guns. The captor was within his rights in burning or sinking such a captured vessel if she was not worth enough to warrant a prize crew, or if—as was the case with the American privateers in 1814, the Confederate raiders in the Civil War, and the Germans in the World Wars—the enemy blockade was too stringent to afford much hope of reaching port for regular condemnation. Such wholesale destruction was avoided if possible, for it meant a loss of prize money. Sometimes the prize might be ransomed for ready cash or a bond. This process was mutually agreeable to the victims, who might continue their voyage, and to the captors, who thus escaped the delays and uncertainties of condemnation. This practice was discouraged by the governments, however, as it put enemy vessels back into circulation.

The overhauled neutral, on the other hand, had different rights and duties. She was bound by international law to submit to visitation and search by a belligerent, which, in turn, was forbidden to destroy the vessel or touch any of her cargo until it had been legally condemned. If the boarding officer found that her papers suggested a contraband or enemy-owned cargo, improper destination, or other irregularity, he might put a prize crew aboard and send her in; he might also take off any enemy military or naval personnel found aboard. Privateersmen were more inclined than regular naval officers to stretch a point to detain a ship in case of any doubt. This nuisance was not fully checked by the proviso that they must pay the court costs in case the vessel was released; and many an innocent neutral was forced into weeks or months of unprofitable idleness by such abuses.

Most of the American prizes taken by the British between 1775 and 1815 were carried into Halifax, Bermuda, Jamaica or some other West Indian island, where the Vice-Admiralty Courts assumed jurisdiction. If the capture took place around British waters, the case was more apt to come before the High Court Admiralty at London. A libel would be filed against the vessel, or her cargo, or both. Captors and owners then had a chance to present their cases through counsel before a judge, acting without a jury. Enemy vessels, being fair prize, offered little problem, although if some of their noncontraband cargo were the property of neutrals, it might escape condemnation. The neutral American vessels taken between 1793 and 1811 meant complications, but the intricacies of contraband and neutral rights are not pertinent here. A condemned vessel or cargo was sold at auction under the orders of the court with the proceeds going to the captor. The loser in the prize court decision, whether captor or victim, was allowed to appeal the case to the Lords Commissioners of Appeal in Prize Causes, who sometimes reversed the original decision after long delays that sometimes stretched over three or four years. The French procedure, with which many Americans became familiar, to their cost, between 1793 and 1811, was similar, but too often degenerated into a judicial farce, especially in the Caribbean.

War-risk insurance rates are an invaluable indication of the actual shifting conditions of wartime shipping and give a more realistic picture, both then and now, than the communiqués of either foe. They are the dollars-and-cents interpretation of the chances of ships getting safely by raiders or mines or blockades; and they are uncolored by propaganda. In those earlier wars, insurance rates on cargoes often ran higher than on hulls, especially in the case of neutrals, because the vessel was frequently released after the condemnation of the cargo. In modern warfare, the rates are much closer, since both hull and cargo almost always share the same fate—either safety or the bottom. In those early troublous times, the American merchants and shipowners were handicapped by the lack of the ample financial concentration represented in the underwriters of Lloyd's. They struggled to spread out their burdensome risks by joining together for insurance. They had, moreover, to act pretty much in the dark on information, which was too often stale and incomplete, for their estimates on the prospects of safe completion of a voyage. Unlike the present rates, those also included the normal marine risks of shipwreck and the like, which were usually about 2 per cent on a voyage to Europe or the West Indies. One really got remarkably ample and generous coverage in those old policies. A New York one of the Napoleonic period read:

> Touching the adventures and perils which we, the assurers are contented to bear and take upon us in this voyage, they are of the seas, men of war, fires, enemies, pirates, rovers, thieves, jettisons, letters of mart or countermart, surprizals, takings at sea, arrests, restraints, detainment of all Kings, Princes or Peoples of what nation condition or quality soever, barratry of the master or mariners, and all other perils, losses and misfortunes, that have or shall come to the hurt, detriment or damage of said vessel, or any part thereof.

War-risk fluctuations will be mentioned frequently because of their pertinence to the subject. One can, for instance, picture the changes in shipping conditions during the American Revolution from the rates paid by Yankee and Tory shipowners; and in 1942 such rates remain the most accurate barometer of the maritime situation. Even with the high premiums sometimes charged, it is small wonder that more than one prosperous merchant was dragged into bankruptcy by underwriting marine risks in wartime.

One feature of the early period of American maritime activity that helped make marine insurance so very hazardous and uncertain—and influenced commerce in general at every turn—was the slowness of communications. Today maritime affairs are again being affected by communications to an extreme degree; this time by their astonishing speed. Even in peace, a mercantile voyage was in those days literally a "venture." One had no idea whether the cargo would reach a glutted market with low prices or an empty one with skyrocketing profits. In wartime, it was dangerous to a degree. Weeks elapsed before news of changes in the naval situation, new restrictive decrees, or even of the declaration of war or peace reached the uneasy shipping circles. Once a captain left port, he was beyond the shipowner's control and entirely upon his own initiative. An owner who learned of serious new developments in international affairs after his ship had set sail could only walk the floor in helpless anxiety for weeks or months. Many a Yankee captain, for instance, first heard of the War of 1812 when he was overhauled by a British cruiser or privateer. New Orleans was not the only battle fought after peace had come in 1815; the *Constitution* fought the *Cyane* and the *Levant* off Brazil several months after that. Even in 1865, the *Shenandoah* destroyed the Yankee whaling fleet in Bering Strait four months after Lee surrendered at Appomattox. Wireless has made all this a very different story in 1939 and 1941. On the whole, however, the development of rapid communication was to help the hunted merchantmen far more than the raiders who pursued them.

Cargoes, like so much else in the old order of things maritime, were not of the same significance in that earlier period as they were to become in modern times. In those days of simpler economy and technique, the various nations were far less dependent upon materials from beyond the seas. Most of them already had within their borders such raw materials as were used for gunpowder, ordnance, and most of the other sinews of those but slightly mechanized wars, although their industry might not always be geared to the production of an adequate supply. Being still primarily agricultural, most of Europe could in normal times raise enough food at home. Practically the only chronic lack of basic strategic materials occurred in masts and naval stores in the cases of England, France, Spain, and Holland. Important emergency shortages might appear, such as our need of munitions in our Revolution, and France's need of breadstuffs at the beginning of its. On the whole, a nation's military effort could not be severely crippled, as it can be today, by cutting off outside supplies. The morale of Napoleonic Europe might be undermined indirectly by the continued shortage of coffee, tobacco, and other "colonial wares"; but the armies of that day were not vulnerable through a curtailment of rubber, copper, manganese, or even staple foodstuffs. In the reign of Louis XIV, the *guerre de course* waged by Jean Bart, Duguay Trouin, and the other Dunkerque corsairs took a toll of English shipping relatively as heavy as the U-boats at their worst in 1917 and 1942; but those lost cargoes were not the lifeblood of England's war effort and security.

The pursuit of a merchantman, then, was more of a nuisance than a menace. Neither the crew of the pursuing raider, hungry for prize money, nor the captain of the trader, struggling to escape, could ordinarily feel that the fate of his nation literally depended upon the outcome of that chase, or of a thousand other similar ones. Commerce raiding, in other words, was ordinarily a purely business matter rather than a prime strategic weapon. The losses, to be sure, were a blow to the mercantile and shipping interests, whether they were sustained directly by the owners or spread out more widely through marine insurance, but the war-risk charges could be passed on to the consuming public through increased prices. In the old days, mercantile war losses might lead to occasional clamor from the business classes, but they never were of a severity to inspire a lobby strong enough to produce a premature peace.

Chapter II

Gunrunning in the Revolution

THE STORY OF OUR WARTIME SHIPPING BEGINS IN 1775, WHEN FOR the first time American ships and sailors had to fend for themselves. True, the colonists had had to defend their vessels from armed violence almost from the very beginning, but always before that year the powerful Royal Navy had been their protector. On scores of occasions, the colonial seafarers had taken measures to make the local sea lanes safe from privateers and pirates; from Dutchmen, Frenchmen, Spaniards, and renegade Britons. Even the first product of Boston shipyards, the *Blessing of the Bay,* is said to have been used as a warship against pirates. The Yankee attack and capture of Louisburg in 1745 was undertaken to cripple the French privateers who were preying on their fishing fleet. But behind all such efforts had always stood the formidable bulwark of the Royal Navy.

Now the Americans of 1775 found themselves not only "on their own" but with that same great navy as their foe. By all the rules, the rebellious colonists should have been in a very tight place, if not helpless before the potential pressure of the Royal Navy. British warships should have found it easy to bottle up American harbors and strangle commerce as effectively as they were to do later. The Royal Navy had, in fact, no other fighting on its hands before 1778 to interfere with its concentration upon that strip of coast. Only a few years before, it had shown itself the most powerful navy afloat with its smashing successes in the Seven Years' War. Yet now it seemed able to accomplish little. Not only did it fail to secure sufficient control of the seas to enable British shipping to come and go safely, but it could not keep the Americans from the sea.

To be able to move about at all was a real triumph for the

Americans with British naval might on the scene. At the same time, the coastal waters were more a "no man's land" than controlled by either belligerent during the eight years of fighting. Around 1780, both the Tories of New York and the patriots of Philadelphia were paying extraordinarily high insurance premiums to the West Indies and back, but this was an extreme situation. By and large, whether Yankee or pro-British, four vessels out of five reached their ports safely throughout the hostilities.

The lost opportunity of the Royal Navy is all the more impressive in view of the urgency of America's needs from overseas. The Revolution has been the only war in which the United States has stood in desperate straits from lack of strategic materials from beyond the seas. The Confederate states in the Civil War were in a similar position, but that was not the nation, of course. In the Revolution, the Yankee problem involved more than the retention of the normal commercial swapping of fish, flour, and tobacco for textiles, hardware, and sugar. Washington's army in fact faced helpless surrender without the gunpowder and other military supplies that were smuggled in past the king's ships.

Yet not even this was the whole story of the American triumph in the supply lines. England's great masts for its navy came from the tall trees of the primeval forests of northern New England, and in those days of wooden ships, masts were a specialized and essential factor in naval supplies. In few places did pines grow of sufficient height and strength for the navy's hard usage. By withholding this vital strategic material, the Yankees struck an effective blow, and one which became increasingly damaging to the Royal Navy.

The war at sea came on only very gradually, unlike the land fighting that kept up a rapid pace following Lexington and Concord in April, 1775. Strange as it seems, that year saw American exports to England heavier than ever before through the action of the Continental Congress, which voted in the fall of 1774 to permit this trade until September, 1775. Imports, on the other

hand, followed a more normal course for trade between belligerents, as the Congress stopped them after December 1, 1774.
Most of the colonies rigidly observed these nonimportation orders, and as a result the imports were the lightest in seventy
years.

But war or no war, all the colonies made the most of the last
chance to export to England. English merchants, for their part,
rushed ships to America to bring back cargoes that would help
reduce the debts owed them by the colonists. New York's exports
to England jumped from £80,000 to £187,000, and Pennsylvania's from £69,000 to £175,000. The Chesapeake region and
the Carolinas increased their already very heavy totals; while
even New England, with its chief port, Boston, closed by the
British, showed a slight gain.

War had by no means ended trade with the mother country
during that initial year, but after that, both sides took steps to
stop this intercourse. At the end of the year, Parliament prohibited all trade with the colonies during their rebellion. On
April 6, 1775, Congress declared America's independence from
the economic side of the British colonial system; and with that,
British imperial regulations no longer could bar Americans
from several lucrative fields. For the first time, the hitherto forbidden trade with France and northern Europe was opened to
them—if the Royal Navy did not prevent it.

Among the men who helped make American independence
possible was one whose name is not familiar to us in that connection. He is well known in our daily round as the inventor
of that common basis of the quick lunch, the sandwich. As First
Lord of the Admiralty during the Revolution, John Montagu,
fourth Earl of Sandwich, probably did more damage to the navy
entrusted to his care than any hostile French admiral was ever
able to do. Under his guidance, the splendid fighting machine
that had thoroughly smashed the French in the last war was but
a ghost of its former self. Its ships were too few and too rotten.
Its admirals were incompetent or disgruntled. During the latter

part of the Revolution, the French, Spanish, and Dutch fleets threatening home waters were some excuse for the navy's troubles. Perhaps Sandwich does not deserve to be the only scapegoat, but the fact remains that for the first three years of the war the only antagonists facing his fleets were the rebellious colonists who entered the hostilities with no navy at all.

Certainly a rigid naval blockade from the outset would have made it impossible for the Americans to carry on, as they did, a respectable amount of sea-borne trade throughout the war. One of Sandwich's colleagues pointed out at the beginning that the proper way to win the war was to cut the Americans off from the outside world, but it took Sandwich a full three years to come around to that point of view. Not until November, 1777, did he send the following memorandum to Lord North. If he had done so in 1775, this policy would doubtless have borne fruit.

> It must not, however, be imagined that any force will be sufficient entirely to execute the purpose of blocking up all the rebels' ports and putting a total stop to their privateering; for along so extensive a coast, full of harbors and inlets, many ships will in spite of all our efforts, get in and out by taking advantage of their knowledge of the coast, of dark and long nights, and events of wind and weather favorable to their purposes. However, we may certainly distress them infinitely more than has been done and throw such burdens upon their trade and privateering as to make it difficult to carry on their trade without considerable loss, which it is to be hoped, together with their want of necessaries from Europe, would soon make them tired of the war.

He went on to discuss plans for seizing further ports as British bases, for blockading still other ports, and for keeping as many cruisers as possible at sea in small squadrons. But when Sandwich belatedly penned these lines, Burgoyne had already surrendered, and within a few months the ships on the North Atlantic station would be busy dodging the French fleet. Yet surprisingly enough, the navy seems to have done a more efficient job along the coast during these later more difficult years, with all the other distractions, than when it had little else to do in the first stages of the conflict. Stirred out of its lethargy, it finally put to sea "everything that would swim," with resulting higher American insurance rates, which suggest it was more risky to escape from port in 1782 than in 1776.

During the intervening years, the Sandwich regime gave a far from vigorous demonstration of sea power. There was almost none of that steady, tedious, grueling blockading, month in and month out, which was to yield such effective results in the War of 1812. Only thirty British warships were on the American station at the time of Bunker Hill. These included a few small two-deckers and a group of little cruisers. One was at New York and one at Portsmouth, while the rest generally hung around Boston. Even if these vessels had kept constantly on the move, they were insufficient in force for a successful blockade of Yankee commerce. Then, and for some time to come, the navy spent most of its time, moreover, tending out on the army—first around Boston, later near New York and Philadelphia. Gradually a few of the scores of ships that had long been lying idle in "Rotten Row" in the British dockyards were refitted for sea. By the summer of 1776, some seventy ships were on the station, and thereafter the number fluctuated between that and ninety until the French entered the war, when it became considerably larger. A few energetic commanders in big frigates, such as Collier in the *Rainbow,* Hamond in the *Roebuck,* and "the demon Wallace" in the *Phoenix,* made things hot for the Americans with their raids, cruises, and occasional harbor vigils; but their activities were spasmodic. Frequent opportunities were available for Yankee vessels to slip out of port with a fair chance of reaching their destination safely.

Some of these gaps in the British cordon were plugged by those forgotten vessels, the loyalist privateers. Their exploits have been passed over by history although the deeds of the British Navy, of the American Navy, and of patriot privateers have all been recounted many times. These neglected Americans, who sailed under royal commissions, were particularly active at New York, where Governor Tryon began to grant letters of marque in September, 1778. Six months later, he had issued 121 of these to vessels which had already brought in 165 prizes, valued at $1,200,000. Some were simply little whaleboats or similar small craft, but they raised havoc in Delaware and Chesapeake Bays. According to one recruiting advertisement for a 16-gun ship, "Seamen of spirit who would prefer rich French prizes to piddling along-shore in boats, have now an opportunity to make their fortunes." Many of the New York raiders belonged to the Goodrich firm which would later, in 1794, operate privateers against Yankee shipping from Bermuda. A few British privateers raided the Maine coast from Nova Scotia in practice for their more extensive operations in 1812, while a few others operated against southern sea lanes from St. Augustine. Altogether, these privateers did much to make the seas more dangerous for patriot shipping, and in some cases were well rewarded for their pains.

With no navy of their own, the patriots had to improvise one as quickly as possible. It was a pretty sorry affair—in the eyes of those who want glamor in their naval history. There was, to be sure, John Paul Jones and his famous *Bonhomme Richard,* but she never came within three thousand miles of America and had only a handful of Americans among her crew. Yet valuable, if prosaic, service was rendered by that motley navy in maintaining vital commercial contacts. It included thirteen built-to-order frigates and thirty-odd converted merchantmen, together with the more numerous smaller vessels of the eleven state navies. Of course, the Continental Navy had to spend some of its time chasing prizes as an inducement to sailors to join its crews; otherwise it could not have competed with privateers for competent seamen. Most of its energies, however, were devoted to convoying merchantmen through the danger zone, sometimes even as far as the West Indies and back. Far less orthodox for a navy was its yeoman service in the conveying of government-owned tobacco to exchange for supplies of munitions or specie, deemed

too precious to be entrusted to ordinary merchantmen. Many
naval vessels were captured or wrecked in the performance of
such unusual duties.

In addition, a swarm of vessels, sometimes estimated at two
thousand, received letters of marque from Congress or the state
governments. Many of them were straight privateers with the
sole purpose of capturing fat merchantmen. Their effect on the
American shipping situation was only indirect. They brought
large quantities of prize goods into port; they forced the Royal
Navy to disperse its forces in convoy duty; and they competed
for crews. Their terrific toll of captures may also have stung
some British shipowners into pressing for an end to the war.

Much as they raised havoc with enemy shipping, these privateers proper are far less pertinent to our story than the letters
of marque or armed merchantmen, which probably equaled
them in numbers. Virtually every British as well as American
merchantman, except the little coaster, carried guns for her defense when sailing laden with cargo. It was worth while to have
a letter of marque because the guns might be put to more profitable use than defense and effect the capture of some weaker
vessel. The accounts are full of such encounters between embat-
tled merchantmen.

Altogether, chaos ruled the seas during those years when no
one was in control. Warships carried freight, and merchantmen
hunted prizes—a topsy-turvy state of affairs. The British themselves were well aware of this, and no one put it more pointedly
than Admiral Arbuthnot, writing from Halifax at the end of
1777:

> I wish it was in my power to give your Lordships a more
> favorable account of the disappointment of the rebels in their
> attempts on our trade, which they have really cut up almost
> without molestation, our cruisers having been looking out for
> their trade . . . while our enemies have been too successful in
> distressing ours in small vessels at hardly any expense.

Time and again, vessels were recaptured and restored to their original flag. Few cases, though, were as extreme as that of the British ship *Thorn,* which was four times seized in the course of five years by three different navies. Her captain declared at Halifax in 1782:

> That in the year 1779 the *Thorn* was taken by the *Boston* and *Deane* ships of Warr; that in 1780 she was again retaken by the *Hind* a Twenty gun Ship, That she was only Five days in the possession of the English, when they fell in with the *Harmion* [*Hermione*] and *Astrea,* Two french ships, who took her and ṣent her into Boston, where she was condemned and Sold, That William Raymond Lee Esquire, purchased her, & were sending the Ship *Thorn* to Lorient in France, with about Fifteen Thousand Weight of Indigo & with Stores and Provisions for the Voyage . . . That he left Marblehead on the 9th of August, Instant, That on the 19th Instant, being Lat. 42°, Long. 54° they fell in with the *Arethusa,* Frigate, who chased the *Thorn* Twenty-five Hours, when they came up, and took the *Thorn* and brought her into this Port . . . That she carried Eighteen Six pounders, That by his Commission paper No. 1, he had full Power and Authority to make Captors [*sic*] and Reprisals.

As far as the British cruisers and privateers on the Halifax station were concerned, the British tonnage that was recaptured was almost equal to the newly seized Yankee tonnage. An analysis of the Halifax Vice-Admiralty libels indicates that between 1776 and 1783, the British libeled there 178 American merchantmen—eleven ships, thirty-one brigs, eighty-three schooners, and fifty-three sloops. This meant a total of some 15,860 tons, judging from the average sizes for those various classes of vessels at that time. The recaptured British merchantmen totaled about 14,000 tons, but they were only half as numerous. The similarity in tonnage was caused by the greater size of the majority of the latter vessels—twenty-two ships, fifty-seven brigs, four schooners, and five sloops. Also libeled at Halifax by the British were twenty-three American privateers and three French vessels, along with two of their own recovered cruisers. Of the 201 American vessels, 140 were taken by British naval cruisers or their tenders; fifty-three by privateers, chiefly from Nova Scotia; seven by shore forces; and one by a transport.

The main significance of this conflict on the seas lay in the need of each side for strategic materials and the fact that each belligerent was in a position to deprive his foe of these essential needs. The Americans were, as we know, desperate for a good many war materials; the British were well supplied except for masts. Yet the Americans parried the blow and got their ma-tériel through the danger zones from overseas; the British did not.

Ever since 1652, the Royal Navy had relied solely for its larger masts on the supply from Portsmouth and later also from Fal-mouth (Portland) in New England. No sooner had the news of Lexington passed up the coast than the men—not only of those two ports, but of the lower Kennebec as well—seized all the masts that were awaiting shipment and carried them far out of the reach of the navy. Falmouth was later burned to the ground for its share in this action. The Admiralty lost little sleep over this loss—and Lord Sandwich did nothing at all about it, for the dockyards had a three-year reserve supply. But the war did not end with the exhaustion of this stock pile; and the navy awoke to its plight at the moment when fresh masts were urgently needed to fit out ships to fight the French.

This complacency was to cost the navy dearly and play its part in the loss of victory. "Time and again throughout the war came the tale of squadrons scattered and great ships rendered useless as spars crashed to the deck, while worn-out masts split open and tumbled into the sea. The plans of admirals miscarried more than once at critical stages of the conflict when the rotting pine aloft gave way in the stress of the winds." Only toward the end did the navy wake up to what it should have done at the first news of the colonial confiscation of the masts; it began to develop the alternate supply that was available in Nova Scotia and was to provide well for future needs.

Military supplies in general and gunpowder in particular were the far more desperate American needs. From the beginning, the colonists had a woefully inadequate stock of supplies for carrying on a war. Not only had British colonial policy deliberately stifled any industrial development, but foreseeing the colonial plight, it had prohibited the export of gunpowder in 1774, at the very moment the colonists were about to look around for what they could find for eventualities. The result was a frantic race at the outbreak of hostilities between the royal authorities and the colonists to the various magazines, with victory sometimes to one side and sometimes to the other. From various sources, domestic and West Indian, a moderate supply was gathered by the patriots, only to have their green soldiers assembled at Boston waste it recklessly. Not enough was left to stop the third British charge at Bunker Hill.

Three weeks after that, Washington ordered an accurate stocktaking. When he saw the appalling report, he was "so struck that he did not utter a word for half an hour." Aside from what the men had in their horns already, only a reserve of nine rounds per man remained, with none for artillery action. Pleading letters were dispatched to the New England governors, urging that "no quantity, however small, is beneath notice." Washington even commissioned a small naval force to try to seize some from British storeships, with scant results. Ways and means were canvassed for gathering saltpeter and for manufacturing a domestic supply. But it was soon clear that only powder from abroad could save the war.

Despite the Royal Navy, this was done—and in good quantities too. A painstaking survey several years ago revealed that by the time of Saratoga in the fall of 1777, 1,454,210 pounds of gunpowder had been imported from abroad, in addition to saltpeter, from which nearly 700,000 pounds more were manufactured. Altogether it was estimated that "well over 90 per cent of all the powder available for carrying on the Revolution during the first two and a half years of the struggle for independence was obtained from outside the country." More than half of those total imports arrived at Philadelphia; but into every colony except Georgia came at least as much as Washington's total stock after Bunker Hill. Along with the powder were muskets, artillery, uniforms, blankets, shoes, and other equipment—all welcome, if not so badly needed. Credit for this success belongs to the well-laid plans of the Continental Congress and to the state governments; but also, in a back-handed manner, to Lord Sandwich.

The sources of that invaluable supply lay in the new colonial trade with France, other parts of Europe, and also the West Indies. Aside from the psychological gratification of revenge upon England for the drastic defeat of France in the recent war, the merchants of Nantes, Havre, and Bordeaux were eager to divert the rich colonial trade from London and Bristol. In particular, they had their eyes on the tobacco trade, which came to about half of the total colonial exports. On the eve of the Revolution, America was shipping some 99,000,000 pounds a year to England, which re-exported 83,000,000 to other countries, taking a handsome profit for that service. Obviously, here the Yankees had something with which to pay for the military supplies and general imports that they were bound to need.

By the fall of 1775, two enterprising Nantes merchants had come to Philadelphia and returned with an appointment as agents for Congress in the matter of war materials. Considerable trading in such supplies was done on private account, but there was a resemblance to present-day practices in the government's active participation in the business. Congress established what today would be called a purchasing commission. It was handled chiefly by Arthur Lee and Silas Deane, who worked in anything but friendly co-operation. Congress held title to many of the cargoes of military supplies brought over; and even to the tobacco and other commodities sent in payment. These were in much smaller quantities than the French had expected. Some of the agents drew a very hazy line between the government transactions and the ventures which they handled on their own account.

The French and also the Spanish governments took a hand in the business too, though appearances of neutrality demanded that it be disguised. In the spring of 1776, Vergennes, the French foreign minister, decided to give secret aid to the colonists. A million livres (about $200,000) were made available to them for munitions, some of which was to be allowed to come from regular French military arsenals. Spain put up another million livres, and yet further funds came from private sources. To cover up the transactions, the business was placed in the hands of the playwright Caron de Beaumarchais. He established the commercial house of Rodrique Hortalez & Co. as a blind, with the idea that the American returns of tobacco and the like would make it a self-supporting venture; but again the lines between government and private business were somewhat hazy.

Risks of the gravest sort were involved in bringing the cargoes of contraband to their destination. Even if the British ambassador, well-informed by spies, did not bring pressure upon the French ministers to remember their neutral obligations, a vessel had to evade one vigilant line of British cruisers on the French coast and another in American waters. Mariners prayed for a gale that would scatter the patrols in the Bay of Biscay and for fog to blanket the approach to the United States. On the high seas, the danger of interception was less.

Numerous private cargoes of munitions had run those gauntlets before Beaumarchais went, under an assumed name, to Havre in December, 1776, to try to get his first shipments to sea. Stored in neat piles along the water front, he had artillery, muskets, and gunpowder from the French arsenals, together with thousands of uniforms and blankets, ready to be lightered aboard the *Amphitrite,* the *Seine,* and the *Romaine* which lay below in the stream. Indiscreetly, the egoist in Beaumarchais could not resist the temptation to rehearse the actors in his popular new *Barber of Seville;* that revealed his identity, and the British ambassador brought instant pressure on the ministry. Beaumarchais, hearing that an order was on the way to forbid the sailings, made frantic efforts to get off at least one ship. A hundred long-

shoremen worked throughout two whole nights in wild confusion to get whatever they could aboard the big *Amphitrite*. The
other two ships were stopped by the port authorities, but she was
able to slip out with 15,000 uniforms, 10,000 muskets, some 75
bronze cannon from the Havre forts, a few mortars from the
Havre arsenal, and a group of French Army officers. The Royal
Navy failed to catch her; and she reached Portsmouth, New
Hampshire, safely.

Eight more of those Beaumarchais cargoes are said to have
reached Portsmouth that spring. In March, for instance, the
Mercury arrived in forty days from Nantes. Her cargo, as it
appeared in the newspapers, must have cheered the Americans:
1,000 barrels of gunpowder, nearly 12,000 muskets, 11,000 flints,
some shoes, and 46 cases of cloth. The local authorities made the
most of their luck; the splendid equipment of the New Hampshire troops is said to have made them the envy of the army
for some time to come.

Meanwhile the house of Basmarein & Rambeaux at Nantes
was plunging heavily into the munitions business. Nantes had
for some time been carrying on a clandestine American trade,
in vessels which it had permission to arm. The first of the
Basmarein ships carried a cargo that had cost $90,000 at Nantes
and had sold for $240,000 in Boston! In June, it was another of
its ships that safely landed Lafayette and De Kalb in South Carolina—along with a cargo.

Such early shipments of Beaumarchais and of Basmarein were
fairly lucky in their passages, with only about one ship in nine
caught. But this good fortune did not last. Before long the British intelligence service in France apparently grew more alert,
and the naval officers on the American station were evidently
reading the newspapers. Whatever the cause, the British frigates
began to pick up ample prize money. Between February, 1777,
and August, 1778, of the sixty-five cargoes Basmarein & Rambeaux dispatched toward America four were wrecked and the
British snapped up thirty-eight. Of those, twenty-seven were
seized while France was still officially neutral. No prize court

would have hesitated long about the contraband status of what most of them were carrying. A difference of opinion on the net losses sustained appeared in a conversation between John Adams and a French dinner guest in the spring of 1779. To the guest's complaint, "We have had so many vessels taken, that many houses and individuals are ruined," Adams retorted that "the loss to trade was not so great, because if half their cargoes arrived, they sold for near as much as the whole would have produced, if it had all arrived; besides that, a great deal was insured in England." Seizures were not the sole difficulty of the French merchants; the anticipated return cargoes of tobacco and other produce, which were to pay for the munitions, were pretty meager. The net result was that Beaumarchais and Basmarein were both wrecked financially. A half a century later, their heirs were still appealing to Congress for relief.

As time went on, direct loans from the French government helped relieve the financial situation as far as munitions were concerned. Gradually, too, a more normal commercial exchange developed. American ships entered the trade along with more French ships which began to bring "luxury goods" to the colonies. Some made the passage safely; a few were captured. Only five vessels in the direct French trade were libeled at Halifax. The brigantine *Elizabeth* was caught off Cape Ann in 1778 with wine and brandy from Bordeaux. Four years later, the 150-ton letter-of-marque ship *Janus,* bound from Bordeaux to Boston with "brandy and bale goods," was lured to capture by the French colors flown by a British cruiser off Cape Cod. The oft-taken *Thorn,* as we saw, was headed from Boston to Lorient as a letter of marque, laden with indigo. Most of the others arrived safely, however, and French luxury goods were soon to be had in almost every port along the coast.

A moderate amount of direct trade developed with certain other nations on the Continent. Trade with Spain had been allowed, with certain restrictions, even under the old colonial system. Some merchants in Massachusetts for some time had had relations with the house of José Guardoqui & Sons at Bilbao,

which carried on a good American business both in military supplies and general articles of commerce during the Revolution.
Most of this trade was in vessels from the North Shore of Massachusetts. Five of these were taken as prizes to Halifax. Bilbao
was the chief port visited, but a few vessels brought back salt
from other Spanish ports and from Portugal. This was perhaps
the most seriously needed commodity in America, once the gunpowder supply was assured, for the old source at Turks Island
was cut off, and it was essential for preserving meat and fish at
that time.

With Holland, most of the trade was indirect because of the
dangerous sea route past England to Amsterdam. The Dutch
goods were usually transshipped from France or the Dutch
island of St. Eustatius in the West Indies. The trade was very
heavy, and so there was plenty of inducement for a few vessels
to risk the direct route. Captain McGee, for instance, successfully
brought the letter-of-marque brig *Amsterdam* from that port to
Boston in 1779; but two years later a cruiser caught him off Cape
Ann, inward bound from Sweden. A few cargoes of Swedish
iron came through safely from Gothenburg in Sweden, but such
crossings were the exception.

As this was a war within the British Empire, the risks of the
Atlantic crossings loomed especially grave for civilians bound to
Europe on official business for the new nation. In a regular war,
such a person is treated as a sort of prisoner of war, much as a
military and naval officer is. Americans of the latter category did
get this preferred treatment even in the Revolution, but political
leaders, if caught, faced possible hanging for treason, or at the
least severe prison terms. The same transatlantic problem faced
the Confederates in the Civil War. Several distinguished Americans took their chances in eluding the Royal Navy during the
Revolution, and all but one crossed safely. Had the transatlantic
clippers been flying in those days, such worries would have been
greatly relieved!

The problem weighed heavily on John Adams, when Congress

appointed him to join Franklin and Deane in France. As Adams recorded his anxious forebodings:

> The dangers of the seas, and the sufferings of a winter passage, although I had no experience of either, had little weight with me. The British men-of-war were a more serious consideration. . . . I had every reason to expect that ships would be ordered from Rhode Island and from Halifax to intercept the *Boston*. . . . The consequence of a capture would be a lodging in Newgate.

Nevertheless, the frigate *Boston*, of the little navy Adams had himself been instrumental in creating, sailed on Friday, the thirteenth of February, 1778, with two future presidents aboard—for young John Quincy went with his father. Captain Tucker's orders warned: "On all occasions have great regard to the importance of his security and safe arrival." Adams himself was distinctly jittery throughout the trip—and with good cause. Three British cruisers were sighted; one gave chase for three days until balked by a midnight thunderstorm. At last, Adams was able to record in his diary: "We have passed all the dangers of the American coast. Those of the Bay of Biscay remain." A week later, the *Boston* turned pursuer and caught a British letter of marque with a cargo worth $400,000. But the worst scare of the trip lay ahead of Adams. As the *Boston* approached the French coast, two British men-of-war were seen bearing down on her. The crew rushed to the guns; capture within half an hour seemed certain to all aboard, but for some reason the enemy ships bore off without attacking. At last, the *Boston* took on her pilot, who brought word that France had declared war. The following June, Adams returned to Boston in the French frigate *Sensible*. This time he rendered thanks to Providence for the fog that blanketed the approach to Massachusetts Bay. That winter he had to set forth again, but this time the crossing in the same ship was without incident and he landed safely in Spain, with fewer nervous qualms.

Silas Deane did not rate a frigate when he sailed from Philadelphia early in 1776, but Congress did provide a naval convoy for his well-laden merchantman until clear of the coast. She made her way safely by way of Bermuda and Spain. He returned in 1778 with a superabundance of protection—in the fleet of D'Estaing. Later in 1776, Franklin had the Continental frigate *Reprisal* at his disposal, but he joined her down the Delaware, secretly to conceal the news of his departure. Her captain landed him safely on the Breton coast after picking up three prizes on the way across.

John Jay did not get over as easily. He and his family were not finally landed at Cadiz to take up his post as minister to Spain until three months after sailing from Philadelphia. Although chased for several days by a British cruiser off the Bay of Biscay, the enemy was not the cause of his major trials. Two weeks out from the Delaware, the rigging of the frigate *Confederacy* somehow became slack, and in three minutes all the masts and the bowsprit had crashed into the sea. A helpless hulk, the pride of the Continental Navy wallowed for two weeks, with her loosened rudder threatening at any moment to batter in the stern. Her captain eventually got up a jury rig and made for Martinique, where Jay was taken aboard the French frigate *Aurore*.

Despite the worries and dangers of these diplomatic crossings, Henry Laurens was the sole casualty. Early in 1780, soon after his retirement as president of Congress, he was commissioned an envoy to Holland, but his difficulties were upon him before he had even left these shores. His bags were aboard a French ship at his home, Charleston, when thirteen British warships prepared to attack the port. Hastily he chartered a little schooner at Georgetown, South Carolina, to get up the coast to Wilmington, North Carolina, where he heard a ship was about to sail for France; but she was not ready. The schooner captain refused to take him farther north for fear of the British. Finally Laurens went overland to Philadelphia, where he obtained passage on the fast little 62-ton brigantine *Mercury* belonging to Congress, and was given a naval convoy of the sloop *Saratoga* and two other warships, to the Grand Banks. The two latter captains refused on the ground that they had to refit, and after waiting for them in vain in the lower Delaware, the *Mercury* and the *Saratoga* put to sea; but the latter was so slow that she was ordered home after six days. Left alone, the *Mercury* fell captive to the British frigate *Vestal* after a chase of several hours on the Newfoundland banks in September. Desperate, Laurens threw his papers overboard tied in a weighted sack, but the vigilant British fished it out before it sank. Laurens was landed at Newfoundland, where lenient treatment seemed in store for him; but he was sent on to London. There he was at once committed to the Tower on suspicions of high treason, and, broken in health, he was held there for nearly fifteen months. That capture was doubly unfortunate for the Americans, because the British found a draft of a treaty between Holland and the United States in Laurens' papers. That gave an excuse to declare war on the Dutch.

In spite of these relative successes of the hazardous Atlantic crossing, Americans more commonly used the roundabout trade route by the West Indies. For every vessel that went straight overseas, scores sailed to the French, Dutch, or Spanish islands for their European cargoes. The big vessels, from those nations in Europe that were neutral during the early part of the war, could shuttle back and forth between their home ports and the Caribbean with relative safety. From the islands, these European cargoes were carried to the United States in the numerous little vessels which the Americans had long had in the West Indian trade. The advantages of this divided voyage were stressed by William Bingham, who made a fortune as agent for the Continental Congress at Martinique.

> Very few French masters of vessels are acquainted with the coast of America, and admitting they were, large ships cannot take advantage of running into small inlets and harbors as lesser vessels may. Besides, all the Continental vessels sail with skilful pilots, which greatly lessens the risk.

Bingham did not add that he missed his 5 per cent commission on those cargoes that went direct.

Besides safety considerations, the broken voyage offered decided economic advantages. The bulk of the munitions, as well as a good part of the general cargoes, was needed in the northern ports, whereas the most valuable commodities for export, such as tobacco, indigo, and naval stores, were produced in the south. A vessel would find it hazardous in the extreme to unload at Boston, for instance, and then skirt the cruiser-infested coast to pick up a return cargo at Norfolk or Charleston. The West Indies, moreover, had long been utilized by the northern colonists for the disposal of products that would scarcely find a market in England. In operating the old "sugar triangle," Yankee vessels had swapped their lumber, fish, or flour at Jamaica, Antigua, or Barbados for sugar, rum, or molasses, which could be swapped again in England for woolens, hardware, and all the other diverse offerings of that rich market. An extra profit could be made in selling to some Britisher the vessel that had made the lucrative long haul across the Atlantic. Even in colonial times the Yankees had not limited their Caribbean dealings to the British islands; despite discouraging legislation, they had found their way to the adjacent foreign sugar islands as well.

Altogether, the setting was perfect for a flourishing entrepôt trade in the Caribbean. With cargoes of every sort brought together from Europe and America in the warehouses of Cap François, Port au Prince, Martinique, St. Eustatius, Havana, and St. Croix (Santa Cruz), each and every vessel was able to carry thither whatever was easiest to collect, and return with whatever was most needed or most profitable. Transshipment of huge quantities of gunpowder, munitions, and specie, and of brandy, gin, and fancy goods took place at these islands, with tobacco, indigo, and naval stores being sent to Europe in payment. Along with this, the local West Indian needs still meant a market for the old northern offerings of lumber, fish, and flour, which could be exchanged for sugar and its by-products. Thus the triangle, in its old as well as its new form, continued as popular in early

American commerce as it was to become in modern American fiction.

In view of the relative safety of the Caribbean detour, it was ironic that the only one of Beaumarchais's early shipments to go by this route was the only one to be captured. This was the ship *Seine,* which had been detained, we recall, by the Havre authorities but managed to get away, after a few weeks, for New England. Blown off the coast by gales, she put into Martinique early in 1777. Bingham, in the interests of safety—and of his own commission—at once removed 217 cases of muskets and 100 bales of camp equipment to transship in smaller American vessels. The precaution was wisely taken, for as soon as she set out to try her luck at some northern port, a British frigate seized her. Although her clearance papers had been carefully fixed for the French fishing islands of St. Pierre and Miquelon, she was carried into Dominica for condemnation.

Congress at times put its new navy to rather unorthodox uses, as we recall. Frequently, naval vessels were sent to pick up military stores accumulating in the Caribbean ports. Captain Wickes in the *Reprisal,* for instance, carried Bingham to Martinique, and then, after beating off an English cruiser, took aboard a large quantity of muskets, together with a supply of linens for the house of Willing & Morris. This round trip was arranged by Robert Morris. Incidentally, although Morris's patriotism and invaluable services were above question, he developed a fine coordination between his right hand, which served Congress, and his left hand, which worked for his Philadelphia countinghouse. Unlike Bingham, who "cleaned up," or Silas Deane, who was "cleaned out," he is believed to have broken about even in his mixture of official and private dealings in the Revolution.

However active business may have been in the French islands, the entrepôt par excellence was the little Dutch island of St. Eustatius or "Statia." Conveniently located at the outer bulge of the Antilles, it was close enough to the possessions of several nations to become a perfect clearinghouse. It could, moreover, be reached from the North American coast without traversing the dangerous bottlenecks to the westward. Holland, fully aware of the lucrative possibilities of neutral trade in wartime, made a free port of its tiny town, Port Orange, and welcomed all comers. The little rock could scarcely produce enough sugar on its seven square miles to load one good-sized ship during an entire year. Nonetheless, 3,182 vessels are said to have cleared from there during a thirteen-month period in the middle of the Revolution. Not only was it used heavily by Amsterdam merchants for their own wares, but traders from all nations assembled there to swap all that they could. The islanders waxed fat on rich commissions and port services. Quite a trade was actually carried on even between the belligerents—England and the colonies—by way of Amsterdam and "Statia."

Long before any of Beaumarchais's munitions were ready at Havre, much of Washington's desperate shortage after Bunker Hill had been relieved by powder from St. Eustatius. Although Holland officially banned this exportation to the Americans, Dutch merchants could not forego the golden opportunity of selling powder to the rebels at "Statia" for six times what it had cost them in Amsterdam. As early as 1774 vessels from the colonies were beginning to load casks of the precious explosive. By the spring of 1776, so the British ministry was informed by its secret agents, eighteen shiploads had gone out from Amsterdam to be transshipped for ports all along the rebel coast. A single vessel that summer is said to have carried 49,000 pounds to Philadelphia.

In connection with its rapidly developing American trade, "Statia" played its part in transforming Baltimore from just another little Chesapeake town into one of the leading seaports of the nation. Abraham van Bibber, a Baltimorean, went to St. Eustatius to procure powder and munitions for Maryland and Virginia. He urged the Chesapeake region to concentrate its tobacco and flour shipments at "Statia," rather than spread them among other ports. He likewise seems to have used his influence, as far as he was able, to direct the return cargoes to Baltimore. The risks of capture on the long runs up and down the Chesapeake were an added problem to the ever-present dangers at sea. Speed was at a special premium, and the ordinary tubby merchantmen were too vulnerable. Baltimore cleverly found the answer by perfecting its fast little "clipper" schooners, and these proved highly elusive in avoiding the Royal Navy. A recent Princeton senior, searching the Baltimore customs records for his thesis, has revealed the fact that in 1780, when Baltimore first had its separate customhouse, one ship, nine brigs, thirty-nine schooners, and eleven sloops cleared for the Dutch West Indies, chiefly to St. Eustatius. This amounted to 4,972 tons or 65 per cent of Baltimore's foreign trade.

Two advertisements in the *Virginia Gazette* early in that summer of 1780 indicate the wide variety of the "Statia" cargoes and the risks involved in bringing them. Obviously the Caribbean port was supplying far more than gunpowder:

> Just imported from St. Eustatia, and for sale by the subscribers in King & Queen County by retail or wholesale, for cash or tobacco,
> A few hogsheads of rum, Muscovado sugar in hogsheads, molasses, allum salt, coffee, Russia sail duck and light canvas, cordage of different kinds, nails of most kinds, German steel, hyson and green tea, pewter, gunpowder, loaf sugar, oznabrugs, files of different kinds, writing paper, &c.
> EDWARD HILL, & COMPANY.

Possibly those goods had had the same narrow escape from condemnation in a British prize court as the cargo that had come from the adjacent Danish entrepôt a week before:

> The ship *Adventure,* Capt. Reeves, of 16 guns and 60 men, in 17 days from St. Croix, with a cargo of rum, sugar, salt &c, is safe arrived in James River. About 40 leagues east of Cape Hatteras, fell in with the brig *Hammond* of 18 guns, and the sloop *Randar* of 10 guns, two privateers from Bermuda, both which he engaged near three hours within pistol shot, and obliged the *Hammond* to strike, but being so much disabled in his sails and rigging, and the wind light, he could not get

possession of the brig before the sloop towed her off, and got clear; what is something remarkable, Captain Reeves had not a man hurt during the engagement. Between the capes he saw eleven sail of privateers, which were in a chain from Cape Henry to Cape Charles, but not one of them attempted to come near him. The brig *General Wayne,* Captain Nicholson; and the schooner *Grand Tiger,* Captain Smith, parted from him the 9th instant, in latitude 22.

Not all were as lucky. Early in 1779, Captain Alexander Mc-Pherson of the Tory privateer *Experiment* reported to his New York agent an encounter with a "rebel privateer" and continued:

> This morning I made shift to take the sloop under her protection. She proves to be the *Nancy* loaded with tobacco from Baltimore, bound for St. Eustatia. I despatch her to inform you that in the course of my cruise I have taken the *Crowfane,* Turks Island to Virginia with salt; *Prince Frederick,* St. Croix to Philadelphia, salt and dry goods; sloop *Jean* from St. Eustatia, a French snow from Cape Francois to Virginia; and a brigantine from Cadiz—the last two in company with the privateer sloop General Matthews, Capt. Forsyth. Made prize of a sloop loaded with salt, burned her after taking out what was valuable and chased a large French brigantine ashore on Ocracoke Bar.

Yet on the whole, the safe arrivals from St. Eustatius and adjacent islands proved the wisdom of the Caribbean detour. At Philadelphia, for instance, in the four weeks from mid-May to mid-June in 1780, seventeen vessels arrived from St. Eustatius, along with eleven from Haiti, five from the other French islands, one from Teneriffe, and three coastwise. Salt was apparently the chief need, and all but two of the vessels from "Statia" contributed to the total of 6,800 bushels. Times had changed since 1776, though, for only two brought gunpowder. Next to salt, liquor was the most common import; Philadelphia's alcoholic content must have increased considerably with the steady arrival of rum, gin, wine, and brandy.

"Statia's" luck was too good to last. The British grew increas-

ingly incensed at this shameless aid to their enemies through the
Dutch port. The treaty draft, fished from the sea at Laurens'
capture, furnished all the excuse necessary to force war on Holland in the last days of 1780. Unaware of this disaster to their
profits, St. Eustatius was enjoying a day of boom trade, with 130
vessels in port on February 3, 1781, when Admiral Rodney
swooped down. The plunder afloat and ashore ran into the millions; but that was not all the British captured. They chased and
seized a rich convoy just leaving for Holland, and keeping the
Dutch flag aloft as a decoy, tricked fifty tobacco-laden American
merchantmen into what they thought was still a neutral harbor.

With that rich trading post gone, West Indian trade lan-
guished for the remainder of that year. By the next year, the
Americans were turning in greater numbers than ever to the
islands of other powers: French, Danish, and Spanish. Tangible
commercial statistics for the Revolution are so rare that one is
tempted to use them when they can be found. The Baltimore
customs records reveal the following tonnage movements from
that port for this readjustment:

	1780	1781	1782
Dutch West Indies	4,900	300	1,300
Danish West Indies	100	300	3,900
Haiti (St. Domingue)	300	100	3,900
Havana	100	—	6,800

Baltimore, from its concentration upon St. Eustatius, naturally
was much shaken by its capture. By 1782, its schooners were visiting Cap François and Port au Prince in similar numbers to
St. Croix and St. Thomas in the Danish Virgin Islands.

The big novelty in 1782, however, was the sudden boom in the
Havana trade. Spain had been slower than the others to open
its big colonial port. Once it did, the Yankees came with a rush.
Havana was more than a market for flour; it was a source of
the hard cash, which by that time was needed more than anything else by the poverty-stricken Congress. Most of the Continental Navy had been captured or wrecked by now; but all that

remained was dispatched for the coveted specie. In July, 1781, for example, Captain Nicholson in the frigate *Trumbull* was sent to Havana with a cargo of flour, but, more important, he was entrusted with a bill drawn on France and Spain for a tremendous amount to be converted, if possible, into silver. The *Trumbull* was scarcely clear of Delaware Bay on the way out when she fell into the clutches of a British cruiser. Captain Barney of the *George Washington* had better luck in 1782 on a similar mission. He brought from Havana to Philadelphia, without mishap, $600,000 in specie, the property of private merchants; but he had stopped on the way out at Cap François to secure a French ship of the line as escort. Early in 1783, a huge amount of specie was brought home safely by the frigate *Alliance,* accompanied by a new cruiser purchased from the French. In this case, British cruisers attacked the convoy, but a big French warship appeared on the scene in time to save the treasure. Cash was even brought by the risky transatlantic route direct from France, one large consignment being landed in Boston and taken overland to Philadelphia in oxcarts guarded by marines.

This recourse to difficult overland freighting over the miserable roads points to the perils of the coastal trade. Vessels from abroad were usually in danger from the British only while running the cruiser gauntlet at each end of their voyages; but the coasters were vulnerable to that peril every minute of their way. Most of the coasters, too, were small vessels, too often unarmed. At this time, however, overland freighting was less prevalent than it would become during the severe blockade in 1814, and again in 1942, when tank car and pipe line, rather than tanker, had to transport oil.

The most ambitious coastal trading lay in the exchange of Carolina rice, indigo, and naval stores for northern produce. Nine of these vessels were taken into Halifax as prizes in 1777 and 1778. Most of them had been plying between Charleston and Boston. Far more common were the coasters along the New England shore, where Maine lumber and firewood were swapped for provisions from the southward. Apples and cider appeared in numerous cargoes. One prize sloop carried into New York was described as "freighted with onions, pumpkins, and the like kind of New England fruit." The normal distribution of imported cargoes along the coast was very hazardous. It was safer to bring in as much as possible directly to avoid extra contact with the British. At Philadelphia in those same four weeks of 1780, with thirty-two vessels in port from the Dutch and French West Indies, only three coasters—two from North Carolina and one from Boston—arrived.

The coastal trade was irregularly extended to some occasional clandestine dealings with the "neutral Yankees of Nova Scotia." This illicit dallying with the enemy would develop into a flourishing business during the years around 1812. Some business was found in the "no man's land" of Passamaquoddy Bay. Several schooners were caught prowling around the Bay of Fundy laden with Carolina naval stores or West Indian goods. One of these, the schooner *Swallow*, anchored off a tiny Nova Scotia harbor and

> asked for assistance to pilot her further in, and stated they were from Halifax. The people discovered the *Swallow* was from New England, with rum, molasses, cotton, cocoa and coffee aboard, and captured her after some resistance.

From time to time, both British and American cruisers and privateers discovered two sets of papers on seized vessels, one showing British registry from Nova Scotia and the other American registry. This practice was said to be particularly common at Salem, while even Congress resorted to it on occasion. Bermuda, with its need of Yankee produce and its own ability to provide salt in return, was another tempting center of irregular trading.

As for the effects of these Revolutionary maritime conditions upon the ports of the American coast, they proved confusing and changeable, to say the least. One feature that complicated matters was that almost every major American port was either

occupied or burned by the British in the course of the war. Only
Salem and Baltimore escaped scot free—and they were able to
reap so much profit from their rivals' ills that they flourished
for years thereafter. Only for a few months in 1776, between the
evacuation of Boston and the attack upon New York, were all
the ports in American hands, and even in that interval British
warships lay at anchor in some of them.

Boston was already in British possession before fighting began,
and so remained until their evacuation in March, 1776. The British burned Portland (Falmouth) in 1775 and Norfolk in 1776;
New London went up in flames later. Newport was occupied
and used as a base from December, 1776, to October, 1779.
Philadelphia was held by the enemy from September, 1777, to
June, 1778. Savannah fell in December, 1778, and remained in
British hands until May, 1782. Charleston was taken four months
later and held until December, 1782. The longest occupation of
all was at New York—from August, 1776, until November, 1783,
after the war was over. That port with its strong Tory atmosphere was the principal base for British operations throughout
most of this time.

These rapid changes of status often spelled danger to inward
bound vessels of both sides as they were apt to blunder into
the enemy. Two British transports loaded with Scottish troops,
for instance, confidently approached Boston in June, 1776, totally
unaware that it was in rebel hands. They learned the news—
from the Connecticut cruiser that captured them in Nantasket
Roads. And such mishaps also befell Yankee vessels more than
once, as we saw at St. Eustatius in 1781.

Incidentally, the crude conditions of navigation played their
part in causing other costly mistakes of this same nature. If
faulty calculation of longitude could get Howe's flagship almost
three hundred miles off her intended course on a short trip from
Halifax to New York, it is not strange that merchantmen sometimes made the wrong landfall with disastrous results. One
unlucky Yankee skipper sailed merrily into what he thought was

friendly Guadeloupe, only to find himself under the British guns of Nevis!

Probably the region that caught the brunt of the coasting troubles was Maine. It had specialized in a single commodity before the war—white pines. These had provided masts, lumber, and cordwood, in exchange for whatever the people required from outside. The gravest of those needs was flour and meal. Maine, too, found its coast too close for comfort to the route of the naval vessels and privateers passing to and fro between Halifax and their favorite cruising ground off Boston. Sometimes for days at a time privateers hung off Cape Porpoise or Casco Bay, harrying the coasters. More than once, the energetic Sir George Collier sent boat expeditions up Maine rivers to capture or burn ships loading masts for France. Cut off from outside foodstuffs by these trade interruptions, little communities were sometimes in danger of starvation. In 1779, a plea came from one town for a bushel or two of seed barley at any price in silver, paper, or lumber. Over half the people, it seemed, had been without bread for a month, with only clams and small fish to stay their hunger. Some were already dead, others helpless, and all in a sort of stupor.

Just south of remote Maine, it was another story. The fifty miles of coast from Portsmouth to Boston was probably able to continue its trade more freely than any other part of the American seaboard. Both Portsmouth and Newburyport did a good business with merchantmen and privateers. Many of the early munitions cargoes from France, we recall, came into Portsmouth. Near-by Salem and Beverly enjoyed even more thriving days. Elias Haskett Derby of Salem and George Cabot of Beverly both fitted out privateers on a great scale and traded extensively with their letters of marque. They were simply modest merchants when the war broke out, but luckier than the average, they were among the most prosperous men in Massachusetts at its close. Boston, too, was the most active and open of the major ports, once the British were gone in the spring of 1776. Even the persistent cruising of the *Milford* and other British cruisers outside the harbor entrance between Cape Ann and Georges Bank did not prevent a flourishing trade, which often left the warehouses glutted with imports.

Newport, on the other hand, never recovered its colonial prosperity after the British occupation. Some of its former trade shifted to near-by Providence. New London did a fair business until it was burned by Benedict Arnold; but the small boats full of Tory privateersmen crippled New Haven and the other Sound ports. Connecticut got along by selling provisions to the army. As for New York, it had plenty of thriving business after the British occupation, but it was all on loyalist or British account. Before that, the presence of the Royal Navy's *Asia, 64* acted as a damper upon its trade.

Philadelphia, which had been the foremost port since 1749, had periods of excellent prosperity, with almost half of the early powder supplies landed there. Its trade was vulnerable, however, because of the bottleneck at the Delaware Capes, which became a favorite lurking place for British cruisers and Tory privateers. Outgoing merchantmen sometimes gathered by the dozens in the river, awaiting a Continental cruiser to convoy them out to sea. For a full year after the British evacuation in 1778, these raiders almost paralyzed Philadelphia's trade. It was said that not one vessel in seven escaped their vigilance; and that flour, salt, and firewood had to be rationed within the city. An embargo on shipping was proposed "to deprive our enemies of their expected prey," but instead the merchants financed a state cruiser to clear the bay. In five months she captured some Tory privateers and recaptured several valuable merchantmen. Her services yielded a clear profit of £449,000, in addition to ensuring that "food, commodities and military stores once more entered the port of Philadelphia in a steady stream." As late as 1781, nevertheless, the Tory privateer *Ladies Delight* captured seven merchant vessels in Delaware Bay.

The circumstances of the Revolution played a strong part in determining that Baltimore rather than Norfolk would thereafter be *the* port of Chesapeake Bay. Norfolk, with one of the finest geographical positions on the whole coast, was crippled by its burning at the hands of the British. Baltimore, on the other hand, made good capital out of shipments of tobacco and flour in its own swift schooners. With more foresight and a few more ships, it was in the power of the British to have blockaded it as effectively as they did in the next war; and to have nipped that budding commerce.

The ports of North Carolina were able to sneak a good many little cargoes in and out. The peculiar coast line has only a few inlets through the great sand barriers, and these are extremely hazardous for large vessels. This aided the colonists and made it almost impossible for the British to check their clandestine trade. Charleston in South Carolina, until captured in 1780, conducted a substantial amount of business, for its indigo was one of the valuable American offerings. It developed a considerable state navy to keep the approaches clear. Savannah's experience was similar, although on a smaller scale.

The risks involved varied frequently, but were generally considerable. Against the already quoted remark that at one time six out of every seven vessels leaving Philadelphia were being captured must be placed the experience of a Newburyport firm that lost only one vessel in thirty voyages to the West Indies. The insurance rates, including both marine and war risks, were as usual a fair barometer, but would probably have been lower had more capital been available. At their best, in 1775, Philadelphia merchants could insure a voyage to Europe for 2½ per cent, little more than ordinary marine rates. By 1781, they were having to pay around 50 per cent on a voyage to Havana, while the Tory shipowners of New York were having to pay the same rate to Jamaica. The normal range during the war lay midway between those extremes—from 20 to 30 per cent. Lloyd's even charged the British government 4 per cent for insuring gold for troop payments conveyed in warships to America. And, too, the profits on successful ventures were excellent. Not everyone could write, as did a Chesapeake merchant in 1777, "Goods are exceeding scarce here, and will sell at any price a man's conscience will let him take," but profits of 100 per cent, before the insurance had been deducted, were common.

Altogether, the Americans did pretty well to keep themselves supplied with munitions, salt, and luxuries from beyond the seas in view of what the powerful Royal Navy might have done to their trade. It was, however, no time for a nervous man to venture himself or his savings in maritime pursuits. According to a French visitor to Philadelphia in the later years of the war, "There was scarcely a captain, or even a common sailor, who had not been taken six or seven times during the war, nor a merchant who had not been more than once rich and ruined."

Chapter III

Neutral Profits

IN THE GENERAL GLOOM OVER AMERICAN COMMERCE IN THE DISMAL years immediately following the Revolution, the solitary gleam of hope lay in the rumors of a pending Anglo-French conflict. One New York merchant revealed his anticipation of neutral shipping profits in the wishful lines that he penned to his Jamaica correspondent late in 1787: "Should a war (O, horrid war!) take place between Great Britain and France, will not your ports be open to us, and our commerce with you as neutrals be an object of consideration?" Not for over five long years did the hoped-for war materialize, but with it came a tremendous boom to gladden the hearts of American shipping circles. The next years were to see soaring profits and high adventure alongside chronic international complications and warfare against both belligerents. This "heroic age" of our merchant marine was a high point equaled only by the more peaceful "golden age" of the clipper ships a half century later.

The merchants and shipowners of 1787 had good cause to long for such neutral profits. After 1783, the Americans had become foreigners in British eyes. To their chagrin, they found themselves forced to view that self-sufficient empire from the cold outside. This was a galling blow to their pocketbooks. After fighting for eight years to be free from the political implications of membership in the British Empire, they complained bitterly at the loss of the old economic advantages. The imperial divorce had knocked askew the old "sugar triangle," the very foundation of the commerce of the northern and middle colonies.

A depressed and at times desperate undertone ran through the commercial letter books of that period. The new nation was too loosely joined to present a united front for collective bargaining with England or other foreign nations. Some states would impose high discriminatory duties, only to find their neighbors luring trade to their ports by liberal terms to foreign shippers. Domestic trade was hampered by the jumbled condition of the various state currencies. It was small wonder that the new federal constitution was welcomed by the merchants. Prewar debts to English merchants and uncollectible fresher debts from Americans were further nightmares. The anticipated commerce with France failed them; in more than one sense the two nations did not speak the same language.

The Americans consequently turned back to London, Bristol, and Liverpool, where they knew what they were ordering and where they could get credit. Yet they could not hope to buy English goods indefinitely unless they were able to export enough to pay for them; and England had scant use for the products of the northern and middle states.

The distraught businessmen of the seaports did try, to be sure, to find new and, they hoped, profitable trade routes for their ships in distant seas. The trail from New York around the Cape of Good Hope to Canton for a cargo of teas and silks was blazed by the *Empress of China* in 1784. At the same time, the *United States* sailed from Philadelphia to begin a lucrative commerce with India. A few years later, the *Columbia* from Boston initiated the fur trade on the northwest coast, near the river which bears her name. Dramatic and important as these voyages were, they involved but a few ships a year; and participation in this new trade was a luxury only the wealthy might afford, because of the amount of capital necessarily tied up for long periods.

Such distant wanderings were not possible for the lesser traders and smaller vessels, which made up by the hundreds the rank and file of the merchant marine; and scant business remained for them in these lean years. With all their vessels and some cargoes barred from the British West Indies, the Americans tried the near-by Caribbean islands of other European powers. The Dutch and the Danes proved hospitable as usual to this

Yankee quest for trade; the French opened a few ports, with certain restrictions, in their rich colony of Haiti (generally called "St. Domingo" by the Americans) as well as in their other islands. Even the rigidly exclusive Spaniards allowed some trading with Cuba and Puerto Rico. The Yankees were able to sell their fish, lumber, and flour as of old, but now all the sugar, rum, and molasses obtained in exchange was, of course, left on their hands for their own consumption.

A major cause of their plight was the loss of the old remunerative transatlantic "long haul," which had, as part of the colonial "triangle," made it possible to get enough sugar, beyond their own domestic needs, in the West Indies to permit shipping the surplus to Europe with profitable freight earnings for themselves as well as that wider market for their own produce in the Caribbean. Between 1783 and 1793, not only the British, but also the French, Dutch, Danes, and Spaniards reserved this "long haul" exclusively for their own vessels. The recovery of the use of this "long haul" under war conditions was to be the secret of the coming prosperity, not only for the small schooners plying the Caribbean but for the average-sized ships trading with Europe. And business would pick up all along the line within the new nation—with special profit to lumbermen, fishermen, millers, and shipbuilders.

At last in April, 1793, a British mail packet brought the long-hoped-for news of war. It was by then already two months old and was to last for twenty-two years with but two short breathing spells. Not until a June night in 1815 was peace to return, when a defeated Napoleon rode away from Waterloo to take refuge with the British Navy, which had contributed strongly to his final downfall. Unlike the latter part of the American Revolution, the rival navies were at no time evenly matched, for the British had the advantage from the outset. Not only did the Royal Navy enjoy a numerical superiority of about 3 to 2 in ships of the line at the beginning, but it was in far better shape than in the days of Lord Sandwich. At the same time, the Revolution had left the French Navy with inexperienced officers and undisciplined crews.

As in 1917 and again in 1941, our sea-borne trade helped involve us in war. The attitude of the people was another story. Whereas in our later wars the people have swung from comparative neutrality to eager endorsement of one side, in 1793 they started off as strong partisans of France, and then their sympathy cooled into real neutrality. As time went on, our neutrality actually was reminiscent of the alleged inquiry of the Irish Free State official, "Whom are we neutral against?"

Both sides were to use and abuse us for two decades. Scarcely was the war under way, when each began to issue a long series of regulations, which seriously affected American trade. Primarily concerned with their struggle against each other, the belligerents cared little about the repercussion of those measures upon the United States except for certain considerations that kept them from going too far. We were the heaviest purchaser of England's manufactures, and with the Continental market now restricted, we were too valuable a customer to lose. Also, our neutral bottoms were convenient for trading with hostile Continental ports. France had even more urgent need of our neutral flag to bring home its Caribbean sugar and coffee and to carry on its coasting trade, for the tricolor became exceedingly risky to fly at sea. We were, thus, very useful, but not, as we thought, indispensable. The Embargo would prove that to our sorrow.

As for ourselves, various reasons caused us to swallow insults and accept humiliating conditions for so long with a fair grace before resorting to armed conflict. Obviously we were far from being the first-rate power we had become by 1914. At the outset, we had no navy at all; even after 1797, it was a very small one. Our envoys at London and Paris were in no position to give orders; the day was still far distant when a British prime minister would cross the Atlantic to discuss American maritime co-operation.

Above all, we found our neutral role an extremely profitable one, with "freedom of the seas" a decidedly practical policy. The records of seizures by the British and French are voluminous and sometimes exciting, but they tend to obscure the financial gains from our freighting and trading throughout those unsettled decades. For every voyage interrupted by seizure, many others terminated in high profits. Part of the gains came from selling a cargo for much more than it cost: a barrel of flour bought for eight dollars at New York would sell abroad or in the West Indies for two or three times that amount. Still more common were the generous freight payments for a vessel's carrying services. One small 78-ton sloop, worth $1,500, was earning $2,500 for a voyage between Boston and Surinam, when captured. That was, of course, an exceptionally high proportion, but the prize records abound in cases where freight earnings amounted to a third or a half of the vessel's value. In those days, too, the same man or men usually owned both vessel and cargo and reaped both profits. Even the national treasury was richer by some $100,000,000 between 1793 and 1812 from customs duties above the annual amount received from peacetime trade in 1792; and in that day, customs duties paid most of the costs of government.

Such good business explains the hundreds of beautiful homes built by merchants and mariners along the eastern coast during those neutral years. The fine old house overlooking Hell Gate, recently converted by New York City into a home for its mayor, was built as a country seat by Archibald Gracie from his shipping profits in 1799. It has its counterparts in the old homes in almost every seaboard town, all the way up the coast to Wiscasset, Thomaston, and beyond.

Statistics always present a dilemma to the author. If they are hard to find, he wonders just what was happening; if they are abundant, he is tempted to exasperate his readers by peppering the text with too many. Nonetheless, it seems best to present here the basic figures for the whole period, as they tell graphically the quantitative side of the story. The statistics of merchant-

COMMERCE, SHIPPING, AND INSURANCE RATES, 1792-1815

The insurance rates included marine risks (normally 2 to 3 per cent at that time) as well as war risks. Rates before 1800 are based primarily on French Spoliation records; after that, on MS records of the Boston Marine Insurance Company, and other scattered sources. Figures show the prevailing range for the year.

				ARRIVALS		SHIPPING IN M TONS		INSURANCE RATES			
	IMPORTS MIL. $	EXPORTS MIL. $	RE-EXPORTS MIL. $	M TONS	% U.S.	TOTAL	REGIS-TERED	GREAT BRITAIN	MEDITER-RANEAN	WEST INDIES	FAR EAST
1792	31	20		658	63	564	411	2	3	2	3
1793	31	26		611	73	520	367	3-10	25		
1794	34	33		608	84	628	438				
1795	69	47		637	91	747	529				
1796	81	67	26	721	93	831	576	6-8	25	6-15	5-6
1797	75	56	27	680	89	876	597	7-10		15-25	10
1798	68	61	33	610	85	898	603	6-9		20-33	
1799	79	78	45	734	85	939	662		6	10-20	
1800	91	70	39	806	84	972	669			10-15	
1801	111	94	46	1007	84	947	632	2½-3	5-6	3-5	6-10
1802	76	72	35	930	84	892	560	"	4-6	2½-3	4-4½
1803	64	55	13	951	82	949	597	"	3½-5	2½-4	4-6
1804	85	77	36	944	87	1042	672	"		3-4	4-5
1805	120	95	53	1010	91	1140	749			"	
1806	129	101	60	1134	93	1208	808	"	"	"	"
1807	138	108	59	1176	92	1268	848	3½-6	3-13		4-6
1808	56	22	12	572	91	1243	808	"	8-12		
1809	59	52	20	684	88	1350	910	4-5	8-10	3-5	5-6
1810	85	66	24	986	92	1424	984	"		3-4	5-9
1811	53	61	16	981	96	1232	768	"	"	"	"
1812	77	38	8	715	93	1269	760	4-15	8	3	5-50
1813	22	27	2	351	52	1166	674	"			75
1814	12	6	.	107	55	1159	674	"			40-50
1815	113	52	6	917	76	1368	854	3			

marine tonnage are now regarded as rather inflated, but, like the other figures, they at least indicate the relative consequences of the various international stimuli. The table on opposite page also indicates the insurance fluctuations.

With a bad harvest in 1792 and with the turmoil of the Terror, France was in peril of going hungry in 1793 and 1794. This gave American exports a real significance at the very outset, in contrast to most of the period, when American vessels were to be more important than domestic offerings. Even before the news of war came to America, the French minister arranged with the American government for credit to buy flour, to be charged against our Revolutionary debt. The eastbound flour cargoes for Bordeaux, Nantes, Lorient, Havre, and other French ports during the next year represented an appropriate partial payment for the munitions shipped westward by Beaumarchais seventeen years before. In each case, their safe arrival was a matter of deep strategic, even more than of commercial, significance.

By the summer of 1793, plenty of risks faced such American cargoes. England, with a chance to strike at France through hunger, declared breadstuffs contraband of war in June, 1793. This was a novel step, for heretofore, food had only been put in that category in cases of close siege. Russia joined in this policy, and with Prussia at war with France, the Baltic granaries were unavailable. The French need for American flour became more urgent, but the British cruisers made its transportation highly precarious.

Out of this situation came the only full-dress naval battle in the first four years of the Anglo-French war. Not daring to risk all their precious American flour in individual voyages, France sent over a small naval squadron under Admiral Van Stabel to convoy all the flour-laden vessels together. For months, the French purchasing commission stored the flour aboard merchantmen anchored in Chesapeake Bay, where other freighters gathered from the French West Indies. Quite contrary to modern censorship of ship movements, the Philadelphia newspapers openly published Admiral Van Stabel's arrival at Hampton

Roads in February, along with the reasons for his trip. Early in April, 1794, fifty French and American ships sailed down from Philadelphia to join the convoy; and a naval officer wrote that they were impatiently awaiting vessels from New York. As it turned out, that brief delay probably saved the flour for France. Finally, guarded by Van Stabel's warships, the completed flotilla of 116 merchantmen sailed out past the Virginia Capes, carrying other items along with 24,000,000 pounds of flour. That would have meant only one loaf of bread for each man, woman, and child, if distributed evenly throughout France, but it would be enough to quiet the hunger pangs of the restless and dangerous Paris mob.

Surprisingly enough, the British Navy was not lying in wait at the three-mile limit outside Cape Henry. Their consuls had been reporting regularly on the convoy; so too had the newspapers; and a frigate was close at hand at Norfolk. A moderate squadron on this side of the Atlantic would have had little difficulty in crushing the French force and capturing the flour ships or driving them back to port. Instead the Royal Navy planned to intercept the convoy on the other side—a very doubtful procedure in that prewireless era.

Realizing that, France decided to risk practically the whole battle fleet—two dozen ships of the line—though the condition of the ships and the inexperience of the officers made them no match for the equal number of British warships under the veteran Howe. The French ships sailed from Brest five hundred miles to sea to meet Van Stabel, under orders to avoid a fight with Howe's powerful Channel fleet unless the convoy were in danger. The two rival fleets, both still unaware of the convoy's exact whereabouts, met in the last days of May; and in the course of desultory encounters, the French admiral drew Howe toward the northwest. It was a sacrifice play but it cleared the way for the flour fleet. Howe badly smashed the French fleet on the "Glorious First of June," as the British called it, and carried off six of its battered ships of the line. But on June 13, Van Stabel triumphantly brought his convoy unscathed into

Brest, after passing directly over the very spot where the British had lain in wait. Flour from the Chesapeake, the Delaware, and the Hudson staved off bread riots in those last weeks of the Great Terror, Robespierre being guillotined just six weeks later.

Meanwhile aggressive privateering in the Caribbean by the British was arousing bitter American indignation. France, fully aware that those waters were too dangerous for its own vessels, had given permission to neutrals to engage in the lucrative and hitherto prohibited "long haul" from its sugar islands to French ports. England struck at this trade suddenly in November, 1793, by authorizing the seizure of any neutral vessels trading to or from the French islands. Two months later the order was relaxed at London, but with the slow communications, tremendous damage was done in the meantime. British warships and privateers seem to have used the order as an excuse for the indiscriminate hauling of hundreds of American vessels into their island ports, where about 150 were condemned. All through the early months of 1794, the American newspapers were filled with lists of unlucky vessels at Jamaica, Antigua, Dominica, Montserrat, St. Kitts, Nassau, and Bermuda.

The Bermudian privateers took the first crack at them, catching them in flank as they came down the coast. They were most irregular according to the reports, looting and destroying before proper condemnation in the Vice-Admiralty Court. Passengers had their trunks rifled and they themselves were thoroughly searched "without discrimination of age or sex." As for the vessel, "they commence unloading her, at their own discretion, starting, boreing, breaking and destroying many things before them, at the same time, turning the crew on shore, and enlisting them on board their privateers," while any captain who objected was "threatened with destruction."

If a Yankee schooner escaped past Bermuda, she found worse dangers in the bottleneck entrances to the Caribbean. Every British island turned out a swarm of privateers. "Everything that will carry from ten to thirty mulattoes and negroes," wrote a

skipper from Dominica, "is commissioned to take Americans."
One was better off if overhauled by a cruiser of the Royal Navy,
whose officers would at least be correct, than by a boatload of
half-breeds. The Spaniards, then allied to England, joined in the
chase. One sea captain was told by a British naval officer that
"the Spaniards and English send all American vessels into port."
Now and then boldness paid. The mate of the sloop *Polly,* taken
into Montserrat, "took the opportunity of weighing anchor
while the prize master was on shore, and made the best of his
way to New London, leaving Capt. Lester, papers, and log book
behind."

Few were that fortunate. Those small craft were pretty helpless against attack. There was no United States Navy to convoy
them. Foreign warships, to be sure, did give protection to more
important American vessels. There was, for instance, that French
help to the flour fleet, some British convoying across the Atlantic, and, as we shall see, varied types of protection against
the Barbary pirates. But the little schooners bound for the
Caribbean were on their own. Unarmed and unescorted, they
trusted only to their own speed, which was too often lacking,
and to their luck.

The island ports were crowded with destitute American sailors
and desperate captains, deprived of their money and sometimes
of their very clothes. Some of the provision cargoes spoiled in
the heat and crews sickened from the stench. At Antigua, an
epidemic ran through the American vessels. There was no money
for doctors and mourning flags were hoisted almost every day.
It was difficult to hire lawyers to defend the cases in the Vice-
Admiralty Courts; and still harder to communicate with home
to have the owners launch appeals from condemnation. Worst of
all was Martinique early in 1794, when the British took the
island. They seized and condemned some forty Yankee vessels,
impressing some of the crews into naval service and locking
up the rest on a prison ship with very short rations.

This last outrage aroused the whole Atlantic coast from Maine
to Georgia. Angry memorials from every seaboard town poured

into Congress. Charleston, for example, reported that thirty-eight of its vessels, with cargoes worth $315,000, had been captured and detained, twenty-five being already condemned, while another thirty-three were "now abroad in the West Indies, fate not known." But the West Indies were not the only scene of maritime difficulties in those spring weeks of 1794. Our mariners were being much harassed by the Barbary pirates and also by French detentions and seizures. Altogether the United States awoke suddenly to what it meant to have no navy, and took the first step toward building one, with the prime purpose of erasing the pirate menace. The government also laid an embargo, the first of several similar measures, on trade with the British. Some hotheads did not want to stop there, but the realists preferred to see what could be done peaceably with England. In May, while Van Stabel's convoy was on the high seas, the chief justice of the United States, John Jay, sailed from New York to try his luck at the Court of St. James's.

The resultant Jay Treaty disappointed many Americans who had hoped for more concessions. Its many provisions do not concern us here beyond certain commercial clauses. Little American vessels of not more than sixty tons were now allowed to trade with the English sugar islands, since they were too small to continue on across the Atlantic with their sugar on the forbidden "long haul." England agreed that a mixed commission should determine claims for damages resulting from unneutral acts. This able group of two Englishmen and three Americans (the latter won the toss for the third member) met intermittently for nearly ten years, sifted hundreds of cases, and argued the technicalities of international law. They awarded British shipowners and merchants $143,000 for damages inflicted by the French privateers fitted out in American ports; and to American claimants nearly $12,000,000 was granted for losses sustained in the taking of grain ships, and in the seizures in the West Indies. That adjudication has been called a "direct and immediate progenitor" of the Geneva commission for the Alabama claims.

The first year of the war had brought more trouble than profit to the Americans, but a glance back at the table of statistics will indicate that by 1795 our commerce and merchant marine were both feeling the quickening influence of our neutral role. For almost three years after the Jay Treaty, American commerce was not seriously molested, although some seizures were made by both sides throughout the period. Shipbuilding was booming all along the coast from the Chesapeake to Maine; and not only at the major ports but in almost every creek and inlet near a good supply of oak and pine. Most of our foreign trade was now in American bottoms, which a few years back had had little more than half of it.

Much of the expanding commerce followed the usual familiar routes. The cargoes of textiles and hardware from England still bulked largest in value; nor was that trade troubled to any extent. Trade with the Continent was on the increase. Occasional valuable shipments arrived from China, India, and the "Salem East Indies," while most numerous were the small vessels in the Caribbean trade.

The sudden jump in import and export figures is somewhat deceptive, for it reflected the new indirect trade between the French sugar islands and France. That was being winked at by the English who opposed the direct "long haul." If the voyage were broken at some American port en route, the vessel was not liable to British seizure. Sometimes such a vessel might carry a cargo all the way from Martinique to Bordeaux safely by the simple expedient of stopping at Boston, New York, or Philadelphia, to go through the formality of unloading the cargo and then reloading it after paying customs duties, most of which would be at once refunded. At other times, large vessels would handle the transatlantic leg of the trade, with smaller ones to distribute through the West Indies that which had been brought from Europe. The records show some strange mixtures of foreign and domestic offerings. The brig *Eliza,* for example, sailing from Philadelphia for Haiti, had in her cargo "flour, oil, gin, brandy, salmon, candles, soap, tea, lard, hams, sausages, almonds, marble mortars, herring, claret, looking-glasses, playing cards, travelling cases, glassware, cheese, fruits, perfumes, sweetmeats and hair powder." Part of the sugar or coffee carried northward in return might be transferred into some ship bound for Nantes or Marseilles.

Such practices swelled our customs statistics with items in which we had only a fleeting—though very profitable—connection. The column of "re-exports" indicated the extent of this entrepôt business. In 1792, the New York customhouse had refunded in re-export drawbacks less than 4 per cent of the duties collected; by 1795, this amounted to more than 25 per cent; and by 1798 to more than a third of the total. During most of the years down to 1807, those re-exports overshadowed the exports of our own domestic produce.

While this new wartime activity gave an illusory inflation to the customs statistics, another very profitable function of the merchant marine did not appear at all on the customs records. This was the "tramp carrying trade" between foreign ports, without returning to the United States. It was stimulated by France's removal of the peacetime restrictions on her coasting trade. Right up to the War of 1812, hundreds of American merchantmen were playing around the Continental ports or even going as far afield as the East Indies and back, without seeing their home ports for years on end.

Even those relatively peaceful years saw some adventures. The 459-ton ship *Confederacy* represented the "tramp" trader of the period, and her path was beset with perils. Perhaps her unusual size made her loom as a rich enough potential prize for many a frigate captain to take a chance on finding grounds for her condemnation in court. Sailing from New York in April, 1795, with provisions and sugar for Havre, she was not fifty miles from Sandy Hook when two British frigates swooped upon her. Sent into Halifax on the charge of carrying contraband in the provision casks, she was released by the Vice-Admiralty Court and her captors had to pay the charges. But near the English Channel, she was snapped up again; and this British frigate sent her into Plymouth on the charge of carrying provisions to

France. Again she was released, and her captain, apparently abandoning the Havre project, went around to London, where the ship was sold to another New York firm which sent her to the East Indies. Leaving London on Christmas Day, she stopped for wine at Madeira, then sold most of her cargo at the distant French colonies of Isle de France and Bourbon, and by June was taking on a cotton cargo at Bombay. She next sold the cotton at Canton, after a stop at Penang, and loading tea, cinnamon, sugar, and chinaware, sailed for Hamburg by way of Cape Horn in January, 1797. She stopped at Charleston and everything pointed to the safe completion of her voyage around the world, when in June, she was caught by a French privateer near the Channel. This was her end, for she was condemned at Nantes on the trivial charge of lacking a notarized crew list. The lucky privateersmen shared the $298,349.68 which ship and cargo fetched at forced sale.

By that time, the lull was over and the Americans were clamoring against the French more loudly than they had protested the British seizures of 1794. At the outset of the war, the French had anticipated lively American co-operation in accord with the Treaty of 1778; but instead, the Jay Treaty came along to anger them thoroughly, as it abrogated the provisions of the other treaty. In July, France decreed that neutral vessels would be treated exactly as they allowed themselves to be by England. In other words, they were to get "least-favored nation" terms: "By this monstrous abuse in judicial proceedings," wrote Secretary of State Pickering, "frauds and falsehoods, as well as flimsy and shameless pretexts, pass unexamined and uncontradicted, and are made the foundation of sentences of condemnation." The only thing the Secretary neglected to call the French was "pirates," but plenty of others were using that familiar epithet.

A long collection of sworn statements, casualty lists, and newspaper clippings accompanied Pickering's message, with details of scores of seizures. Most of them leave an impression of petty plundering, shameless irregularity, and occasional brutality. Here are samples of what Americans were reading in their newspapers during the fall of 1796 and the spring of 1797.

The brig *Glasgow,* Codwise, of New York, being bound from Jeremie to Port-au-Prince, was captured and carried into Leogane. The captain was confined on board his vessel, his crew were excited to assassinate him; and on the fifteenth day of his confinement, having ventured on shore, he was taken up, placed in the fort, and there detained thirty-six hours, without provisions. After a detention of sixty-eight days, seeing no prospect of a trial, he abandoned his vessel, and returned home.

The brig *Two Sisters,* Captain Worth, from Norfolk for Leogane, was brought to by a French privateer, to the leeward of Hispaniola. Captain Worth was ordered on board, and, when there, the captain of the privateer, offering a paper written in French, ordered Captain Worth to sign it. On his refusing, the pirate drew his cutlass and swore he would cleave his scull if he did not immediately put his name to the paper; but Captain Worth persisted in refusing, reasoning on the absurdity of his signing a writing in a language he did not understand. The privateersman then turned to the sailors (two Italians) and commanded them to write their names; they could not write; he then forced them with threats, and a drawn sword over their heads, to make their marks at the bottom of the paper. He then directly hailed the brig, informing that she was a good prize, as the men had signed a declaration that she was bound to Jamaica.

There were lying at Petit Guave, on the 10th November, seven American vessels, which had been captured in pursuance of orders of the Commissioners at the Cape, making all Americans bound to or from British ports, lawful prize. They had been lying there from two to three months, during which time their cargoes were taken from them, without the form of a trial; more than three-fourths of the men (captains and sailors) fell a sacrifice to the fever, and the remaining fourth were more like walking ghosts than men; most of them destitute of money and unable to give a decent burial to those who die.

The psychological effect of such items, repeated week after week, may well be imagined. Probably fifty of those small schooners and brigs, together with all their ladings, did not represent as much value as the single freighter *Robin Moor* sunk in 1941; but their crews were twenty times as numerous, and their loss intimately affected communities all the way along the coast. The pressure upon Congress from outraged constituents was correspondingly much more personal and intense. The widespread indignation burned at a whiter heat than it had at the British seizures in 1794. Also the naval preparations, stimulated by that previous crisis, were assuming really tangible form and looked stronger in contrast to the depleted French cruisers than when compared with England's naval might.

But for the moment Congress tried a repetition of the Jay venture as a peaceful solution. Three commissioners were sent to Paris to encounter Talleyrand's shameless demand for a heavy bribe through his emissaries "X, Y, and Z." When word of the infamous "X.Y.Z. Affair" reached Congress, it prepared for more drastic measures. The French, in the meantime, had begun to seize vessels on our very coast.

The result was the "undeclared naval war" with France which lasted from 1798 to 1801. Interesting in itself, it is doubly so because of its close parallel to the naval situation with Germany in the summer and autumn of 1941. Perhaps it was a coincidence that President Franklin D. Roosevelt advocated, and wrote the foreword of, the seven fat volumes of naval records of that "war," published by the Navy Department. They provided ample precedents, anyway, for the patrolling and convoying on dangerous sea lanes, the arming of merchantmen, the "shoot-at-sight" orders without declaration of war which the President directed on that later occasion.

Congress took a number of radical steps between April 27 and July 7, 1798 to provide naval protection for shipping. Merchantmen were authorized to receive letters of marque, entitling them to carry guns, to beat off French privateers or cruisers (on the ground that the miscarriage of justice in French ports nullified the usual rights of visitation and search), and to make prizes of any vessels that they should capture. A separate Navy Department was established and a force of ships assembled to seize any French warships or other armed vessels anywhere on the high seas. Unlike regular war, however, unarmed French merchantmen were not to be molested.

For various reasons, this did not become a declared war. Congress was seriously divided; and war would make the whole merchant marine more vulnerable. In the hope, too, that France might come to terms, it was stipulated that these emergency measures would cease at once whenever France should "cause the commanders of all French vessels to refrain from the lawless depredations and outrages hitherto encouraged."

The naval force available for these various protective devices was not large. Two of the crack 44-gun superfrigates, the *Constitution* and the *United States,* along with the smaller *Constellation,* were not yet quite ready for sea. Further construction was started, and in the meantime some fast revenue cutters and armed merchantmen were used in the service. In a year, the navy consisted of thirty-three vessels of varied sorts.

Benjamin Stoddart, the new secretary, worked overtime to whip this navy into shape. Since its meager forces would have been spread too thin if American shipping were to be protected on all runs, he wisely concentrated upon our own coasts and upon the West Indies, the site of the major depredations. Most of the trouble in those waters came not from French cruisers, but from the privateers, which were able to bully defenseless merchantmen but could not and would not stand up against a well-armed warship. As our infant navy was too small to provide regular convoys to and from the Caribbean, the vessels were used to patrol the principal dangerous bottlenecks where the shipping was most vulnerable.

The first capture, made by the *Ganges* in July, 1798, not far from the present site of Atlantic City, was the French privateer *La Croyable.* Before long, the French realized that our coasts were too risky for comfort and fell back on the West Indies, nearer their bases. Our navy was down there too; it seized a few dozen privateers and recaptured numerous merchantmen. Also, the *Constellation* fought and won the only two regular frigate duels of the "war," capturing the *Insurgente* in 1799 and defeating the stronger *Vengeance* a year later. The important result of this naval activity was that the privateers grew less bold in their former richest hunting grounds, and though Yankee vessels were still seized as prizes, it rarely happened on the more frequented runs.

The armed letters of marque were particularly valuable on routes distant from the strong arm of the navy. Altogether, more than a thousand of these armed merchantmen were commissioned, ranging from the *Providence* with thirty-four guns, down to the *Reindeer,* which carried nineteen wooden guns and one real one. Early in 1799, the ship *Mary* of Boston, with Captain Gamaliel Bradford in command, fought off several French privateers near Malaga with her ten guns without losing a man. That summer, the *Mount Vernon* of Salem with twenty guns had a four-day running fight off Gibraltar, in which she beat off a small French warship, escaped from two pursuing frigates, and then pounded a privateer into submission. Her voyage proceeded calmly after that and netted a profit of $100,000 on a $43,000 investment. Even in the West Indies, the letters of marque often had to fend for themselves, as the embryo navy could not be everywhere at once; their own guns saved more than one of them from what would have been inevitable prize courts.

While the "undeclared war" thus diminished the French depredations, it did not end them, and some of the most lurid tales came from the later period. Early in March, 1800, the unarmed ship *Mary* of Baltimore was seized by three barges of Negroes off Haiti. Her crew were sent ashore, stripped, and their hands tied behind their backs. The captain managed to break away, escape a volley of musketry, and hide in the woods. The next morning, he crept out to find bodies of six of the crew, naked on the beach, hacked and mutilated beyond recognition, while scattered about were the looted contents of trunks. Twenty miles up shore, he found the cave where the *Mary's* cargo was hidden; and then coming upon a boat without oars, drifted over to a safer shore.

In March, 1800, on the very day that the *Mary* was despoiled, three American commissioners reached Paris to negotiate peace terms, and by the end of September the "Convention of 1800" was completed. Though Napoleon and the Senate wrangled over details for another year, the original terms put an end to the French interference with our commerce, and our navy was recalled from the West Indies.

Altogether the infant navy had done a good job. In less than three years, it had captured one French frigate and beaten another; captured 111 privateers and sunk four more; recaptured more than seventy merchantmen; reduced seizures drastically; induced Talleyrand to hint at the desirability of peace negotiations; and generally built up respect for the untried nation. All this had cost six million dollars—only about a quarter of the customs duties collected during those same years.

The war-risk figures confirm Secretary Stoddart's boast that the navy had more than paid for itself through the reduction in insurance rates. In the summer of 1796, before the French started their heavy raiding, the rate for the West Indian voyage was about 6 per cent. By the end of the year, it had more than doubled. During 1797, premiums fluctuated between 15 and 25 per cent. By the summer of 1798, just as the navy was going into action, they reached their peak at 30 to 33 per cent, a fivefold increase in two years. The results of naval protection were soon apparent. During the spring and summer of 1799, the rate ranged from 15 to 20 per cent, and by the beginning of 1800 had fallen still farther to the vicinity of 10 per cent. Here was tangible evidence of the wisdom of the policy and of the effectiveness of the measure.

The American commissioners at Paris had failed to secure one thing which Jay had successfully extracted from the British six years before—compensation for private damages caused by the seizures and condemnations, estimated at some twenty millions. Eventually in 1803, the United States government agreed to pay those claims as part of the Louisiana Purchase deal. England had paid promptly the 1794 damages, but through no fault of France, the "French Spoliation Claims" were not settled by Congress until the end of 1915. Congress argued for years that this payment was a moral obligation, but even when bills were eventually passed for the investigation of the claims, Presidents Polk and Pierce vetoed them. At last in 1885, the Court of Claims was authorized to judge the validity of thousands of claims. Old papers had to be dragged from attics and offices; and by 1891 Congress began to approve the first payments. Now and then one encounters someone who recalls receiving a government check for his great-grandfather's share of a schooner seized in Haitian waters a century before. By 1905 the payments totaled nearly four million dollars, but thousands of cases were left on the docket for another ten years in spite of continual Congressional agitation. By the end of 1915, when the Court of Claims had cleaned up the docket, 6,479 cases had been handled, involving 2,309 vessels. Of these, 4,626 were settled in favor of the government and 1,853, totaling $7,149,306, for the claimants. The old merchants and mariners of 1798-1801 had received far better service from their new navy than from other branches of their government.

Everything looked bright in the American seaports in the spring of 1801, for France was behaving again and schooners could clear for the West Indies without fear of condemnation or mayhem. To make matters better, England needed American grain to offset a bad harvest. This was not the desperate need of the French in 1794, but nevertheless a good business opportunity. The demand was so heavy and shipping so busy elsewhere that flour commanded a freight of more than four dollars a barrel, and at that rate, one eastbound crossing would virtually pay for a ship. Imports, exports, re-exports, and shipping movements struck their highest level yet. More than a million tons of shipping entered our ports, with imports almost four times what they had been in 1792 and exports more than four times as large. Our merchant marine was approaching a million tons in size, the equivalent, perhaps, of nine thousand vessels, and almost two-thirds of it was registered for foreign trade.

Then, to the general disgust of mariner and merchant, England and Napoleon patched up a peace in the autumn. The news "instantly operated like the hand of death upon all business" over here. The definitive peace of Amiens in 1802 deepened the gloom. And to make bad matters worse, England had a bountiful harvest. The American ardor for neutral profits had not been dampened by eight years of seizures and uncertainties, and men hoped that "France and England would get at loggerheads" again, for then "the chance would be good." Those prayers were quickly answered; the peace proved to be only a temporary truce, and high adventure lay ahead for American ships and seamen.

But the second round of the Anglo-French conflict, recommencing in 1803, was a more serious matter for the Americans as well as for the belligerents. Napoleon gave France a more stable government, increased its naval strength, and sent its victorious armies into almost every nation of the Continent. England, between the threat of invasion and the loss of its European markets, was in no mood to be complaisant about the role of neutrals. With sea power its most potent weapon, Britain used it vigorously and effectively.

During the first phase, our chief troubles had come from undisciplined swarms of British and French privateers; now we were to encounter sweeping national policies carried out in a more orderly but, at the same time, more ruthlessly thorough manner. For a while, American sea-borne trade flourished as never before; then came the series of violent interruptions, when it was caught between the rival belligerent measures.

One distinctive new feature was Britain's wholesale and very successful use of blockades. Instead of relying simply upon cruising at large to catch the enemy or neutrals at sea, warships were kept on constant vigil off scores of ports. On the grand scale, powerful fleets of ships of the line held continual watch to prevent any concentration of the rapidly increasing French forces, which might gain control of the Channel long enough for Napoleon's Grand Army to be ferried over to England in flatboats. As Mahan expressed it, "Those far distant, storm-beaten ships, upon which the Grand Army never looked, stood between it and dominion of the world." The Americans were more concerned with the lesser cruiser forces stationed off neutral ports, which in time meant American as well as European. Day in and day out, they waited to check the comings and goings of merchantmen as well as of stray French cruisers.

This expanded role of the Royal Navy called for more ships, and that, in turn, meant more sailors. Many Englishmen were deserting the "floating hell" of their naval service for the freer life aboard the American merchant marine, which, too, was growing rapidly and offered higher wages. To England, American naturalization did not count; "once an Englishman, always an Englishman." Britain claimed the right to recover its seagoing subjects wherever it might find them, in port or even on the high seas. It was not always easy to recognize bona fide Englishmen in an American crew, but the Royal Navy generally allowed itself the benefit of any doubts. Such was the galling practice of impressment that eventually helped to goad the United States into war in 1812.

Impressment was no novelty, though it became acute about 1803. For more than a century, the Royal Navy had relied upon abductors and press gangs, who had long spread terror through all the seacoast towns. Its service was so unpopular that most men in their right minds refused to join voluntarily. The American colonists, protected by an act of Queen Anne's time, had opposed any attempts violently. John Adams in 1769 had secured a verdict of "justifiable homicide" for a Marblehead sailor who had killed a British frigate lieutenant while resisting impressment. Even before the current war began, the United States was protesting the snatching of men from its vessels in British ports. The outcry grew when early in 1796 officers from H.M.S. *Regulus* removed five men from the crew of an American ship by force, not in port, but on the high seas. That precedent rapidly spread into general practice.

Congress, contending that a nation's merchantmen under its flag were an extension of its territory, tried to mitigate a situation which it lacked the power to check. Among other things, it provided American seamen with certificates of citizenship, which the British scorned as often being forged and too easily negotiable. According to a senator's later comment, if a sailor had a "protection," the British called it a forgery; if not, they considered the lack as proof of noncitizenship.

The dispute missed a satisfactory settlement early in 1803, when the American minister at London took tactful advantage of a temporary lull in the fighting to promise to bar British seamen from American merchantmen if impressment were stopped. Only the consent of Lord St. Vincent, a tough old sea dog in charge of the Admiralty, was needed, but his quibbling balked the solution; and in a short time England was in the thick of war again. Later, a bill was introduced in Congress to declare impressment piracy, with the death penalty, and with a bounty of two hundred dollars offered to any American seaman for killing anyone trying to impress him; but action was postponed.

Meanwhile, the seizures did not stop. By 1806, American seamen were being taken within sight of Sandy Hook. A little tragedy was re-enacted hundreds of times during these years. An American vessel would be forced to lay to, with topsails helplessly backed, while a boat came over from a British cruiser. Even the toughest foremast hand must have had his moment of terror when the boarding naval lieutenant came over the side. If his visit meant the seizure of ship or cargo, that was a matter for the captain and owners to worry about; at least the case would go through the forms of legal trial at some Vice-Admiralty Court. But if the lieutenant called for a line-up of the crew, the future liberty and happiness of any one in that group might depend upon the snap judgment of that haughty young man of twenty, inspecting the anxious line of sailors. Even a Maine twang or a Georgia drawl might not save a likely looking top-mast hand if the officer pronounced him an Englishman. Off he went for forced service in His Majesty's fleet, where enlistments never terminated save through disability or death.

Along with the outraged protests against impressment of Americans and the thousands of cases listed in the official rec-ords, one batch of testimony denied the existence of the practice. The New England shipowners, as time went on, became wor-ried over the impressment dispute because it seemed to be drag-ging us into trouble with England, the very last thing they wanted. Thereupon they solemnly asserted that in all their years of shipping experience, they had never, or almost never, heard of an American sailor's being impressed. One wonders if Wil-liam Gray, the leading shipowner of the country, had his tongue in his cheek when he said that, or whether the epidemic of native American impressments was merely a figment of the Adminis-tration's imagination.

American cargoes, as well as seamen, were running afoul of the Royal Navy. The encounter of the *Ann Alexander* of New Bedford was, to be sure, both pleasant and profitable, but cir-cumstances were rarely as mutually beneficial. In 1805, eighteen days out from New York, and laden with flour, tobacco, salt fish, apples, and a deckload of lumber, she met the British fleet off Cape Trafalgar, just after the great battle which had left some of the ships rather battered. That deckload of lumber was a godsend for temporary repairs; a boat from the *Victory* brought over an officer who paid well for it, together with some flour and apples, in good English gold.

The *Ambition,* which had left Sandy Hook at just about the same time, had a more usual experience. She was engaged in that indirect trade, which had been so profitable for eleven years for American shipping, between the West Indies and the Continent. In May, Isaac Clason of New York had sent her to Havana with $34,000 in specie and a cargo of flour, butter, and brandy, valued at $13,000. By mid-August she was back in New York with 1,420 boxes of sugar and fifteen tons of logwood. The usual farce of carrying part of the cargo ashore to pay customs and then restowing it with contents untouched was gone through. With the property now valued at $75,000, a gain of more than 50 per cent over the original shipment to Havana, and with new officers and crew, the *Ambition* sailed for Amsterdam. Her orders were to sell the sugar and logwood, buy a hundred pipes of "Geneva" (gin) for Clason and send it back to New York, while the rest of the proceeds were to be remitted to London "in unexceptionable bills of exchange."

Had there been cable or wireless, the *Ambition* would never have been allowed to sail upon that second leg of her journey. After eleven years of winking at this indirect trade, Lords of Appeal in Prize Causes had just handed down a devastating decision in the case of the *Essex,* which had been intercepted on a similar voyage from Barcelona to Havana by way of Salem. She was condemned on the new ground that she was really engaged in a "continuous voyage" between two enemy ports. The captain of the *Ambition* knew nothing of this when His Majesty's gun brig *Haughty* (a most appropriate name for the purpose) overhauled her "seven leagues south of Falmouth" and sent her into Plymouth with a prize crew.

England's reasons for the change of policy were strongly set forth in a book, *War in Disguise; or The Frauds of the Neutral Flags,* written during the anxious months when invasion scares put England in no mood to humor even its best customer. The author, James Stephens, who had had ample experience in the prize courts of the West Indies and London, argued that England was letting slip through its fingers one of the main advantages of sea power by letting its enemies trade with their sugar islands in neutral bottoms. Not a single enemy merchantman dared appear on the high seas, yet France received its sugar from Guadeloupe more cheaply than England could bring it from Jamaica. He charged that the Americans did not really own those sugar cargoes but simply gave neutral coverage for a consideration. He further pointed out the very recent modest circumstances of many of those merchants, comparing them with the German shoemaker, who suddenly became nominal owner of 150 vessels. Also this carrying trade was aiding Napoleon's navy, for he need not detach warships, as England must, to guard distant sea lanes.

The ubiquitous cruisers of the Royal Navy, along with British privateers, were soon snapping up American merchantmen all over the seven seas. The chief crop once more came from the West Indies, but this privateering epidemic was conducted on a more orderly basis, with legal condemnations in the Vice-Admiralty Courts at Jamaica and Antigua. In European waters, vessels bound for Amsterdam and Rotterdam were picked up off the Dutch coasts, and the *Hare,* for example, another Clason ship, was caught leaving blockaded Cadiz with a load of salt and sherry. In more distant seas, the brig *Cora* and the ship *Penman* were instances of the far-flung arm of the Royal Navy. The former was caught with a load of Java coffee just after she sailed from Samarang, and the latter was taken in the Indian Ocean while trading between Batavia and Muscat.

A tramp-swapping voyage to far less conventional ports eventually came to grief through the suspicious vigilance of a British frigate captain. Mathias Nicoll, sailing from New York in 1806 in his ship *Cotton Planter,* stopped first at Madeira and Teneriffe to dispose of the flour and oak staves in his mixed cargo. He moved on to the slave stations of the African coast. At Senegal and Goree, he bought thirty-four Negroes, paying for them by the sale of his rum, brandy, and tobacco, together with the sterling bills of exchange received in the wine islands. Picking up some salt in the Cape Verde Islands, the slave ship headed for South America. At the mouth of the Rio Plata, she had to wait while a British expedition attacked Buenos Aires. Nicoll made a side profit salvaging a partly wrecked American ship. Then at

NEUTRAL PROFITS 91

Buenos Aires, he sold his slaves and salt—the latter innocent cargo netting twice the profit of the Negroes. With the proceeds, he bought a cargo of jerked beef and cleared for Charleston. Off Antigua, the ship was brought to by the frigate *Latona*. Nicoll confidently pointed out that he was bound to a neutral port; but to his consternation, he was shown some of his own letters, intercepted from another ship, in which he had written, "I feel fully persuaded that the sooner my beef arrives in Havana, the greater price it will bring." Those damning words transferred the profits of the voyage to the *Latona's* captain and his subordinates. Nicoll comforted himself with the thought of his insurance coverage: "Premiums dig deep in profit, but are frequently repaid with heavy interest."

By 1804 American vessels did not have to travel beyond their own coast to meet British cruisers exercising control of the seas. They were beginning to haunt the immediate approaches to the major American ports. The *Guerrière*, which in due time would receive her punishment, stood watch near Boston Light. A squadron was posted to check the comings and goings in Chesapeake Bay. Most conspicuous were several cruisers patrolling the waters around Sandy Hook. The frigate *Leander*, the most persistent of this last exasperating group, made herself particularly obnoxious. As one of her midshipmen later described her annoying routine:

> Every morning at daybreak, we set about arresting the progress of all vessels we saw, firing off guns to the right and left to make every ship that was running in heave to, or wait until we had leisure to send a boat on board "to see" in our lingo, "what she was made of." I have frequently known a dozen, and sometimes a couple of dozen, ships lying a league or two off the port, losing their fair wind, their tide, and worse than all their market, for many hours, sometimes the whole day, before our search was completed.

Inward bound New York vessels from the West Indies and abroad were boarded within sight of Sandy Hook light and sent to Halifax under prize crews. Seamen were impressed by the dozen from British as well as from American merchantmen.

The climax was the attack by the *Leander* on the little sloop *Richard* as she came up the Jersey coast about a quarter of a mile off Sandy Hook on April 24, 1806. The *Leander* started firing without warning; one shot landed forty feet ahead; another flew directly over the sloop; and as she obediently started to heave to, a third shot struck the quarter rail. A splinter carried off the head of the helmsman, John Pierce, brother of the master. His headless body was viewed by angry crowds on the New York water front before being laid in state at the City Hall. A huge mass meeting passed vigorous resolutions against the "repeated outrages committed by foreign ships of war at the mouths of our harbors." Within ten days, President Jefferson issued a proclamation calling for the arrest of the *Leander's* captain, forbidding the captains of all three men-of-war from ever again entering United States waters, commanding the ships to leave, and barring any shore assistance in the form of food, pilotage, or repairs. The squadron did not depart at once; incoming vessels continued to be seized.

While England was thus continually arousing American anger, France was relatively well behaved during the first four years of the renewed war. Against an estimated total of 528 British seizures in this early period, France was charged with only 206, of which many occurred in the vicinity of Haiti. There, France, with some cause, was nursing a definite grievance against the Yankees for their lively business of swapping munitions for coffee with the "rebel blacks," who were gradually driving Napoleon's forces from that troubled island. In 1806, a French admiral chased a small convoy of those coffee-laden vessels northward, blustering that he would hang every captain and supercargo from the yardarms of their vessels in New York harbor; but a convenient gale off Hatteras drove him to sea with his bold threats unfulfilled.

While the British frigate *Leander* was annoying the port of New York in 1806, a New York ship *Leander* was arousing equally righteous indignation among the Spaniards. She was one of those Haitian gunrunners temporarily diverted to carry the Venezuelan adventurer, Miranda, on a revolutionary drive against the Spanish Main. Sailing from New York, with the apparent connivance of the government, she had aboard a group of young Americans who thought they were going to New Orleans as mailguards, but who found themselves incarcerated in Spanish dungeons when the coup failed.

During all this, American shipping and commerce were both flourishing as never before. Even if a few hundred vessels were seized, thousands successfully completed their highly profitable voyages. Combined imports and exports, which had been only $52,000,000 in 1792, had risen to $205,000,000 by 1801. With the peace interval, they slumped to $110,000,000 in 1803. Then they started up again; $162,000,000 in 1804, $215,000,000 in 1805, $221,-000,000 in 1806, and finally hit the high-water mark of $246,000,-000 in 1807, a level not touched again until 1835. Just about half of that amount represented the almost $60,000,000 worth of sugar, coffee, and other products, which counted once when arriving and again when leaving as re-exports. It was the last boom year of that trade, which kept on despite the British attack on the "continuous voyage." Sugar imports came to 110,000 tons; coffee, to 29,000 tons. Of the re-exports of those Caribbean products, Holland was the heaviest consumer, followed by France, Italy, and Spain, while Cuba, in turn, absorbed a large amount of the re-exports from Europe. A particular reason for the high 1807 total was a sudden boom in domestic exports. In a single year, cotton jumped from 35 to 63 million bales, flour from 782,-000 to 1,249,000, and wheat from 86,000 to 1,173,000 bushels. Great Britain, which took only one-thirtieth of the re-exports, purchased nearly half the domestic offerings in exchange for its textiles and hardware.

With more cargoes than ever, shipping naturally rose to new heights. The flour exports alone were enough to fill four hundred ships or a thousand schooners. The amount of entering tonnage, too, made 1807 a banner year, with a record not equaled until 1835; 1,176,000 tons, the equivalent of some 250 vessels daily, arrived from foreign ports, with an equal number cleared. American vessels made up 92 per cent of these huge shipping movements; and the figures do not include the many vessels that spent years abroad in the rich carrying trade without returning home.

With vessels paying for themselves in one voyage or two, shipyards great and small were working overtime turning out everything from sloops to ships. Less sensitive to external stimuli than imports, exports, or shipping movements, the merchant marine did not reach its maximum until 1810, but it did attain a new high in 1807 with 1,268,000 tons, roughly the equivalent of 10,000 vessels, requiring some 65,000 mariners. More than two-thirds of that total was registered for foreign trade. If old Adam Seybert's estimate of fifty dollars a ton per year for freight earnings was valid, the profits were tremendous. In that boom year the federal government made enough in customs duties more than to cover all its running expenses.

All along the coast from Maine to Georgia every maritime community was still enjoying the rush of the thriving business boom, blissfully unconscious of the blight that was about to descend. As one traveler recorded his impressions of the bustling activity of New York harbor:

> The port was filled with shipping and the wharves were crowded with commodities of every description. Bales of cotton, wool, and merchandize; barrels of pot-ash, rice, flour, and salt provisions; hogsheads of sugar, chests of tea, puncheons of rum, and pipes of wine; boxes, cases, packs and packages of all sizes and denominations, were strewed upon the wharves and landing places, or upon the decks of the shipping. All was noise and bustle. The carters were driving in every direction; and the sailors and labourers upon the wharves, and on board the vessels, were moving their ponderous burthens from place to place.

Chapter IV

Withdrawal from the Sea

Two months later, all that was changed. With its commerce at flood tide, America suddenly withdrew from the sea. In the dislocations and readjustments of the next seven years, that exuberant atmosphere of 1807 would never be recaptured. Every schoolboy knows why—Berlin and Milan decrees, Orders in Council, Embargo, Nonintercourse, Macon Act, and War of 1812.

John Lambert, the traveler who described the rushed and thriving port scenes in November, returned in April to find a hopeless inertia along the water front:

> The coffee-house slip, the wharves and quays along South-street, presented no longer the bustle and activity that had prevailed there five months before. The port, indeed, was full of shipping; but they were dismantled and laid up. Their decks were cleared, their hatches fastened down, and scarcely a sailor was to be found on board. Not a box, bale, cask, barrel or package, was to be seen upon the wharves. Many of the counting houses were shut up, or advertised to be let, and the few solitary merchants, clerks, porters, and labourers, that were to be seen, were walking about with their hands in their pockets . . . a few coasting sloops, and schooners, which were clearing out for some ports in the United States, were all that remained of that immense business which was carried on a few months before. . . . In fact, everything presented a melancholy appearance. The streets near the waterside were almost deserted, grass had begun to grow upon the wharves.

The same stagnation would have been found in a dozen other ports, from Portland to Savannah and around to New Orleans. Soup kitchens and other relief agencies alone found plenty of

customers. Unemployed seamen, who had not found their way
to Canada, were "on the town." But plenty of other people were
in a similar fix; shipwrights, longshoremen, and clerks were also
suffering from the sudden dislocation of their livelihood. In-
solvent debtors by the hundreds crowded the jails, with now and
then a suicide. Farmers felt the drop in the price of wheat from
$1.45 to $1.00 a bushel and of flour from $7.13 to $5.25 a barrel.
Southern planters did not escape, with cotton at thirteen instead
of twenty cents a pound.

This puncturing of the balloon of merchant shipping did not
come from a clear sky. Even in those booming summer months
of 1807, dark clouds were gathering on the distant horizon, while
nearer home the British cruisers were increasingly insolent. No
longer content with overhauling merchantmen, they were now
highhandedly insulting American government armed vessels,
even warships. A revenue cutter, for example, with Vice-Presi-
dent Tompkins aboard, was fired upon as she left Chesapeake
Bay for New York. A naval gunboat, approaching New York,
also came under British naval fire and was forced to send a midshipman over to the two waylaying cruisers. The customhouse
barge was sent to warn them off, only to be boarded and searched
in insolent fashion. A deeper humiliation awaited the frigate
Chesapeake off the Virginia Capes in June. Halted on the high
seas by the fire of the British *Leopard,* which killed and wounded
several men, she was forced to bow to the seizure of four de-
serters aboard her. This was the last straw for the aroused nation,
particularly when England postponed immediate disavowal of
the affront and replied instead with orders for increased impressment.

Far more significant in ultimate effects was the use to which
Napoleon was putting those same summer months of 1807. His
recent smashing victories had made him master of much of the
Continent, but in those preaircraft days, a few miles of salt water
kept England safe from his armies. Attempts to defeat it through
Ireland, Egypt, and direct invasion had all failed; its gold was
still financing the Europeans, who kept on fighting him. Now

he had found a grandiose project to bring his most persistent enemy to its knees. This was nothing less than drying up the source of its gold by closing all the ports of Europe to its manufactures and products from beyond the seas, whether borne in British or in neutral vessels. Napoleon had announced this program in the Berlin Decree of December, 1806, but he had been too busy to act until he stopped fighting the Russians on the same June day that the *Leopard* overhauled the *Chesapeake*. Four weeks later he secured the co-operation of the Czar at their famous conference on a raft in the Niemen; and soon afterwards, most of the Continent had been persuaded or compelled to close all ports from the Baltic to the Mediterranean.

England, faced with the loss of its valuable Continental markets, countered vigorously with new Orders in Council in November. By these, no vessel might trade with the ports involved in Napoleon's Continental system without first stopping at a British port to unload her cargo and pay duties upon it, before being allowed to reload and proceed. In December, Napoleon struck back from Milan with another decree; any vessel, which submitted by entering a British port or was visited by a cruiser of the Royal Navy, was to be a fair prize.

At first glance, those rival systems suggest the blockades of the World Wars of the present century, when England, Germany, and others have tried to starve their enemies into submission by cutting off vital supplies of sea-borne products. Quite to the contrary, neither the Continental system nor the Orders in Council were aimed at actually cutting off supplies from the foe. They were instead primarily financial measures. Napoleon sold Continental produce to England in order to drain away its gold more rapidly. England, in its turn, supplied the Continent with sugar, coffee, and tobacco, for its policy of "no trade except through England" was not to deprive the Continent of such articles, but to see that Britain alone reaped the entrepôt profits. Obviously, if such rival decrees were enforced at their face value, neutrals would be getting no more profits from their carrying trade. Their vessels faced a quandary: If they submitted to the

British regulations, they risked seizure in any European port, but if they tried evasion, they were fair game for the ever present cruisers of the Royal Navy. According to Mahan:

> The imperial soldiers were turned into coastguardmen to shut out Great Britain from her markets; the British ships became revenue cutters to prohibit the trade of France. The neutral carrier, pocketing his pride, offered his services to either for pay, and the other then regarded him as taking part in hostilities.

All this put Yankee shipping and its rich profits in such jeopardy that the government worked strenuously to obtain a relaxation of either or both of these belligerent measures. Jefferson's solution was the negation of "freedom of the seas." By withdrawing American vessels from foreign trade, he hoped not only to avoid war and prevent seizures, but also to show Britain and Napoleon that those neutral bottoms filled an indispensable need. In that way he expected to find that the harsh regulations would soon be relaxed.

Three days before Christmas, Congress embodied this new withdrawal policy of Jefferson's in the celebrated Embargo Act that was to become effective immediately. It forbade any American vessel to clear from an American port for a foreign destination. Except for certain British goods prohibited by another act just going into effect, American vessels already abroad might bring in cargoes, but once in, could not legally clear for foreign ports again. Messengers were rushed up and down the coast to instruct the customs collectors to put the law into operation immediately. Congress knew that if a week's advance notice were given, scarcely an American vessel would be found still in port at the end of that time.

The northbound courier, by dint of hard riding, reached New York before dawn on the fourth day to give the city one of the liveliest Christmas days in its history. By seven that morning, printed handbills with the text of the act were being distributed. As McMaster described the ensuing excitement:

On a sudden the streets were full of merchants, ship-owners, ship-captains, supercargoes, and sailors hurrying toward the water-front. Astonished at this unusual commotion, men of all sorts followed and by eight o'clock the wharves were crowded with spectators, cheering the little fleet of half-laden ships which, with all sail spread, was beating down the harbor. None of them had clearances. Many were half-manned. Few had more than part of a cargo. One which had just come in, rather than be embargoed, went off without breaking bulk. At the sight of the headings on the handbills, the captains made crews of the first seamen they met, and, with a few hurried instructions from the owners, pushed into the stream.

In spite of this scramble, hundreds of vessels failed to get away. By one estimate 537 were left in port, 666 by another. Several arrivals were given in the *Evening Post* the day after Christmas, but their announcement was followed by the ominous statement, "No Clearances in the Future."

The utter stagnation that spread over the ports was what one would expect from reading the Act; but it tells only part of the story. William Gray of Salem, the prominent shipowner, co-operated fully with the law, and his example was widely followed. On the other hand, a good many others displayed keen ingenuity in evading the stringent provisions. As a result, a considerable amount of clandestine trade managed to move about in spite of vigilant customs officers and Congressional tightening of the regulations. The adroit practices thus developed were to continue for several years to come as Embargo gave way to Nonintercourse, and to the War of 1812. Doubtless many a New Englander justified this shameless flaunting of national policy on the comforting ground that the Embargo was only a partisan measure of Jefferson's and his crew anyway. The Federalists were not slow in capitalizing this profitable opposition to the Republicans.

The coasting trade that was still legally open offered the richest chances for evasion. Vessels clearing for coasting voyages had to post bonds that the cargo would be delivered in a port in the United States, "dangers of the sea excepted." That qualifying phrase proved a godsend to Yankee ingenuity; naturally, a vessel in distress could seek any haven! The result was an amazing epidemic of broken spars and leaky hulls during the early months of 1808.

Such accidents, of course, excused refuge in any port a vessel might reach—anywhere from Halifax down past Bermuda and Nassau to the Caribbean. Once in port, it might well prove necessary to sell the flour cargo to pay for the repairs. Altogether, such misadventures did much for Yankee pockets, emptied by the Embargo rules. On one occasion, flour that cost five dollars a barrel in the Chesapeake sold for forty dollars at Antigua. One mariner was even blown so far off his coasting course that he found himself—and his tobacco cargo—in England. The British, needing American flour in their Caribbean islands, were extremely hospitable to these storm-tossed sailors. The royal cruisers carefully avoided them, and the port officials were most understanding about irregular clearance papers.

Whalers likewise were permitted to clear under the Embargo; and they made profits, with less need for misadventures. One Bostonian set out after whales—or so he said—but he carried five hundred casks of bacon. He brought back from Halifax one cask of whale oil—and several hundred bales of Yorkshire woolens.

Maine, we recall, had always needed some flour from the southward, but suddenly this need seemed to have grown a hundredfold. Never before had such a procession of flour-laden coasters cleared for its ports as during the Embargo, nor did they head for the usual ports. Instead they sailed past Portland, snubbed Thomaston, Castine, and even Machias, until further eastward, they came to Passamaquoddy Bay. There the United States met the British Empire, but no one was exactly sure where among its islands the frontier ran. Campobello—where a president would later summer—was definitely on the New Brunswick side, and Eastport was clearly in Maine, but all the rest was a no man's land, with dozens of sheltered coves where clandestine traders in flour or broadcloth would find nothing more than the twenty-foot tides to worry them. Customs officials thereabouts developed an attitude of tolerant broadmindedness; perhaps for good cause, as an American collector wrote that his house would be burned if he tried to interfere. The Maritime Provinces helped to facilitate the trade by frequent helpful decrees. Halifax had more reason to bless the Embargo than any other port, except perhaps Quebec which was fed by smuggling over the inland border. Both became flourishing entrepôts, as they exchanged Yankee products for the wares of England and its sugar islands.

Almost as potent a lure as "Quoddy" for the coasters was Amelia Island, fifteen hundred miles or so to the southward. A flat and desolate little place, connected with the mainland at low tide, it lacked "Quoddy's" crisp beauty, but had something else in common—it lay just over the border at the opposite end of the coast. It was part of Spanish Florida; but only a mile or two away, on the opposite side of the frontier river mouth, was the little port of St. Mary's, Georgia. Cotton-laden schooners by the hundred slipped down the coast to St. Mary's. It was a simple matter to boat their cargoes over to Amelia and bring back overseas imports from the square-riggers that flocked to that barren anchorage. Federal authority was pretty well diluted by the time it reached that outer edge of things; even an occasional revenue cutter could not prevent the shameless leakage that went on at Amelia year after year.

A further opportunity to side-step the Embargo arose when Congress, yielding slightly to maritime pressure, permitted clearances in ballast for foreign ports for those merchants who wanted to bring home property stranded abroad. Some 590 such permits were granted. Soon thereafter, a hundred American vessels were counted in Havana harbor, where ideas of what constituted stranded property were seemingly pretty elastic.

John Jacob Astor did not stoop to such petty practices. He cleared his ship *Beaver* from New York for Canton in August, 1808, at the height of the Embargo with the full blessing of Jefferson and the Treasury Department. His mission, according to his tale to them, was simply one of international courtesy; a Chinese mandarin, stranded by the Embargo, had requested passage home. Other merchants, infuriated at the permission, insisted that Punqua Wingchong was nothing but "a Chinaman picked up in the Park" or "a common Chinese dock loafer," and that, anyway, high-class Chinese never left their country. The *Beaver* went her way and was home again in ten months with "two hundred thousand dollars more than she left with."

Meanwhile, customs officials all along the coast were busy checking violations of the Embargo. The collector at New York launched eighty-eight prosecutions on this account, in addition to a similar number for evasions of the law restricting British imports. Constantly changing instructions from Washington, however, were almost as exasperating to the customs men as to the merchants, who could never be sure whether their shipments were liable to seizure or not.

Many merchants were fortunate enough on Christmas, 1807, to have their vessels abroad; and they kept them there. Some of them, of course, ran afoul of the decrees, which had caused the Embargo, but plenty earned higher freights than ever with competition radically reduced. Napoleon's Bayonne Decree of April, 1808, which ordered the seizure of all American vessels entering ports under his immediate control, increased the risks. His argument was that such vessels must be Britishers in disguise, since all genuine Americans were detained at home by the Embargo.

In March, 1809, during the last week of Jefferson's presidency, Congress finally repealed the Embargo. Then and since, men have been divided in their estimates of its wisdom. It had at least accomplished what Jefferson had had in mind when he wrote, "This exuberant commerce brings us into collision with other powers in every sea, and will force us into every war with European powers." The wholesale seizures that would otherwise have probably resulted from the belligerent decrees were radically reduced. Few seamen were impressed, and dangerous "incidents" were safely avoided. That aspect of the voluntary abandonment of "freedom of the seas" was enough to encourage similar legislation in neutrality acts in later years. On the other hand, the Embargo did not succeed in forcing any concessions from either Britain or Napoleon. American shipping services and markets proved to be less indispensable than Jefferson had hoped. The mills of Lancashire suffered from short rations; the West Indies worried about their food supply; and England seemed almost entirely cut off from foreign markets when the Act went into effect. By an unfortunate coincidence, from the American point of view, Spain and Portugal with their extensive colonies became available as British markets a few months later. Napoleon, too, found that he could get along without American shipping. Both his decrees and the Orders in Council remained in full force.

The end of the Embargo did not bring complete freedom of action; in its place Congress substituted Nonintercourse. Altogether, trade with England was permitted for only fifteen months between the enactment of the Embargo and the end of the war in 1815. Still expecting its restrictive measures to cause the belligerents to modify their decrees, Congress continued to forbid trade with British and French territories as long as the oppressive measures remained in force, but elsewhere it now permitted American shipping to go freely. This Nonintercourse lasted from March, 1809, to May, 1810; and for a few months in the summer of 1809 trade was permitted with England through negotiations with the British minister, but his work was disavowed at London.

Nonintercourse was superseded by Macon's Act, which allowed free trade with the proviso that if either France or Britain ended its obnoxious regulations, the United States would co-operate by renewing Nonintercourse against the other. Napoleon duped the Americans into believing he had suspended his decrees, and consequently trade with British territories was again prohibited in May, 1811, and was not resumed before war was declared in 1812.

During this interval, a good many Britishers still tried to play the Amelia Island game, with ample co-operation from the Americans. In 1811, Stephen Girard sent his ship *Good Friends* to London, where she took on a valuable cargo, crossed with a British convoy, and joined the dozens of vessels waiting at Amelia for a change in the American regulations. Early in 1812, a body of Americans captured the island, and the *Good Friends* headed northward on a "coasting voyage." The American customs authorities, however, seized her in the Delaware for violation of Nonintercourse and sued Girard for penalties totaling $900,000. He recovered the vessel, and early in 1813, after the war started, dispatched her to the Continent; but she was captured by British cruisers, just twenty years after her launching and as the first war news was reaching America.

Meanwhile, with its regained access to the sea under Nonintercourse, American commerce was adjusting itself to new sea lanes in place of the run to England, which was still barred by law, and to the Caribbean, where the spread of British conquest sharply reduced the old sugar trade. Napoleon's wholesale seizures made his ports unpopular even in the intervals when trade was allowed with France. Instead, American vessels were finding their way to the small North German ports of the North Sea near Hamburg; to Russia, either by the Baltic route or by Archangel; and to the Spanish and Portuguese ports of the Peninsula, where Wellington was fighting.

One Yankee mariner visited all three regions during these years and left a record of exceptional value because of its comprehensive detail. Not only did he tell—and tell well—the usual run of sea adventures, but he also gave full particulars of his cargoes and of the business methods abroad. Captain George Coggeshall, native of Milford, Connecticut, later privateersman and author, had already had his full sum of excitement before this in the Caribbean and had also built up a good reputation among New York shipowners as a skillful mariner and a shrewd trader in foreign ports.

Tonningen, a little river port near the North Sea, was one of those most frequented in Germany by the Yankees, while Napoleon kept Hamburg, Bremen, Amsterdam, and the usual centers closed. One of Coggeshall's voyages for the great New York merchant, Archibald Gracie, was made here in August, 1809. Like several other foresighted merchants, Gracie had sent his vessels southward to load cargoes while prices of export commodities, cut off from the markets, were very low; then everything was ready for their sailing as soon as the Embargo was lifted. Coggeshall sailed from Petersburg, Virginia, in the ship *Virginia* with 550 hogsheads of tobacco, ten of which were his private "adventure." He found that the revival of trade was making such a heavy demand for seamen that their wages had jumped from $6.00 to $28.00 a month. Proceeding to "Falmouth [England] for orders," he learned that his destination was to be Tonningen via Heligoland. The latter island in the North Sea had been recently seized by England as a convenient base for slipping goods in licensed neutral bottoms into Continental harbors. Off Dover, the *Virginia* was visited by a British gun brig, whose suspicious commander "hesitated some time, whether he should send me into some port or let me go. . . . After a vexatious and scrutinizing examination, I was allowed to proceed." At Heligoland, Coggeshall presented his letters to a merchant who helped him secure a pilot. The latter merited the epithet "extortioner," but was eventually beaten down from the price of $500 to $400 for the four-hour job of guiding the ship some twenty-five miles into the Eyder River towards Tonningen. Another American captain, failing to get a pilot of his own, agreed to split the fee if he were allowed to follow the *Virginia*. Forty or fifty other American vessels were already anchored below Tonningen. Gracie's correspondents at Amsterdam and Hamburg advised Coggeshall to discharge the tobacco and have it forwarded to the latter port. He rode over in a springless wagon, noting with delight that the country was peopled with inveterate smokers—an excellent prospect for his tobacco cargo. And so it proved, for the profit was 1,000 per cent! After seven weeks, he sailed for New York in ballast.

Voyages to Russian ports presented more complications, with the longer water routes and the frequent necessity of having to winter there because of ice conditions. The Czar, however, had begun to lose his enthusiasm for the Continental system as scarcities began to pinch and trade profits disappeared. England, moreover, was desperate to sell whatever it could to the Continent, and with its own emblem too risky to show, gave licenses and naval convoy into the Baltic with a free hand to neutrals. Many proved to be bastard neutrals, flying flags of little German states, such as Knyphausen and Pappenburg, whose tiny merchant marines expanded almost a hundredfold overnight, for a few scratches with a pen and a generous fee could clothe a London ship or a Bordeaux brig with the sacred protection of neutrality. But plenty of genuine neutrals—Swedes, Spaniards, Portuguese, and Americans by the hundreds—headed for whatever Russian or other Baltic port was reported safe for the moment by the British secret service. Sometimes a single vessel, and on occasion a whole convoy, would be caught by Danish privateers or navy, or now and then by French privateers. Also, a port might prove a trap and hundreds of vessels be seized.

Beginning moderately, this business grew in leaps and bounds for the Americans. From $12,000 in 1806, our Russian exports rose to $842,000 in 1809, $3,975,000 in 1810, and $6,137,000 in 1811. Boston took the leading role, with more than half the business coming from Massachusetts ports, which first gathered the cargoes from various points along the coast and the West Indies. The *Pacific,* for example, bound from Salem, was carrying a $31,000 cargo of cotton, flour, rice, tobacco, sugar, and rum when caught and condemned by the Danes in 1809; and the brig *Hope,* of Marblehead, with cotton and coffee for St. Petersburg, was sent into Copenhagen (by French privateers) and condemned "on suspicion of being on English account and sailing with convoy." Altogether seventy American vessels were condemned by the Danes, but many more were merely detained and then allowed to proceed.

When possible, the voyages were planned to escape being frozen in by entering the Baltic in June and returning home in September, but Coggeshall was among those who had to winter in Russia. In the summer of 1810, he left New York in the fast schooner *Eliza* with a mixed cargo, including sugar, coffee, rum, molasses, and nankeens. She was cleared "for Gothenburg and orders," to give one of the partners, living in Copenhagen, a chance to report on the current dangers. There, after a five weeks' stormy crossing, Coggeshall was advised to join the British naval convoy through the tortuous, Dane-infested bottleneck of the Baltic, and then push on to some Russian port, as "no American property was safe on the Prussian side of the Baltic." Late in October, the *Eliza*, along with some ten other American vessels in a total of six hundred merchantmen, was part of the last convoy of the season, guarded by a seventy-four and a few cruisers. Once clear, Coggeshall sped ahead to reach Riga two days before the port froze in.

Altogether there were twenty-three American vessels wintering in Russia that year, with eight at Riga. The crews were housed near the ships; the officers and supercargoes took apartments, to enjoy several cold but pleasantly social months—though that year one supercargo blew his brains out after gambling away most of the cargo entrusted to him. By the end of February, loading began with iron bars, casks of tallow, and a few tons of hemp for ballast; then the more valuable part of the cargo was brought over on sledges from St. Petersburg—"sheetings, drillings, diapers, canvas, ravens' duck, etc., etc." The ice broke in April, and in May, the *Eliza* started homeward with a cargo worth $45,000. Again, after running over to the safer zone by the Swedish coast, Coggeshall had to await the gathering of a convoy of fifty merchantmen, which was guided by a British frigate and two sloops to Gothenburg. The *Eliza* was back in New York in forty-nine more days—after an absence of a full year, of which half had been spent in port.

By 1810, many Yankee vessels were avoiding the delays of convoying and the troublesome Danes by using the longer route around the North Cape to Archangel. Sixty were in the White Sea that year, three frozen in from the year before; and they hailed from sixteen ports between Portland and Charleston. Although New York had the most, with fifteen, a full half came from the hundred-mile strip of shore between Boston and Portland, with ten from Salem, and seven from Boston. Half of them had come straight from the United States, mostly from their home ports, but the others had detoured by the wine islands, for instance, or the Peninsula or North Sea ports. A year later, sixty-five American vessels visited Archangel, along with only two Russian vessels, two Prussian, and one from Hamburg. The trips from America ranged from about forty-three to seventy-seven days; in contrast, convoy delays lengthened Coggeshall's to eighty-three days to the nearer Riga.

Meanwhile, larger numbers of American vessels were becoming familiar with the ports of the Peninsula, where England needed flour for Wellington's army and where some queer things were happening in the grain trade. Short of grain even at home, England would have been in a sorry mess had it not been for Napoleon and the American flour shipments! Napoleon in 1810 was allowing the export of a huge amount of grain from France, and according to some writers this saved the British from starvation. Napoleon justified himself on the ground that the sale further drained England's gold—the main objective of his Continental system. Our grain trade with the Peninsula was about equally gratifying to the British who had an army to feed there, and to the farmers, millers, and shipowners of America who profited from it. From a mere 76,000 barrels in 1807, these flour exports jumped to 233,000 in 1810, to 835,000 in 1811, to 938,000 in 1812, and, most amazingly, as we shall see, continued to rise in 1813 to 972,000, when we actually fed redcoats while fighting England.

There was good money in the business, as Captain Coggeshall could testify. In November, 1811, he sailed from Philadelphia in Gracie's new 525-ton ship *America*. Twice as big as the average ship, she carried 5,382 barrels of flour. After a tussle with a drunken and semimutinous crew in the Delaware, Coggeshall made a slow, thirty-eight-day passage to Lisbon. There he sold, at fifteen dollars a barrel, the flour that had cost only nine dollars, making six hundred dollars on his own private venture of a hundred barrels. Returning to New York in January ballasted with sand, he set out again in the same ship in March with three thousand barrels of flour and twelve thousand bushels of Indian corn. Contrary and baffling winds delayed him from reaching Lisbon until May—a lucky chance, for news of the prewar embargo of the United States reached Lisbon just before him and boomed prices. Two weeks earlier, he would never have been able to sell the flour, which had cost $9.50 a barrel, for $20.00; while the corn jumped from eighty cents to three dollars a bushel. The cargo sold for exactly double what it had cost five weeks before.

This long period of maritime complications finally culminated in the War of 1812. This was not an inevitable outcome; in many ways, some might say it was not even a sensible one. Its slogan was "Free Trade and Sailors' Rights"; but the situation at sea in 1812 was far less serious than it had been five years earlier. England did not want the war; neither did the Yankee shipping interests, any more than they had wanted the Embargo. The declaration was the work of the young "war hawks" in Congress who saw a chance to grab Canada while England was preoccupied on the Continent. Also, British intrigues with the western Indians gave added ground for complaint. Within a week after war was declared, the assassination of a stubborn British prime minister cleared the way for the repeal of the Orders in Council: England confidently expected that with that stumbling block removed, the Americans would call off their war. Neither side would compromise on impressment; and so the war went on its sorry, indecisive course. It antagonized seagoing New England to the point of considering secession; and it ate up many years of neutral profits.

One's impressions of the War of 1812 depend largely upon whether one studied an American, a Canadian, or a British textbook in school. If American, the war means *Old Ironsides* whipping the *Guerrière* and *Java;* Perry's victory on Lake Erie in the fresh-water process of humbling the pride of the Royal Navy;

and Andrew Jackson's mowing down the redcoats at New Orleans—after peace had come. In Canadian textbooks, one would never recognize the same war. There, the same lengthy pages are devoted to the conflict, but they tell of army after army of aggression from the "States" sent over the border only to be thrown out by a handful of heroic regulars, militia, and Indians! As for the British schoolchild, he scarcely hears of the war at all, except as a rather bothersome and inconclusive side show to Wellington's victories.

As far as each goes, these accounts are all true enough, but they omit one of the most striking features of the strange conflict. At no other time in its history has the United States been cut off so completely from the sea as it was by the Royal Navy in 1814. However galling our frigate victories may have been to British pride and however costly the raids of our privateers upon British shipping, the fact remains that the war saw the American merchant marine cooped up so thoroughly in its home ports that even little coasting sloops ran grave risks in slipping from New Haven to New London or from Cape Cod to Boston. The frigates and the privateers have had their due share of recording for posterity; the sorry tale of the American merchantmen needs more attention, if the maritime lessons of the war are to be appreciated.

This rigid British blockade in 1814 was a serious economic nuisance, but it was not the strategic tragedy it would have meant in 1776 or 1777. Thanks to the stimulus given industry by the Embargo and subsequent trade interruptions, the United States was better prepared to endure this strangling of its commerce. No longer was the nation dependent upon munitions imports. In the three fiscal years, 1812-14, only about 100 tons of gunpowder were imported as compared with 650 tons in 1805-07, while in the year ending in September, 1814, 53 pounds were the total. Meanwhile, sloop loads of Du Pont powder from Wilmington were being carried up and down the coast at the outbreak of the war. Later on, as the blockade tightened, the powder had to be hauled overland.

Both sides had become well rehearsed in their maritime war roles during the preceding turbulent years. Not only were the British frigates well drilled in patrolling European waters, but they had become well acquainted with our harbor approaches. American merchantmen, too, had had plenty of practice dodging British cruisers and American regulations. The Embargo showed the possibilities of "Quoddy" and Amelia Island and accustomed the people to get along with curtailed imports and exports. It had also fostered a Yankee spirit of defiance of governmental regulations, for "Mr. Madison's War" was fully as unpopular to the eastward as "Mr. Jefferson's Embargo" had been.

That attitude was well reflected early in April, 1812, when Congress decreed a ninety-day embargo to keep shipping in port to save it from wholesale seizures should war come. The seaboard had a week end to get ready—and it made the most of it. The hectic scramble on Christmas Day of 1807 was re-enacted in port after port. Scores of vessels slipped away to sea from New York; "had the city been in flames, property could not have been moved off with greater expedition." Down at Norfolk, Captain Elijah Cobb upon his arrival on Saturday went at once to the customhouse for a clearance for Lisbon. The collector grudgingly granted it with the warning that no vessel could be unloaded and re-loaded in forty-eight hours and that he would be prevented from sailing after noon Monday. Apparently Cobb pressed every available Negro around town into service as a longshoreman; anyway, the vessel was emptied in record time and her hold filled with flour barrels, destined to sell at double their cost in Portugal. With two hours to spare, Cobb cast off in triumph and headed for Hampton Roads; then the wind died down. At the stroke of noon, he saw the customs barge, manned by sturdy rowers, bearing down on him. Just as they came uncomfortably close, a breeze sprang up and he cleared the Capes in safety.

Like the others who got out of American ports in a rush, and those already overseas, Cobb found it was also difficult to get back home after war was declared. Slow communications and the small United States Navy did their part in simplifying this wartime problem of the merchant marine.

Today a declaration of war reaches most ships at sea within a few hours at the most, warning merchantmen to scramble for cover, and enemy cruisers to begin to prowl. In 1812, many vessels of both sorts knew nothing of the war for days, weeks, and even months. The Americans, having made the declaration, were able to steal somewhat of a march on the British before they heard of it. New York merchants dispatched a swift pilot boat to Gothenburg to warn our shipping in the Baltic. A naval squadron, sent to sea within three days, chased the British frigate *Belvidera* off the coast. This was the Royal Navy's initial warning; it took the *Belvidera* five days to warn the base at Halifax, and the war had been going a full month before the Admiralty learned of it. Some of our ships, too, in the Orient and South Pacific first heard of the war as they neared home in 1813.

The American Navy worked hard to bring our shipping safely home. At first glance that looked like a hopeless task for sixteen American warships against the six hundred in the Royal Navy, even with that Navy preoccupied in European waters. The London *Times* scornfully dismissed our Navy as "a few fir-built frigates with stripes of bunting, manned by sons of bitches and outlaws." Luckily we had the three supercruisers that Joshua Humphreys had designed so wisely eighteen years before—the *Constitution,* the *President,* and the *United States;* and England could not match those forty-fours. They were some 30 per cent stronger than the largest British frigates and could show their heels to any lumbering ship of the line. They gave the American naval forces an influence out of all proportion to their numbers, by affecting British strategy throughout the war. From the first, they kept England from planting a frigate in front of each port to catch all homecoming freighters, for with Commodore Rodgers at sea with two forty-fours and some smaller cruisers together as a squadron, the Halifax frigates dared not be out alone. Consequently, most American ports were left unblocked during those critical summer months when the merchantmen were crowding homeward.

Not all of them escaped. The war was but six days old when Captain John Jordan of Portland, in the brig *Malcolm,* heading for home with Madeira wine, met the *Belvidera* hurrying to Halifax with the news of the war. The *Malcolm* soon found herself in Halifax, also, the first prize in the Vice-Admiralty Court. The next day, the frigate likewise seized the ship *Fortune,* bound for Newburyport with salt from the Cape Verdes; and she added her share to the prize money of the lucky officers and crew of the first royal warship to hear of the war.

The heaviest concentration of American shipping overseas was in the flour fleet at Lisbon, where speculation over the imminence of war had run riot since the news of the preliminary April embargo had arrived. With news lagging a full month behind events, the captains, supercargoes, and merchants were in a bad quandary; some were sure war would not come, others were for laying up their ships in safety, and some decided to run for it. Among the last was Coggeshall in Gracie's *America.* With the flour proceeds of this and the other three Gracie ships in port dispatched to London by the Gracie correspondent, Coggeshall decided to push on alone, ahead of the other vessels and a little out of the regular westbound shipping lane. He offered each of the mates a new suit of clothes if the *America* beat the others into port. For five days, Coggeshall fretted with impatience in an exasperating calm, with the sea as smooth as a mirror. Then a good breeze sprang up from the southward. On July 15, off Nantucket Shoals he learned from a passing schooner that the war was four weeks old. Unable to make the shelter of the Sound around windy Montauk Point, he was forced to sail along the exposed south shore of Long Island, a nerve-racking approach to New York, with the likelihood of British frigates being near by.

I had no cargo or money on board, except two thousand Spanish dollars, belonging to myself—the avails of my own private adventure. This specie I put into small bags, and got one of the boats ready, with a select crew, to start for shore at a moment's warning. . . . My plan was, if we met with an English cruiser, and could not avoid capture, to run the ship on shore, set fire to her, and then escape to the land in the two remaining boats. During the whole of this day we had light, variable winds, and fine weather. We steered along shore, in eight or nine fathoms of water, and in the afternoon passed near Fire Island, where we boarded a sloop, laden with wood, but to our disappointment, could get no positive information about the war, or whether there were any British cruisers off Sandy Hook. At 10 p.m. we got close in with the Hook, where we took a pilot, and soon learned that nothing had been heard of the *Eliza Gracie* or the *Oronoko*. The next morning, July 17th, we got safe up to New York, rejoiced at our good fortune in having thus escaped the enemy. About a week after our arrival we heard, with regret, that the *Oronoko* and *Eliza Gracie* had both been taken by Admiral Sawyer's fleet. They sent the *Oronoko* into Halifax, and burned the *Eliza Gracie*.

Elijah Cobb had also been less lucky in returning from Lisbon than he had been in beating the embargo at Norfolk; his first knowledge of the war came from his capture by a British cruiser off Newfoundland.

But for every vessel caught during that homecoming, many more made port safely. Altogether less than forty merchantmen were taken into Halifax by the end of September. Of these, seventeen were from Liverpool or Ireland and many were released because of British cargoes or because they had sailed before war was declared. Eight were from Lisbon, Oporto, or St. Ubes; eight from the Mediterranean; two from Spain; and one from France. The brig *Betsy*, en route from Naples to Boston, was caught by the *Guerrière* and her captain was still aboard the frigate during her famous duel with the *Constitution*. For the Baltic, the pilot boat from New York had spread the alarm so well that the ship *Merchant*, with iron from Gothenburg to Portsmouth, was the only victim. Other captives came from farther afield; such as the brig *Federal* with ivory, camwood, coffee, palm oil, and old copper from Africa for Boston, and the ship *Malantho*, heading for

Baltimore with 259 tons of copper, 9 bales of furs, and $43,000 in specie from Chile.

Particular concern was felt for the ships at Canton or Calcutta, which could not reach home before the spring of 1813 because of the seasonal monsoon. One merchant found he could not secure New York insurance in January, 1813, without great difficulty and cost; 75 per cent was the rate asked for the same route that had been but 6 per cent the year before. Several vessels remained at Canton "for the duration," but some made port safely by avoiding the major harbors and heading for the smaller ones along the New England coast. The *Sally,* for instance, inward bound from Canton in April, first learned of the war from a fishing boat off Cape Cod, and successfully made for Plymouth "to give the Pilgrim capital its greatest sensation since the *Mayflower* landed."

By that time, most of the Yankee vessels were back from their wanderings. Some would be converted into privateers and a few others, as well-armed letters of marque, would try to fight their cargoes through to foreign ports. The great majority, though, would lie idly at anchor, with topmasts down and inverted barrels—"Mr. Madison's nightcaps"—protecting their mastheads, as in 1808, to signalize the stagnation of our sea-borne trade.

The best prize money for the Royal Navy was won in the first three months. A detailed analysis of the 450 American merchantmen libeled in the Halifax Vice-Admiralty Court during the whole war shows that the situation in those months differed completely from the rest of the twenty-nine. Out of forty-nine full-rigged ships captured altogether, twenty-eight were taken in those three months, along with eighteen of the sixty-eight seized brigs. The captures up to the seventeenth of September, when the *Federal* and *Melantho* were caught, were less than 13 per cent of the total number of the war, but that 13 per cent represented almost a quarter of the total tonnage. Thereafter, most of the captures were little coasting schooners or sloops with far less valuable cargoes.

Altogether, the first phase of the war at sea had gone pretty well for the Yankees. The navy had drawn the British away from the harbor entrances long enough for most of the shipping to get home safely. The three famous frigate duels also occurred in 1812—the *Constitution* and the *Guerrière*, the *United States* and the *Macedonian*, the *Constitution* and the *Java*.

But those victories were not to continue. England was plentifully supplied, not only with more than a hundred other frigates, but with ships of the line and lesser cruisers. Admiral Warren was sent over late in this first year with an offer of peace and with a hundred warships at his disposal. When the former broke down over the old bugaboo "impressment," he began to use the latter with effect. From that time, the maritime situation for the Yankees steadily deteriorated: 1813 was bad; 1814 was infinitely worse.

Meanwhile, the most "phony" aspect of those strange years flourished at a great rate. Flour from our Middle States continued to feed Wellington's army in the Peninsula. This trade had the active support of London—for obvious reasons—and at least the passive acquiescence of Washington with its eye on the farm vote. Numerous arguments were heard at Washington against this provisioning of the enemy army, but Thomas Jefferson justified it with a typical rationalization:

> If she is to be fed at all events, why may we not have the benefit of it as well as others? . . . Besides, if we could, by starving the English armies, oblige them to withdraw from the peninsula, it would be to send them here; and I think we had better feed them there for pay, than feed and fight them here for nothing. A truth, too, not to be lost sight of is, that no country can pay war taxes if you suppress all their resources. To keep the war popular, we must keep open the markets. As long as good prices can be had, the people will support the war cheerfully.

During the first half of 1813, 165 American vessels arrived at Lisbon alone, and many of them returned safely later in the year with cash and ballast from Lisbon or with salt from St. Ubes. The British supplied licenses that were supposed to afford freedom from British capture, both going and coming, and for a while such vessels were insured at the very low rate of 5 per cent but some mariners found to their cost that their licenses gave them protection from neither the British nor American navies. After 1813, Britain was able to get grain from Baltic granaries and both governments shut down on the peculiar practice.

In the same way, the British encouraged Yankee vessels to bring food to their West Indian islands, and many were tempted by the high prices down there. In 1813, for example, the Vice-Admiralty Court at Halifax released four vessels bound from the British West Indies to Maine ports. Even more extensive was the shameless indirect trade that was revived through Amelia Island and Passamaquoddy. The intricate inland waterways in the south afforded "the most convenient part of the world for illicit trade"; bales of cotton once more were sneaked south from Charleston and Savannah to be swapped for imports brought by dozens of square-riggers to Amelia.

In the north the entrepôt trade was welcomed by Nova Scotia and New Brunswick. Either indirectly through "Quoddy" or directly to St. John or Halifax and protected by licenses from naval seizure, it rapidly became so extensive that the American government shut down upon it. Arguing that because of the rigidity of the British blockade no normal shipments were safe and others were obviously counting upon the connivance of the enemy, an embargo was laid on all American vessels, whether on foreign or coastwise voyages, from December. 1813, to April, 1814.

In this queer wartime trading with the enemy, the British were ready to give as well as to take. Woolens from Leeds furnished greatcoats for the United States forces fighting Britain as well as for Napoleon's Russian campaign. A cruiser duel took place off Monhegan in September, 1813, from just that sort of business. Some Portland merchants, importing English woolens and blankets for our army, arranged to have a full cargo brought down to the Kennebec from St. John in a neutral Swedish brig. To make the voyage doubly safe, they paid one hundred pounds to the commander of the British naval gun brig *Boxer* to convoy the illicit cargo down the coast. For a while, the cruiser actually towed the brig. Then, just to make things look correct in case anyone were watching from shore, the *Boxer* fired a few shots as the two separated off the Kennebec. Unluckily for the conniving British, the American gun brig *Enterprise* heard those shots, and, heading for the scene, battered the *Boxer* into submission in a half-hour's brisk gunnery the next afternoon. Both commanders fell in action and were buried side by side in Portland's Eastern Cemetery. In the effects of the British captain were found his payment for protecting those woolens en route to the American Army.

By early 1814, the whole seaboard was feeling the pressure of the Royal Navy as it imposed what Mahan called

> the noiseless, steady, exhausting pressure with which sea power acts, cutting off the resources of the enemy while maintaining its own, supporting war in scenes it does not appear itself or appears only in the background, and striking open blows only at rare intervals.

Off every major port was a squadron on tedious, persistent patrol duty. In an attempt to coop up the American forty-fours, the average blockading force had to consist of three or four frigates, strengthened by a ship of the line or two. The sheltered anchorages in Chesapeake and Delaware bays made this duty fairly easy for the British there, but the long sandy angle off New York, with no ports of refuge for a hundred miles to the east or south, meant ticklish work in stormy weather. The people of Southampton, Long Island, watched one cruiser pound to pieces in a gale but carefully rescued the few survivors. Off Boston Light, it was cold and disagreeable in fog, rain, and snow. Only occasional shore raids to "cut out" or destroy shipping enlivened the tedious months. Now and then, detached cruisers lurked off headlands, which coastal shipping had to round. Even by the spring of 1813, the cordon was so tightly drawn that the letter-of-marque schooner *Ned,* coming from France, was driven away from Chesapeake Bay, from the Delaware, and from Sandy Hook and only reached New York by the Sound after eluding a squadron off New London. It was all an old story for the British; they had had twenty years of practice around Europe and almost half that much on the American coast itself. Their eternal vigilance bottled up not only most of our merchantmen, but most of the navy as well.

A few privateers supported the strangling blockade. In the north, a score or so from the Maritime Provinces raised havoc with the New England coasters and fishermen. The hundreds of Yankee privateers are not part of our story, but that handful of Bluenose raiders, repeating on a larger scale their Revolutionary exploits, terrorized the eastern coasting trade. Their captures were out of all proportion to their numbers: 149 prizes as compared to the Royal Navy's 249 among the vessels libeled at Halifax.

The most celebrated was the small 67-ton *Liverpool Packet* from the Nova Scotia port of that name, an ex-slaver taken on the Guinea coast. Mounting five guns, she put to sea in September, 1812, and at once snapped up three vessels from overseas. Then she began her distinctive work by sailing for Cape Cod to intercept the Boston coasters. In five days, she bagged five schooners, and the angry Bostonians began to talk of a Cape Cod Canal. The next month, her loitering off Salem caused scores of determined men to parade to martial music as they went to man a pursuit vessel; but before they got to sea, she was gone. Always elusive and exasperating, one day she seized a schooner off Portland and sent a half-burned boatload of fish drifting ashore; the next day, she caught a sloop off Point Judith, 250 miles away. When she went home for Christmas, twenty-one of her prizes lay at anchor in the harbor. In June, 1813, a stronger Portsmouth privateer brought her to a day of reckoning; but she had sent thirty-three prizes, valued at $150,000, back to her home port, not to mention numerous others destroyed or re-captured.

For a while, neutral shipping was not molested by the block-aders, unless they carried contraband. As a result, foreign ship-ping, which had amounted to only 6 per cent of our arriving tonnage in 1812, rose to 32 per cent in 1813 and 44 per cent in 1814. In this war, Europeans performed the same neutral carrying services for Americans that the latter gave Europe in the pre-ceding two decades and would render again in the twentieth century to warring nations. The neutral traders came in con-siderable numbers. Swedish ships carried iron and glass from Gothenburg and Karlskrona, or sugar, molasses, and rum from Swedish St. Barts in the West Indies. The Spanish brought salt or fruit from Cadiz, or coffee, sugar, and molasses from Cuba and Puerto Rico. By Portuguese vessels came salt from Lisbon or St. Ubes and a few cargoes from Brazil. Occasionally, a neu-tral even arrived from far-off Batavia. They all carried away flour, tobacco, and other American produce. Some American ves-sels were transferred to neutral registry.

Early in 1813, the blockade barred neutrals, too, and cargoes were now hit as well as shipping. This was inaugurated in Chesapeake and Delaware bays in February; the commerce of Philadelphia and Baltimore was dried up quickly for the dura-tion of the war. In March, New York came next, when the iron-clad blockade was extended to Sandy Hook and all southward. But New York still had the back-door approach through Hell Gate until November when the barrier was stretched to include the Sound almost to New London. The rest of New England was rewarded for its antiwar stand for six months more, as Boston and other eastern ports flourished as entrepôts for neu-tral traders. But by May 30, 1814, the blockade held the whole coast in its harsh grip from New Brunswick to Florida, while trade was further strangled by that embargo the United States placed on all its own shipping during the winter of 1813–14.

The year 1814 was unique in American maritime annals with commerce and shipping movements practically at a dead standstill. Even the dull statistics are almost eloquent on that point. In millions of dollars for the fiscal years ending September 30, imports which had reached a peak of 138 in 1807 had fallen with the Embargo to 56 in 1808; they stood at 22 in 1813 and slumped to 12.9 in 1814. Exports likewise dropped from 108 millions in the boom year 1807 to 27.8 in 1813—a rare year when they exceeded imports—and then to the all-time low of 6.9 in 1814. Re-exports dwindled away almost to nothing, the nation needing all that it could get from beyond the seas. Georgia alone doubled its volume and stood first among the states—but that was old border-running to Amelia Island. New England, with its delayed blockade, almost held its own.

The terrific impact of the blockade fell with full force upon New York, Philadelphia, Baltimore and other ports of the Middle States which not only lost the lucrative job of feeding Wellington's redcoats, but were cut off almost completely from the sea by the British. In that single year the Chesapeake exports fell from $6,994,000 to $268,000 and New York's from $8,185,000 to $209,000, while Philadelphia, which had a total of $3,577,000 in 1813, did not export a single cent's worth in the following black year.

American shipping was similarly squeezed almost out of activity. The tonnage of vessels arriving from foreign ports had reached a peak of 1,059,000 in 1807, had dropped to 525,000 under the Embargo, but rose a bit in 1812 to 667,000; now it shrank to 237,000 in 1813 and dropped to the bottom in 1814, with a mere 59,000 tons. The amount of capital tied up in idle shipping was enormous. Because the smaller a vessel was the better her chance of slipping through the blockade and the less the investment hazarded in a risky venture, only fast little brigs and schooners dared the overseas run. By 1814 smaller schooners and sloops alone even skirted the coast. The average size of all the merchant prizes at Halifax was 139 tons in 1812-13 and only 73 tons, barely half that size, in 1814-15. The average brig fell from 180 to 137 tons, while the schooners, which made up the bulk of the list, dropped from 93 to 68 tons with some less than 30 tons.

Behind these arid figures lie many a high adventure and many a minor tragedy. Captain Coggeshall, as always, missed nothing important during all those troubled years. He made a typical armed trading voyage to France in the letter-of-marque schooner *David Porter,* in which he owned a quarter share. Arming her, and with a crew from the idle blockaded navy, he slipped down from Providence to Newport late in 1813, and made a dash for sea during a blizzard. He was chased by three naval brigs, but reached Charleston, where with his customary acumen, he sold his salt cargo, which had cost 65 cents a bushel, for $1.50. Reloading with enough bales of compressed cotton to give gross freight earnings of $23,300, he slid out for Bordeaux just in time to escape the new embargo. Once clear of the coast, he scarcely saw a sail, for "the risk of capture between Newport and Charleston was infinitely greater than in going to France." But only a bad gale saved him from the Royal Navy in the Bay of Biscay, and he had to rush into a tiny fishing port thirty miles from Bordeaux. In the spring he sailed into the Bay to loot the cargoes of several British transports; by then it was futile to try to send prizes home through the blockade. Strip or burn them was the custom. Coggeshall, with business of his own in France, sent the *David Porter* back to Boston under the mate and shipped some wine and brandy home on his own account aboard the letter-of-marque brig *Ida.* He started home later in the year in command of another letter of marque, the *Leo;* but his luck had run out. He did capture some British vessels before losing his topmast off Lisbon; but then a frigate overhauled him and he was sent to Gibraltar a prisoner. Yet, never daunted, he escaped just as the war ended!

By a coincidence, the arrival of his wine and brandy was recorded by another storyteller. Lieutenant Henry Edward Napier of H.M.S. *Nymphe,* 38, wrote, "Yesterday [June 30] we chased the *Ida,* letter of marque, but could not catch her," so Coggeshall, as usual, made his tidy profit. The *Nymphe* was one of the small squadron blockading Boston—with particular care that the *Constitution* would not escape. Napier's journal (recently ably edited) pictured the tedious blockade routine of patrolling from Cape Ann to Cape Cod from early May to August, 1814. Sometimes the Britishers ventured ashore to destroy small boats or purchase provisions ("You may always buy a Yankee"); sometimes they raided Boston harbor itself in little tenders; occasionally they overhauled Nova Scotia privateers to impress sailors; and always they were on the lookout for prize money. During those summer months only one good prize came their way—a Portuguese brig bound from Boston to Brazil with dyewoods and sugar.

The bulk of Napier's journal, however, confirms the prize lists from Halifax—very few American vessels were at sea except miserable little coasters. Early in June, for instance, the *Nymphe* went up to Cape Ann and Napier led a boat expedition:

> I went to Halibut Point in Ipswich Bay for the intention of lying in wait, like a spider for flies, for the coasters from the northward and southward, all of which make that point; took an empty sloop of an hundred tons. The master miserably poor and this his all. Let him go, making a virtue of necessity, for it was nearly calm and I should not have been able to tow her out to the ship.

and, a week later, still on Cape Ann:

> Went into the harbor of Annisquam, burned two vessels, let one go clear because she belonged to an old man who had a wife and eight children and had lost $20,000 within two years. Destroying this, his last, would have ruined him. Spared another, as I told them, because her name was the *Federalist,* but the truth is she was aground alongside of the town and I could neither get her off, or set fire to her there, without burning a number of poor people's houses.

Now and then, they encountered little vessels from the eastward, carrying British licenses along with their American flag. One sloop from "Quoddy" for Rhode Island was allowed to pass, but the *Three Sisters* from Frenchman's Bay for New London was not so lucky, for her license had expired. The sloop with her cargo of shingles was burned, although

> the bulk of the property belonged to three unfortunate females who were then on board. They told us that their employment the last twelve months had been keeping a school at Mount Desert, the people of which place being almost unacquainted with money, had been in the habit of paying for their children's schooling in shingles . . . which thus collected, they had embarked on board the *Three Sisters* intending to sell them at New London, where they hoped to receive $75 for their year's labor.

The seasick schoolteachers were sent ashore in a fishing boat, "to their great delight, particularly as the Captain and officers made up by subscription nearly the amount of their loss." Aside from burning vessels or sending them to Halifax as prizes, the British went to the petty length of ransoming some vessels, particularly fishermen, for cash. Off Cape Cod, Napier wrote:

> Made the unfortunate master of a fishing boat, who formerly had permission to fish and came out, trusting to that protection, pay $200 for a ransom. The poor creature has a wife and seven children, no money, and was in debt for his salt and fishing lines even. He with great difficulty scraped up by sixpences and shillings the amount of the money at Provincetown and came on board with tears in his eyes. This is an ungenerous war against the poor and unworthy of Englishmen. I am ashamed of Captain Epworth's conduct.

"Provincetown," he remarked, "formerly famous for its whaling, now completely cut off from all trade and at the mercy of any person." Nor was it alone: "Salem suffers severely from the war, as formerly there was no less than twenty East Indiamen sailed out of this port, now hardly a coaster of fifteen tons escapes being captured." Had the *Nymphe* been able to catch one of those fat Indiamen laden with pepper or tea, Napier would have enjoyed his prize money without a qualm, knowing that the loss would probably fall upon some insurance company. But these small sloops were different: "Making prize money resembles killing a sheep; one likes to eat it but cannot bear the distress of the animal's death."

Such was American commerce at its lowest ebb. Save for the clandestine activity around Quoddy and Amelia, the coast was dead. By autumn, the blockaders were even snapping up boatloads of cordwood bound for Boston. Longer coasting voyages were becoming constantly more rare. Schooners found it generally too risky to continue carrying cotton from Charleston to Providence or tar and pitch from North Carolina to Boston, with return cargoes of imported wares brought in by neutrals. Even the high profits of such voyages, if completed safely, did not make them worth the hazards. In the month the war started, for instance, a hundredweight of rice had cost $3.88 in Charleston and $4.38 in New York; by the fall of 1814, rice was a drug on the market at Charleston at $1.12 and commanded $10.00 in blockaded New York. So dangerous was coasting that much of the trade was being carried overland in wagons despite the bad roads. Oxcarts arrived at Charleston "forty-six days from Philadelphia"; and elsewhere along the coast the "horse marine" plodded its slow, weary, and costly way.

Seagoing New England's long mutterings against "Mr. Madison's War" were by that time including discussions of secession at Hartford. Federalist papers damned the stupid strangling of commerce and the ruination of the merchant marine. Strangely enough, British papers were full of similar cursings from seaport merchants, whose shipping was in turn being terrorized by Yankee privateers close to their shores. The shipping communities of both nations were heartily sick of the war, when a British cruiser brought the news of peace to Sandy Hook on a stormy February night in 1815. New York went wild with joy—without a thought as to who had won! If the War of 1812 had accomplished nothing else, it had shown the folly of two trading nations fighting each other. But the twentieth century would show that it was not a lasting lesson.

Chapter V

Pirates

OUR HIGHEST OFFICIALS HAVE ALWAYS FLUNG THE EPITHET "PIRATES" pretty freely at anyone who disturbed our shipping activities. The technical meaning of the term has never seemed to deter them when their ire was aroused. "Pirates" has been the outraged cry from the seventeen nineties to recent times. It mattered little whether the offenders were British or French privateersmen, Confederates aboard the *Alabama,* or German U-boat captains. To be sure, the methods of these various raiders have been irregular at times, but they were definitely not pirates. Technical piracy does not include legally commissioned depredations by regular belligerents.

From time to time, though, our shipping has known the horrors of being harassed by real pirates. They have interfered in American "freedom of the seas" until in each case the navy eventually gave them the quietus. In the colonial period, we had to contend with Captain Kidd, Blackbeard, and scores of their ilk. After independence, three sets of pirates have menaced our sea lanes. For thirty years, the well-organized piracy of the Barbary States of North Africa made trade with the Mediterranean and the ports just outside Gibraltar, hazardous in the extreme. No sooner was there relief from this menace than unorganized and brutal West Indian half-breeds swarmed along our own shores to prey upon shipping to Cuba and the Gulf. Meanwhile, our vessels to the Far East went armed for nearly a century in dread of the Malays lurking in the Straits of Sunda and elsewhere in the eastern seas.

The Barbary States developed piracy into one of the most profitable—and most persistent—rackets in history. From about 1500 until after 1815, Morocco, Algiers, Tunis, and Tripoli alternately plundered and blackmailed other maritime states—and were allowed to get away with the habit. Relatively few of their victims were forced to "walk the plank," but their fate was almost as black. It was found to be more profitable to hold them captives for ransom and in the meantime work them hard. Whether plunder of its vessels or blackmail of its treasury was to be the keynote of any nation's relations with the Barbary States depended on the latter's interpretation of whether they were at "peace" or at "war." If at war, a country was in constant danger of having its shipping seized, its coasts ravaged, and its subjects enslaved. The payment of sufficient blackmail, on the other hand, might permit it to enjoy a precarious "peace." Even heavy blackmail payments did not always accomplish this, for the pirates were careful never to be at "peace" with too many nations at once. "If I were to make peace with everybody," declared the dey of Algiers, "what should I do with my corsairs? What should I do with my soldiers? They would take off my head for want of other prizes, not being able to live upon their miserable allowance."

England suffered the "war" of the Algerines and of Morocco's Sallee rovers during the lowest ebb of its naval annals in the half century after the Armada. Scores of English merchantmen were seized, and the corsairs even raided the British coasts to carry off captives. In one episode in 1625, two vessels from the infant colony at Plymouth were snapped up in the Channel. Parliament at last in 1646 sent an agent to Algiers to redeem hundreds of the poor enslaved victims and had to pay what they had fetched in the slave markets. One, Mary Bruster from Ireland, cost the government £139 to free her; a London shipwright, Thomas Thomson, was worth £130; ordinary seamen cost about £50 apiece; and one, Elizabeth Mancor of Dundee, was held at only £20. Admiral Blake bombarded Algiers thoroughly in 1655, but even that did not stop the ravages. In 1678, for instance, a Harvard graduate, sailing from America, was never heard of again after being captured by Algerines. By the eighteenth century, however, England's payments, coupled with the presence of the Royal Navy, brought relative security to its shipping. Its American colonies naturally shared this "peace" and soon developed a good trade in fish and flour with Spain and Portugal.

But the loss of this protection was one of the prices America paid for its independence. In fact, it was openly suggested that that severance from the British Empire involved an even more positive liability to American shipping. England seemed to be buying more than protection; the pirates were almost perpetually at "war" with the small states of Italy and the Adriatic, and apparently could be "persuaded" to attack the Scandinavians, the Spaniards—and the Americans. It proved an exceedingly effective way to reduce potential rivalry in the Mediterranean carrying trade. This was one reason why the North African "scourge of Christendom" was allowed free run of the seas for such a long period; certain powers found the pirates too useful to wish to co-operate in their destruction. Franklin in 1783 heard London merchants paraphrasing Louis XIV in the remark: "If there were no Algiers, it would be worth England's while to build one." Lord Sheffield, in his anti-American commercial tract of that same year, wrote, "It is not probable that the American States will have a very free trade in the Mediterranean; it will not be to the interest of any of the maritime powers to protect them there from the Barbary States."

The first Barbary attack on the Stars and Stripes came in October, 1784, upon the brig *Betsey* bound to Teneriffe. She was captured in the Atlantic by the Moroccans and carried into Tangier, but her crew were not enslaved. As a result of Spanish intervention, the brig as well as the crew were both released after six months. This was mild, and intended as a warning that the Americans might find it well to make a "peace" treaty with Morocco. The hint was taken, and at the moderate cost of less than ten thousand dollars, a consul was established at Tangier; and thereafter the Moroccans behaved fairly well.

It was not such a simple matter when Algiers struck at the new nation. This was the most powerful and aggressive of the raiders and its victims met the hardest treatment of any. In this same year, Algiers was in a particularly cocky mood after having beaten off a combined naval attack of Spanish, Portuguese, and Italian warships; and in the following July, 1785, Spain removed its patrol from the Straits of Gibraltar after making a sudden peace. The Algerines wasted no time in cruising out into the Atlantic to the menace of all and sundry; and specifically to the schooner *Maria* from Boston and to the ship *Dauphin* from Philadelphia.

Off Cape St. Vincent just outside Gibraltar, the *Maria* was boarded by a band of the ferocious Algerines. They were out for the richly laden Portuguese vessels bound for Lisbon from Brazil, but missing them picked up whatever came their way. The six members of the *Maria's* crew were stripped of shoes and clothing by greedy pirate hands as they were driven into the filthy, stuffy hold of the pirate cruiser. Already captive below decks, seized from little Portuguese prizes, were thirty-six men and one Spanish woman "who seemed perfectly reconciled to her situation and endeavored to reconcile everyone to theirs."

At Algiers, the unfortunate group were given dirty clothing, swarming with vermin, and marched through the streets to the delight of a mob, avid for a glimpse of the first Americans. Three miserable days later, they were put up for sale in the slave market; most of them were bought by the government, including the woman—for the dey's harem. Another corsair caught the *Dauphin* that same week, "fifty leagues west of Cadiz." The fourteen aboard her likewise went into slavery. Only the captains received preferred treatment—if it could be called that. They were taken to the British consul's house to work in the garden and otherwise "to serve as domestics . . . suffering every indignity that inhumanity could devise to render their situation humiliating in the extreme." Eventually, our chargé d'affaires at Madrid was able to arrange for them and the mates to live in fair comfort in a small house by themselves, but the sailors were left at hard grueling labor in the Algerian heat or in special jobs around the palace.

The news of these men's imprisonment stirred the United States to keen interest in their fate. John Adams in London exchanged views on the matter with Thomas Jefferson in Paris. George Washington presented their case to Congress. In 1790 an agent was sent to Algiers to redeem them at $200 a head; but he was met with contemptuous laughter for the low price. The Algerines set the ransom at $6,000 for the two captains, $4,000 for the mates, and $2,000 apiece for the seamen, an average of $2,833 per man. The United States would not have haggled over the exorbitant prices if the freedom of the men had alone been at sake, but future policy had to be considered. If the government paid out such sums without a definite treaty of "peace" with Algiers, the corsairs would unquestionably find it good business to seize all the American shipping upon which they could lay their hands.

Early in 1792, the prisoners sent a pathetic petition to Congress, praying

> that you will consider what our sufferings must have been for nearly seven years captivity, twice surrounded by the pest, and other contagious distempers, which has numbered six of our brother sufferers in the tills of mortality, and we remain employed in the most laborious work, far distant from our friends, families and connections, without any real prospect of ever seeing them more. . . . Owing to the melancholy situation to which we are reduced, one of us, James Hormet, has been deprived of his senses and confined in a dungeon; the rest remain destitute of almost all the necessities of life.

They had. been, they continued,

> For a considerable time flattered with the expectation held up to us that we would be released from captivity, as soon as it could be done consistent with propriety, and the interest of our country.

Congress eventually voted the necessary money and appointed John Paul Jones to conduct the negotiations, but he died before the appointment reached him at Paris.

There matters stood in the fall of 1793, when the Algerines swooped down on American commerce to catch eleven vessels. This time Portugal was responsible for leaving the corsairs free to sweep into the Atlantic by removing its naval patrols from the Straits, after concluding a sudden peace with them. This was the largest single haul of Americans made by the Barbary pirates. All the vessels, with their officers, crews—more than a hundred strong—and cargoes were carried to Algiers as prizes. Here the new slaves were put to hard labor along with the long-suffering survivors of the 1785 raid.

The routes and cargoes of some of these unlucky vessels give an idea of the kind of shipping that would continue to be exposed to the Barbary menace for many years to come. Four were engaged in the old flour and grain trade to the Atlantic ports of Spain and Portugal. The ship *Prudent* of Philadelphia and the brig *Polly* of Newburyport were bound to Cadiz, while the brigs *George* of Rhode Island and the *Olive Branch* of Portsmouth were heading for Lisbon. Of the four traveling the more vulnerable route past the Barbary coast itself, the schooner *Jay* of Colchester was going toward Boston with a typical Mediterranean cargo of "raisins, figs, wines &c" from Malaga, and the brig *Minerva* of Portsmouth was bringing "sundries" to New York from Leghorn. Several were engaged in the new "tramp carrying trade" between Continental ports, such as the ship *Thomas* of Newburyport with "sugar, wooll & sundries" to Amsterdam, and the schooner *Dispatch* with "sugar, indigo, sasparilla &c" for Hamburg.

These wholesale seizures caused consternation in more places than their home ports. The merchants of Lisbon and Cadiz were aghast to see their valuable American trade jeopardized. American consuls spread warnings in every direction for Yankee vessels to remain in port. Insurance rates on American bottoms jumped to 25 per cent at Cadiz; and one overdue ship from

Philadelphia could not be covered at 50 per cent. Portugal reversed her "peace" stand to rush warships to the Straits "in order to shut up the hell hounds that were lately let loose upon our unfortunate countrymen," while other Portuguese along with Spanish warships provided convoy protection well out into the Atlantic. American vessels stranded in English ports returned home in ballast, because the English would not trust their cargoes to them; and Lloyd's raised its rates for the Atlantic crossing to 10 per cent. Rumors even circulated that the next summer would find corsairs raiding America's own coasts!

Many Americans blamed the English for this situation, believing that it was designed to cripple us in the competitive carrying trade. There was some ground for this suspicion. The disastrous treaty between Portugal and Algiers had been arranged by the British. British merchants in Cadiz were charged with forming a $400,000 pool to purchase captured American grain cargoes at Algiers at bargain rates. The Royal Navy was so busily impressing men from American vessels at Cadiz that several had been "strip't of their men in this way, and are expected to lose the convoy for want of hands to man them."

But it is to those piratical forays that we owe the founding of our navy. The news of the Barbary depredations reached the United States along with the news of those wholesale British seizures in the West Indies. Just as two crushing militia defeats at the hands of the Indians a few years before had given us our regular standing army, so now our navy came into being with "An Act to provide a Naval Armament" which was passed by Congress on March 27, 1794. But the passing of an act does not place warships on the high seas; and in the meantime the United States had to buy peace as speedily as possible or abandon all commerce in the Mediterranean region.

At last a treaty was signed at Algiers in 1795 which included a heavy down payment as well as annual tribute of naval stores and various "presents" for the grasping Algerines. Delay followed delay in procuring cash for the redemption of the 1785 and 1793 captives—and that was not finally effected until 1796. Only twelve of the twenty-one men captured in 1785 ever returned to the United States; seven had died of the plague; one of consumption; and one in the madhouse. Some of the others had been already redeemed with money raised by their friends. "Peace" was also soon arranged with Tunis and Tripoli.

Consuls were dispatched to Barbary to try to keep the Mediterranean safe for American shipping, which was now venturing in increasing numbers into those dangerous waters. It was estimated in 1796 that American vessels in that trade were earning $1,200,000 in freight, half of which was clear profit. But should a vessel fall into the hands of the corsairs, $60,000 would be lost, half of which represented ransom—and with sums like that at stake it was obvious why the government was ready to pay for peace while its navy was building.

Upon the shoulders of the three consuls rested the burden of safeguarding the Mediterranean for this valuable shipping. Two of these, both Irish-Americans, were survivors of those long years of Barbary imprisonment. Captain Richard O'Brien of the *Dauphin,* chief spokesman for the captive Americans, had been lieutenant of an American privateer in the Revolution and now became consul general at Algiers, serving until 1803. James Leander Cathcart, a foremast hand on the *Maria,* was only eighteen when she was captured, but harsh imprisonment was no novelty to him. He had been a midshipman on a Continental frigate taken by the British, and he had escaped from the notorious prison ship *Jersey* at fifteen. He had side-stepped many of his companions' hardships at the hands of the corsairs, for he had learned the language on a previous Mediterranean voyage. Instead of toiling at hard labor, he had soon risen in the dey's service from clerk of the marine to clerk of the galley slaves, and from keeper of the prison tavern to become chief Christian secretary. In the last position he was able to help materially with the treaty of 1795. He returned as consul at Tripoli, where he remained until war broke out in 1801. The third consul, stationed at Tunis, was William Eaton, an energetic, aggressive Dartmouth graduate and ex-soldier.

At best, it was a precarious peace that this trio were able to maintain. If payments fell in arrears or if anything else irritated the pirate ruler, he would unleash his whole corsair navy to pounce upon vessels from Leghorn, Smyrna, Malaga, or Barcelona. These rulers were not the sort to inspire much confidence. One American described the dey of Algiers as

> a huge, shaggy beast, sitting on his rump upon a low bench, with his hind legs gathered up like a tailor or a bear, who extended his fore paw as if to receive something to eat. . . . The animal seemed at that moment to be in a harmless mood; he grinned several times, but made very little noise.

Such men had to be humored or cajoled constantly by the consuls, who had no cable line to communicate with Washington and had to handle emergencies on the spot.

The rapacity and low cunning of the pirates meant constant problems, and at its best the task was humiliating. In 1796, for example, the treaty cash was slow in arriving, and all that held the dey in check was the promise of a new thirty-six-gun frigate. Accordingly, the *Crescent* had to be built at Portsmouth. Time and again the pirate chief or one of his high retainers would insist upon the gift of some particular sort of jewel, whereupon our minister at London or Paris had to busy himself to find just the right one. The crowning insult occurred at Algiers in 1800 when the frigate *George Washington* brought the annual payments. The dey ordered that she carry his embassy, bearing his tribute to the sultan, to Constantinople and that she make the trip under the Turkish flag. It was a bitter pill for Captain Bainbridge of the *Washington* but O'Brien pointed out:

> The consequences of a positive refusal would be war immediately by this regency on the United States. The ship under your command would be detained, and detention and slavery would be the fate of yourself, officers and crew. The vessels,

property and children of the United States would be captured and condemned in this city of bondage.

Consequently, Bainbridge made the humiliating trip with the following unpleasant shipmates: "Ambassador & suit, 100; negro men, women & children, 100; 4 horses, 150 sheep, 25 horned cattle, 4 lions, 4 tygars, 4 antilopes, 12 parrots; funds & regalia amt. nearly one million of dols."

Occasionally in these years an individual American vessel was seized by a Barbary corsair, but the crews were not enslaved and the vessel, with such of her cargo as had escaped casual looting, was restored. The corsairs did not want the Americans to forget the danger to their shipping, in case they were tempted to become slack in their payments. Thus the "peace" was kept, but the menace was ever present, and many times only the zeal and adroitness of the resident consuls kept the situation under control.

In 1801, however, Tripoli got out of hand and started a head-long course to war. The pasha found his raiders short of potential victims, because he had made "peace" with several former enemies and the shipping of others dared not appear within range. He was tempted, too, by the rich and apparently unprotected American commerce; some eighty merchantmen were venturing into the Mediterranean, and the exports to Italy alone had risen to two millions. The pasha had been guilty of some of those occasional earlier seizures. In fact his flagship, commanded by a renegade Scot, was the former Boston merchant-man *Betsey*. Now he insisted that as the price of peace he must have a fine new frigate, like the one given the dey of Algiers. Foolishly the pasha announced his demands in a six months' ultimatum.

He did not reckon with the new American Navy; threats were no longer going to reap rich rewards for the Barbary pirates. Those warships, authorized in 1794, had been ready for sea four years later but until now had been needed in the West

Indies against the French. That trouble ended just in time to reply to the pasha with iron instead of gold.

There is no need to retell here the exploits of our infant navy in Tripolitan waters. Boys by the thousands have thrilled at the burning of the *Philadelphia,* the loss of the *Intrepid,* and the other deeds of daring for which Decatur, Reuben James, and many another bold young man had a destroyer named after him in later days. It is not so generally known, however, that the Swedish Navy, during the earlier part of the war, co-operated with the American in the action against Tripoli and aided in safeguarding the commerce of the two nations.

At last our merchantmen were having something more tangible than consular tact and tribute payments for their protection. Long before war was declared, Cathcart at Tripoli was warning consuls in other ports to hold American vessels until convoy service was available. When Morocco too joined in the war for a while, such protection was especially essential around Gibraltar. The system was for the navy to pick up merchantmen outside the Straits, sometimes as far away as Cadiz and Madeira, and escort them up the inner coast of Spain, dropping off those bound to Malaga and Barcelona, then others perhaps at Marseilles or finally at Leghorn. Sometimes two dozen vessels would be at Leghorn at one time, so rapidly had its American trade grown. On the passage home, the merchantmen would again be offered safe convoy until well out into the Atlantic. The merchant captains reacted differently to this service. According to the Gibraltar consul, "There are several American vessels here but afraid to go without convoy." On the other hand, a naval officer claimed at Leghorn in 1802 that some had refused to wait for his convoy, two others sailed with him but "instantly left me & shaped their own course," while a third held back "in consequence of a ball he was to be at on that night."

Nevertheless, in spite of the imperfections of the system only one American merchantman apiece was the record of the corsair states in the war. The brig *Franklin* was seized by the Tripolitans in June, 1802, while bound from Marseilles to the

West Indies. The brig was left at Tunis while her officers and
men were carried captive through the Swedish-American blockade into Tripoli. Some of the crew were released at once as
being British; the rest, four months later at a price. A year later
the brig *Celia,* of Boston, bound from Barcelona to Malaga, fell
afoul of a Moroccan corsair. Luckily, Bainbridge in the *Philadelphia* encountered the pirate shortly thereafter; he released the
captured crew and overhauled the brig to restore her to Captain
Bowen at Gibraltar.

Yankee sailors were still worried about the pirate threats to
their liberty. Hidden away among the thousands of policies insuring hulls and cargoes in the records of the Boston Marine
Insurance Company, one now and then appears assuming the
risk, for instance, of

> three thousand dollars on the personal liberty of the said
> Eleazer against the risk of captivity by Mahometan Cruizers,
> on board Ship *Hannah,* of and from Boston to port or ports
> of discharge in the Mediterranean, and at and from thence to
> her port of discharge in the United States, or Great Britain.

Eleazer Johnson paid seventy-five dollars for that policy in 1801
at the rate of 2½ per cent. The rate for the cargo on that same
ship was 5 per cent one way to the Mediterranean, for the British
or French might also desire the cargo. Two weeks later, Daniel
Sargent took out a similar policy for Thomas Hill, Jr., at 2 per
cent, which was the standard rate until 1812 when it jumped to
5 per cent. The amount of the policy would pay a ransom.

Even after Tripoli made peace, the navy continued its effective protection in the Mediterranean, until the summer of 1807
when it was recalled because of tension with the British at home.
The trade with the Italian ports was heavier than ever in that
boom year; our exports thither totaled nearly three times what
they had been when Tripoli declared war. Yet, although the
route to Leghorn was most open to pirate attack, insurance
rates had dropped during the six years from 6 or 7 per cent down
to 4½ per cent. This was decidedly reasonable, since it also cov-

ered the risk of seizure by the warring British, French, and Spanish. Altogether the navy had done a remarkably effective job of commerce protection. Without its presence it is doubtful if our Mediterranean commerce could have flourished so successfully.

This was obvious by what happened as soon as the last cruiser sailed homeward from Gibraltar. The Algerines put out to sea immediately, and in the autumn of 1807 captured three American merchantmen near the Straits. Two were carried into Algiers and were soon released, the dey being "apparently satisfied with the commotion he had stirred up." The third vessel, the schooner *Mary Ann* of New York, never reached Algiers. Captain Ichabod Sheffield and his men set upon the pirate prize crew, threw some of them overboard, put the rest adrift in a boat, and took the schooner safely on to Naples. The consul at Algiers, however, had to pay $18,000 indemnity for the missing prize crew.

For the next few years, under Embargo, Nonintercourse, and new Napoleonic decrees, our Mediterranean trade dwindled away, while the Algerines did not venture outside to bother the growing flour trade with Lisbon and Cadiz. By 1812, however, the British again aroused them against the American mariners, but they caught only one prize, the brig *Edward* of Salem. Her unlucky crew were enslaved throughout our war with England.

With the peace early in 1815, our navy was free to return at once to the Mediterranean. After picking up several Algerine cruisers, Decatur appeared before Algiers with a squadron. On June 30, just thirty years less one month after the *Maria* and *Dauphin* had fallen into Barbary toils, he exacted a treaty which completely reversed the old relations. Algiers was hereafter to treat American shipping with due respect without being paid for its good behavior. In fact, instead of receiving ransom for the *Edward's* captive crew, the dey had to pay ten thousand dollars indemnity for the seizure. Decatur then moved on to Tunis and Tripoli where he secured similar treaties, while Bainbridge, following along with another squadron, further cowed the pirates. This aggressive attitude was a potent factor in breaking up the old system of blackmail. Not only did it keep the Mediterranean safe thereafter for the Yankees, but it set an example soon emulated by other nations. A British fleet bombarded Algiers in 1816, and, with the French occupation of Algeria in 1830, the Barbary piracy passed into history.

Meanwhile, closer to our own shores, another piratical scourge was operating on the principle that "dead men tell no tales." This West Indian piracy, like the Barbary one, was a constant threat to vessels and cargoes, but even more of a source of terror to crews and passengers. Instead of seeking live prisoners to be worked or ransomed, the Caribbean pirates indulged in a sadistic orgy of beatings, torture, rape, and murder. Many vessels simply vanished without a trace; occasionally a lone survivor electrified the nation with a horror tale of wholesale butchery.

This West Indian piracy, at its worst from about 1818 to 1825, was almost impossible to eradicate because it was informal and decentralized. The Caribbean, of course, had a piratical tradition almost as old as that of Barbary. The wealth of the Spanish Main had always lured freebooters of many nations; Drake, Morgan, and d'Ollonais had less distinguished imitators by the thousands. There was no counterpart of the Barbary ruler, who could unleash or recall his corsairs at will. Instead, mongrel boatloads of pirates scourged the Caribbean on their own and had to be liquidated one by one—an interminable process. Some operated in the grand manner with the black flag flying over fast, powerful cruisers. The "little man" had his innings, too, with his open boat, armed with a single swivel and packed to the gunwales with brigands. He too could swoop down on a becalmed brig and hastily disappear with his booty to an island lair.

Just as peace was settling down upon most of the world's sea lanes in 1815, the struggle for Latin-American independence gave a new impetus to those irregular operations in the Caribbean. The new revolutionary governments appreciated the value of having Spanish shipping constantly harassed, but they had few sailors or vessels of their own. They showed a shameless readiness to grant privateering commissions to vessels which never visited any of their ports from Cartagena to Buenos Aires—and in many cases, did not have a single Latin-American sailor aboard. Many American privateersmen, who found themselves at a loose end with the return of peace and the loss of their legitimate letters of marque, eagerly grasped this alternative to humdrum peacetime trading. Many of the French "privateers," too, which had caused much havoc around 1798, were identical with the pirate craft which now made themselves dreaded. Baltimore rapidly became a center of this new lawlessness as batches of blank privateering commissions began to arrive from the revolutionary ports to the southward. Merchantmen began to tell of being hailed, in good Maryland or New York accents, by the South American privateer *True-Blooded Yankee* or the *Fourth of July*. Late in 1818, a Baltimorean wrote to a New York friend: "Privateers continue coming and going to this port as to their home. Two arrived this week, one of which landed at midnight eight dray loads of gold and silver."

Very quickly the situation went from bad to worse, as the Latin-American privateers took on more and more of an international aspect. The privateer *Heroine,* captured by a Portuguese frigate, for example, numbered among her crew forty-two British, twenty-six South Americans, nineteen North Americans, ten Frenchmen, seven Italians, six Spaniards, four East Indians, three Swedes, two Prussians, two Dutchmen, an African, an Austrian, a Greek, a Portuguese, and a Russian. Originally these privateers were expected to confine their attentions solely to the shipping of their hostile mother countries, but according to a New York editorial in 1817, "They board and overhaul everything they meet and the character of the vessel is generally determined by the number of Spanish dollars that may be found on board." Although the Caribbean was the principal center of their plundering, they sometimes cruised far out into the Atlantic. In 1818, the ship *Robert,* bound from Liverpool to New York, was stopped in mid-ocean by "one of these patriot picaroon cruisers," which poured a broadside into her. The pirates swarmed aboard to loot the ship, taking her provisions, slashing the rigging, and robbing the steerage passengers, "besides treating them very ill, and in Spanish, threatening the females."

The weakness of Spanish rule in Florida and the remoteness of the Gulf from all effective authority gave the privateers plenty of bases from which to operate with little danger of interference. New Orleans was a pirate hangout for a while. In 1817, a Scottish adventurer, who styled himself "Sir Gregor MacGregor," raised some men and money at Savannah and other southern ports, procured some Latin-American privateering commissions, and seized Amelia Island. At this old smuggling entrepôt, he was joined by the high sheriff of New York County. Later the island was taken over by Louis Aury, a Gulf pirate, and became a lively "privateering" base until the United States Navy intervened, when operations were shifted to more secret places. Meanwhile, Jean Lafitte, who had aided Jackson at New Orleans with his pirate crew, was committing irregularities from his base at Barataria near the Gulf.

By 1818, this "fag end of privateering" was more and more becoming outright piracy. The strong, seagoing cruisers were being outnumbered by little open boats operated from hidden shore bases against any merchantmen becalmed in their vicinity. Cuba, from its strategic position commanding some of the bottleneck entrances into the Caribbean, was the worst center. The pirate craft were dangerously thick around Cape San Antonio, its western tip. They hung on the flanks of the vessels bound to Havana and Matanzas. They haunted the Windward Passage and extended their operations over to Haiti and even to Puerto Rico. Those coasts had hundreds of small coves and inlets, from which the lurking boats swept out and then could retire quickly to be hidden behind rocks, trees, and undergrowth. Spanish rule in Cuba was less weak than in Florida or Texas, but it was inclined to be complaisant toward local pirates. For one thing, the merchants of Havana and other Cuban ports found good profit in handling the pirate loot. And the Cubans could justify their

practice as reprisal for the participation of the Baltimore privateersmen in the raids on Spanish shipping.

This new piracy was a particularly grave danger to American
ships with some of our most traveled sea lanes running through
the danger zone. The threat to our trade from the Barbary
pirates had been a minor consideration, for less than one-tenth
of our shipping used the Mediterranean; but probably more of
our vessels were coming and going past Cuban waters than anywhere else. In contrast to the twenty-odd American vessels that
fell into Barbary hands in the course of thirty years, it has been
estimated that some five hundred vessels, with a property loss of
twenty millions, were seized by the West Indian pirates, while
many more were stopped and molested.

Cuba's sugar and New York's "cotton triangle" were the mag-
nets for these southern sea routes. The United States was finding
in Cuba a substitute for the lost sugar trade of the British West
Indies and French Haiti. Every year an increasing number of
vessels were making their way to Havana, Matanzas, and other
Cuban ports. New York port was enterprisingly bringing southern cotton north for transshipment to England from its own
docks and sending south in exchange both northern products
and its own imports. This practice, which was helping to push
New York into first place among ports, was giving a tremendous
impetus to the longer coasting voyages down past Florida to
New Orleans, Mobile, and the other Gulf ports. Ten years after
the pirate period, one-eighth of the total tonnage arriving at the
port of New York came from the Gulf and from Cuba. While
these cargoes may not have equaled in value the textiles and
hardware reaching New York from Liverpool, the southern trade
was carried on in little brigs and schooners; consequently the
number of vessels and sailors exposed to the pirate menace was
greater than on any other run.

Not all cargoes found the same favor with the pirates. Silver
or gold or kegs of Spanish dollars made their eyes gleam. The
many cases of torture arose from their efforts to learn if such
treasure were hidden aboard a ship. Dry goods and other "mer-

chandise" that represented considerable value in small bulk were their next choice. Although not as easily negotiable as silver, they could be disposed of through "fences" in Cuba. Sugar and coffee, too, were a source of profit; such cargoes, it was said, sometimes started northward from Cuba several times, only to be recaptured and resold at Havana or Matanzas to another Yankee purchaser. Loads of lumber or baled hay, on the other hand, were enough to drive pirates to rage. Useless as loot, such a disappointing cargo was more than once set afire by the disgusted cutthroats.

Notices of piratical seizures or visitations began to be common around 1818 and 1819. These have been collected from the files by the score and reproduced by several authors. Some of the earlier vessels got off easily, occasionally losing nothing, sometimes merely being robbed of a keg or two of silver. But this did not last; the next step was the maltreatment of crews. They might be beaten up, or an officer might be suspended by the neck in the hope of making him divulge the hiding place of treasure. By 1822, the pirates passed on to actual murder. As the merchants of Portland complained in a memorial in 1824:

At first they were content to plunder and maltreat the crews of our vessels, without proceeding to actual murder. Of late, however, they have not stopped short of the most brutal and inhuman outrages. In some instances, whole crews have fallen victims to their barbarous and unrelenting fury.

The brig *Aurilla* of Gloucester, for example, en route from Baltimore to New Orleans, was boarded by two pirate schooners off Salt Key (Cay Sal) between Cuba and Florida on May 16, 1822. The captain and crew were ordered below; then they were brought up, one by one, to run the pirate gauntlet past the windlass, which was smeared with blood to indicate the murder of those ahead. This process yielded enough information to give the pirates fifty thousand dollars' worth of merchandise and money. One passenger, suspected of concealing money, was stabbed, blindfolded, hoisted to the yardarm, and lowered into the sea.

Several Negro slaves were part of the cargo; the women were all raped. After that, the *Aurilla* was allowed to go on her way.

A month later the crew of another coasting schooner had a still more horrible experience. A passenger alone survived to tell of the fate of the *Mary*, which was bound from Philadelphia to New Orleans. Off the southern coast of Florida, she was over-hauled by pirates. Her guns sank one boatload, but another, filled with "horrid looking wretches" swarmed aboard. Two of the crew were killed in the assault. The narrator was bound to the mainmast—being too well dressed to throw overboard, ac-cording to the pirates. With some eighteen thousand dollars in gold and silver secreted under a plank in his cabin, and fifteen thousand dollars in banknotes sewn into the lapel of his coat and into his cravat, his feelings may be easily appreciated as he was forced to watch this grim scene:

> Over my left shoulder, one of our sailors was strung up to the yardarm, and apparently in the last agonies of death; while before me our gallant captain was on his knees and begging for his life. The wretches were endeavoring to extort from him the secret of our money; but for a while he was firm and dauntless. Provoked at his obstinacy, they extended his arms and cut them off at the elbows. At this human nature gave way, and the injured man confessed on the spot where we had concealed our specie. In a few moments it was aboard their own vessel. To revenge themselves upon the unhappy captain, when they had satisfied themselves that nothing else was hid-den, they spread a bed of oakum on the deck, and after soaking it through with turpentine, tied the captain on it, filled his mouth with the same combustibles, and set the whole on fire. The cries of the unfortunate man were heart-rending, and his agonies must have been unutterable, but they were soon over. . . .
>
> On casting my eyes towards the schooner's stern, I discovered that our boatswain had been nailed to the deck through his feet, and the body spiked to the tiller. He was writhing in the last agonies of crucifixion. Our fifth comrade was out of sight during all this tragedy; in a few minutes, however, he was

brought upon the deck blindfolded. He was then conducted to
the muzzle of the swivel and commanded to kneel. The swivel
was then fired off, and his head was dreadfully wounded by the
discharge. . . .

The passenger's own turn was next. The banknotes were found
in his lapel, but as the pirates scrambled for them greedily, a
sudden squall sent them scurrying back to their own vessel.
Still bound to the mast, the solitary survivor was soon aware
that the *Mary* had been scuttled and was sinking beneath him;
but at the last moment, a passing ship discovered his grim plight.

Coasting voyages usually sound uneventful, but with this sort
of adventure ever lurking in the offing, it took plenty of courage
to travel by sea along the southern coast in the twenties. Sometimes a derelict schooner or brig was found drifting with all on
board murdered; other vessels, probably scuttled or burned,
simply "went missing." Among the latter was the one that sailed
from Charleston with Aaron Burr's daughter Theodosia among
her passengers. The vessel was never heard from; perhaps she
sank off Hatteras, but many wondered if the pirates had found
another victim.

One cause for the popularity of such a brutal policy lay in the
increased activity of the navy. The Gulf squadron, based on New
Orleans, hunted the pirates from the outset, and by 1821 the
force around Cuban waters was being strengthened. Meanwhile
Congress was being deluged by demands for better protection of
our shipping. In 1823, Commodore Porter took seventeen naval
vessels to the West Indies "for the purpose of repressing piracy,
and affording effectual protection to the citizens and commerce
of the United States." This was not the simple problem of blockading a few ports with cruisers as it had been in Tripoli. Since
the larger warships were not suited for inshore work, a force of
smaller vessels had to be improvised. Nine schooners were included in the squadron, along with five 20-oared barges that
could follow the pirates in shallow water to their lairs. Porter's
flagship the *Sea Gull* was the first steam war vessel to go into

actual service; she had been a Connecticut river steamer. It proved a trying task, even with the co-operation of the British Navy, to police the hundreds of miles of potential lurking places and to bring the culprits to heel. Also the Spanish authorities in Cuba and Puerto Rico generally continued to be unco-operative. Yellow fever, added to casualties in action, meant a heavy toll in lives. By the end of 1825, the Secretary of the Navy was at last able to report that the situation was well in hand. He was right; a few sporadic outbreaks occurred later, but that was the last bad year of West Indian piracy. Once again, the navy had done its part well, if slowly, in keeping the sea lanes safe.

A final act in this chapter occurred at New York in 1831. The brig *Vineyard,* bound northward from New Orleans with several barrels of silver aboard, was seized by a mutinous crew who murdered the captain and buried the treasure in the sands of Coney Island. The culprits, when apprehended, were found to include one of the most extensive practitioners of piracy in the West Indies. Charles Gibbs, who came originally from a good Rhode Island family, had drifted into piracy and become leader of a gang which operated a squadron around Cuban waters. He claimed that out of forty vessels captured between 1818 and 1824, twenty of the crews had all been murdered. One of these was a Dutch ship, from which he spared one passenger, a girl whom he forced to be his mistress until, fearful that she might betray him, he did away with her too. The public was incredulous at his fantastic confessions until they were corroborated by Captain Kearney, whose naval vessel had interrupted Gibbs's gang in the act of despoiling three vessels at Cape San Antonio in 1821. Gibbs was hanged at New York on April 22, 1831. By that year a greater volume of traffic than ever was passing safely through the erstwhile zone of terror.

For a brief interlude in 1827, the navy was recalled to the Mediterranean again to protect our merchantmen from pirates. This time it was the Greeks, who had lapsed into piracy during their war of independence from Turkey. The navy provided convoys and quickly wiped out a few nests of troublemakers.

But on the other side of the world, pirates had long lurked and continued to lie in wait for many years to come. For many years American shipping ran the distant peril of being caught by the ferocious Malays around the bottleneck of the Straits of Sunda or by the pirates infesting the China coast. All vessels went well armed in those eastern seas, even at a time when our merchantmen were forbidden on other runs to take anything more than small arms. Vessels bound for Canton were generally larger than the average and were manned by sizable crews. Because of the guns that were carried stripped for action, the size of the vessels, and the number in the crews, relatively few merchantmen encountered trouble in these tropic waters; and most of those that ran afoul of pirates were able to beat off the attacks.

One exception was the ship *Friendship* of Salem, which was overrun and looted by the Malays as she lay waiting for a pepper cargo at Quallah Battoo, Sumatra, in 1830. Several of the crew were killed in the rush of the attack and others wounded. A few dived overboard and after wandering in the jungle made their way back later to find the ship intact. To make the Malays think twice before trying such a thing again, the U.S.S. *Potomac* was sent out on a punitive expedition two years later. American guns reduced Quallah Battoo to ashes. While an ever present threat, piracy in the Far East was never as serious a danger to the American vessels as it was nearer home.

It is to the credit of the American mariner that crews were never lacking to man ships during the most dangerous hazards of Barbary slavery, Caribbean torture, or Malay ambushes. Marine insurance, always a sensitive barometer, reflected the increase and decrease of piratical activity on these various routes, but, as in the case of impressment and seizure in the Napoleonic period, the perils did not drive American shipping from the seas. The navy, in each case, played its part in that successful clinging to the sea lanes by the persistent Yankees.

Chapter VI

Reversed Roles

The Civil War was a strange interlude in the usual attitude of the United States toward "freedom of the seas." Forgetful of its past championship of that policy, it quickly utilized the advantages of sea power in the best British manner. A strangling blockade was imposed on Southern sea-borne trade, while troops and supplies were moved by water wherever possible. All this was not done without spectacular opposition from Confederate raiders in a vigorous *guerre de course* against the Union merchant marine. The damage inflicted was more serious in its repercussions on Northern morale than in actual destruction of vessels.

The Union role, therefore, had much in common with that of England and Germany in their modern wars. Jefferson, Madison, Wilson, and Franklin Delano Roosevelt all had plenty to say against interference with neutral rights on the high seas, but Lincoln found his own country the infringer of those rights. Between 1861 and 1865, the United States was the aggressive blockader, seizing neutral vessels engaged in trading with the South. Federal judges condemned British vessels on the very same grounds that the High Court of Admiralty had used against Yankee neutrals in the past; and the British protests simply paraphrased Jefferson's and Madison's tirades against such "piracy." Fortunately, each side had sufficient sense of humor and proportion not to press its case too hard; each undoubtedly realized that it was playing the reverse of its usual role, and that in wars to come would likely be back on its old side of the fence. For the time being, the North had scant patience with its former theories of "freedom of the seas."

That tedious vigil off the Southern ports proved even more fruitful in results than the Royal Navy's similar rigid watch in

1814. The Confederacy, unlike the United States at that earlier time, did not have enough industrial development in its own states to sustain the war effort without overseas supplies. By preventing its sale of cotton in exchange for war materials and food, the Union navy contributed materially to the final victory.

The old British practice of moving troops and supplies by sea to avoid overland lines of communication was employed to excellent advantage by the North. Sea-borne movements not only tended to keep the enemy in doubt as to destinations but proved cheaper, easier, and far less vulnerable to attack. A safe line of retreat was at hand, too, should things go wrong—Dunkerque was no novelty in the history of combined strategy. From the opening week of the war, when the North's attention was drawn to the danger of overland communications through doubtful cities by the mobbing of a Massachusetts regiment in Baltimore, the water routes began to be used. Expeditions were taken by sea to the Peninsula campaign, to the Carolina coast, to New Orleans, and elsewhere without hindrance.

The Northern merchant marine made possible both the effective blockade and the sea-borne communications. Its vast quantity of sailing vessels was drawn upon to some extent for carrying coal and other heavy supplies but its steamers were invaluable. Steam vessels were still in a minority in the merchant fleets of the world, and most of these were small vessels engaged in river or harbor work, where changing winds were most bothersome. Luckily, however, the North had a few score good-sized coastal steamers and even a handful of ocean liners.

The owners, most of whom were New Yorkers, were among those who made the most money out of the war. Especially was this true of those who chartered their ships to the navy or army at $1,500 to $2,000 a day. Marshall O. Roberts, for instance, a leader in the isthmian steamship business, bought the 1,750-ton *Empire City* at auction from his old company for $12,000, and, without counting in his naval charters, received $833,000 for her services to the army alone. His 2,123-ton *Illinois* earned some $414,000 in charters alone and was finally, at Lincoln's express order, sold to the army for $442,000, although the latter was well aware that she was not worth it.

Whatever they cost, those steamers were indispensable to the Northern effort. The navy had but a few dozen vessels of all types when the blockade was proclaimed on April 19, 1861; and most of those were on distant stations. If the blockade was to be effective before new warships could be rushed to completion, armed steamers were needed to take up immediate patrol stations off the Southern ports. South they went—everything from ocean liners to East River ferryboats, and they did their job well. Hundreds of other steamers, some almost too rotten to float, were used as transports and supply ships.

New York was not only able to furnish most of these, but its highly developed shipyards and marine-engine works on the East River made possible the wholesale construction of new warships that constantly reinforced the navy, until at the close it numbered some seven hundred vessels. Out of 199 naval vessels built during the war, a quarter of the hulls and a third of the engines were built at New York, which also provided twenty-two of the twenty-eight ready-made steamships of over one thousand tons purchased for the navy, and 111 of the 257 smaller steamers. Altogether, the role of the port of New York, between its shipping and shipbuilding facilities, was an essential one in winning the war.

The effects of the Confederate raiders, however, proved more significant, as far as American commerce was concerned, than the blockade and the transport service. They were few in number but they dealt Yankee shipping such a deadly blow that it failed to recover until World War I, a half a century later. Just as in 1814, when the shipowners of Britain had howled to high heaven at the depredations of Yankee privateers upon their vessels, so now the New York Chamber of Commerce was issuing frantic complaints against the Southern raiders that were dotting the seas with the flaming wrecks of local sailing vessels. To the eastward, lamentations rose in similar vein from one shipping port after another. History was certainly repeating itself fifty years later; on both occasions the navies of those frantic shipping circles, the Royal Navy in 1814, and the Northern navy in the sixties, were strangling by rigid blockade all the commerce of the enemy. Yet their own shipowners and merchants scarcely noticed that successful blockading in their horrified concentration upon the lesser activities of the enemy raiders. Those Confederate raiders fell into three groups—the privateers, the lesser cruisers, and, most devastating to Union commerce, the British-built *Alabama* and her consorts.

The first to appear—and to disappear—were "the last of the privateers." Privateering had been abolished by international agreement by the European powers in 1856 at Paris, but the United States had not participated. Panic spread through Northern shipping centers at President Jefferson Davis's announcement in April, 1861, that the Confederacy would grant "letters of marque and reprisal." Lincoln threatened five days later that any such vessels would be regarded as engaged in piracy. The crew of the captured privateer *Savannah* were actually put on trial for piracy at New York but were saved from the gallows by the Confederate ultimatum that a corresponding number of captured Union officers were being held as hostages and would suffer a similar fate.

A small and mongrel assortment of vessels operated out of Southern harbors, chiefly New Orleans, Charleston, and the North Carolina inlets. They were augmented by some vessels from the North Carolina state navy. A few privateers made a tidy profit. They caught some forty Yankee victims, more than half of which were condemned by regular prize courts in Southern ports. By the summer of 1861, the practice died of malnutrition because of the increasing difficulty of getting the prizes through the tightened blockade into ports—and the consequent dearth of prize money. Only a lone privateer, the *Retribution*, once a tug on the Great Lakes but now refitted as a schooner, was left by early 1863. In January she seized the schooner *Han-*

over and in February the brig *Emily Fosdick* in the Bahamas—
a final act in the history of privateering.

The rest of the Southern raiders, although often denounced as
privateers or even as pirates, were all formally commissioned
warships of the navy of the Confederate states, and in many cases
their commanders were officers of the "old navy." The *Sumter,*
a former passenger steamship of the New Orleans-Havana run
and the *Nashville* of the New York-Charleston line were passenger steamers seized in Southern ports. The *Georgia,* built to
order in a British yard, was such a shoddy piece of work that
she lasted for only three months of active service in 1863. In the
latter part of 1864, two other British-built vessels were the block-
ade-runners *Tallahassee,* alias *Olustee,* and the *Chickamauga.*

The bulk of the effective raiding was the work of the "big
three"—the *Alabama, Florida,* and *Shenandoah.* All were large,
fast vessels, equipped with both steam and sail, and built in
England. Despite the protests of the vigilant Northern minister
at London, the British government did not stop them from
slipping out to sea, where they received their armaments from
other vessels from England. The *Alabama,* justly the most celebrated, left the Mersey in July, 1862, to be commissioned off the
Azores four weeks later, and was steadily "on the go" under
Captain Raphael Semmes until sunk by the *Kearsarge* off Cher-
bourg in June, 1864. The *Florida* had an even longer nominal
career—between March, 1862, when she sailed from England,
and October, 1864, when she was rammed and captured by the
Wachusett in the neutral harbor of Bahia. She spent, however,
a good part of her time lying idle at Nassau, Mobile, and Brest;
and her chief activity came between February and August, 1863,
when she was aided by a series of tenders as sub-raiders. The
Shenandoah left England in September, 1864, ostensibly on a
merchant voyage. Early the next year she visited Australia, and
then went north to accomplish her chief damage in the Bering
Sea.

Most of these raiders' victims were burned at sea. A few were
allowed to proceed after giving a bond payable to the Confed-

eracy six months after the war. The usual reason for such surprising clemency was the presence of more passengers than the raider cared to take aboard, or of a neutral cargo. It was also a means by which the raider could rid herself of an accumulation of prisoners from destroyed ships. By the time the raiders were at sea, the blockade had become too tight to reach the ports with prizes, as the privateers had done earlier. Semmes used Cuba for his early captures, but Spain restored the vessels to their owners. One vessel he succeeded in selling in South Africa, but under rather irregular circumstances. The bulk of the captured vessels was put to the torch—much in the same way as were the British victims of American privateers in 1814. The procedure was pretty much a regular ritual. The doomed vessel was stripped of whatever the raider wanted in rigging and stores and the officers and crew were taken off as prisoners. Combustibles were then set ablaze in cabin and forecastle or other enclosed places.

Altogether some two hundred Northern vessels would be burned, scuttled, or sent in for condemnation between May, 1861, when a privateer caught the lime-laden *Ocean Rover* from Rockland below New Orleans, and July, 1865, ten weeks after Appomattox, when the *Shenandoah* burned her last victims. The intervening years saw few weeks when at least one raider was not at work, but after the privateering interval, four were the most ever to be cruising at any one time. The peak of this destruction at sea coincided with the "high tide of the Confederacy" in the six months before Gettysburg. The story of that raiding has been told many times by eyewitnesses and by recent authors, but always from the viewpoint of the raiders themselves. Their point of view often reminds one of the little boy who stood with tears in his eyes before a picture of lions devouring Christian martyrs: "One poor little lion," he sobbed, "didn't get any martyr." Our concern here is for the hunted Yankee square-riggers.

The old American merchant marine was at its peak, as far as size was concerned, at the outbreak of the war. The combined stimuli of the California gold rush, the flood of Irish and German immigration, the increased European demand for wheat and cotton, along with various other factors, had more than doubled it between 1846, when it stood at 2,562,000 tons, and 1861, when it reached 5,539,000. Nearly half of the latter was registered for foreign trade, a level that would not be reached again until 1918. At the conservative British estimate of forty dollars a ton, the total American tonnage represented an investment of almost a quarter of a billion dollars.

Much to the disadvantage of the Confederacy, most of that shipping was owned in the Northern ports. New Yorkers were among the heaviest investors, as was obvious from the fact that the majority of the vessels used in the blockade hailed from that port. In fact, exactly half of the entire registered tonnage belonged to the two ports of New York and Boston, while four-fifths of it hailed from the three states of New York, Massachusetts, and Maine. As a result, those ports and states bore the brunt of the marine losses in almost exactly that proportion.

On the other hand, only one-ninth of the registered tonnage was owned in the Confederate states—and this was just about the amount that hailed from the two small Maine districts of Bath and Portland alone. One cause of this was that the carrying trade for the South had been largely in Northern bottoms. It was claimed that the Yankees got forty cents out of every dollar that the planters received for their cotton. In shipbuilding, the South was at a worse disadvantage. Out of 148 new square-rigged ships, barks, and brigs built during the last year of peace, one was launched at Norfolk. Not another one slid down the ways along the whole Southern coast from Virginia around to Texas. The South had one asset: it was able to raid Northern vessels with slight fear of reprisals. Beyond the few Northern vessels seized in its ports at the outbreak of the war, it had very little shipping of its own to be endangered.

Yet the germs of decay were already at work in spite of the fact that the nation's merchant marine reached its maximum size at this time. It was relatively weaker than it had been in 1854, when it almost equaled the British in tonnage and surpassed it in quality and performance. In those few intervening years, with the panic of 1857 and the overproduction of clippers, the earning power of American vessels had decreased, while foreigners in general and the British in particular had forged ahead. England's old handicap from lack of native ship timber was lessened by the increased use of steamers and iron hulls, where she had a distinct advantage. An increased volume of our carrying trade was already in foreign hands before the war started, and this amount grew rapidly from the threat of Confederate raiding.

An unusual result in this preponderance of foreign bottoms, especially in the transatlantic trade, was the continued prosperity of Northern commerce while Northern shipping was being depleted by raiders. The commerce of the port of New York, for example, was actually heavier during the war than it had been in the four preceding years! Unlike its isolation by the rigid British blockade in 1814, the North had no trouble whatsoever in exchanging whatever commodities it pleased with foreign countries, as the neutral vessels plied back and forth without hindrance.

Thus the Confederate raiders, for all their depredations, had scant influence upon the outcome of the war, while the Northern blockade exercised a deadly pressure upon Southern military performance. Also, the North, being industrial, had no serious need for strategic materials from beyond the seas; a moderate amount of muskets and woolens for uniforms were imported early in the conflict, but they were not at all vital.

Unlike the dearth of figures for the Revolutionary period, the annual reports on Commerce and Navigation give a wealth of detail for the fiscal years from July 1, 1861, to June 30, 1865. The raiders' toll of 150 American vessels engaged in foreign trade represented only one voyage in two hundred. Their fifty coasting victims probably indicated a still lower proportion. Omitting the shipping with British North America, where the constant comings and goings of little fresh-water or coasting craft give a misleading picture of the whole, 29,521 American vessels and 28,937 foreign ones entered or cleared on foreign voyages during the war years. Their cargoes, valued at two billion dollars, were almost evenly divided between imports and exports.

The raiding hit with particular force the pride of the merchant marine, the clipper ships and other large seagoing sailing vessels. The bulk of the tonnage lost was in sixty-four full-rigged ships and sixty barks, which were like ships except for their labor-saving fore-and-aft rig on the third mast. Only one steamship was destroyed; these were less numerous and from their nature could escape more easily. The rest of the losses concerned much smaller vessels—thirty-odd brigs and forty-five or so schooners.

The ships lost measured several times the average tonnage of the Napoleonic period, sixteen of the victims being more than a thousand tons. The largest was 1,767 tons, which was only fifteen tons smaller than the celebrated *Flying Cloud*. The average was about five hundred tons, as compared with the 118 tons of the American prizes taken into Halifax in 1812. In value, too, these latest losses represented "more eggs in one basket," most of the largest vessels being estimated at $65,000 to $90,000, with the cargoes of even greater value. In the final American estimates under the Alabama Claims, the highest casualty, combining the vessel, her cargo, and her freight earnings, was rated at $530,000, while five others were put at more than $400,000. The average for that whole group was about $120,000 as compared with about $25,000 in the Napoleonic period and with nearly $3,000,000 for the *Robin Moor,* the first American vessel torpedoed in World War II.

The blows fell upon some sea lanes much more heavily than upon others, although none of the major fields of commerce escaped scot free. Altogether, the transatlantic run yielded some twenty-six victims totaling about 16,200 tons; the Far East and Africa, twenty-seven of 22,500 tons; the Cape Horn route to San Francisco, six of 5,000 tons; the Caribbean, thirty of 8,300 tons; the rest of Latin America, twenty-seven of 14,700 tons; the coastal trade, fifty of 15,500 tons; and the whalers, forty-three of 12,800 tons. The largest ships and most valuable cargoes were caught on the Far Eastern and West Coast runs which, with the whalers, suffered the heaviest relative damage.

Except for a few brief forays, the lucrative North Atlantic shuttle was subjected to heavy raiding for only a single month out of the forty-eight months of war. Had not the cream of the trade of the New York sailing packets with the rich cargoes of specie, woolens, silks, and other "fine freight" already passed to the neutral steamships of the Cunard and other foreign lines, that story would have been different. More keels plowed this sea lane than any other foreign one, and the value of the cargoes was more than that of all the rest combined. In fact, the British trade alone came to a billion dollars, half the grand total for the four war years; and that of the rest of Europe, to a third of a billion more.

But even over ordinary cargoes the Stars and Stripes were flying less and less, and the threat of raiders accelerated the trend. In the trade with the old Hanse ports of Hamburg and Bremen, only 38 out of 1,336 vessels entering or clearing at our ports were American. In the French trade, our vessels dropped from 681 in the first year of the war to 55 in the last, while in the British, they fell from 1,716 to 398 in those same years.

Confederate raiders, consequently, did not find it a happy hunting ground. This proportion of neutral flags was higher than on any other run—73 per cent for the last war year and 62 per cent for the average. It was not healthy to raid neutrals; and they might spread the alarm of the raider's presence. Even American vessels when found did not always prove good prizes. On this run in particular at this time, they were apt to have cheap cargoes or none at all; or to be carrying neutral property; or even to be loaded down with immigrants, so that burning was not feasible. Almost the only brisk business for American bottoms was in carrying wheat or flour because of crop failures abroad at the opening of the war. For a while Europe was almost as dependent upon Northern breadstuffs as upon Southern cotton. But the return cargoes which might have proved tempting raider fodder were lacking. Some of the grain fleet came back in ballast; some brought cheap ladings of British coal; and a few of the packets still carried immigrants, although the steamships were rapidly weaning even that business away.

The first distinguished victim on the Atlantic shuttle was the 1,462-ton clipper *Harvey Birch* of New York, the second largest of all the vessels destroyed. She was burned by the *Nashville* in November, 1861, as she was returning in ballast after delivering grain to Havre.

Eleven months later, the North Atlantic caught its only systematic punishment when the *Alabama* cruised westward from the Azores almost to Sandy Hook to catch the autumn grain fleet. In October, the ship *Brilliant* bound from New York to London with grain was destroyed by Semmes of the *Alabama,* who felt a momentary twinge of pity at the sad mien of Captain Hagar, forced to watch his uninsured life savings go up in flames. Before the month was out, seven other Yankee captains had shared his experience. News, however, spread too rapidly on the Atlantic shuttle for the *Alabama* to continue this successful pace. The *Lafayette,* caught later in the month, carried New York newspapers with the story of the burning of the *Brilliant* less than three weeks earlier. The forewarned shippers had doctored the *Lafayette's* documents to make her cargo appear to be British property, but the job was too hastily and clumsily done to fool the wily, legal-trained Semmes, and she was put to the torch just the same.

Semmes shortly abandoned these too-frequented waters after deciding that his coal was running too low to risk a raid on New York. Thereafter the Atlantic raids were infrequent and not serious. The Black Ball packet *Isaac Webb* was accosted by the bark *Tacony,* a tender of the *Florida,* in June, 1863, near Nantucket Shoals, but her 750 immigrants saved her. The next day, the ship *Byzantium* with English coal was warned by a Union cruiser of the presence of this "pirate bark," but the fog shut down, and when it lifted, the bark was upon her. Both the *Byzantium* as well as a Yankee bark, outward bound for Londonderry, went up in smoke. The next summer found the *Talla-*

hassee spreading terror in those same waters and numbering among her victims a bark laden with pig iron for Scotland, a schooner with coal from Cardiff, and the packet *Adriatic*. The last was not saved by her immigrant cargo; her 170 terrified passengers were taken aboard the raider and she was burned. Union naval bases were too close to Nantucket Shoals for these to be more than brief "hit-and-run" affairs.

The Far Eastern trade offered better hunting for the raiders. Two-thirds of the shipping flew the American flag and was fair game, while the individual cargoes, especially those homebound, were exceedingly rich. Above all, in the wide and empty expanse of the Pacific and South Atlantic, the raiders profited from the midway developments of the "age of speed," which enabled them to operate under more advantageous circumstances than the cruisers either of earlier days or of modern wars. Steam gave them superior speed to their quarry, which was still under sail, yet ocean cables and wireless were not hampering them by spreading the alarm to merchantmen or by summoning enemy war craft, a situation that was greatly to hinder raiders of the future. Nor was there the constantly passing shipping of the more crowded Atlantic shuttle to spread word of their cruising, nor nearby shores to speed the alarm by telegraph.

The natural consequence of this combination of circumstances was a heavy toll of Far Eastern shipping. About one American vessel in 70 was caught on that run, whereas only one in 340 was the score on the Atlantic shuttle, and one in 450 in the Cuban trade. Also, the largest victims of all—as well as the most valuable—were lost on this Eastern route.

Although it was still most respectable to import tea by the cargo in one's own ships, the aristocratic China trade was no longer our sole interest in the Orient. Whereas commerce with Japan was still disappointingly meager a decade after Perry's visit, a lively interchange had sprung up at Manila, largely in American bottoms. India, too, sent much, especially in rice and cotton no longer obtainable from our South, but it wanted little that we had to offer in return. With Australia, it was the exact reverse; all sorts of supplies were needed there but no adequate return cargoes came from "down under." This led to a mixed-up pattern of tramp voyages. Africa, on the other hand, took a moderate amount of mixed cargoes and also generally had products for the return voyage.

Just a year after her raiding splurge on the North Atlantic, the *Alabama* reached the outer limits of her wanderings in the Eastern seas. In November, 1863, she caught the largest prize of all, the 1,767-ton clipper *Winged Racer,* in the Straits of Sunda between Java and Sumatra. That cargo of sugar, hides, and jute had cost $190,000 at Manila but was expected to realize $252,000 in New York. Instead, it was looted by the Confederates and she was set afire.

The next day, not far from Batavia, another clipper ran afoul of the *Alabama,* and her beauty was ruthlessly put to the torch—but not before she had led her destroyer a chase, which almost saved her. She was the 1,098-ton *Contest,* a record breaker on the Cape Horn run in her day and still with enough speed to make Semmes admit that "it was the first time that the *Alabama* had appeared dull." The chase lasted for hours and only a sudden calm betrayed the fleeing ship. Her cargo of lacquer ware and novelties from Japan was destined for the firm of Abiel A. Low and Brothers, of New York, her owners. Low, who was head of the New York Chamber of Commerce, had already lost another clipper, and he led the pack in denouncing the Confederate "pirates." Semmes, in sarcastic response, sent him his special compliments by a released vessel.

Barely dodging a lone Union cruiser in those seas, the *Alabama* proceeded into the straits of Malacca, and not far from Singapore added to her list the ship *Sonora* of Newburyport in ballast for a tramp voyage. The *Sonora* had been lucky before this encounter. While some twenty big American vessels were lying idle in Singapore because shippers feared to use them, she had kept busy. She had carried a cargo from New York to Melbourne, had gone to Hong Kong, and when caught was proceeding to Burma to load rice for Europe under a $32,000 charter, which was more than half her value.

The favorite hunting ground of the raiders of this Far Eastern trade was, however, closer home in the South Atlantic, where it narrows somewhat between the bulges of Brazil and Africa. Here they could lie in wait both for the clippers rounding the Horn to California and the shipping bound to the farther ports of South America. This region, too, was sufficiently remote to avoid effective Union pursuit. The first half of 1863 found the "big three" all there at once, while the *Sumter* and the *Shenandoah* likewise haunted these waters in their turn.

Early in her career the *Florida* there burned three rich Far Eastern victims, averaging almost half a million dollars apiece in value. In February, 1863, she caught Abiel Low's 1,362-ton clipper ship *Jacob Bell* homeward bound with teas. The next month, it was the 941-ton *Star of Peace* on her way from Calcutta to Boston with a general cargo, including saltpeter for the Du Pont powder works. The third capture in April was the 420-ton *Oneida*, a little old ship bound from Shanghai to New York, but with a cargo of great value.

At the same time the *Florida* was busily making hauls in the trade between New York and San Francisco. This trade was not quite what it had been at the height of the gold rush a dozen years before, but until the transcontinental rail connection was opened in 1869, most of the general cargo for the West Coast was still going by square-riggers around the Horn. Foreign vessels were barred from this "coastal" trade, and with ships and cargoes just about as valuable as those from the Far East, the *Florida* found plenty of loot. Unlike the China trade, where vessel and cargo had the same owner, these were common carriers representing the new trend toward divorce between shipowning and cargo. The *Commonwealth*, for example, one of these victims and a common carrier, had a mixed cargo for San Francisco valued at $470,000 and belonging to 217 merchants—quite a difference from the Lows' sole ownership of the clipper *Contest* and her cargo. The *Crown Point*, also destroyed by the *Florida* on this run, and the *Tycoon,* caught by the *Alabama* in that same 1863 season, had similar ladings almost as valuable.

Vessels trading with South America found it dangerous going "down between the bulges" in that spring of 1863. Four vessels, carrying guano (bird dung) from the Pacific, made the least fragrant of the Confederate bonfires. But the raiders had compensation, as far as smell was concerned, when they set fire to some of the cargoes of Rio coffee. Even in the early months when the *Sumter* was abroad consuls in Brazilian ports found cargoes were scarce for vulnerable American ships down there. Wool shipments from Buenos Aires went in smoke, too; one of the last of the South Atlantic losses, burned by the *Shenandoah* at the beginning of her career late in 1864, was bound from England to the Argentine.

In the Caribbean, where trade with Cuba ranked second only to that with England in value of cargoes sent and received, the major raiders did little. Materials of every sort from lumber to railroad cars went southward, while sugar and molasses came back. Almost three-quarters of this trade was in American bottoms—good raider fodder; yet 9,500 American vessels came and went during the war, with exactly twenty-two seized. The catch lay in the small size of the vessels, for their individual cargoes were not of sufficient value to tempt the raiders. Besides, too many Union warships were close at hand for comfort. More than half even of the luckless twenty-two were taken in flank by little privateers as they passed the Carolina coast in the opening months of the war. The trade with the other Caribbean islands ran a similar course.

A counterpart to Amelia Island sprang up at the Mexican port of Matamoras, just over the Rio Grande from Brownsville, Texas. Vessels by the score were carrying supplies, sorely needed by the Confederates, from New York to the little neutral border port and bringing back much-desired Southern cotton. Exposure by the *New York Herald* and a couple of Congressional investigations did not prevent this clandestine trade from increasing tenfold during the war. Naturally, the Confederate raiders granted immunity to such vessels, just as the British had winked at similar Yankee trading a half century before; that illicit commerce was too useful. The *Clarence,* a tender of the *Florida,* encountered such a trader in the schooner *Albert H. Partridge,* laden with arms and clothing; but she was allowed to proceed unharmed after signing a bond to deliver the cargo where it would surely fall into Confederate hands. Such vessels fared worse at the hands of Yankee cruisers, whether they flew the Stars and Stripes or shifted to British registry. And if Matamoras was another Amelia Island, Nassau was another "Quoddy." So too were Havana and Bermuda with their shameless leakage from Northern ports to circumvent the blockade.

But the raiders missed the richest possibilities of all in the Caribbean—the gold from the California mines between Panama or Nicaragua and New York. Liners were conveying nearly three million dollars a month at the beginning of the war. Yet the raiders never caught what would have been the closest counterpart to an old Spanish treasure ship. Even one such capture would have been invaluable to the shaky Confederate finances. Shortly after his transatlantic sweep, Semmes headed south for just such a prize and late in 1862 caught one of the liners, Vanderbilt's *Ariel.* To his chagrin, she had but a trifling amount of cash in her safes for she was headed the wrong way. With more scruples than later U-boat commanders were to show, the disappointed officers of the *Alabama* did not even feel free to burn the ship because of her five hundred passengers, half of whom were women and children. The boarding officers returned to their ship minus their uniform buttons, which the women had begged to have as souvenirs. Later the Union navy provided its only convoy service of the war for these treasure ships. Yet the fear of capture worked for the Confederacy more effectively than its raiders: the flow of gold to New York was cut more than two-thirds. Most of the balance went directly from San Francisco to England under the British flag, while some was brought overland under cavalry escort.

In the coastwise trade, too, the fear spread by the raiders did more damage than their actual captures. Several times raiders swept up the coast and about fifty vessels of various sorts were destroyed, but each time panic spread from port to port. The war was brought to the very harbors of the North. The merchants set up such a clamor that the Confederates had good reason to hope that enough naval vessels would be sent to their succor to relax the blockade. Chambers of commerce demanded harbor protection and coastal convoys, but as in later U-boat forays near the coast, the Secretary of the Navy refused to detach warships from service more essential to victory.

The first coastal attacks came from Carolina privateers, whose plunder included some chartered army and navy transports bound southward with coal and other heavy supplies; but the chief onslaught occurred in 1863, that victorious moment of the Confederacy on sea as well as land. With the three major raiders burning their fat prizes in the South Atlantic and with Lee's army invading Pennsylvania, a succession of sailing vessels under some of the *Florida's* men on detached service swept up the coast from Hatteras to Portland.

They left a trail of burning hulks. Lieutenant Charles W. Reed, with twenty men and one gun in the brig *Clarence,* captured off Brazil, set out to raid the Union base at Hampton Roads. He caught some vessels off Hatteras, including the bark *Mary Alvina* bound from Boston to New Orleans with "3200 bbl. pork, beans & c" for the Union army, but he found Union vigilance too keen for his original project. Transferring his flag to the bark *Tacony,* he proceeded up the coast, destroying shipping along the way. None of his prizes was particularly valuable, but the impact on Northern nerves was tremendous. Although the Navy Department would not detach warships from the blockade, hectic week-end preparations at the Philadelphia, New York, and Boston navy yards sent some thirty regular or improvised naval vessels out to hunt the raider. Even the yacht *America* was made ready for the chase. Panic spread when the newspapers told of what was happening to the incoming transatlantic ships—the *Isaac Webb,* the *Byzantium,* and others—in encounters, already mentioned, with the "Pirates off Nantuckett." Headlines, rivaling those about Lee's sharp advance, told of "The Oceans Lit up by the Rebel Sea Devils." Less sportsmanlike than his usual conduct was Reed's burning of six Gloucester fishing schooners. Boston merchants offered ten thousand dollars reward for the capture of the *Tacony* and fitted out a vessel for the pursuit; but the New York Yacht Club, in the spirit of business as usual, held its annual regatta, undismayed, between Barnegat Bay and Fire Island.

But the navy and its cohorts were by now hunting down the wrong vessel! The resourceful Reed, finding the pursuers too hot on his heels, shifted his men to the schooner *Archer* and sent the *Tacony* up in flames. The *Archer's* bold career was soon ended by her actual invasion of a Northern port. Sliding into Portland harbor, the *Archer's* crew seized the revenue cutter *Caleb Cushing* as she lay in port and headed to sea with her. This latest shift in vessels was thwarted by the energetic defense authorities. With no naval craft at hand, they rushed soldiers and guns aboard the New York and Boston passenger steamers, and before they were clear of Casco Bay, were already gaining so rapidly on the fleeing cutter that Reed blew her up—and submitted to capture.

Meanwhile the *Florida* herself had been heading northward, capturing several valuable vessels on the way. Within fifty miles of New York, she had a successful brush with an improvised Northern cruiser, but finding too many more in the vicinity, hurried south to Bermuda. By the time the good news of Gettysburg and Vicksburg had come, the North found that the worst of its maritime menace had also subsided.

There were some further coastal scares, with the *Florida* back again for some of them; but the closest to the *Tacony's* exploits were the hit-and-run raids out of Wilmington by the fast British-built blockade runners, the *Tallahassee,* alias *Olustee,* and the *Chickamauga.* In the summer of 1864, the *New York Herald,* headlined "Operations at the Entrance to our Harbor," along with news of Farragut at Mobile Bay and of Sherman at Atlanta. The *Tallahassee* scuttled a coasting schooner off the Jersey coast, rather than spread the alarm to the shore by the flames from her burning hulk. Then she suddenly appeared off Fire Island, near the very entrance of the unsuspecting port of New York. The plan was to dash into the East River through Hell Gate and to set fire to the shipping at the crowded wharves. An unobservant pilot, on the lookout for business, came aboard before spying the Confederate flag and "a more astonished man never stood on deck of vessel. He turned deadly pale and drops of perspiration broke from every pore." Seizing the pilot boat *James Funk* as a decoy, the raiders caught "no less than six vessels in as many hours," including another Sandy Hook pilot boat. Ironically, the harbor raid had to be abandoned because a Hell Gate pilot was not to be found. Turning eastward, the *Tallahassee* continued her destructive course from Nantucket up the Maine coast to the Bay of Fundy. She caught some transatlantic shipping, as we saw, and also burned many coasters laden with lumber or Cape Breton coal. Despite the naval vessels swarming on her trail, she found her way from Halifax safely back through the blockade to Wilmington.

Two months later, rechristened the *Olustee,* she was through the blockade again. Off the Delaware Capes she destroyed six vessels, including an army transport brig, luckily not full of troops, bound from Fortress Monroe to New York. The transport's captain and crew, because of her military status, were deposited in a Southern prison. Hotly pursued by a Northern cruiser and with coal nearly gone, the *Olustee* had to rush back to port, but again made good her escape. Meanwhile, the *Chickamauga* was also out of Wilmington, raiding within fifty miles of Sandy Hook and off Block Island. She destroyed several coasters and vessels in the Cuban trade; but by late autumn all was finally quiet along the seaboard.

The coastal raiders had had to hit and run in fear of the warning spread along shore by the telegraph to Union bases;

but the other cruisers did a thorough and devastating job against the whalers without interference. Of all American shipping, the whalers, scattered through remote seas, caught it hardest, losing almost a tenth of their fleet. For generations, New Bedford and Nantucket had done a thriving business with whale oil—in heavy demand for illumination in America and Europe—brought in by little second-hand vessels from their adventurous prowlings. The Civil War years brought ruin to this flourishing trade. Even without the Confederates, petroleum was fast becoming a serious rival. The first Pennsylvania refinery started operations in 1859, but by 1864 the exports alone, aside from domestic consumption, amounted to twenty-one millions—sure proof that kerosene was fast replacing whale oil in the lamps of the world.

In the meantime the whalers were apt to return from their three- or four-year voyages with catches worth a quarter of a million or more. In and of themselves, the vessels were not valuable. Most of them were ships or barks, ranging in size from 350 to 450 tons with an average value of about $15,000 to $25,000; many were old second-hand packets or traders. The *Alabama* began their systematic destruction immediately after she was commissioned in 1862. The Azores, a popular haunt of the whalemen on their way to more distant seas, was her first scene of operations. Within a few weeks, eight whalers had gone up in flames; and the *Alabama* turned to westbound grain ships. She was to catch several other whalers in the course of her long career; privateers were to get three in the Gulf; and the *Florida* destroyed two. The real nemesis of the whalers, however, was the *Shenandoah,* which took over the *Florida's* orders to cruise primarily against whalers in the Pacific when the latter was seized at Bahia.

Leaving Melbourne, Australia, early in 1865, the *Shenandoah* swooped down on four whalers in port at Ascension Island, now Ponape, in the Carolines. Leaving there in April just as Lee was surrendering at Appomattox, Captain Waddell cruised over toward Japan and picked a solitary victim. Late in July, he came upon a big concentration of whalers in the Bering Sea. After burning one, he accosted a trading schooner fresh from San Francisco and saw a newspaper dated April 15 with a telegraphic report of Appomattox but with plenty of implications that the Confederates might not be through fighting. Giving himself the benefit of any doubts about the war's being over, he proceeded to his work of wholesale destruction. Eleven vessels were burned in less than a week, with two spared to carry the crews home. Two days later, eight more were put to the torch by a vessel that had never been within two thousand miles of the country whose flag she flew. An officer of the *Shenandoah* wrote of that last grim and distant act of Confederate raiding:

> The red glare from the eight burning vessels shone far and wide over the drifting ice of those savage seas; the crackling of the fire as it made its devouring way through each doomed ship fell on the still air like upbraiding voices. The sea was filled with boats driving hither and thither with no hand to guide them, and with yards, sails and cordage, remnants of the stupendous ruin there progressing.

Slow transmission of news was responsible for that ruthless destruction; but it caused, too, an interesting aftermath in New York. Months passed before word of the Bering Sea disaster reached the home ports, but rumors of the presence of the *Shenandoah* in the Pacific worried some of the New Bedford marine underwriters. They hastened to New York to secure reinsurance on their risks. On the ship *Nassau,* one of the final eight burned, for example, the Union Mutual Marine Insurance Company of New Bedford hedged its $25,000 risk by reinsurance policies of $17,000 with the Atlantic Mutual and of $2,000 with the Metropolitan Insurance Company of New York. Although the *Nassau* and other reinsured vessels were already gone at that time, the reinsurers had to pay the losses.

In all the different wars, marine war-risk rates make, as we have seen, a fairly accurate gauge of the fluctuations in control of the seas; but in the Civil War, they have more than such an academic interest. They did more damage to the Northern merchant marine than did the actual burnings by Confederate raiders. Yankee shipping at this time suffered from an exact reverse of the conditions that had piled up neutral profits between 1793 and 1812. In the Civil War, American cargoes sought neutral bottoms because that meant cheaper insurance rates, just as earlier, European belligerents had used neutral American vessels to the latter's profit.

The panic in Northern shipping circles produced rates much higher than the actual losses warranted. By and large, the destruction was not high; it averaged less than ½ of 1 per cent. Even in the Far Eastern trade, it came to less than 2 per cent. The tonnage destroyed by the raiders was almost exactly equal to that otherwise "lost at sea" by shipwreck and other causes, which were covered by ordinary marine insurance, for which the rates were considerably lower than the war risk of 1863. The Chamber of Commerce at New York published the following record of war-risk rates (not including regular marine coverage) through the critical summer of 1863:

	ATLANTIC COAST	EUROPE	WEST INDIES	SOUTH AMERICA	PACIFIC	EAST INDIES
1861	½	½	½	½	½	1¼
1862, JAN.-JULY .	½	½	1	½	½	1½
JULY-DEC. .	1	1	2	2	2	2
1863, JAN.-APRIL .	3	3	3	3	3	3
APR.-JUNE .	4	3	4	5	5	5
JUNE-AUG. .	4	3	3	7½	7½	7½

Similar figures are not available for the later period. Even in those earlier years the figures sometimes went as high as 10 per cent on the distant runs. The rate on the old *Oneida,* bound from Shanghai to New York, in 1863 was 12 per cent.

Obviously the rates in general were too high judging from the size of the profits of some of the companies. The Atlantic Mutual, leader in New York underwriting circles, advertised that its marine and war-risk business yielded profits of $1,740,000 in 1862, of $2,630,000 in 1863, and of $2,732,000 in 1864. At that, a few more burnings such as the *Star of Peace* or the *Oneida* might easily have wiped out a year's profits. It was the practice among mutual companies to set the rates high enough to leave a probable margin of safety—and then to refund to the policy-holders their share of the surplus earnings. That margin had, of course, to be a substantial one with the likelihood of further enemy raiders slipping out of British ports at any time before an insured vessel had completed her voyage. The Atlantic Mutual's refunds amounted to 40 per cent in each of those war years. The position of the underwriters is easily understandable, but in the meantime the high rates had done their damage.

They placed American vessels at a serious disadvantage in the competition with neutrals for cargoes. A margin of 5 or even 3 per cent made quite a difference in a commercial transaction. If a shipper could save that much on insurance by employing neutral bottoms, he was likely to do so, particularly if he were a foreigner. For that reason American vessels suffered most keenly in the European trade. To offset this, the Yankee shipowners often had to absorb the cargo war risk themselves, in addition to the war risk they were paying on their vessels and freight earnings. That solution, which cut deeply into shipping profits, did not remedy the situation completely; even though a shipper might ultimately be reimbursed for destroyed cargo by the insurance companies it was a nuisance not to have that cargo arrive on time, as it would on a neutral vessel. The idle Yankee vessels that Semmes saw at Singapore unable to secure cargoes had their counterparts in many another port during the war years.

Such were the circumstances that produced the "flight from the flag." Increasingly common after mid-1863 were notices such as the following in the marine news columns:

> Ship *Saratoga* of New Bedford, 542 tons, has been sold on British account, to hail from St. John, N. B.
> Bark *Hudson,* late of New Bedford, has had her name

changed to *Hae Hawaii,* and now hails from Honolulu, for which port she will sail in about 10 days.

Schooner *Chief of Barnstable* has been sold to Spanish parties for $6,500.

Ship *Henry Clark,* A1½, 512 tons, built at Kennebunk in 1857, has been sold at about $20,000 to go under the British flag.

Ship *Martin Luther,* A1½, 984 tons, built at Searsport in 1855, has been sold at Genoa on private terms to go under the Italian flag.

Even some of the newly built shipping was sold directly to go under foreign flags, as for instance this item from Portland:

Bark *Artemesia* (new) recently built by B. W. Pickett of Cape Elizabeth, 447 tons, sold the past week to Claudio Lanicrold of Valparaiso for $43,000.

For every vessel the raiders destroyed, the Yankee merchant marine lost eight others as an indirect result. A moderate amount of tonnage was being transferred to foreign registry before the war. In the first war year, it had amounted to 117,000 tons. By the second year, ending in June, 1863, it had grown to 220,000 tons. Then it suddenly jumped, in the panic of the "great terror" and its attendant high war-risk rates, to 300,000 tons for the third year, but dropped back to 133,000 tons for the fourth year. This meant the loss to the American merchant fleet of 1,613 vessels, about 774,000 tons.

The blow fell hardest on the big sailing vessels, the full-rigged ships and barks which had been the pride of the old merchant marine and the mainstay of the foreign trade. During the course of the four war years, 990 ships and barks were "sold foreign"; 213 were "lost at sea," about half of them being destroyed by the raiders; and 55 condemned as unseaworthy. Meanwhile, only 378 new ones were built, leaving a net loss of 880 of the big square-riggers.

After the war, these vessels could never return to American registry, because Congress, acting in behalf of the shipbuilders rather than of the shipowners, refused to change the registry laws forbidding the transfer of foreign vessels to American ownership. Unlike the blockade which helped bring victory to the North, the Confederate raiders did not affect the war's outcome, but they had a disastrous effect in the black years of American shipping after the war.

A picture of the sinking *Alabama,* which sold well in the North, carried the inscription, "Built of English oak, in an English yard, armed with English guns, manned by an English crew, and sunk in the English Channel." That hinted at the bitterness which the Northerners felt at England's shamelessly unneutral attitude in connection with the raiders. The vessels had been allowed to slip away from England despite the protests of Charles Francis Adams, our minister at London. British colonial officials had stretched neutrality in their ports when the raiders came in to coal and refit. In denouncing the raiders, the Northern press had been almost as violent against England as against Semmes and his fellow "pirates." There were demands for compensation; a precedent was ready at hand in the awards made by the commission created by the Jay Treaty.

Finally in 1871, England agreed in the Treaty of Washington to submit the question of damages for unneutral conduct to an international arbitration commission. This group met at Geneva in 1872 to analyze the Alabama claims.

Probably the total direct damage to Northern shipping and cargoes amounted to somewhere between twenty and twenty-five million dollars, about one-fifth of which represented the vessels themselves. The victims totaled nearly 100,000 tons; of that, the *Alabama* alone got about one-third; the *Florida,* with her tenders, and the *Shenandoah* accounted for another third; while the remaining third was shared about equally between the lesser cruisers and the privateers. The Americans claimed plenty. Not only did they want damages for losses actually caused by those raiders, but also the amounts paid in war-risk insurance in general, and even the United States Navy's expenses of $3,375,000 for fitting out vessels to chase the raiders.

The commissioners whittled this down to the damages inflicted by the *Alabama,* the *Florida* and her tenders, and the *Shenandoah* after leaving Australia. The claims of the insurance companies were thrown out, unless they had lost money in the war period. The extravagant claims of the whalers for the oil and bone that they *might* have caught had they not been destroyed were radically reduced. The final award came to $15,500,-000, including interest. It was a good bargain for England at that—to have reduced so effectively the competition of the American merchant marine, not only during the war but for a half century thereafter.

The Americans almost had a chance to return the compliment in 1878, when England and Russia were on the verge of war over the Balkan situation. Three powerful raiders, designed to prey on British shipping, were built on the Delaware on Russian account. Presumably, they would have been used to inflict heavy damage on England's far-flung commerce while American neutrals would have been in a position to have picked up plenty of cargoes. The United States would doubtless have still found it to be a good investment even had the government been assessed damages afterward. The Anglo-Russian crisis was smoothed over, however, and the Russian-American raiders missed their fun.

Part II

THE WORLD WARS

Chapter VII

The Changing Order

THE RAIDS OF THE "ALABAMA" CAME EXACTLY MIDWAY BETWEEN the strangling blockade of 1814 and the outbreak of World War I in 1914. Ships and cargoes changed infinitely more during the latter half century than during the former. By 1914, steam and steel had generally supplanted canvas and wood in merchantmen as well as warships. By 1939 and World War II, the airplane was making itself significantly all-important to the functions of each. Open sea lanes, moreover, had become more vital than ever to the nations of Europe and, to a somewhat lesser extent, to our own prosperity. Supplies of oil, rubber, copper, and scores of other commodities were required by the spread of the Industrial Revolution and its effects upon developments in warfare. Some nations, like England, even had to look beyond the seas for foodstuffs for their increasing industrial populations. Synthetic rubber and other ersatz products had begun to point to a future when nations might achieve more self-sufficient destinies, but that time had not come in 1914, nor was it completely here in 1939.

During those fifty years before World War I, the United States had withdrawn from the high seas. For a while after the Civil War, its navy as well as its merchant marine fell off in alarming fashion. Eventually the navy revived, but the return of the American merchantman to the seas was longer delayed. Most of the nation's flourishing foreign commerce continued to be carried under alien flags to the profit of alien shipowners.

By the turn of the twentieth century, most of the cargoes were being transported in tramp steamers rather than in square-riggers. The smudges of black smoke belching from the funnels of the stubby little freighters lacked the romantic appeal of the billowing clouds of white canvas of the old ships and barks; but the tramps were more economical and infinitely more dependable. Those sturdy steam freighters concern us more here than the great luxury liners that sped past them on the high seas. Forming the rank and file of the world's merchant marine, they transported most of the cargoes that kept the Allies going in World War I and were the most common submarine fodder. Along with some of their more streamlined successors, they enacted a similar role, to meet a similar fate, in the second world conflict.

The introduction of these steam freighters was an important factor in the shifting of the carrying trade from American to English vessels. Lack of adequate timber at home had hampered England in the building of the old sailing vessels in competition with the Americans. Now these conditions no longer mattered, for England had ample iron, plenty of coal, and a well-developed steel industry. The opening of the Suez Canal in 1869 stimulated the demand for steamers, for they could plod steadily through the Red Sea where the fickle breezes, or utter lack of breezes, baffled the efforts of the square-riggers. The volume of freight to be carried to and from India and the Far East by the new short cut was tremendous. England could send the freighters out with a profitable maiden cargo of coal, which was always in demand at hundreds of scattered ports throughout the world. By the eighties, the yards of the Clyde and the Tyne were turning them out in such quantity that it was jokingly said they "built them by the mile and cut them off and closed the end with a few rivets to suit the customer." By 1883, steam tonnage had caught up with sail in the British merchant marine; thirty years later, its sailing vessels had all but disappeared.

Almost anyone who has visited a seaport knows how those old freighters looked. The upper lines of the sturdy black hull, often streaked with rust, rose at the bow and stern as well as amidships. Here the bridge and officers' quarters were surmounted by lifeboats, ventilators, and a single funnel painted with the owners' colors. From the wells between those "three islands" rose two substantial masts, no longer designed to carry sails on lofty yards, but often made ugly by apparatus for hoisting cargo into or out of the hold. Below, in a labyrinth of steel and brass, were the engines. Many of the older freighters were content to push along at eight or nine knots; eleven might be their utmost capacity—and that consumed some twenty-five tons of coal a day.

The cost of the coal—a new operating expense—was more or less offset by the saving in wages and food for the crew in these steam freighters. The old square-riggers had been expensive in that respect because of the number of men needed to go aloft to handle the sails. A full-rigged ship of moderate size took at least twenty men; a tramp steamer twenty times her size was able to get along with thirty. Some of the latter were used on deck, and others in the "black gang" engaged in the grueling task of shoveling coal from the bunkers into the insatiable furnaces beneath the boilers.

Steamers, relieved from dependence upon the whims of the winds, could operate with a regularity impossible in sailing vessels. They traveled the shortest distance between two ports without wasting extra hundreds of miles in tacking against head winds. They developed new sea lanes across former dead areas where, because of the prevailing winds, sailing vessels never could travel. Now and then, a speedy square-rigger, with a good following wind, might sail right past a plodding tramp, but the tramp was apt to arrive first at the ultimate destination. On the shuttle between America and England, even the hard-driven Yankee packets used to average three weeks on their faster eastbound passage, while five to six weeks, sometimes even eight to nine weeks, were needed bucking the winds on the westbound passage. A slow nine-knot tramp, on the other hand, could be relied upon to make the crossing in either direction within two weeks and consequently could make more trips, carrying many times the amount of freight, in the course of a year.

The tramp proper, of course, seldom spent her time simply shuttling back and forth across the Atlantic. She prowled all over the world, picking up cargoes wherever they might be found. In the popular mind, all those little freighters were "tramps"; actually, the phrase indicated a function rather than a type of vessel. As time went on, an increasing number of cargo steamers, identical with tramps in every respect, settled down to regular line service between different ports. Such cargo lines provided stability and regularity of service on all the major sea lanes, while the tramps could be used to meet special seasonal demands, such as the movement of cotton, wheat and sugar. England strengthened its position with those cargo lines and let foreigners take over much of the tramp work.

As years passed, the primitive tramps were being overhauled on the sea lanes by more efficient freighters whose engines could develop several extra knots of speed with little if any extra consumption of fuel. This meant a quicker "turnaround" and consequently more paying cargoes in the course of a year. The progress would be easily apparent if one compared a Glasgow tramp of 1885 with a sturdy Hog-Islander of 1919 and a streamlined C-2 freighter of 1942. The gradual substitution of oil for coal was a blessing for the stokers—"much more intellectual sort of work, you know"—and in many ways, comfort, speed, and efficiency were increased. Despite new watertight compartments, however, submarines could and did send the new ships to the bottom almost as quickly and easily as the old veterans.

As far as commerce destruction went, the new developments meant "more eggs in one basket," a single sinking in this century being usually more costly than a dozen in earlier days. The average ship of 1800 had cost from $12,000 to $15,000; the big clippers ranged from $75,000 to $90,000; but the steam freighters, from a fairly modest start of around $250,000, ran up to ten times that amount. With their greater cargo capacity, the potential loss from a single torpedo was obviously much increased.

Tonnage has become a complex matter in modern times—a "Liberty Ship" is rated at about 10,500 tons when she is launched, 7,200 tons if she is sunk, and only 4,400 tons when she enters or leaves port! It had been much simpler in the old days when vessels were generally described by a single standard, the official "old customhouse measurement," which indicated their total cubic capacity. In recent times, with engines and passenger accommodations to complicate matters, the same vessel may be reckoned by several different standards, to the confusion of the layman. Most common of these standards are gross, net, and dead weight. *Gross* and *net* tonnage are official registry measurements based on cubic capacity in tons of 100 cubic feet. *Gross* tonnage is the direct counterpart of the old measurement, giving the total enclosed capacity. It is the common basis for comparing the merchant marines of different ·nations and for war losses. *Net* tonnage represents the amount remaining after the space used for machinery, officers' and crew's quarters, and navigation purposes is deducted. It is used in our official figures of tonnage entered and cleared. *Dead-weight* tonnage is unofficial, but is the standard most useful to shipping men, for it refers to the actual cargo capacity on the basis of weight. The ordinary ratio of net, gross, and dead weight for freighters is about 3 to 5 to 8, or 5 to 8 to 12; as a rule of thumb, one adds 50 per cent to gross to get approximate dead weight. The psychological element of inflation has not been lost upon the Maritime Commission, nor upon the Shipping Board before them, for they give their statistics in dead weight—a building program of twenty-three million tons sounds more impressive than sixteen million gross tons. Of course, "displacement" would inflate the figures still further. Indicating the weight of the water displaced by the loaded ship, it is the normal basis for measuring warships, but it is seldom used in the merchant marine except to make a cruise ship seem larger than she really is. All tonnage figures cited hereafter will be gross unless otherwise specified. That measurement gives a basis of comparison with the ships of earlier days, and is used in the most important international official statistics.

The fixed ratio for tonnage falls down when one comes to passenger liners, whose dead-weight cargo capacity is relatively much smaller. The *Robin Moor,* for instance, a typical Hog Island freighter built in 1919 and the first American vessel torpedoed in World War II, measured 4,999 tons gross, 3,057 net, about 7,500 dead weight, and 11,450 displacement. Her cargo capacity was almost as large as that of the much bigger and faster passenger liner *Kronprinzessin Cecelie,* later the American transport *Mount Vernon.* She measured 18,732 tons gross, 7,564 net, 8,300 dead weight, and 32,130 displacement, which was more than the largest battleship in World War I.

A new specialized type of freighter was just beginning to make its appearance around the turn of the century and has grown steadily in importance and usefulness. The tanker developed quickly to keep pace with the tremendous new demand for gasoline and fuel oil. As the oil industry grew to gigantic proportions, it was, of course, much more economical to transport large quantities of oil in a ship's huge tanks than to continue the use of tin cans and barrels as in the old days of the kerosene trade. With its superstructure and stack pushed back to the stern and with only the bridge amidships, the tanker was not a beautiful vessel by any standards. It might be a "clean" one, carrying the dangerously explosive gasoline, or a "dirty" one, with fuel oil or crude petroleum; some even carried molasses at times. In 1900, the world's merchant marines contained only 182 tankers of more than five hundred gross tons, and some of those were sailing vessels. In the course of thirty years, the tankers increased almost tenfold in number, while the total number of vessels remained almost stationary. They grew steadily in size as well as in numbers, with the seagoing ones averaging around eight thousand gross tons by 1939, and a few reaching almost double that size. A glance at the makeup of our seagoing merchant marine in 1914 and 1939 will show how very important the tankers had become by the latter date.[1] The "Esso" fleet, even without the little local distributing vessels, totaled almost 600,000 tons, which made it the largest private unit in our merchant navy; even the mighty British merchant marine had only three units with greater tonnage, and two of those consisted of tankers. Because

[1] See p. 314.

of the special importance of their services, the tankers were sin-
gled out as submarine targets in both World Wars, especially
the second.

The crack passenger liners, which monopolize the public's attention, were not such novelties as the tramps and tankers. The
international race in size, speed, and luxurious appointments had
begun back in 1850 between the Cunard and Collins lines.
Steady improvements continued, with the largest ships being
built for the transatlantic run to New York. At the eve of World
War I, the speed record was held, and would be kept for twenty-
two years, by the Cunarder *Mauretania,* built in 1907, with her
ill-fated sister ship, the *Lusitania,* as runner-up. Each had cut the
Atlantic crossing to less than five days. By 1914, Germany had
produced the 54,000 ton *Vaterland,* later the American transport
Leviathan.

After that war, the international quest for bigger and faster
ships quickened. Between 1933 and 1939 the "blue ribbon" for
speed was won in turn by the German *Europa,* the Italian *Rex,*
the French *Normandie,* and the British *Queen Mary.* The last
two cut the crossing below four days, averaging better than thirty
knots. Both exceeded 80,000 tons, but were surpassed in size by
the 85,000-ton *Queen Elizabeth,* completed after World War II
started. These costly vessels threatened to become "white ele-
phants"; designed for the passenger trade, they carried very little
freight. In wartime, they made themselves particularly useful as
troop transports; the *Leviathan* could carry 12,000 at one time. It
looks as if these were the last of those great vessels of extreme
size, speed, and luxury; they will feel more keenly than any
others the competition of the still faster and increasingly enjoy-
able transoceanic air travel.

Midway between the crack liners and the freighters were the
smaller liners designed for the Far Eastern, African, and South
American runs, and for secondary service on the North Atlantic.
Ranging normally from 10,000 to 25,000 tons, many of them were
fast, and most of them carried cargo as well as passengers. Such
vessels were pressed into service in wartime as auxiliary cruisers

to reinforce the naval patrols. The Germans used them with some success as commerce raiders in World War I; and the British armed them as auxiliary cruisers in both wars.

With such rapid development of steamships, the old sailing vessels were steadily being crowded from the seas. Steam tonnage overtook sail tonnage in the United States in 1892, nine years after England, and nine years before the American tonnage of iron and steel caught up with that of wood. A few big square-riggers managed for a while to compete with the tramps on long runs where the coal consumption was large, particularly in the grain trade to Britain from Australia and the American West Coast. Some of these old sailing vessels were American, some were Scandinavian, and a considerable number came from France, where they were well subsidized. The United States also went in for some huge coal schooners around the turn of the century. These included several big five- and six-masters and one seven-master of 5,218 tons. With the day of the sailing vessel well on the wane before World War I, its crying need for tonnage called the "windjammers" out onto the sea lanes for high profits and for what seemed one final burst of usefulness. With the coming of peace, they were left to rot in port and had all but disappeared before World War II. Its even louder cry for tonnage, however, was to call some forth from retirement and even to lead to the building of some new ones.

While other nations had been forging ahead with the new types of shipping, the United States had lagged far behind; between the Civil War and World War I came that dark age of our merchant marine. The panic produced by the Confederate raiders, as we know, had accelerated a decline already well under way, while recovery had been prevented by the stubborn Congressional persistence in refusing to modify the old law that denied registry to any vessels built abroad or transferred from foreign flags. This policy, which favored American shipbuilders at the expense of American shipowners, even denied readmission to the hundreds of square-riggers that had been transferred to foreign flags during the Civil War. New ships had become more costly than they were in the old days of wooden vessels, with the fashions changed to steam and steel. Besides, American sailors were accustomed to better food and wages than foreigners were; and that higher cost of manning the merchant vessels further widened the differential.

In the coastal trade, from which foreign vessels had been barred by law since 1817, a respectable amount of shipping was maintained under the American flag. It was protected from foreign competition, but at that, high costs of construction and operation hampered its competition with the railroads.

Our rapidly expanding foreign trade, however, belonged almost completely to vessels under other flags. British, Scandinavian, German, and Greek tramps crowded our ports. The cream of the passenger trade passed to the crack liners of the Cunard, White Star, Hamburg-American, North German Lloyd, and French lines. A few such liners belonged to American companies, but much American capital went into foreign lines. A few moderate-sized liners flew the Stars and Stripes on Caribbean runs and in the protected trade to Hawaii, but Americans could not compete at all in the tramp trade. Altogether, the United States tonnage registered for foreign trade amounted to only 1,066,000 tons in 1914, less than half of what it had been in 1861, and only a trifle higher than the 981,000 tons of 1810. That lack of American-flag shipping would create serious problems as soon as Europe became involved in a major war. The boom in ships, stimulated by World War I, would bring American tonnage, as we shall see, to new heights, but again in the second of the great wars, there would not be enough ships for the needs of our war commerce.

Naval vessels, in the meantime, had changed fully as radically as the merchantmen. The mongrel fleets of the Civil War period had ranged from old-fashioned sailing frigates, through wooden steam cruisers, to steam ironclads. By 1890, a new type of speedy vessels with steel hulls, and, in many cases, substantial armor, had become fairly general throughout the navies of the world;

and by the time of the World Wars, this radical development had gone infinitely further.

For a while after the Civil War, the American Navy partook of the same dry rot as the depleted merchant marine. While European nations were busy with constant experiments in steel hulls, armor plating, and rifled guns, the United States Navy calmly patrolled the seas with obsolete wooden cruisers. Its officers were under orders to save coal by using sail whenever possible. This unenterprising apathy did not last; by the mid-eighties the first of the "new navy" was appearing on the seas, and by 1898, there were enough modern ships to smash Spain's weaker navy.

Incidentally American shipping did not suffer in that brief conflict beyond one bad scare. While Cervera's fleet was at sea, panic swept the coast; underwriters offered war-risk policies both on shipping and against coastal bombardment. The rates for the latter were one-fourth of one per cent for New York City above 42nd Street, one half of one per cent downtown, and one per cent along the New Jersey coast. The premiums were all "velvet" for the insurance companies: no merchantmen were sunk, and the enemy was never near the shore.

For the next sixteen years, the navy continued to expand. At the outbreak of war in 1914, it stood fairly close to the German Navy, which had been brought by a spirited naval race to about two-thirds the size of England's. By 1939, our navy was tied for first place on the seas with England's.

The capital ships of the modern navies, like the old ships of the line, would not be as intimately concerned with commerce problems as would the lighter vessels. During the decade before 1914, the new battleships were "all-big-gun" affairs, following the fashion set by the British *Dreadnought*. With powerful 14- or 15-inch guns and heavy armor, they were still designed for fleet fighting in line of battle. Similar to them in size and appearance, but with protective armor reduced to give greater speed, were the battle cruisers, a new type which would not stand up well in battle. Most of these new capital ships would lie watching for each other from their rival North Sea bases during World War I and seldom appeared upon the sea lanes. In World War II, they would be found on the sea lanes more frequently both as protectors for commerce from the threats of enemy capital ships and as potential raiders themselves. Their usefulness was becoming questionable, however, and *Punch's* reference to "H.M.S. Unriskable" reflected the chronic worry over torpedoes and air attacks. They came through the first war and part of the second with but slight casualties; then in four days, capital ships of two, and perhaps three, great navies were sunk by air attack. Thus it was conclusively demonstrated that, without air protection, the capital ships no longer represented maximum force upon the seas.

Merchant shipping in modern wartime became more familiar with the dozens of armored and light cruisers, counterparts of the frigates and sloops of earlier days. With guns of considerable power and range, and often capable of good speed, they were well equipped for the old cruiser functions of protecting, controlling, or raiding commerce.

Even more intimate would be the acquaintance of the merchantmen with the new destroyers, which were to prove their best friends against submarine attack. These were really small cruisers, although originally designed to destroy torpedo boats. The latter were fast small boats developed with the torpedo in the late nineteenth century for darting in to attack bigger warships. To counteract them, the navies evolved a somewhat larger type of vessel, originally called the torpedo-boat destroyer. But these destroyers could also perform the original function of attack, and so the separate torpedo boats for attack were no longer needed for a while. As time went on, the destroyer became one of the most useful naval types. With its sleek, slender, and vulnerable hull, it could travel at high speed and carry a moderate armament. The destroyers of 1914 measured about 1,000 tons displacement. By the second war, some of them were more than double that size, relatively much tougher in construction, and capable of traveling almost forty knots. Aside from its primary function of protecting or attacking capital ships, the destroyer was versatile; it could be used for many of the purposes of a light, fast cruiser and proved especially valuable for the protection it could give merchantmen on dangerous routes.

With World War II the torpedo cycle started all over again with the reappearance of the torpedo boat. This time it was a little scooter whose motors could drive her at terrific speed. Our tiny P.T. boats of this type showed their worth during the Japanese attack on the Philippines.

Even more radical than the transformation of surface craft were the new devices for waging war beneath the seas and above the seas. Americans played a prominent part in developing the mine, the submarine, and the airplane, but all three were to be used with deadly effect by the enemy in both World Wars. The mine was the least novel and the least destructive of the three. The submarine was the big surprise which transformed sea warfare in World War I. The plane, less effective in that war, had a tremendous, far-reaching, and revolutionary effect on the sea lanes in the second.

Mines were an old story from the past, but only with the invention of high explosives did they become really deadly instruments of war. They were big iron globes, a yard in diameter and filled with TNT, moored a few feet below the surface of the water. These insidious weapons were ready to blow up any ship that hit them. Inshore "controlled mines," exploded by electric current from the shore, could be operated with some discrimination as to victims, but the more common "contact mines," sown at large in the shipping lanes, were equally disastrous to friend, foe, or neutral. Frequently they broke loose and drifted far away; sometimes they sank vessels long after peace had come. The chief safeguard against them lay in the constant sweeping of ship channels by pairs of trawlers, with a wire drag between them. Mines sank more than a million tons of shipping in the first World War, and were again somewhat menacing in the second.

By November of 1939, moreover, a new kind of mysterious mine began its deadly work close to England's very shores. The east coast from Harwich down to the cliffs of Dover, even the much traveled entrance to the Thames itself, was littered with the half-submerged wrecks of big vessels blasted by explosions that often ripped right through them from keel to topsides and sometimes broke them in two. A Dutch liner, bearing refugees, was shattered with eighty-five lives lost; an 11,000-ton Japanese liner was sunk; Italian, Danish, and other neutral vessels were victims, along with Britain's own ships. Twenty-seven sinkings in that one month and various other battered ships crawling into port had the British desperate and puzzled. Mines were obviously guilty, but not ordinary mines nor ones laid in the usual manner. No German surface craft would dare come so close to shore, and the waters were too shallow for any regular submarine minelayer. At last a watcher on the Essex coast solved part of the puzzle: One moonlight night he saw a plane flying barely a hundred feet above the water just offshore. With a splash, a heavy round object landed in the water. A dauntless "suicide group" carefully took apart the first one that was found intact and learned that it was not the conventional contact mine at all—the kind that exploded when a ship bumped into it or caught one of its antennas. Instead this was a magnetic mine. The mere presence of a steel hull near one of these was enough to draw a little needle around to a contact point to effect the explosion.

Learning at last what the problem was, the British set about solving it. Ten thousand seamen from the fishing fleet went out in their small wooden smacks to drag the dangerous waters. This "splinter fleet" stuck to its tedious job, with machine-gun bullets from German planes spraying their decks. Science, too, added its bit, and produced the "De-Gaussing Girdle" or "chastity belt." This was a strand of wires suspended around the ship's upper hull, carrying an electric current to nullify the workings of the mines. Motorists on New York City's West Side Highway stalled traffic the following spring as they slowed down to view the 85,000 ton *Queen Elizabeth,* girdled with the first of these to be seen over here.

While the possibilities of the destroyer and the mine were generally appreciated by 1914, the submarines' deadly potential power remained a mystery. They had been initiated into naval service around the turn of the century, but the various navies had only very vague ideas about their usefulness. When the Germans were driven from the surface of the sea soon after the war began in 1914, they started to develop their underseas boats or U-boats into particularly devilish commerce destroyers. The sinking of some 5,700 vessels in the first war was followed in the second by more continued and heavier raiding by larger and faster subs than those known in 1914.

The early U-boats were relatively small and slow with a cruising range of only a few hundred miles. Being originally designed for surprise attacks on warships, they carried in the beginning only a few torpedoes as weapons. Eventually their striking power was increased by the disappearing gun, which could sink a large number of merchantmen with shells without exhausting the precious supply of torpedoes. By 1917, and Germany's intensified submarine warfare, those slow pioneers were succeeded by others carrying a dozen torpedoes, mounting two guns, and with oil capacity to cross the Atlantic three times. By World War II, they were more efficient and further perfected, but the general technique of submarine warfare was pretty much the same. The chief new developments were the use of planes and "blimps" for scouting, and for both raiders and hunted to travel in groups. In the early years, lone submarines prowled the sea lanes after lone freighters. By 1917, the merchantmen had found themselves infinitely safer in convoys under naval protection; and by World War II, the subs were traveling in "wolf packs," which lay in ambush along the convoy routes to shoot their torpedoes into the massed vessels of a convoy.

Submarine warfare necessitated radical changes from the old methods of search and seizure by surface cruisers or raiders. The cramped quarters of the U-boats made it rarely possible to carry men for prize crews or to take aboard prisoners. As a result, it was generally necessary to sink prizes instead of sending them into port for condemnation. The best fate that officers, passengers, and crew of a prize could expect was time enough to get safely off in the lifeboats.

But drifting far at sea in lifeboats was not the worst that was soon to face submarine victims. The U-boat was far more vulnerable to attack than the surface raider. While lying on the surface during the time its boarding party was visiting and searching its victim, it was in extreme danger itself. Its victim might turn upon it and sink it with a single shell or ram it fatally. For that reason, the practice grew of sinking merchantmen without warning. Also the arming of merchantmen acted as a boomerang in this respect—for those guns mounted on their stern justified in German eyes the orders to sink without warning, regardless of the loss of life of innocent persons. A submarine would lie submerged, to launch its deadly torpedo at the unsuspecting merchant vessel. Sometimes a sharp-eyed lookout might spot the periscope or the telltale streak of bubbles of an oncoming torpedo in time for a fast liner to zigzag sharply and escape; but a slow little freighter could not move that fast. Rarely, however, was there any warning before the torpedo ripped into the fragile hull; then only minutes were left those, not already dead or maimed or trapped, to get off the vessel as best they might before it sank.

The new practice was denounced from its inception as both cowardly and barbarous. Naturally it ran counter, just as did the new remote blockade of the British, to the provisions of international law that were based upon conditions of an earlier day. In particular, the old stipulations were violated that all persons aboard a vessel must be made safe before she was sunk.

Whatever the ethics of the matter, this new submarine form of warfare called upon raiders and victims alike for constant bravery seldom before demanded at sea. Submarine crews faced continuous terror and discomfort; they lived for weeks on end in stuffy, vulnerable, cramped quarters with the ever-present hazard of facing one's last hours helplessly breathing in chlorine at the bottom of the sea, with perhaps ears and eyes bursting from the unbearable pressure. Courage, too, was needed by the sailors serving the merchantmen. Particularly precarious were the chances of escape for the "black gangs" far down in the stoke-holds, and for the tanker crews, who faced agonizing death in flaming oil aboard their exploding vessel or in the burning seas about her.

Various antisubmarine devices were developed, such as the depth bomb, the camouflage of merchantmen and warships, sound detectors of various sorts, the return to the old convoy system, and, gradually, the use of planes or "blimps." Of these, the depth bomb, or "ash can" was filled, like the mine, with three hundred pounds of TNT. Ever ready at the sterns of patrol boats they were dropped on the spot where a U-boat was suspected to be lying beneath the water. The explosion of the depth bomb, magnified in its effects under water, might easily crush in the hull of a submarine, or at any rate disable her.

To locate that spot where a submarine might be submerged, the sound detector became invaluable. This delicate instrument revealed the presence and direction of U-boats from the sound of their propellers. The combination of the depth bomb and detector, along with convoying, camouflaging, and the use of plenty of destroyers or subchasers by the Allies in 1917, helped to bring the intensive submarine warfare of the Germans under control.

With the outbreak of World War II came the chance to see what the intervening years had done to submarine warfare. The optimists believed that new detecting devices had made the de-fense of the merchantmen far easier and with other improve-ments had cut down the offensive power of the U-boats. In the first six weeks, these cheerful souls suffered some severe jolts. The Royal Navy itself was impudently and successfully attacked by the bold U-boats. A great aircraft carrier went down at sea, but, what was more astounding, a submarine sneaked into the supposed security of the naval base at Scapa Flow to sink an anchored dreadnought. The detecting devices did not work as well against the U-boats as had been expected because their propellers had been adjusted, and they, too, used detectors to search out their victims. They learned to lie in ambush with their engines stilled along the convoy routes, and could wait submerged until their detectors brought them the sound of approaching propellers. No longer did they have to betray their presence by having their periscopes visible above the water. Unseen, they could blindly shoot their torpedoes into the massed vessels of a convoy with usually fair success at hitting something. In the same way, as we shall see, the use of planes worked for the submarines as well as against them. The new submarines, moreover, proved to be much more durably built.

As a result, submarine warfare on the whole followed pretty much the same pattern as in the earlier war, in spite of the improvements both in the submarines themselves and in the protective methods used against them. All in all, the U-boats were successful when the Allied navies had other work to occupy them. The number of their victims dropped whenever those navies concentrated on the patrolling and convoying of any submarine-infested sea lane; this was the same general story of both wars.

The latent possibilities of the ten-year-old airplane had been still less recognized than those of the submarine in 1914; and even in 1939 many surprises were in store as its versatile achievements unfolded in the war years. Its use in the first war was only incidental compared to its dominant position in the second. A few merchantmen were bombed or machine-gunned from planes in the North Sea; one German raider carried a seaplane for scouting; and planes sometimes guarded convoys on the home stretch.

By 1939, the transformation was tremendous; in various ways the plane was working far-reaching changes in the conception of sea power. The fleet, as well as the army, that lacked air protection was almost helpless against an enemy well equipped with planes. One need not say that air power had supplanted sea power, but rather that the plane had joined the ship as an indispensable ingredient of sea power. The surface warship, whether tough battleship or fragile destroyer, was rendered vulnerable. The plane was an indispensable part of fighting on sea as well as land; and the airplane carrier took her place quickly as one of the most important, if not the most essential, elements of a first-class navy.

In fact, the most effective naval unit, as the second war progressed, was no longer the squadron or fleet of great "battle-wagons," but the "task force" based around one or more carriers, escorted by various other types of vessels, including cruisers, destroyers, and sometimes a battleship or two.

In the constant struggle between submarine and merchantman, the plane could both run with the hares and chase with the hounds. As a scout, it could warn a convoy or lone ship of the presence of danger; under right conditions it could detect a lurking U-boat from the air, even when the latter was completely submerged beneath the water. On the other hand, it could widen the hunting range of the submarine or surface warship by spotting potential prey from afar. Not only could it scout, but it could strike as well, by bombing or machine-gunning either merchantmen or U-boats, not only at sea but sometimes, also, as they lay motionless in port. The lighter-than-air "blimp" could also be used for some of this aerial work. It was excellent near its home shores because it could hover almost stationary over a spot to watch for submarines, or amble along at the slow pace of a convoy, but it was of course too vulnerable if enemy planes were anywhere about.

But fighting and protecting were only part of the story of the plane at sea. It proved, too, to be a dependable method of transporting passengers, mails, and cargoes of certain kinds across the oceans with new speed, and above all with safety from interception or destruction by enemy cruisers or submarines. American commercial aviation had grown enormously in the years before 1939. Shortly after the last war, fliers had begun to span the oceans by air. A vast network of international airways, involving some hops across salt water, grew rapidly between the wars. European lines spread to the Far East, down through Africa and across to South America where the Atlantic was narrowest.

The two most ambitious all-ocean routes, however, were the work of our Pan American Airways. It had already expanded in eight years from a 90-mile Key West–Havana hop to a 32,000-mile system covering most of Latin America, when, on November 25, 1935, its *China Clipper* flew out through the Golden Gate for the first transpacific service. The great plane—capable of carrying a sixteen-ton load, including forty-eight passengers, at 150 miles an hour—stopped at Honolulu, Midway, Wake, and Guam on its 8,200 mile flight to Manila, completed in sixty flying hours. The service was soon extended to Hong Kong, where it connected with the British system. By the beginning of 1940, a second Pacific run to New Zealand was also in operation.

Pan American also blazed the way across the North Atlantic, where regular service dates from May 27, 1939, when its *Yankee Clipper* took off at New York for Lisbon by way of the Azores. Unless delayed by fog, these huge planes could make the scheduled crossing in some twenty-six hours, in little more than a quarter of the time consumed by the *Normandie* or *Queen Mary* in their record "blue ribbon" passages. On this route, as on the Pacific, a remarkable record for safety and regularity was established. During the war, as we shall see, an African service was added, and all the Pan American routes were used for various new war services, from ferrying bombers to the transportation of surprisingly heavy cargoes by plane. Undoubtedly the emergencies coincidental with war would accelerate the development and wider use of planes for numerous undreamed-of purposes that would have seemed impossible during normal times.

The combination of planes, mines, and submarines required a new blockading technique, which England was not slow in perfecting. This new method of remote control was different in

many ways from the squadrons close inshore that had blockaded European and American ports with such success a century
before. In 1914, memories of 1793 to 1812 were awakened when
England resumed its time-honored control of neutral shipping
to capitalize the advantages of sea power once again in this
new war. In the Napoleonic period, it will be recalled, the British were ready to supply the enemy with anything except munitions as long as they could take their own profits from the trade.
Now they exerted all their resources, naval and otherwise, to
cut the enemy off completely from outside supplies and markets.
The Germans did not have enough surface vessels to attempt
the same sort of control and so turned to the submarine blockade.
The old regulations of international law, based on the close
blockade by surface vessels, did not fit the British any more than
it did the German methods. The rigid blockade which England
successfully established was to prove, like that imposed by the
North upon the South in the Civil War, one of the major causes
of ultimate victory in World War I.

Nature played into England's hands in exercising this new
remote control. Most of the Continent's naval and commercial
contacts with outside seas could be controlled by the blocking
of four narrow entrances. Gibraltar and Suez were the keys to
the Mediterranean, but, more important, the Dover Straits and
the north-about passage cooped Germany in the North Sea. The
new devices of mines, submarines, and such, made it too risky,
of course, to keep squadrons hovering immediately off the entrance to a port, but with the asset of these narrow entrances,
remote control could prove effective against the Central Powers.
While the Grand Fleet at Scapa Flow in the Orkneys kept watch
lest the capital ships of the German High Seas Fleet broke loose,
the lesser vessels of the Dover Patrol and the Tenth Cruiser
Squadron maintained constant vigil to check the comings and
goings of any vessels attempting to trade with Germany or adjacent neutrals.

Thousands of cargoes from America, along with everything
else bound into the North Sea, had to pass the vigilance of those

cruisers patrolling its two entrances. If anything aroused suspicion, the vessel was ordered to undergo examination at the Downs near Dover, at Kirkwall near Scapa Flow, or at one of the other British control stations. They had to wait idly, losing valuable time and freight earnings, while officials at London pored over their papers, censors went through their mails, and inquisitive naval ratings prowled below decks hunting for hidden gold, letters, or German passengers. It was even charged that, in going through the mailbags, the British extracted American commercial information, which they used to their own advantage.

The early days of World War II saw the temporary revival of these practices. Kirkwall and the Downs again did a flourishing business. By the end of 1939, the British boasted that they had seized half a million tons of cargo destined for Germany; again Americans and other neutrals raised protests without effect. But in this war, Dunkerque changed the whole control picture. Suddenly in the early summer of 1940, the control stations were all but closed because Germany had the whole western coast of the Continent. With German bombers just across the Channel, it ceased to be safe to concentrate so many ships where they would be vulnerable targets. Holland, Denmark, and Norway, moreover, were no longer neutrals, and had no excuse in British eyes for any sort of trade. Consequently even if the control stations had remained safe, there was little business for them anyway.

As a result, another variation in blockading technique made control even more remote. Now Britain pushed it back into the ports beyond the seas, where the cargoes started their dangerous trips. British consuls or other officials in overseas ports took over the control of neutral shipping by issuing navigation certificates or "navicerts" for cargoes and ships engaged in trade with the constantly diminishing group of neutral nations. This practice had been tried in 1918 but upon a more modest scale. A vessel and cargo that were thoroughly covered by these certificates would not be molested by any British patrols. This navicert system controlled, too, the increasing use of the plane for transatlantic mailing of articles of small bulk and great value; "aircerts" made it possible to regulate that mode of transportation which was out of reach of naval patrols. Designed to meet the leakage of supplies into Germany, this navicert system amounted to a rigid ration, based on the prewar imports of each commodity by the neutral nation to which it was consigned. As soon as Spain reached its quarterly quota of cotton imports, for example, or Sweden its allotted amount of copper, no further navicert was available for such goods until the next three-month period. In addition, neutral firms and shipowners, especially in Latin America, were black-listed if they were suspected of having dealings with the enemy. These new methods of remote control were administered by the Ministry of Economic Warfare and proved even more effective, although less colorful, than the old system of visitation and search.

As for the time-honored convoy system, returned to use in the two World Wars, it will be recalled that it had been effective in earlier encounters but had long dropped out of general practice. The old objections to convoying delayed its use in the early years of the first war. Valuable time was wasted in traveling to the assembly port and in waiting there for the convoy to gather. Faster vessels, too, were slowed down to the speed of the slowest ship of the convoy, which might make but seven or eight knots, unless the convoys were arranged according to the speed of the vessels—a complicated arrangement and still more time-consuming in port. Port facilities, too, were overtaxed by the sudden arrival of large numbers of vessels at once with consequent unloading delays. In the beginning of the first war, too, the Admiralty questioned whether the officers and equipment of the usual freighter were adequate for the complicated defensive zigzagging and blacked-out night sailing in close formation without many collisions. It was obvious that half of a vessel's carrying and earning capacity was apt to be wasted by the delays of the convoy system, but it would, on the other hand, be gone for good if she lay at the bottom of the sea. The fast liners, which could outsail any U-boat, were relatively safe, but the slow little tramps had scarcely a chance.

After a successful experiment with daily convoys of colliers on the short cross-Channel run to France and a safe trial escort from Gibraltar, the Admiralty, pressed by the United States, finally agreed to try the system on the transatlantic run in the spring of 1917. For a while, because of the scarcity of escort vessels, it was used only for shipping bearing vital cargoes *to* England, as the loss of empty returning vessels was considered less vital. A cruiser or old predreadnought battleship was often assigned to the less perilous ocean crossing, but at the edge of the danger zone, three or four hundred miles from the British Isles, a flock of destroyers would be on hand to take up the task. The "train" of merchantmen sailed in parallel columns, with intervals of several hundred feet between the ships. The most valuable vessels or cargoes were normally placed in the center; the least precious would get the "coffin corners" at the rear, where they were most vulnerable to submarine attack. The destroyers hovered around the outer edges, constantly on the watch for periscopes. As time went on, admission to general transatlantic convoys was usually refused to vessels slower than eight knots or faster than fourteen. On some runs, special convoys were arranged for steamers of medium speed, but the swift liners usually crossed alone until they reached the danger zone.

In World War II, there was none of that dawdling about the convoy system; it was put into effect immediately and proved by its results to be well worth all the delays and annoyances. A typical major convoy of this war often consisted of twenty-five to thirty merchantmen or transports, sailing with intervals of 800 yards between the columns and with the vessels about 400 yards apart. At the head of the middle column would be the "convoy commodore," often a retired naval officer of high rank. A regular cruiser or a converted liner might lead the convoy, while two or three destroyers guarded the flanks and another brought up in the rear to protect the "coffin corners." Often two or three ship-based planes were further safeguards, as they could fly overhead to give advanced warning of the enemy's presence. Should a submarine be spotted, the merchantmen would scatter by prearranged signals; and then if the warships had successfully dealt with the raiders or U-boats, the convoy would reassemble to continue on its way. "Blimps" were used in the coastal convoys, forced on the United States by the aggressive U-boats in 1942.

One woman, who crossed the Atlantic on a westbound convoy during October, 1941, described the workings of the elaborate defense system in meticulous detail. Traveling on an empty 15,000-ton Norwegian tanker, she told of the eight miles of bombed and ruined docks of her unnamed English port of debarkation. Little Dutch boats were tending the barrage of balloons moored to buoys for the purpose of keeping dive bombers away. Some of the ships also carried such balloons, whose heavy cables would imperil the swooping planes. During the first two days of the voyage, the tanker was joined by groups of vessels from other ports, until altogether there were thirty empty tankers and twenty cargo ships, of which only six were loaded in this westbound passage. Planes flew constantly over the vessels as they fell into formation, while destroyers, camouflaged in blue, white, green, and gray, kept constantly close by, with small corvettes ranged at a distance. On the fourth day, the merchantmen were marshaled into eight long columns, with the commodore's ship leading the fourth group. At his orders, the convoy practiced emergency zigzagging, turning 45 degrees to port and then quickly to starboard. One cargo ship carried a small plane that could be catapulted into the air to engage the enemy; this was more or less of a suicide plane, since it could not again land on the ship's deck, and the flier had to take his chances with a crash landing in the sea. A Panamanian tanker and an American freighter joined the convoy at sea. Off Iceland, two American destroyers were added to the British escort; but one of them, which was identified as the *Kearney,* left that night and was attacked by a submarine two nights later. Mid-October found them in the danger zone west of Iceland with a U-boat to port. The destroyers and corvettes rushed toward the spot, while everyone put on lifebelts preparatory to abandoning ship. The tanker rocked with the explosion of sixteen depth bombs; but after two hours, the convoy resumed its normal course unscathed. Early the next morning, the escort departed and the convoy broke up. "So we parted, Panamanian, Icelandic, Norwegian, English, Dutch, and American, each to its own destination, each now on its own."

An outstanding feature of the "new order" was the revolutionary change in the transmission of news at sea. Formerly, the speed of communication across the oceans or to ships at sea had been limited by the time it took some fast vessel to transmit it. This meant a news lag of weeks and sometimes months, many times with disastrous results to a vessel in ignorance of whether her country was at war or peace. Cruisers and merchantmen, as we have seen, often sailed for weeks unaware of news vital to their safety, or blundered into ports that had long since fallen into enemy hands. New policies of seizure were slow in being carried into effect or stopped, while merchants lived in constant uncertainty as to the fate of the cargoes they had ventured on the deep.

By 1866, with the permanent transatlantic cable, America and Europe had been linked together in instantaneous communication. The Pacific, too, was spanned not long afterward. This affected commerce by bringing distant ports into competition; a buyer was able to shop around on three or four continents in a few hours before deciding which offered him the best bargains. Shipowners could exercise remote control over their vessels, as they wandered from port to port, and were able to find the best charter rates available. Naval forces could be marshaled into action more quickly. Dewey, for instance, had clung close to the cable station at Hong Kong in 1898 awaiting news of the declaration of war against Spain.

But the cable did not bring the ships at sea into that instantaneous contact until wireless telegraphy and its offspring, radio, came into use. They had had to depend on the old slow transmission of messages until after that December day in 1901 when Marconi heard at Newfoundland the three dots of the Morse code "S" from across the Atlantic at his wireless station in Cornwall. The maritime possibilities of the new device were obvious. The first considerations were for safety at sea, dramatically illustrated by the answer to the S O S from the sinking *Titanic* after an iceberg smashed her hull in 1912. By the outbreak of war two years later, about one-tenth of the world's merchantmen, chiefly liners, were already equipped with those early wireless sets that had a range of only a few hundred miles. In the years between the wars, the spread of wireless and then radio to the vessels on the high seas was extended to most oceangoing vessels.

Naturally, the navies made the most of the opportunity to maintain constant control over their scattered warships. Some officers apparently resented this encroachment on their old freedom of action. As one complained, the cable had made them "nothing but damned errand boys at the end of a telegraph wire." Nonetheless, all had to recognize the advantage of knowing the latest events from the flashes that came through the air in code or "in the clear."

In sharp contrast to the weeks of ignorance in 1812, almost instantaneously in 1939 naval vessels and merchantmen knew war had come. In the early hours of April 9, 1940, hundreds of Danish and Norwegian mariners, scattered all over the world, scratched their heads in bewilderment at radio orders to stand by for further instructions. Fifty years before they would have gone on their way, as unsuspecting neutrals, straight into the hands of British cruisers or German U-boats. A few months before, the whole world was following, on their radios, play by play, the battle of the *Admiral Spee* with the British cruisers off the Rio Plata, before the *Spee* took refuge in a neutral port. Early in 1815, in a surprisingly similar action, our frigate *President* was captured by British cruisers only about fifty miles from New York, but the city did not learn of the affair until the news trickled in from Bermuda weeks later. Again in 1939, the crew of the American freighter *City of Flint,* seized by the Germans, lay at the remote port of Murmansk, ignorant of what their fate was to be, until they tuned in on a short-wave broadcast from New York. And so it went, on hundreds of occasions.

The half century between the wars saw the beginning of vital changes in the nature and significance of cargoes as well as of conditions at sea. The same era of invention and technology that produced the tramp, the fast liner, the dreadnought, the submarine, and the plane was also responsible for the automobile and much else in the line of steel production. The result was a need for overseas products that destroyed the old relative self-sufficiency of the nations. Aside from the normal peacetime articles of commerce, whose loss would be a nuisance and an annoyance, these new developments involved many strategic commodities vitally necessary to the prosecution of war. In the past, almost any nation with a reasonably well-developed industry could produce within its own borders most of the necessary military and naval matériel. Inadequate industrial development, rather than lack of essential raw materials, had made the Americans vulnerable in the Revolutionary War and the Confederates in the Civil War. Abroad, masts and naval stores had been almost the only strategic materials required by European countries from overseas, even if they had not enjoyed being deprived of coffee, tea, and sugar.

By 1914, and ever more radically so by 1939 that situation was changed. In the later period, even the United States was to find itself on short rations for some commodities essential to the prosecution of war. On the whole, nature had blessed the United States and also Russia with plentiful supplies of most raw materials; and the former had, besides, the added advantage of a huge industrial system that could be efficiently converted into war production. Rubber and tin were the two most important products which the United States lacked, but there were others.

Nevertheless, it was not only better supplied than most of Europe, but it had additional sources available in the nations to the southward.

Oil was a prime essential to the warring nations of the twentieth century. With armies changing from horse to motor transport, with the ever-increasing use of the plane on land and sea, and with the shift from coal to oil in ships, that latter commodity was one of those that became of transcendent importance. The great powers of western Europe produced almost no oil within their borders. There were wells in Rumania and in the Russian Caucasus region, but much of the oil supply had to be brought by sea from the Persian Gulf, the East Indies, and, above all, from America.

Rubber, too, had become a military necessity as well as a cushion for innumerable civilian comforts. Tires for armies consumed a huge amount, and although the tires of 1939 wore much longer than their primitive ancestors in 1914, the need was enormously increased through the tremendous ramifications of mechanization. Rubber was required also in artillery construction and in gas masks, to mention but two of innumerable uses. In World War I, the Germans envied their enemies' waterproof coats and boots in the endless days of rain on the Western Front; but in the interval they had brought synthetic rubber to a high production, and in the second war, it was the United Nations who were caught potentially short.

The ever-increasing use of steel for military and naval purposes made much of Europe more dependent on foreign supplies than it had been in the old days of cast and wrought iron. Most of the powers, except Italy, had a fair amount of coal. Most of them, too, had a reasonable supply of iron ore, for Germany could draw upon Sweden to supplement its own stock. The fashioning of armor plates, gun barrels, projectiles, machine tools, and so on, however, called for minerals far scarcer than coal or iron. Manganese, chromite, tungsten, and tin were not to be found west of Russia, nor adequately even in the United States; copper, nickel, and lead were scarce in western· Europe;

so, too, in most of the nations, were zinc, mercury, bauxite (for making aluminum), antimony, mica, and certain other minerals.

Food was not the least of the worries of nations in modern wartime as we shall see. Germany and some of the other nations of the Continent were by no means self-sufficient, but the stoppage of foreign trade for them meant a gradual tightening of the belt, rather than the swift starvation that faced England in World War I. In the vegetable field, outside of foodstuffs, there was a very uneven distribution of silk, cotton, jute, and wool— all with important wartime uses from parachutes and high explosives to sacking and uniforms.

Various chemicals played their part, too, but there is no point in extending the list into its further minute details. It should be amply apparent by now that armies and navies were in no position to function at their best unless a constant procession of cargo ships, or perhaps in time cargo planes, could bring commodities from other continents. Ingenuity, of course, made up for some of the deficiencies in World War I by means of ersatz products, and went miraculously further in the second conflict. The Germans had uncanny ability along that line, but their enemies were not too far behind. Even at that, the day came in the first war when the lack of copper cut down the accuracy of German artillery fire, and in the second, the Axis partners had to keep up a fast rate of conquest to prevent their military effectiveness from being impaired in other respects. Germany's wide conquests, however, made it less vulnerable to blockade after June, 1940.

In view of that general need of overseas products, it is small wonder that in both World Wars America would be called upon to furnish the products of its industries and agriculture. Each side tried to damage the other by stopping its sea-borne trade. for success in the Battle of the Atlantic went far toward victory.

Conditions were fairly similar in the two wars, and for that reason we shall consider in the next chapters the various phases of those two struggles from a topical approach. In order to understand why our nation took such a keen interest in the situation on the seas, and why, in large measure, maritime happenings brought it into each conflict, we must first "go ashore" to see how the United States produced vitally important cargoes. After that, we shall go out on the sea lanes, first to that essential main line across the North Atlantic, and then to more distant routes, where the epic struggles to "deliver the goods" to far-flung battle fronts continued unremittingly throughout each war. In those efforts to have our cargoes safely transported overseas, the ships of neutrals and of allies were of as keen concern to us as were our own, but each war saw huge emergency shipbuilding programs give us extra vessels of our own. Consequently, we shall finally consider the desperate efforts to scrape together enough tonnage to offset sinkings, and the effects of that struggle upon our revived merchant marine.

Chapter VIII

Arsenal and Granary

The attacks were well planned and valiantly conducted. The infantry did splendidly, but the conditions were too hard. The want of an unlimited supply of high explosives was a fatal bar to our success." Those bitter words in the London *Times* of May 14, 1915, were from its military correspondent. He had just watched his old battalion go into action near Lille with 29 officers and 1,090 men—and come out the next day with one officer and 245 men. The rest were all killed, wounded, or missing; but the French infantry on the right had carried their objectives with slight losses. The French artillery pieces had pounded the German defenses with a high explosive shell every minute for four full hours, leveling the enemy barbed wire and crushing the machine-gun nests. The British had had only "H.E." shells enough for forty minutes of such bombardment, with the tragic consequence of those terrific losses. After that fight, it was worse; the artillery, it was said, had only about four rounds of high explosive per gun left. In his later memoirs, the correspondent wrote:

> I shall never forget the look on our soldiers' faces when they came out of the trenches after a long hammering by the German artillery, to which ours, at this time, could make little reply. It was a look of utter and complete weariness and it haunted me. They seemed almost dead to the world.

His message to the *Times* proved to be "high explosive" in itself. Before the month was out, it produced a major cabinet shake-up and a new Ministry of Munitions in England. More to the point here, it gave a tremendous boom to the munitions orders from America for shells in general and for high explosives in particular.

A quarter of a century later, almost to a day, British troops struggled in that same region against the same enemy and superior matériel. Once more, the British were caught short in essential equipment. Their troops, heroic as always, had scant air protection against enemy dive bombers nor were they prepared to combat the huge array of tanks and other mechanized apparatus of the German blitzkrieg. Again the call for help went across the seas, not so much for high-explosive shells this time, as for planes and tanks.

Under such circumstances America was twice called upon to become not only the "arsenal of democracy" but the granary as well. Three if's stood in the way of effective fulfillment of those roles. Only if America were able to produce the essentials in adequate amount; if enough shipping, supplemented in the later emergency by transport planes, were available to carry it; and if those ships were able to cross the seas in safety would the United States be able to "deliver the goods." The situation on both occasions somewhat resembled the American Revolution, when France and its neighbors sent strategic materials across the Atlantic before becoming involved in the conflict themselves. The circumstances differed, to some extent, from the long neutral period during the French Revolutionary and Napoleonic Wars, when our main offering, and our main concern, was with our shipping, even though it spent much of its time carrying foreign cargoes. Now with a scant merchant marine at the beginning, our interest lay—a fact that cannot be overstressed—in the safe arrival of our cargoes, even though most of them were transported under foreign flags.

During those earlier neutral years between 1793 and 1812, we had traded fairly freely with both sides and had strenuously maintained, to the limit of our meager strength, our right to do so. In the World Wars, practically all our material assistance went to only one side in the conflict. In theory, we were ready in 1914 to trade with anyone who could come and get it, but the

Royal Navy stood in the way. In 1939, that same navy and our already embittered attitude toward the Hitler regime blocked trade with Germany.

During the first months of the earlier war, our direct trade with Germany was limited to a few cargoes of cotton. In normal times the cotton crop had been fairly evenly distributed in three directions: domestic industry, England, and central Europe. With that last market gone and the English market temporarily out of action, the Southern planters saw the price of cotton fall from nearly twelve cents in mid-July to six cents in October; and it cost them nearly eight cents to raise it. The contraband status of cotton was doubtful, since most of it went for harmless peaceful purposes, although it could be used for the manufacture of explosives. Under strong Southern pressure, the government wrung from the British the grudging permission to ship cotton direct to Hamburg or Bremen, in exchange for aniline dyes badly needed over here.

All sorts of difficulties were in the way. No German freighter dared cross the Atlantic. England could not, even if willing, send its vessels into hostile ports, and it discouraged other neutrals from offering their services. That threw the burden upon the few seagoing American freighters, but the dangers of the mined North Sea prevented marine and war-risk insurance until the government underwrote the trade. Even when all that was arranged, British consular officials hung around the docks to X-ray the bales, to be sure they hid no contraband and to seal the hatches. The first cargo in the *Greenbriar* reached Bremen in January, 1915, and was followed by several others, until in March, England shut down on the trade. Altogether, 242,000 bales were shipped, less than a tenth of the normal amount.

Meanwhile, an American concern shipped a cargo of foodstuffs from New York for Hamburg in the *Wilhelmina* to test the British policy toward food as contraband. They found out; she never got beyond Falmouth, where the British insisted upon buying her lading.

Only once again was there to be direct trade. A Bremen capitalist conceived the idea of a line of merchant submarines that might make high profits by bringing aniline dyes and returning with rubber, tin, and nickel. His unarmed *Deutschland* arrived at Baltimore in the summer of 1916 and was received with enthusiasm for her dyes but with certain worries over her successful crossing of the Atlantic. She swapped valuable cargoes and returned in safety to make a second trip later in the year. Obviously the United States had shown its willingness to trade with the Germans if they could come to its ports, but it was not ready to exert itself to force its cargoes through to German ports. The undersea commerce did not continue: when the *Deutschland* went to sea again, she was the *U-155* of the Imperial Navy.

With direct trade too difficult, the Americans used the back-door route through the adjacent neutral countries—Scandinavia, Holland, and, for a while, Italy. Cotton exports to those neutrals jumped during the first eight months of the war from a peacetime level of 473,000 bales to 2,142,000, most of the surplus obviously intended for the Germans or Austrians. Copper, being more directly linked with Germany's munitions needs, did not get through to the neutrals but was seized by the British. Our exports to Holland and Scandinavia doubled, as a whole, between 1913 and 1915. For a while, large quantities of foodstuffs went by this neutral detour, but England gradually clamped down on all this trade by placing each neutral on a quota that did not exceed its normal peacetime importation of each commodity. With this side closed, the United States turned with a clear conscience to trade with the Allies; and until late in 1916 the supplies moved freely with relatively little hindrance from submarines.

In the second war, the trade with Germany did not even approach the modest total of the first. Little direct trade was attempted after hostilities commenced, while Britain's navicert system, as we have seen, severely curtailed neutral leakage. There was, to be sure, a moderate amount of roundabout trade through Italy while it was still neutral. Not wishing to goad the Italians into hostility, Britain tolerated some exceptions. The same, to a lesser degree, was true of Spain. By and large, however, the British blockade cut off American supplies very thoroughly from the Axis.

Gradually in both wars, the United States assumed England's historic role in past Continental conflicts of "Paymaster of the Allies." It was a fairly slow evolution from loudly proclaimed neutrality to whole-hearted co-operation; while during each interim, Britain and its allies were often hard put to it to pay for their huge purchases.

In 1914, the State Department was more ready to sanction munitions shipments than loans to other nations. Bryan, then Secretary of State, wrote to President Wilson in August to say that "money is the worst of all contrabands because it commands everything else." Soon afterward he told J. P. Morgan that loans, although legal, were inconsistent with the true spirit of democracy. Bryan, however, was more definitely neutral in his attitude than others in the government. By October, it was being suggested privately that banking credits might be extended. In the course of 1915 and 1916, two billion dollars' worth of American securities held abroad were sold back to this country, and a billion dollars in gold arrived from overseas. Even those sums did not pay for all the munitions, wheat, and other exports. During the summer of 1915, the house of Morgan floated a half billion dollar Anglo-French loan to American investors, and in 1916, another slightly larger one was negotiated in Wall Street. By the beginning of 1917, however, the Allies had borrowed up to the hilt; "alike in cash and credit they had come to the end of their tether." They still had an increasingly desperate need of supplies, with no apparent way of paying for them.

The entrance of the United States into the war was a godsend to them. The Federal Government immediately made large loans, altogether totaling some nine billions, about half of which went to England. Thus were the Allies enabled to carry on their extensive purchases of American supplies.

Only a fraction of those loans was ever repaid. Eventually

every borrower, except Finland, defaulted on its payments. This created considerable bad feeling during the postwar decades. Many agreed with President Coolidge, "They hired the money, didn't they?" Others pointed out that while the money had come from American taxpayers, nearly every cent of it had been spent over here and had come back to American pockets, with businessmen, workers, and farmers all sharing the war prosperity.

By the mid-thirties, a review of the status of those loans produced a change in our foreign policy, reminiscent of the days of Embargo and Nonintercourse. A Congressional investigation of wartime munitions profits aroused widespread attention, and was followed by books and magazine articles on *Merchants of Death*, and the like. A feeling grew that those huge profits of 1916, together with the fear of the Allies' not being able to repay their private loans in defeat, helped push us into the war. At the same time, the sinking of American vessels in the war zone and the loss of American lives on belligerent vessels were emphasized as other potent factors in ensuring our participation. Many felt that the game had not been worth the candle and that a repetition must be prevented.

Out of that upsurge of disillusion came the Neutrality Act of 1935, which, like the Embargo and Nonintercourse Acts, involved a deliberate self-denial of freedom of action in neutral trade. This act, with its modifications of the next two years, prohibited direct or indirect sale of munitions and the granting of loans to belligerents; it also forbade Americans from sailing on neutral vessels. If retained and enforced, such a law would obviously have prevented a repetition of the "arsenal of democracy" role.

But with the outbreak of war in 1939, President Roosevelt immediately began to campaign for a repeal of such hampering legislation—and only partially succeeded in the Neutrality Act of November, 1939. This revision made American profits possible by substituting the "cash and carry plan" for the absolute ban on the muntions traffic. By this the United States might sell munitions to any belligerent which would pay for them without the aid of loans, would take title to the goods before shipment, and would carry them away in ships that were not American. It also forbade vessels under the American flag from entering any belligerent zones, as designated by the President; prohibited the arming of American merchantmen; and repeated the ban against Americans sailing on belligerent vessels. With the Royal Navy in action, there was every indication that England and its allies, but not Germany, could take advantage of these modified terms.

As far as munitions went, the Act did not go far enough to satisfy the British; its effects upon American shipping will be considered later. Strain as the British did to send Scotch whisky, tweeds, and heirlooms to New York, and to push their export business everywhere, it was a losing game to try to build up dollar credits enough to pay for all they needed after Dunkerque. By the spring of 1941, they were a billion dollars in arrears on munitions already ordered. To meet the deficit, holdings in some big American corporations had to be sold.

Unlike the previous war, however, their worries were to be shortly lifted. This time, the United States Treasury came to their aid even before the nation entered the war. The prohibition of loans to belligerents went overboard with the Lease-Lend Act which became law in March, 1941, after a stubborn fight in the Senate. Instead of the direct, formal loans of the last war, with provisions for repayment, the new measure was vague and flexible. It empowered the army, the navy, or other government agencies "to manufacture in arsenals, factories, and shipyards under their jurisdiction . . . any defense article for the government of any country whose defense the President deems vital to the defense of the United States," and "to sell, transfer title to, exchange, lease, lend, or otherwise dispose of, to any such government any defense article." This made outright gifts entirely possible. The United States, remembering its past experience, acted now upon the principle that if a friend needed money which was unlikely to be repaid, it was better to get the credit for generosity at the outset instead of whistling vainly for the return of one's cash. Such a policy, too, gave the donor more voice in controlling the situation than when the borrower spent what he considered "his own" money. The immediate beneficiaries were England, China, and Greece, but Russia and others were added later. The original appropriation of $1,300,000,000 steadily rose; nearly $4,500,000,000 were spent in the first fifteen months. By mid-1942, expenditures were already at the rate of eight billions a year, while England and America created several joint boards to combine their production into a "single integrated program, adjusted to the strategic requirements of the war."

The new arrangements pleased the beneficiaries, but occasional sour notes were injected into Anglo-American harmony. By the summer of 1941 complaints were heard that England was using some of the lease-lend material to compete with Americans in export markets. The British expressed concern, and soon announced that their previous intensive drive for increased exports would be to cut "to the irreducible minimum" to avoid unfair competition with American exporters in American markets.

A few months later, howls arose from American exporters, forwarders, and shipping brokers because of the drying up of their commissions in handling freight and shipping. England's lease-lend business was under the control of the British Ministry of War Transport, which even planned to take over local distributing offices and warehouse facilities. Concern was not limited to the immediate loss of revenue; it was argued that if America's elaborate forwarding and shipping setup were thus allowed to lapse, the nation would be severely handicapped in the postwar race for markets. Congress finally transferred this business to American hands. American forwarding units, composed of the men experienced in the business, were established in the various ports. That was one of the advantages of the lease-lend system over the international loans of the previous war.

Despite the friction, lease-lend stimulated business. Its widespread impact on the nation was indicated in the analysis of goods delivered by a convoy at a British port late in 1941:

A dozen or more attack bombers from Santa Monica, Calif.; big sacks of beans from Hansen, Idaho; tubs from Chicago marked "Wisconsin Brand" cheese; piles of brown cartons labelled "Seedless Raisins" from Fresno, Calif.; citrus fruit from Lake Wales, Fla., and hams from Chicago. . . . Also, machine tools from Michigan City, Ind.; aircraft parts from New Haven, Conn.; fire extinguishers from Brooklyn; dried apples from San Francisco; lard from St. Louis; canned pork from Chicago; boxes of fiber from Wilmington, Del.; insulation material from Trenton, N. J.; tank tracks from Chicago; and peanuts from Georgia.

Meanwhile munitions of all sorts were pouring into scattered war fronts from the Burma Road to Archangel and the Red Sea.

Lease-lend was becoming, by September, 1942, more than a one-way affair. In return, England, Australia, and New Zealand agreed to furnish munitions and supplies to American forces stationed there; so, too, did the Fighting French in their African and South Sea colonies. Not only would this relieve shipping, but according to one London paper it gratified the British to be giving something in return for what they were receiving.

Returning to that role in the first war, we find artillery shells were the first crying need of England and its partners, with ready-made guns, rifles, and machine guns next. German foresight had provided a fairly adequate supply of artillery ammunition; the French, too, had a moderate amount; but the British and Russians were woefully shorthanded. In recent wars in Europe, the expenditure of such ammunition had not been large, but the new methods of warfare used up enormous quantities. In two weeks of the Neuve-Chapelle attack in 1915, for example, the British artillery shot away more shells than it had used in the whole Boer War. Unfortunately, Lord Kitchener, British war minister at the time, still thought in terms of his old campaigns and turned a deaf ear to the pleas of the staff in France for more shells. He reportedly snapped at one general that the army ought to be able to take positions without artillery. As for rifles, the

British had only two-thirds enough for already recruited infantry; and production of trench mortars and hand grenades had scarcely begun.

As the ordnance authorities proceeded with "leisurely red-tape methods," which scarcely tapped Britain's vast industrial potentialities, that *Times* exposé appeared; and the nation awoke. Lloyd George became Minister of Munitions in the cabinet shake-up, and things began to hum. But in the meantime, immense quantities of munitions had to come from the United States if anything were to be done in the field.

Russia, too, turned to the United States, but its lack of adequate ice-free ports on the open ocean was as usual a liability. Its plight was still more desperate because Russian industry was still in its infancy and the enormous reserve of man power was of little use unarmed. With magnificent courage, the Russians went into battle and came out with appalling casualties, often having had to use clubbed rifles against the splendidly equipped Germans and tear down barbed wire with their bare hands. During the first three months, for example, their artillery had used nine rounds a day, with the munitions plants turning out only seven a day; by the first of December, barely a week's supply was left in reserve. And everything else was lacking too.

That was the situation in the spring of 1915 when the munitions orders began to pour into the United States. In addition to several already well-established munitions companies, some of the big steel plants, railroad-equipment works, and electrical concerns were prepared to adjust to the new demands, along with a vast array of lesser plants. Not only were they ready, but they were eager. The steel and iron business was suffering a severe depression during the early war months, with only half their normal operation. Quickly sounding out the State Department, they were unenthusiastically told there was no legal bar to munitions exports. A few sent representatives to pick up orders in Europe, but this proved unnecessary, as the nation was soon invaded by purchasing commissions from the frantic Russians, the less urgent French, and, by April, the British, who appointed

J. P. Morgan and Company to do their business. By the end of that month, New York was buzzing with rumors of the impending rush of orders.

The statistics of that boom seemed staggering in those days before billion-dollar expenditures had become commonplace. The munitions exports jumped from $40,000,000 in 1914 to $1,290,000,000 in 1916; and altogether the Allies purchased some four billion dollars' worth of munitions during the four years of the war. After the spring of 1917, the munitions sent over on American account further swelled the total.

Most strategically situated of all the American companies to take advantage of the new opportunities was the great Du Pont powder concern, with more than a century of munitions experience behind it. Altogether, it is said to have manufactured 40 per cent of all the explosives used by the Allies. Its production jumped from a little over two million pounds in 1914 to 399 million in 1918, while its employees increased from 5,000 to 100,000 during that time. Bethlehem Steel also, after ten lean years, produced not only shells by the million and a substantial portion of the artillery sent from this side, but went into extensive shipbuilding and other production of war materials. The Remington Arms Company, and its subsidiary, the United States Metal Cartridge Company, did an enormous business in rifles, machine guns, and cartridges. The Winchester Repeating Arms Company produced almost two billion units in rifles, bayonets, and cartridges. And those were but a few of the leaders among the firms working on Allied orders. United States Steel, Anaconda Copper, International Nickel, General Chemicals, Central Leather, General Motors, and scores of others saw their businesses grow mightily.

By 1916, the profits were soaring—and would go still higher with the nation's own entrance into the war. The government, however, managed to beat down some of the high prices charged the Allies and also slapped on a heavy excess-profits tax. It is estimated that 21,000 new millionaires were created in the United States. Labor, too, in its more modest way profited well, with wages at levels far above anything to which the workers had been accustomed. The most conspicuous symbol of labor's new affluence was the widespread wearing of silk shirts. This prosperity increased the interest in the Allied cause, and, as those who sponsored the later neutrality legislation thought, helped to draw us into the war. America, anyway, became decidedly interested in seeing that the sea lanes remained open; it had no intention of having those supplies sent to the bottom of the ocean.

The same *Times* correspondent who had reported the impotence of the British artillery in May, 1915, had a far different story to tell of the early attacks of the Somme drive in July, 1916:

> I was very much surprised to find that our artillery had all the fun to itself. I have not seen such inequality of artillery since the old Natal days, and I cannot swear that a single German shell came over us, while the mass of our artillery was hard at work.

Such was the result overseas of the acceleration of industry in American and British factories.

Nine months later, the supply lines between the American munitions plants and the batteries of the Western Front were in grave jeopardy from the U-boats. In those spring weeks of 1917 when it looked blackest, the United States entered the war; and a radical overhauling of the munitions situation was necessary. A second threat to the Allied supplies was America's own need of its munitions output. There was, besides, an ominous shortage of tonnage between the sinkings and the rival claims of foodstuffs. At the same time, as Assistant Secretary of War Crowell later wrote:

> The Allied governments had molded their military programs in reliance upon the continuation of this source of supply. Their troops were on the front and in conflict with the enemy. Failure of supply meant disaster.

A compromise was reached which took into account the rival needs and the tonnage shortage. Since the British and French plants were in a position to turn out finished products, raw and semimanufactured materials were to be transported overseas. Even the American Expeditionary Force would be equipped with guns, ammunition, and planes from the former stocks. Occasionally one hears that the United States could not even equip its own forces in France; though technically true, it must be interpreted in the light of that compromise. Actually for every dollar's worth of Allied war materials used by the A.E.F., the United States shipped five dollars' worth to the Allies between the spring of 1917 and the Armistice.

The Allies, by this time, were fairly well supplied with rifles, field guns, and shrapnel; the crying needs were for smokeless powder, high explosives, big shells, and six-inch howitzers. These went across the submarine-infested Atlantic after experts had carefully reckoned, as we shall see, how best to pack them in the freighters to utilize every inch of space at the maximum. American industry, meanwhile, was being geared for an overwhelming supply of munitions for 1919 and 1920, but the collapse of Germany prevented the full force of that industrial effort from being realized.

Munitions shipments, of course, involved more risks than the transportation of tamer cargoes. German sabotage efforts extended to the water front. Time bombs were found attached to the rudders of munitions ships loading at New York, and it is believed that several blew up at sea because of this. The New York police finally unearthed an active ring engaged in this practice. The big munitions depot at New York was Black Tom, a narrow neck of land stretching into the bay from the Jersey shore toward the Statue of Liberty: the dangerous cargoes were there transferred from freight cars to lighters and then to the waiting ships. One night in 1916, the watchman fled in terror at the sight of a blaze in one of a string of fourteen munition-loaded freight cars; the devastating explosion was heard in Philadelphia, ninety miles away. Extensive postwar investigation and litigation pinned the blame for the $22,000,000 loss upon German saboteurs.

Accidents happened, too. In December, 1917, a French munitions ship, with two whole holds filled with TNT, was entering Halifax harbor, en route from New York to Europe, when an outward-bound Norwegian tramp, laden with Belgian Relief grain, somehow crossed to the wrong side of the channel and crashed into her bow. The deckload of benzol ignited and spread below; seventeen minutes later a terrific blast leveled two square miles of the hapless port; 1,500 were killed, and tens of thousands made homeless, while a howling blizzard descended.

The same calls were made upon the United States a quarter of a century later. High explosives, small-arms ammunition, and shells were still needed but they paled into insignificance along-side the new demands for planes and tanks; and these weapons were more complicated to make and far more bulky to transport. Once again, England and its allies were caught short for the new type of warfare. The Germans, disarmed in 1919, had a chance to start afresh in 1933, unhampered by obsolete equipment, and by 1939 were far in the lead in the instruments of war essential for their swift-striking blitzkrieg.

As early as 1936, the British, alarmed at Germany's rapid prog-ress in the air, saw with dismay that a few miles of salt water no longer made them secure as it had for centuries past. Plane for plane and flier for flier, the Royal Air Force was at least a match for the German Luftwaffe, but in numbers it was des-perately behind. Despite their concern over planes, the British somehow failed to step up plane production to Germany's rapid output. As a result, Germany entered the war with some seven thousand combat planes to England's bare three thousand, while France, which had coddled its labor and bungled its air policy, was far behind both in quantity and quality. With their plane factories vulnerable to enemy bombers, and with the need of so many so fast, it was for planes that England first looked to America for help.

At the outset, however, things moved slowly. Early in Novem-ber, 1939, after the United States had removed its flat neutrality ban against munitions exports to belligerents, seven purchasing missions arrived in the country to place orders. They moved cautiously, however. American manufacturers hesitated to enlarge their plants unless they were paid enough to cushion themselves against a sudden end of hostilities; the belligerents, who had to pay cash for their purchases, were loath to use too much of their precious foreign exchange at such high prices. The British consequently limited themselves to only a portion of the $175,000,000 orders for plane engines and parts, while France ordered most of the balance with a moderate number of guns, shells, torpedoes, submachine guns, horses, blankets, and trucks as well. Things continued to move slowly for several months, since the full implication of Germany's swift and masterly overrunning of Poland was lost on the Allies.

As in the other war, it took the British about nine months to appreciate how short they were of essential war materials. After the terrible consequences of blitzkrieg in the battles of Flanders and France in the spring of 1940, they had no further illusions on that score. In Flanders the 130 British fighter planes were as nothing against the German dive bombers swooping down to machine-gun the overmatched troops. Nor was that all; the tank, Britain's own invention of the last war, had been ably adapted in large quantities by the Germans into their Panzer or armored divisions that slashed and encircled the bewildered Allies. France succumbed quickly and completely; the British in the "miracle of Dunkerque" managed to save an unbelievable number of their men, but they had to leave behind in enemy hands nearly all their inadequate equipment. According to Lord Gort, the British commander:

> It was clear from the outset that the ascendancy in equipment which the enemy possessed played a great part in the operations. . . . The days are past when armies can be hurriedly raised, equipped and placed in the field, for modern war demands the ever-increasing use of complicated material.

It was a pity that it took such a disaster to impress that fact upon the British High Command. The English became terribly aware of the necessity for planes in night after night to come, when swarms of German planes inflicted horrible punishment upon their cities.

America's opportunity to make up the deficiencies was obvious. Most of the nation's own necessary military equipment was still only "on order," while England was hard pressed to pay for what it wanted. Many of the regular aircraft manufacturers swung into action with radically increased output, and a good start was made with tanks; but the Axis superiority still remained, on land and in the air.

By the spring of 1941, England's financial worries were lightened when lease-lend legislation put vast American funds at its disposal, and President Roosevelt announced his purpose to make the United States the "arsenal of democracy." But things were not yet moving fast enough. In August, Senator Byrd lashed out at the "general confusion and delay" in the production program. At the same time, a new and very urgent plea for American help came from the Russians, who had lost much of their equipment and industrial setup to the invading Germans.

Before the year was out, the United States itself was in the war, with heavy needs of its own in the Pacific. Congress, which had already voted the unprecedented sum of 68 billions for war preparations, quickly jumped the total to 150 billions, and it would not stop there. An overwhelming supply of materials was promised in a new "Victory Program" for the United Nations. This, *Time* sarcastically remarked, was "at once the greatest mess of wishful thinking and the greatest production dream in United States history. It multiplied astronomically impossible figures by five and hoped that each figure would show up in something hard, tangible, useful or deadly." Yet, unreal as the program may have looked at first, it began to approach reality by the summer of 1942.

Most dramatic of the efforts to speed up production was the sudden conversion of the great automobile industry to war purposes. "Modern warfare," said Stalin, "is a war of motors. The war will be won by him who will have an overwhelming superiority in the output of motors." Nothing in the world could approach the American plants that were turning out more than four million cars a year. By the end of 1941, the production of private cars was stopped and the plants retooled for war matériel. No such drastic step had been necessary in the last war; "shrapnel shells can be made by anyone with a lathe who can get the steel to work with." But planes and tanks required infinitely complicated processes; more than 300,000 rivets, for instance, were required in every big bomber. The assembly-line technique, developed by Ford, was adjusted to planes, formerly "custom-built" affairs, and to much else. Subcontracts for hundreds of lesser gadgets were awarded to smaller firms in the general speed-up. The Detroit area became the nerve center of the accelerated program, but hundreds of new plants and greatly enlarged old plants made defense areas of many other parts of the country from coast to coast. By the late spring of 1942, General Motors announced that it had accepted more than a thousand orders and contracts involving

> one-third of the machine guns, more than one-third of the Army trucks, more than half of the Navy's Diesel engines, two-fifths of the aviation engines, more than one-fourth of the tanks, three separate types of complete airplanes, numerous parts for planes produced by others, guns and gun parts of many sizes from .30 calibre to five inch, and shells and cartridge cases.

The other big motor companies had similar versatile records, distinguished particularly by Ford's enormous new bomber plant at Willow Run and Chrysler's "tank arsenal."

Other concerns likewise adjusted themselves to the new demands. Procter and Gamble, for instance, added munitions to their soap output. A wallpaper plant was converted for the manufacture of incendiary bombs. A zipper plant, a bed manufactory, and some hosiery mills began to turn out gas masks. A cash register company went in for fuses and shell parts, and a Midwest stove company shifted over to lifeboats! The government, too, built big factories for small arms in the Midwest, safe from bombing raids; one of them was said to have the capacity to produce more ammunition in one month than the whole United States made in the last war.

By the middle of 1942, it was claimed that American war production, plus the stimulated industry of Britain, was already topping the output of the Axis enemies. American planes, whether with American or Allied pilots, began to figure more prominently over land and sea on far-flung war fronts, and their production figures began to reach amazing totals. The national output of planes had jumped from 212 in May, 1939, to 480 in May, 1940; 1,331 in May, 1941; and almost 4,000 in May, 1942.

It was the same story with tanks and much else. Some 12,500,-000 Americans were employed in the war industries. The Department of Commerce, commenting on the trade statistics for the first third of 1942, pointed out that "finished manufactures," which had accounted for only 6 per cent of our exports in 1821, 12 per cent in the Civil War, and 48 per cent in the boom year 1916, had jumped to 70 per cent, at the expense of foodstuffs, raw materials and semimanufactured goods. The "workshop of the world," it went on to say, had obviously shifted to this side of the Atlantic. But along with the summer crop of enthusiastic statistics came an official dash of cold water, with a warning from the new head of the Office of War Information that the nation was "not yet more than ankle deep in the war," that amazing though our production had become, it was not enough "measured against what we need to have," and that we had not given our allies "as much help as we had led them to expect." Close upon that, the British Minister of Production called attention to England's heavier per capita production than America's, and to the fact that England had had to rush planes, antiaircraft guns, barrage balloons, and submarine chasers over here upon our entry into the war.

The increased complications involved in producing planes and tanks were only the beginning of serious problems, as we shall see. Their bulk alone posed a difficulty in transportation even if the lack of tonnage had not been a daily headache. To make the situation worse, the munitions faced far longer journeys than the three thousand miles to France of the previous war—and that increased the tonnage troubles. The worries did not end with the finding of cargo space, for we shall find numerous dangers lurking along those lengthened routes, and in the ports at the end of them, before those munitions reached the scenes of action and were in condition to use.

In food, as in munitions, the part played by America and the vessels of the Atlantic shuttle was a factor in the final victory. In both wars the United States helped to feed as well as to arm the Allied peoples. England's need of overseas wheat and meat in World War I was more excusable than that of munitions, which with adequate foresight that great industrial nation should have been able to have at hand. The old decision to sacrifice agriculture for industry had thrown the country into chronic dependence upon distant lands for the feeding of some forty million mouths. Only a fraction of that food was produced at home. This was the result of the victory of industrial over agricultural interests in the years since the repeal of the Corn Laws in 1846. In strengthening its position as "workshop of the world," England had shifted more and more of the population from field to factory and had let the products of its industrial cities pay for the food from abroad. It depended on America and the dominions of the South Pacific as well as on Europe itself. It will be recalled that as early as 1862 England had needed grain from America, and as time went on this situation grew more acute and might easily have proved disastrous in the first war.

With war cutting off trade with many of the countries that furnished its food and with the tonnage shortage curtailing distant supplies from the Far East, England turned more and more to Canada, the Argentine, and above all to the United States. Nor was England alone in this; European harvests were generally bad in 1914. France and Italy, normally fairly self-sufficient, had millions of men called from the farms to the trenches. Greece was cut off from its usual Russian sources. Belgium, occupied by Germans, needed large quantities of relief. Some of the neutrals sought food also from beyond the seas.

As far as England was concerned, sugar was its first worry. Two-thirds of the supply was beet sugar from Germany and Austria, since the British sugar islands had long since ceased to raise enough cane. The United States and Cuba came to the rescue, with imports to Britain rising from 11 per cent in 1913 to over 63 per cent in 1918; but even with that, British consumption had to be reduced one-third.

Frozen meat suffered, too, because of the length of the haul from the Plata and the longer one from the South Pacific dominions. Many of the refrigerator ships were eventually put on the shorter American run, where they could bring troops as well. As a result, imports from the United States rose from less than 2 per cent to over 31 per cent. More than three-fifths of the imported eggs, butter, cheese, and other dairy products had come from the Continent, but fodder shortage and navigation difficulties naturally reduced that supply drastically, except from Denmark. Imports from the United States and Canada rose accordingly, but at that the British supply was cut almost in half by the end of the war.

American hogs, however, did a more thorough job than the cows and hens. Bacon was the one major food commodity that came in greater quantities to England than before. Over 40 per cent had come from Denmark in 1913, and over 45 per cent from the United States; in 1918, the Danish hogs furnished $\frac{2}{10}$ of 1 per cent, and the American over 83 per cent of the imports. Psychologically, it was not a satisfactory substitute for roast beef, but it was compact to ship, required less refrigeration, and did a good job in offsetting the loss of protein in the British diet.

Grain was the paramount food problem. The British government decided that whatever might happen to other foodstuffs, its people were to have plenty of bread, at any cost. It was the only important food not rationed, and although the price of wheat went up steadily, Englishmen could still buy the four-pound loaf for eleven pence to fill the gaps in their reduced meals. To keep this price for the consumer, the government spent millions in its "bread subsidy." That loaf, to be sure, was no longer pure white bread, but unpalatable though it might be to many, it was the first line of defense against starvation.

The whims of the weather naturally made predictions difficult about the grain supply. The farmers might increase their acreage but no one could be sure whether the yield would be twelve or seventeen bushels an acre or whether crop conditions would be similar across the seas. After the first hectic weeks of uncertainty at the outbreak of the war, the American grain supply caused no further concern for two years. The 1914 crop, which was a failure abroad, was plentiful in America, and the American farmer found that with the stimulated war demand, he had come into his own. Exports nearly doubled and prices climbed. In 1915 the wheat fields yielded seventeen bushels an acre, producing the nation's first billion bushel crop. With shipping conditions still fairly good, England and its allies had plenty to eat.

The rosy picture did not last; just as the munitions worries lightened at the end of 1916, the food troubles multiplied. The American crop failed, with a yield per acre of only twelve bushels; this was less wheat than Americans alone had used the year before. Unless Europe were to starve, the United States must go on short rations. The total crop, which had come to 891 million bushels in 1914 and to 1,025,000 million in 1915, was merely 636,000. Wheat rose to $2.00 a bushel, and in one hectic day of speculation in May, 1917, to an all-time high of $3.25. And, to make the situation worse, the submarines were on the rampage, and both wheat and the tonnage to transport it were going to the bottom of the Atlantic.

So bad were the sinkings in that spring that in March one-sixth of all the sugar shipments and one-eighth of the wheat were sunk. In May, England's wheat reserves touched their lowest point, with barely a three weeks' supply in the government reserves. A temporary respite came in the fall, when the sinkings were reduced, but our 1917 crop was just as disappointingly small as the 1916. To build up a food surplus for Europe, Americans began to eat substitutes for white flour in their bread, to observe "meatless days," and to go short on sugar. Bad weather and a coal shortage slowed up the transatlantic shipments in January, as did the prior claims of the A.E.F. on the ships.

The British food administrator cabled Herbert Hoover, who held that same position here, that an additional 75 million tons, about 300 normal shiploads, must come if there was to be food enough to win the war. Nothing happened; and late in January, the Allied premiers cabled President Wilson:

> It is our deliberate conviction that food shortage with its effect on the morale of the population which has been one of the principal causes of the breakdown of Russia, is the greatest danger at present threatening each of the Allies.

Europe was begging for bread and Hoover offered them bacon—tremendous quantities of it. Eventually, after England agreed to cut down on the grain used in brewing beer, the United States released enough wheat to stave off the threatened bread rationing. Nature did her part; the 1918 crop was a good enough one to aid materially in the feeding of the starving postwar Continent. At any rate, thanks to the United States, the Allied peoples had had far more to eat than the hungrier Germans and Austrians in those lean war years.

In the interval between the wars, both England and Germany remembered their hunger pangs and saw to it that they were equipped for fairly substantial, if monotonous, menus when war returned. Although the British had not profited adequately by the munitions lessons from the first conflict, they proved that they had learned much about preparedness against hunger. The specter of starvation that had haunted Englishmen during the earlier U-boat raids had no counterpart in the first three years of the second war. Nevertheless, England was still dependent upon America for the foods essential to a balanced diet, even though the basic barriers to starvation had been strengthened.

The British wheat supply underwent the main change between the two wars. While the sea lanes were still open in peacetime, England apparently laid in a huge reserve stock. In addition, more land than ever was given over to raising a domestic supply of grain, more than six million extra acres being brought under cultivation, and the wheat yield jumped two-thirds over the pre-war level. The British food authorities clung to their policy of the last war in providing the people with plenty of bread, but this time the grain ships from across the Atlantic were less needed; it was reckoned, in mid-1942, that those domestic crops saved at least five million tons of shipping. The raising of potatoes and other vegetables further reduced dependence upon overseas supplies. The 1942 harvest promised to be a bumper one, but of course there was no certainty that such luck would continue. Altogether, England was producing two-thirds of all its food, as compared with one-fourth before the war.

That increased British self-sufficiency was bad news for the farmers of the United States and Canada, who had the greatest grain surplus in history on hand early in 1942. A huge "wheat pool," to provide for starving peoples during or after the war, was announced, but in the meantime our farm bloc threatened the national price structure with a clamor for higher prices.

The protein part of the British diet was the chief lack in this second war. With the crops being fed directly to the people, the poultry and livestock lacked their usual feed, with a consequent sharp reduction in eggs, milk, butter, and meat products. For a while, to conserve exchange, England went to the Empire for these products, until certain of the lease-lend funds were earmarked for food for Britain. With the slogan "food will win the war and write the peace," our Secretary of Agriculture announced a program to change American farm efforts from wheat and cotton to more diversified crops. Lease-lend funds were spent for such things as powdered, evaporated, and condensed milk, cheese, dried eggs, poultry, beef, and veal. By the late summer of 1942, England's requirements in meat from the United States appeared to be on the increase, because of the need once again to save tonnage by reducing the long hauls from the Argentine and the South Pacific. In addition, many millions of cases of canned tomatoes and peas, with lesser amounts of beans and corn were sent across. To the heavily rationed British, such cargoes spelled relief from a very monotonous diet. Every ship sunk meant just that much less chance for variety in a bread and limited vegetable routine. On the whole, nonetheless, American food was far less important strategically than it had been in 1917 and 1918.

Russia, too, received food supplies as well as tanks and planes, for tremendous dislocations followed the German invasion. Food for unoccupied France posed a difficult question; the British blockade policy frowned upon the suggestion. It was generally realized, however, that American food would count for much in a starving Europe after the war, and might well help to "write the peace."

Munitions and food were by no means the sole significant contributions. During World War I, some half a million horses and a quarter of a million mules went across to the British Army, with additional numbers to the other Allies. In World War II, motorization of the armies radically reduced this need, but oil and the other ingredients for mechanized warfare more than took the place of those animals. Although the United States was the greatest oil producer in both wars, the Allies normally used other sources—especially the Middle and Far East. The sweep of Japanese conquest in the third year of the second war cut off the latter, and Hitler's main objective was the former. As those supplies became lost or more vulnerable, the demands upon American oil fields correspondingly grew.

Much else crossed the Atlantic; even to millions of garments collected as "Bundles for Britain" to clothe bombed-out victims, and these, ironically, sometimes passed in mid-Atlantic cargoes of expensive English woolens bound westward to bolster England's purchasing power. But whatever the cargoes, they were significant factors on the road to victory, and their safety on those dangerous sea lanes was of prime strategic importance.

Chapter IX

U-Boats on the North Atlantic

THE MONTH OF JULY, 1914, THE LAST OF THE OLD ERA, HAD ONLY
an hour or so to live. Four days out of New York, the cabin passengers on the German luxury liner *Kronprinzessin Cecelie* were
dancing through the summer evening as the great ship plowed
her way toward her first British port of call, only eight hundred
miles away. Suddenly the helm was put about and the engines
drove her at top speed back toward America. The mystified passengers were quickly informed by Captain Polak that war was
impending in Europe, and he had been ordered back to New
York.

In earlier years, the ship would probably have blundered on
into enemy hands, but now the wireless had sent the warning.
The fog grew thick but the speed did not slacken. The pleas for
caution by the passengers, who had the *Titanic's* fate fresh in
their minds, fell on deaf ears. The captain had more than his
passengers' nervous chills to worry him; a cargo of gold, worth
twice as much as the five-million-dollar liner herself, was aboard.
She was a prize in ten thousand for the British and French
cruisers, whose wireless messages were crackling through the fog,
far too close for comfort. Efforts at capture were foiled, and the
Cecelie won her race a few hours before England declared war on
Germany. Early on August 4, she was piloted to an anchorage at
Bar Harbor by a passenger, who knew the waters from having
yachted on that rocky coast.

For the first time in fifty years the seas belonged to the raider;
and the hunted scurried to cover. Many other German merchantmen were less fortunate than the *Cecelie*. A British admiral, so it
is said, kept the day-by-day position of each and every one of
them—wherever they might be all over the world—marked upon

a globe at the Admiralty. At any rate, hundreds were snapped up on the high seas or in enemy ports, while the rest clung to the safety of neutral harbors or home waters. Almost overnight, the German merchant flag disappeared from the high seas, not to reappear for more than four years.

The hectic uncertainty of the first days of war endangered more than German merchantmen. Rumor placed three German cruisers and some armed liners in the North Atlantic. The dense August fogs shielded fleeing British liners, too. The *Mauretania* strained her engines to a new record of twenty-seven knots, in a race for the safety of Halifax. A British cruiser escorted the *Olympic* to Sandy Hook and returned with the *Lusitania*.

Meanwhile, lesser vessels by the hundreds lay idle in port, with accumulating cargoes clogging the water fronts. Shipowners feared to risk their vessels, and exporters their cargoes, on that apparently perilous ocean. Remembering the *Alabama* situation, when worry over enemy raiding did more damage than the raiding itself, the British government took quick steps to counteract the stagnation. It announced government war-risk insurance on hulls and cargoes at a flat moderate rate—at a moment when the private marine insurance men of Lloyd's and the New York market were not yet ready to risk their capital. By this prompt action, vessels soon began to move. By the middle of August, the Admiralty called the North Atlantic safe, and before long the private companies were quoting rates of 1 per cent. For six months, shipping came and went across the Atlantic virtually undisturbed.

Those stormy three thousand miles were as usual the most important of the sea lanes and the real "life line of the British Empire." Unlike the route past Gibraltar and Suez to the East, there was no substitute, however roundabout, for the Atlantic shuttle. That fact gave special significance to the Battle of the Atlantic in both wars, as well as to what occurred in the adjacent European waters. The other more distant sea lanes will be considered later.

As for the relation of the United States to the shipping situation, it was, both as neutral and belligerent, markedly different from what it had been in the past. In earlier days, we had had vessels enough not only for our own cargoes but also for a considerable share of the belligerent carrying trade; but in both these wars our vessels were too few at the outset for more than a fraction of our own shipping needs. As our cargoes had become more vital than our own shipping to us, so naturally our interest centered more on the foreign vessels carrying those cargoes. Their services had become absolutely necessary to us if we wanted to get our munitions and food overseas. Other contrasts with our earlier years of neutral profits occurred in our modern periods of neutrality from 1914 to 1917 and from 1939 to 1941. In 1914, with German shipping quickly out of the picture, our attention centered, beyond our own meager seagoing fleet, upon the thousands of Scandinavian or other neutral vessels, and upon the belligerent merchantmen headed by England's tremendous aggregation of liners and freighters.

While American trade with England and most of the Continent was little disturbed during the first six months, the North Sea was a different matter. Mines laid first by the Germans and later by the British made traffic highly dangerous. The German mine fields even in the first week of the war extended over to the coast of England, and by fall the British had thoroughly mined the southern end of the North Sea. Later the situation became worse when submarines began to lay mines up to the Thames approaches. England kept mine sweepers at work to maintain "swept channels" for its own east-coast shipping, and in order to force neutral vessels into its waters for inspection.

Here, three of these American steamers engaged in that brief direct cotton trade with Germany went to the bottom early in 1915. Except for a sailing ship sunk by a raider off Brazil, these were the first American victims of the war. The insurance rates as usual reflected the dangers. Although at the end of 1914 the rate on neutral vessels to the west-coast British ports was only ⅜ of 1 per cent, it was double that amount to the North Sea ports, five times as much to Holland, and eleven times as high to Scandinavia.

Another hazard to overseas trade lay in the remote-control methods of the modern British blockade, which we have already noted. In 1915 some five thousand neutral vessels were subjected to delay and search at the northern control stations alone, while others were undergoing similar treatment at the Mediterranean stations. As England tightened its contraband regulations to prevent leakage into Germany through adjacent neutral states, it purchased or condemned many American cargoes bound for such destinations. The Admiralty judges, with a good sense of humor, cited Civil War precedents of American condemnations of British vessels. Those American decisions in turn, it will be recalled, had been based on British "continuous voyage" precedents, when American vessels had been condemned by the Admiralty courts in the Napoleonic period. Those British actions naturally hit heavily at American profits; and, as we have seen, the United States soon saw that roundabout sales to Germany through the ports of neutral neighbors were out of the question, along with direct trade.

Americans began to recall impatiently their strenuous upholding of "freedom of the seas" against similar British practices a century before. Then the United States had had little or no navy to back its claims, but this time it was well aware it was in a position to demand what it had had to plead for earlier. The mere threat of an embargo, in view of the desperate British need of munitions and foodstuffs, would have quickly modified the blockade methods. With a navy almost as strong as Germany's, we could, moreover, have easily played havoc with that blockade. The governor of Texas, anxious about cotton exports, demanded such action with his call for "American ironclads to England's doors."

But the United States government refused to use either of those trumps. The sting of the occasional strong protests by the State Department was removed by the manner in which Page, our strongly pro-British ambassador, presented them to the Foreign Office, or by what the President's confidential adviser murmured to the British envoy at Washington. As a result, the reassured British carefully delayed their replies until some incident had stirred up anti-German feeling; then they would calmly announce the continuation of their policy. The man in the street railed at times at the activities of the Dover Patrol and the Tenth Cruiser Squadron, but the British felt safe in persisting with the blockade, although they took care not to flout Americans too openly. They were much embarrassed, for example, when the Hamburg-American freighter *Dacia* was transferred to American registry and sailed for Germany with a cargo of Texas cotton. Such use of Germany's interned ships naturally irritated the British; yet they hesitated to seize her. Ambassador Page, of all people, rescued them from their dilemma by a convenient hint; it was as the prize of a French cruiser that the *Dacia* was taken into Brest. No such compromise nor tolerance marked the American clamor for "freedom of the seas," however, when German countermeasures endangered American trade.

The *Glitra* was a humble little British freighter with a prosaic cargo of coal, iron plates, and oil, but she provided an important "first time" in maritime history as the first merchant victim of the new submarine warfare. In October, 1914, en route from England to a Norwegian port, she was stopped by a German U-boat and her crew was given ten minutes to abandon ship. Thousands of merchantmen were to follow her to the bottom of the sea in this war and the next, as the Germans, driven from the surface of the seas by superior British naval strength, perfected their submarine tactics.

Two weeks after the sinking of the *Glitra,* England proclaimed the North Sea a war zone, which warned the Germans that their food supply was in danger. A group of German naval officers quickly drew up a memorandum urging the use of U-boats to threaten, in turn, England's overseas supply lines in the same way—by sinking merchantmen. The day before Christmas, Admiral von Tirpitz, the tough, bewhiskered naval chief, was quoted by an interviewing journalist as saying:

England wants to starve us! We can play the same game. We can bottle her up and torpedo every English or Allied ship which nears any harbor in Great Britain, thereby cutting off large food supplies.

The U-boats did more than anything else to draw the United States toward war; to the British, they were a godsend in that respect because they distracted attention from the less dramatic but more thorough interference with American cargoes at Kirkwall and the Downs. There is neither room nor need here to follow play-by-play the intricate steps by which President Wilson and the State Department met the submarine situation—from our first announcement in February, 1915, that Germany would be held "to strict accountability," down to the final declaration of war in April, 1917.

Early in 1915, the Germans ended the six months of tranquillity on the Atlantic by proclaiming a war zone around the British Isles. They hoped to frighten away neutral shipping with the warning that it might inadvertently "suffer from attacks intended to strike enemy ships," because of "misuse of the neutral flag ordered by the British government." That very week, in fact, the *Lusitania,* on one of her last crossings, took advantage of that time-honored ruse to fly the Stars and Stripes as she neared home waters. The submarine campaign of 1915, however, came to little in comparison with the terrible efficiency of the attack launched just two years later, when there would be no pretense of sparing neutrals.

The U-boats were at their new work in earnest by the end of February, but at that time Germany had only about twenty-one seagoing ones available. Some of these lurked in the Channel, and some in the northern waters between Ireland and Scotland, but their chief hunting grounds were the "Southwest Approaches" where the main sea lanes converged. The ocean floor along the south coast of Ireland and the southwest tip of England was soon littered with the shattered hulls of freighters and liners, but judged by later standards these losses were small. Not until May did the monthly totals approach the damage that had been caused by the surface raiders in distant seas during the previous autumn; even in August, at the highest, the total was only 185,000 tons.

For the moment, the United States felt no serious concern over the wastage of tonnage and loss of cargoes. The underwriters did not raise the rates on belligerent ships between New York and Liverpool, which had been ½ of 1 per cent at the beginning of the year, beyond 1¼ per cent during the first ten weeks of the campaign, while neutral shipping was considered twice as safe. American attention at the outset was focused upon individual cases involving American vessels or the loss of American lives, and neither were numerous.

In fact, as far as our shipping was concerned, the U-boat lagged behind other methods of commerce destruction. One American vessel had been sunk by a raider, three had been destroyed by mines, one had even been attacked by a seaplane, before a U-boat torpedo hit the new tanker *Gulflight* in May, 1915. On her way from Texas, she blundered into a gun fight off the English coast between a British patrol boat and the *U-30*, which loosed a torpedo. The crippled tanker, however, managed to make port with two of her crew killed and her captain dead of heart failure. So, too, did the freighter *Nebraskan* after she was torpedoed later that month. In fact, only one American vessel was actually sunk by a submarine that year—the small ex-British steamer *Leelanaw*. The fourth American victim of 1915 was the auxiliary sailing ship *Pass of Balhamas,* recently transferred from British registry and with Archangel her intended destination. She had the rare experience of being captured, but not sunk, by a U-boat, and was sent into a German port. She was, moreover, at the time of her encounter with the submarine already in charge of a prize crew: the British were taking her into Kirkwall! A yet more thrilling future lay in store for her. When she returned to the high seas, she was Count von Luckner's raider *Seeadler.*

Washington was much more concerned about the loss of American lives—that was the basic reason for protesting more vigorously against U-boat sinkings than against British seizures. As soon as the submarine campaign had been announced, the German ambassador at Washington urged the State Department to warn American passengers against sailing on belligerent vessels. Secretary Bryan was inclined to agree with him, but was overruled; the government upheld the right of an American to sail wherever he wanted to go. Since the State Department would do nothing, the German embassy in a public advertisement in the newspapers warned Americans of the dangers of sailing on belligerent liners. This notice, denounced by the American press as "insolent," first appeared in some fifty papers the first of May.

It apparently did not worry the 149 Americans and 1,108 other passengers who chose to sail from New York aboard the fast crack Cunarder *Lusitania,* instead of transferring to an older, slower American liner leaving that same day. A series of blind chances led the *Lusitania* to her tragic fate six days later. Had Captain Turner, warned of the presence of submarines by an Admiralty wireless, utilized the full power of his engines—some of the fastest afloat—to steer a zigzag course away from the dangerous Irish headlands, probably no submarine could have caught his ship. Had Lieutenant Schweiger of the *U-20*—on his way back to Germany from the Irish Sea, short of oil and with only two "not very good" torpedoes left—not happened to notice the great liner, all would probably have gone well. But Captain Turner slowed down, at just the moment the *U-20* was close at hand, to take his bearings on that foggy day, and the starboard side of the *Lusitania* presented a too tempting target. She sank in eighteen minutes; a speed that amazed everyone, for the *Titanic,* with her hull slashed by an iceberg, had stayed afloat two hours, and the bulkheads of many a small torpedoed freighter had kept her up for some time. The cases of cartridges in the *Lusitania's* cargo could scarcely have been the cause. Confusion of the worst sort reigned on the decks of the stricken liner; there had been no lifeboat drills and even their launching was bungled. In her final plunge, she carried down 1,195 of the 1,959 passengers and crew; 94 of the 125 children were lost, and

124 of the 149 Americans. A shudder of horror and indignation swept the United States, undoing months of zealous German propaganda.

For a year and a half after the *Lusitania,* the "main line" was not seriously molested. For a while, the Germans refrained from torpedoing passenger liners, even though some of them were openly carrying considerable quantities of munitions. In the summer of 1915, when the sinkings of that year were at their heaviest, the White Star liner *Arabic* was sunk with the loss of two Americans among the forty-four victims, and in the spring of 1916 German-American diplomatic relations were complicated by the deaths of more Americans in the torpedoing of the French Channel steamer *Sussex.* Ordinary little freighters by the dozen, some of them laden with American munitions or grain, went down during that summer of 1915, but by fall the sinkings tapered off and were not serious again until October, 1916, when the average monthly toll rose to 175,000 tons for the next four months. Altogether during much of 1915 and 1916, most of the shrapnel, high explosives, and wheat from American ports reached England safely.

The submarines were not idle during that lull on the North Atlantic; they had shifted their activities elsewhere. The quiet waters and narrow bottlenecks of the Mediterranean made it an ideal field for operations. The Germans even sent down a considerable amount of submarine parts by rail to the Adriatic coast, where they were assembled. By the fall of 1916, war-risk rates to the Mediterranean were three times as high as to England; and Britain began to send much of its shipping by the longer but safer alternate route around the Cape of Good Hope. Of the three American vessels sunk by U-boats to the end of 1916, two were lost in the Mediterranean trade.

But with the end of 1916, the comparative calm of the sea lanes was gone. The storm broke with the German decision to use their U-boats to the limit to put England out of the war. The terrific waste of life at Verdun and the Somme in 1916 had gained almost nothing for either side. Jutland had kept the High Sea Fleet still cooped up in the North Sea. And in Germany, the relentless British blockade was compelling "women and children, the sick and the aged, to suffer for their country pain and privations which endanger the life of the nation." Von Tirpitz persuaded his government that his submarines could win the war quickly and cheaply. By this time he had 115 of them, more efficient in every way than the earlier ones, and more were on the ways. Also, the earlier squeamishness about neutrals was now over.

In its new campaign of unrestricted submarine warfare, Germany announced that every vessel of any sort found in the waters around England and France or in the Mediterranean would be sunk. The one exception was permission for the United States to dispatch one ship each week to Falmouth, England, provided several minutely specified regulations were followed. Three days later, the United States severed diplomatic relations with Germany.

The U-boats went to work with deadly effectiveness. They laid mines close inshore to drive the shipping out to sea away from the protection of the patrol boats; and there sank them by the score. From Fastnet, that "rugged lonely rock with its tall lighthouse," off the tip of Ireland, on past Kinsale, and off the end of Cornwall, they cruised in tireless relays. Although they centered their efforts as usual here, where Britain's sea lanes converged, the northern route and the approaches to France were not much safer. The losses hit 540,000 tons in February and did not drop below that again until September. Not only were the Germans successfully sinking a considerable part of the British merchant marine with its cargoes of precious foodstuffs beneath the waves, but this time they were frightening off many neutral cargo carriers. The dauntless Norwegians stuck to the dangerous work, but most others dared not risk their ships.

Even some Americans kept their vessels home until permitted by Congress to arm them. That permission was granted in March, after being delayed by a Senate filibuster, and once more our vessels sallied forth in number, this time with guns on their sterns and naval crews to man them. The *Aztec* was the first to sail; but her gun crew had no time to fire a single shot before a U-boat sank her off the French coast.

She was by no means the first American victim of the new acceleration in submarine warfare. More of our tonnage was sunk and more seamen lost in February and March than in the whole preceding thirty months of the war. Before that diplomatic break in early February, the Germans had been extremely forbearing where American vessels and American lives were concerned; our losses, such as they were, had been rather in cargoes aboard foreign vessels. Raiders, mines, and submarines together had taken only twelve American vessels, of some 34,000 tons, which was less than 1 per cent of the total of 4,300,000 tons of the destroyed neutral and Allied shipping. In these two months, however, U-boats alone sank nine ships of 36,000 tons; and in contrast to the loss of seven American sailors in the earlier period, sixty-four perished. Altogether, the United States lost 216 of its citizens and twenty-one of its vessels before it declared war on Germany on April 6, 1917.

Within two weeks of that declaration, the submarine warfare reached its fastest tempo. The blackest day of the whole war at sea was April 19, when nineteen British vessels were lost. The total sinkings of that terrible month amounted to 881,000 tons, of which 847,000, representing 395 vessels, were sunk by submarines. Of every four vessels sailing from England in those weeks, one never returned. Hard put to it to find enough tonnage before that, the British now faced desperate days with the food stock dangerously low. Berlin was jubilant at the cheap and easy way to victory found by Tirpitz.

That April sinking rate, however, was not retained nor repeated, thanks in part to the United States Navy. England had lacked the destroyers necessary to patrol the sea approaches. It had used small boats of every sort, laid mines to catch the subs, and originated the mysterious Q-ships, which looked like harmless freighters but could suddenly open up their sides to fire naval guns. These were not enough without plenty of destroyers, and the Admiralty could only spare a hundred or so of them for this duty. It was a welcome sight for the Queenstown base, therefore, when the first squadron of American destroyers steamed in early in May. The sleek little four-stackers at once took up their designated stations in those dangerous waters. A flock of converted American yachts soon assumed similar tasks along the French coast, and later a swarm of efficient little subchasers joined in the work.

The reduction in sinkings was achieved by more than that reinforcement in war vessels. There were the various other antisubmarine devices which we have already considered—the depth bomb, the sound detector, the camouflage painting of vessels, and especially the resurrection of the convoy system. The first regular transatlantic convoy sailed from Hampton Roads in May, and consisted of twelve freighters escorted by a British cruiser. Ten of these arrived safely together, but two of the tramps, being too slow to keep up, dropped out of line; one was torpedoed, but the other reached port four days late. By summer, the system had spread to numerous important routes. Every four days, a convoy sailed for England from Hampton Roads and from Gibraltar; every eight days, from New York, from Sydney on Cape Breton, and from other ports. Service was provided up the African coast, past the dangerous bulge at Dakar, and through the Mediterranean, by then the riskiest of all the major routes. "From the first," wrote the official British historian of *Seaborne Trade,* "the success of the convoy was unmistakable." Out of 205 ships in twelve July convoys, all but two reached England safely. Throughout the remainder of the war, the losses of convoyed vessels was considerably less than 2 per cent.

Among the lone vessels not sailing in convoy, sinkings continued high throughout the summer of 1917. England had weathered the desperate spring crises, however, and although the loss of tonnage continued to be serious, the threatened starvation

SHIPPING LOSSES AND WAR-RISK RATES, 1914-1918

Average New York cargo war-risk rates, compiled from N. Y. Journal of Commerce. *Rates in percentages (2.50 = 2½%). Rates from N. Y. except transpacific from West Coast. Sinkings totals for the pro-Allied belligerent and neutral vessels.*

BELLIGERENT RATES

	SINKINGS (M GROSS TONS)		GREAT BRITAIN WEST	FAR EAST VIA				RIO
	TOTAL	U. S.		SUEZ	CAPE	PANAMA	PACIFIC	
1914								
Aug.	62		2.00	6.00	6.00	6.00	6.00	5.00
Sept.	98		"	7.50	7.50	7.50	7.50	7.50
Oct.	87		1.00	4.00	3.00	4.00	4.00	3.50
Nov.	19		.75	3.00	"	"	2.50	2.50
Dec.	44		.62	1.25	1.25	1.25	.75	"
1915								
Jan.	47	3	.50	1.00	1.00	1.00	"	1.00
Feb.	59	4	1.00	.62	.62	.62	.37	2.00
Mar.	80		"	"	"	"	.25	.75
Apr.	55	3	1.25	"	"	"	"	"
May	120		2.12	.37	.37	.37	.37	.14
June	131		1.62	.50	.50	.25	.25	"
July	109	1	1.25	.37	.37	"	.14	.17
Aug.	185	1	"	.50	.50	.25	.10	.12
Sept.	151	1	"	.37	.37	.20	"	"
Oct.	88		"	.62	.62	"	"	.50
Nov.	153		"	2.00	2.00	"	"	"
Dec.	123		1.00	5.00	"	"	"	"
1916								
Jan.	81		"	"	"	.33	"	.10
Feb.	117		.87	"	"	"	"	2.00
Mar.	167		1.00	"	3.00	"	.12	"
Apr.	191		1.50	4.00	2.00	.12	"	1.00
May	129		2.50	4.50	1.50	.25	.10	"
June	108	2	1.50	3.50	"	"	"	.37
July	118		1.00	3.00	.50	.15	.08	.10
Aug.	162		.75	"	"	"	.12	.12
Sept.	230		.87	4.00	"	.10	"	.06
Oct.	353		2.00	7.00	1.50	.75	.10	1.25
Nov.	311	11	3.00	8.00	1.00	1.00	.50	.50
Dec.	355		7.00	10.00	3.00	2.00	.25	3.00
1917								
Jan.	368		6.00	"	2.75	"	.12	8.00
Feb.	540	4	9.00	15.00	8.00	3.00	"	5.00
Mar.	593	20	10.00	"	7.00	"	"	3.00
Apr.	881	22	"	"	5.50	2.75	.87	4.00
May	596	18	"	"	5.00	"	"	3.00
June	687	20	"	17.50	4.00	2.00	.62	2.50
July	557	27	"	"	"	1.50	"	"
Aug.	551	6	"	"	"	"	"	1.50
Sept.	351	13	8.00	"	"	.37	.37	1.00
Oct.	458	16	7.00	"	3.00	1.00	"	.75
Nov.	289	16	"	"	"	.37	"	.50
Dec.	399		6.50	"	"	"	"	.37

SHIPPING LOSSES AND WAR-RISK RATES,
1914-1918—*Continued*

BELLIGERENT RATES

	SINKINGS (M GROSS TONS)		GREAT BRITAIN WEST	FAR EAST VIA				RIO
	TOTAL	U. S.		SUEZ	CAPE	PANAMA	PACIFIC	
1918								
Jan.	306	2	6.50	17.50	3.00	.37	.37	.17
Feb.	318	9	4.50	"	"	"	"	"
Mar.	342	4	3.50	"	1.50	.20	.17	"
Apr.	278	2	3.00	"	1.25	"	.20	.12
May	295	13	2.50	15.00	"	"	.17	"
June	255	28	"	"	2.50	2.00	.12	2.00
July	260	5	2.25	"	2.00	.50	.20	1.00
Aug.	283	46	"	"	"	1.00	.50	"
Sept.	187	14	2.50	"	"	1.50	1.50	.20
Oct.	118	9	2.00	"	1.75	1.00	1.00	.12
Nov.	17	3	1.75	"	1.50	.62	.62	.12
Av. to Nov. 1918	Belligerent		3.48	8.92	2.37	1.21	.69	1.47
" " Apr. 1917	"		2.16	4.26	2.10	1.32	.80	1.72
" " " "	U. S. Ships		1.71	3.70	1.44	.68	.24	.44

had been averted. From the 881,000-ton peak in April, the sinkings fell to 596,000 in May, rose to 687,000 in June, stood at about 550,000 in July and August, and then, feeling the effect of the antisubmarine efforts, dropped to 351,000 in September.

The New York war-risk insurance figures reflected this improved situation. Instead of a flat figure for a particular route, such as would be drawn up by a central committee of underwriters in the next war, the premiums covered a considerable range, depending upon the speed of the vessel, her armament, if any, and, more important, whether or not she sailed in convoy. By the summer of 1917, belligerent vessels for once commanded a lower rate than neutral ones. Thus a fast armed British liner could at one time be insured for less than half the rate on a little unarmed neutral tramp, sailing on her own. Early in November, 1916, just before the revival of U-boat activity, the rates to Liverpool and other west-coast British ports stood at ¾ to 1 per cent for American vessels; 1 to 1¾ per cent for other neutrals; and 1¾ to 2 per cent for belligerents.

SHIPPING LOSSES AND WAR-RISK RATES, 1939-1942

Cargo rates established by American Cargo War Risk Reinsurance Exchange; compiled from N. Y. Journal of Commerce. *Total sinkings of pro-British shipping not announced after July, 1941. Australian rates, previously slightly lower than Far Eastern, substituted after January, 1942. "A": "rates quoted upon application."*

BELLIGERENT RATES

	Sinkings (M Gross Tons)		Great Britain West	Far East Via				Rio
	Total	U. S.		Suez	Cape	Panama	Pacific	
1939								
Sept.	189		7.50	7.50	4.00	3.00	2.50	3.00
Oct.	211		5.00	5.00	3.00	2.00	1.00	2.00
Nov.	165		6.00	"	2.50	"	"	"
Dec.	196		"	"	"	"	.75	"
1940								
Jan.	200		4.00	2.50	1.50	1.25	"	1.00
Feb.	218		3.50	"	"	1.00	"	.50
Mar.	98		"	"	"	.75	"	"
Apr.	135		"	A	1.00	"	"	"
May	249		"	"	"	"	"	.37
June	538		7.50		3.00	1.00	1.00	"
July	399		10.00		4.00	2.00	2.00	1.00
Aug.	387		"		"	"	"	"
Sept.	432		"		"	1.50	1.50	"
Oct.	424		"		"	5.00	2.00	2.00
Nov.	358	5	"		"	"	"	.75
Dec.	313		"		"	"	"	"
1941								
Jan.	288		"		4.50	1.75	1.50	"
Feb.	339		"		"	1.50	1.00	"
Mar.	501		"		"	"	"	"
Apr.	597		"		3.50	"	"	.50
May	504	5	"		"	2.00	2.00	"
June	366		"		"	"	"	"
July	210		"		"	"	"	"
Aug.			"		"	"	"	"
Sept.		5	"		"	"	"	"
Oct.		5	"		3.00	"	"	"
Nov.			7.50		"	"	"	"
Dec.		35	"		7.50	10.00	10.00	2.00
1942								
Jan.		33	"		"	"	"	1.50
Feb.			"		5.00*	6.00*	6.00*	"
Mar.			"		"	9.00*	"	4.00
Apr.			10.00		9.00*	12.00*	"	7.50
May			"		A	"	"	10.00
June			"			"	"	15.00
July			"			20.00*	7.50*	20.00
Aug.			"			25.00*	"	25.00
Sept.			"			17.50*	"	17.50
Av. to Dec. 1941 Belligerent			8.06	....	3.30	1.79	1.41	.89
" " " " U. S. Ships			....	....	1.44	.74	.69	.13

* Australia

During the first three months of 1917 the distinction between belligerents and neutrals temporarily disappeared. The minimum rate for fast liners continued almost without break at 8 per cent, but the maximum rates steadily increased during the spring and summer. Naturally the underwriters had no way of foreseeing that the worst was over by May. In February, the top rate was 10 per cent (five times what it had been in the corresponding period of the 1915 campaign); in March, it rose to 12 per cent, and by mid-May, a split developed between the belligerents—presumably armed—whose rate never went above 12½ per cent, and the neutrals, whose rates ranged from 8 to 15 per cent in mid-May, 10 to 16 per cent in mid-July, and, at their peak, from 15 to 20 per cent late in August. By mid-September, all the rates began to drop, with the liner minimum falling to 5 per cent, and thereafter going almost steadily lower. By March, 1918, the belligerent rates had fallen to 3 to 4 per cent, and the neutrals to 5 to 6 per cent. On the eve of the Armistice, crossings could be insured at less than 2 per cent.

These New York cargo rates, of course, represent only one of several schedules. They were fairly similar to the private London rates, with which they were in constant competition. Both were more sensitive barometers of sea conditions than were the British and American government rates, which were often deliberately set lower than circumstances actually warranted in order to keep shipping moving; but many shippers clung to the private underwriters with their higher rates in order to avoid red tape. In addition to these cargo rates, each of the four groups also had separate scales of hull quotations, generally on a monthly basis. Finally, both the cargo and the hull were also covered by separate marine insurance, for ordinary sea risks. All quotations, unless otherwise indicated, represent private New York cargo rates.

Equal security had not been achieved in the Mediterranean, where the Greek rate hit a top of 25 per cent in July, 1917, and was still averaging 15 per cent at the beginning of November, 1918. Underwriters tell of one tobacco cargo from Smyrna that could not be fully covered at the original quotation of 35 per cent; the balance required a premium of 50 per cent, probably the highest American rate since the War of 1812.

Meanwhile, the Americans had been wrestling with an Atlantic problem that involved the greatest shipping movement in history—the safe transportation of two million men and more than seven million tons of supplies across three thousand miles of dangerous seas. The Germans had already discounted the fact that the United States would probably enter its naval forces in the war against them, but the possibility of American reinforcements on the Western Front did not worry them. It seemed unlikely that we could train sufficient troops or find enough ships to transport them. Even if we did both, the U-boats—so the Germans confidently expected—would keep any great numbers from landing in France. Yet we accomplished all three impossible tasks. The gathering of the supplies, as well as the soldiers, was the job of the army, but the crossing, procurement, manning, and protection of transports and cargo ships fell upon the Cruiser and Transport Force of the Atlantic Fleet. As the Secretary of the Navy warned Admiral Gleaves, commander of the Transport Force: "Admiral, you are going on the most important, the most difficult, and the most hazardous duty assigned to the Navy."

The navy did not have to be told that; it was taking no chances. A heavy fog hung over the entrance of New York port on that June dawn when the first large installment of the A.E.F. slipped away. The ten small passenger liners loaded with soldiers and marines, and the four freighters with supplies sailed in four separate groups out through the submarine net at the Narrows and past Sandy Hook. Along with these ten ships, and carrying extra men and supplies, went four regular cruisers, thirteen destroyers, and six other vessels, including converted yachts, armed colliers, and a former German liner-raider, the *Prinz Eitel Friedrich,* renamed the *De Kalb.* It was feared that U-boats were especially hunting transport convoys; and that suspicion was right.

Three times the submarines struck. The first attack came at night, eight days out and north of the Azores. A keen lookout in the first section saw the bubbling tracks of the first torpedoes rushing toward the *De Kalb*; by deft twisting, she dodged them. The other ships had veered off at full speed at the warning; in the morning, they reassembled, and resumed their course. The second section's turn came four days later. A destroyer charged a U-boat at twenty-five knots, and dropped a depth bomb when she submerged. The debris that floated to the surface indicated that that was the end of that submarine. The third blow was aimed at a cargo ship in the last section loaded with five thousand tons of ammunition below and a deckload of gasoline, hay, and other inflammables. She was turned adroitly and the torpedo passed through her wake, fifty yards astern, while a near-by collier opened fire at the periscope.

The Germans sowed the approaches to Brest with mines, but Gleaves made his way to St. Nazaire. Additional air and surface protection joined the convoy as it neared its destination. The precautions were worth while; and according to one officer, "We didn't lose but one horse, and that was a mule."

That perfect record was not broken; the rest of the two million men, who were convoyed eastward by the Naval Transport Force were guarded with the same painstaking care. Some American troops, who crossed under other auspices, were less fortunate. About two hundred were lost in the torpedoing of the British liner *Tuscania,* and in the merciless shelling of the American freighter *Ticonderoga* by a U-boat. Three army transports were sunk on their return trips, when less protection was thought necessary; and their loss indicated what might have happened had the seemingly excessive safeguards been reduced on the eastbound passage. The very fact that such a gigantic task was accomplished so safely should not blind one to the dangers involved in troop movements by sea. Other nations were less fortunate in that war; and World War II showed that it is no safe and simple ferry service.

By the summer of 1918 the danger zone was suddenly brought close to America's own shores. The cruising radius of the early U-boats had been too short, but by 1916 the two cargo-carrying voyages of the *Deutschland* had demonstrated that the Atlantic was none too wide for the new submarines. More serious, the *U-53* that fall dropped in at Newport, where her commander made a punctilious courtesy call upon Admiral Gleaves; the next day she sank four British steamships and two neutrals close to Nantucket Lightship. This gesture was perhaps designed to warn neutral United States of the danger of fighting Germany. No others appeared until the spring and summer of 1918. Our coast then experienced punishment similar to that inflicted by the *Liverpool Packet* in 1812 and the Confederate raiders.

Late in May, the *U-151,* a sister ship of the commercial *Deutschland,* sowed mines at the entrances of Chesapeake and Delaware bays, cut two telegraph cables off New York, and sank four steamers and six schooners, totaling nearly 20,000 tons. Before she returned to Kiel, ten more vessels were added to her total. The day she reached there, the *U-156* set out for some bold exploits. The mines which she laid at the entrances to New York port caught a distinguished victim in the cruiser *San Diego* off Fire Island. Two days later, vacationists on a Cape Cod beach saw the *U-156* shatter the Lehigh Valley tug *Perth Amboy* and sink her tow of four barges with shellfire. The sub headed north to sink several luckless fishing craft; then returning southward, she caught a Belgian Relief ship and picked off a lagging British freighter from the "coffin corner" of a New York convoy.

Following her from Kiel a week later came the 380-foot *U-140,* largest of the German submarines of that day. After sinking a 10,000-ton tanker, she impudently went after the Diamond Shoals Lightship off Cape Hatteras; then, lying in wait, she caught several vessels as they rounded that dangerous cape. While pursuing a zigzagging Brazilian liner, she was seen by an American destroyer, which wracked her from stem to stern with fifteen depth bombs; but her damage was not fatal. In mid-August, the *U-117* raided the swordfishing fleet on the Georges Bank—sinking nine of the small vessels—and caught some tankers on her way south to sow mines off the Jersey and Carolina coasts. One of those got the battleship *Minnesota* but she managed to limp into port. The former *Deutschland* cruised in the vicinity of Halifax; the sixth sub sent to America did not come close to our shores.

Altogether, the six submarines sank 91 vessels, half of which were American, and took 368 lives in the process. Although they caused only momentary panic along the coast, Chambers of Commerce pleaded for protection as in 1863; submarine nets were placed in harbor entrances; mysterious signals and supply bases were suspected all along the shore. But no more than in 1863 or in 1942 were the raiders successful in withdrawing naval vessels from other more vital duties. At first, the navy tried to keep the raids secret, but that became difficult after a boatload of survivors landed at the Atlantic City boardwalk with a Shriners' convention in full swing. The 1918 experience on the whole was child's play compared with the grim work of the U-boats when they returned again to American waters in 1942.

Meanwhile, the submarine menace had pretty well subsided overseas. The base at Zeebrugge on the Belgian coast had been blocked by the daring sinking of two old cement-laden cruisers in a British midnight raid in April, led by the man who would organize similar commandos in the next war. Later in the year, the United States Navy laid tens of thousands of mines to block the U-boats from using the north-about passage between Scotland and Norway. This less dramatic job probably played its part in further undermining the morale of the submarine crews already shaken by the loss of sixty-six U-boats in 1917 and by a steadily increasing total in 1918. As usual, the falling war-risk rates indicated the corresponding drop in merchant sinkings, which reached a low of 118,000 tons in October.

Thus the Allies managed to keep the sea lanes open and save England from starvation. But that had been achieved only at heavy cost. The British had lost 7,632,000 tons of shipping; followed by the neutral Norwegians with 1,180,000; the French with 915,000; the Italians with 759,000; the Americans with 339,-

000; and then sixteen other belligerent or neutral nations with lesser losses. The rise and decline of the sinkings are evident from the annual totals: 1914: 319,000; 1915: 1,312,000; 1916: 2,305,000; 1917: 6,078,000; and 1918: 2,528,000. Beyond dispute, the submarine had proven its effectiveness as a commerce destroyer, and one that cost relatively little in man power and money. The U-boats had lost only about five thousand men in destroying more than five thousand ships. Their total of more than eleven million tons of shipping destroyed was ten times as great as that done by mines, and twenty times as great as by surface raiders. Planes, prophetic of the future, had in this war sunk a mere eight thousand tons. But the struggle was not over; twenty-one years later, each side would pick up the fight on the sea lanes again, where they had left it late in 1918.

For the second time in a quarter of a century, the United States became in September, 1939, a neutral spectator of a great war. Once again Germany and England were battling on the sea lanes—but on different terms, for the changed alignment of the powers left England bereft of most of its former allies and pretty much alone.

On the seas, some familiar features were repeated, with slight variation, as both sides applied lessons they had learned from World War I. German liners tried to race to safety through the British cordon. The Royal Navy once again sought to strangle German imports and exports. Both sides laid mines freely; and the struggle of U-boat against convoy was picked up almost where it had been dropped in the fall of 1918. Several new elements, however, made the North Atlantic crossing more risky than it had been in the last war. Surface raiders dared show themselves this time on the "main line" as added threats to convoys. The airplane, too, brought many new complications, such as the risk which merchantmen ran of being bombed while lying in belligerent ports. This last consideration explains why the minimum war-risk rates to west-coast British ports, which had fluctuated around 1 per cent for two whole years in the last war, remained around 5 per cent during the first eight months of the second war, and then doubled.

During the late August days when war clouds were gathering, three great liners, under three soon-to-be belligerent flags, slipped into New York between a Monday evening and the following morning. The old 45,000-ton *Aquitania*, built just as the last war was starting, was berthed next to the 83,000-ton *Normandie*, largest of all the vessels on the seas and one of the fastest; and not far downstream lay the 51,000-ton *Bremen*, also a "blue ribbon" winner when she was new, ten years before. All was set for the three to get off to their return journeys in record time. The North German Lloyd officials were prepared for a record turnabout to put the *Bremen* to sea on the next tide. In nine hours, she was ready; but the customhouse refused clearance papers. Instead, upon orders from Washington, all three ships were thoroughly searched for arms and gun emplacements. On the surface, this might seem like impartiality, but the Germans hotly protested the "outrageous" conduct; and with some cause, for while the British and French liners had little to fear at sea then, rumor placed two British destroyers awaiting the *Bremen* off the port. After two days of search, the clearances were finally granted. The *Normandie* never used hers; she lay more than two years in the North River slip, where her flaming hulk finally settled over on its side. The *Bremen*, with her band playing "Deutschland über alles," bravely sallied forth for one of the most exciting of all transatlantic crossings; the *Aquitania* followed her an hour later. While the *Bremen* plowed along at thirty-two knots, her captain kept his crew perilously suspended over the side, painting her great hull a dull gray. Hearing that there was a British warship every ten miles between Iceland and Ireland, he eluded them by steering northward into the cold and foggy Arctic, to eventual safety in the then friendly Russian port of Murmansk.

On the second day of the war, the westbound passenger liner *Athenia* went down a few hours out from Britain, from mine or U-boat or some mysterious cause; two major units of the

Royal Navy were sunk by submarine within the first weeks; and the war at sea was on at about the tempo of the late months of 1918. The immediate use of convoying this time kept the supply lines from being seriously molested in those early months. The British optimistically announced that sinkings had dropped from 78,000 tons in the first week of the war to 5,000 tons in the fourth. The total for September, 1939, was almost identical with that of September, 1918, when the situation had again been pretty well in hand.

The U-boats seem to have been on their best behavior: "We are not so barbarous, are we? Except that I need a shave," laughingly remarked a sub commander when he stopped an American freighter in September, and allowed her to proceed after inspecting her. Evidently politeness did not pay; a heavy toll of lost U-boats, which approached the record of the fall of 1918, was resulting from the detector devices and increased vigilance.

By October, convoys on the North Atlantic had, for the first time, more than U-boats to worry them, with enemy surface raiders at large on these crowded sea lanes. Germany, stripped of its High Sea Fleet at the close of the last war and forbidden to build any warships over ten thousand tons, had not thrown off the restrictions in time to have enough warships to challenge England to a full-dress action like Jutland. This meant, however, that the Germans no longer had to conserve their battle strength, but could scatter their units to break up convoys.

Besides, the three pocket battleships *Deutschland, Admiral Scheer,* and *Admiral Graf Spee* now presented exactly the same sort of problem to England that the *Constitution* and our other two forty-fours had been in 1812. Both groups were a sort of supercruisers, faster than regular battleships and stronger than ordinary cruisers. They were built within the prescribed 10,000-ton limit, but with clever ingenuity, as much gun power, armor, and speed had been concentrated as could possibly be managed. As a result, it was reckoned that the British and French together had only five warships combining speed enough to match the supposed thirty knots of these cruisers, and armament enough to meet their 11-inch guns. Three such vessels at large could raise havoc with the convoy system. Destroyers or light cruisers had been adequate protection against U-boats as long as they were in sufficient quantity, but such light craft could never singly hope to stand up successfully against a pocket battleship.

By October, it was clear that the *Deutschland* was at work on the Atlantic shuttle, while the two newer vessels were probably operating on remote routes. She gave the United States its first maritime "incident" of the war when she encountered the freighter *City of Flint,* plowing eastward alone from New York to Manchester with a cargo of oil, machinery, and other nonmilitary contraband. The *Deutschland,* in a position to employ the more conventional seizure methods that were impracticable for U-boats, placed an officer and an armed prize crew aboard the *Flint,* and also transferred to her the captured sailors from a British freighter that she had sunk. The *Flint,* however, was not reduced to the status of a full-fledged prize, for her captain was allowed to retain command of the ship but had to follow the directions of the German lieutenant.

This unusual anomalous status was to produce plenty of international headaches, as the *Flint,* under German orders, slid from one northern port to another. She first turned up at a Norwegian port with a Danish flag painted on her side over the Stars and Stripes, but the ruse did not fool the port authorities, and she had to move on quickly. At last, she came to Murmansk where she remained some time while Russians, Germans, and Americans debated her disposal. The German guard, anxious over the probable result of this wrangling, ordered her on her way again to try for refuge in neutral Norway before the Royal Navy caught her; but two small Norwegian naval vessels intercepted her. Instead of eventually reaching a German port with the prize, the German crew found themselves interned in Norway, and the *Flint* free for an eventual safe return to Baltimore.

The *Rawalpindi* had a more tragic encounter with the *Deutschland.* This was a big 16,000-ton P. and O. liner, withdrawn from her warm Suez run and sent to the cold waters of the North Atlantic as an auxiliary cruiser of the British contraband control. Six weeks after seizing the *Flint*, the *Deutschland*, accompanied by a smaller cruiser, came upon the converted liner south of Iceland. The pocket battleship opened fire at ten thousand yards with her 11-inch guns; the *Rawalpindi* bravely replied with the four 6-inch guns of her starboard battery. It was a desperately hopeless encounter, even before the other German warship began pounding her frail hull from the port side. Yet her naval reserve crew fought stoutly on until her last gun was silenced and she was ablaze from bow to stern; only a few of her men got away in boats before she turned turtle and sank. That brave exploit was repeated just a year later, when another converted liner, the *Jervis Bay*, engaged in convoy duty, made a sacrifice play by engaging a pocket battleship at equally hopeless odds, to delay her until the freighters of the convoy could escape.

The presence of these powerful supercruisers on the high seas made it necessary for some of the biggest battleships and battle cruisers of the Royal Navy to devote themselves to convoy duty. Lesser war vessels, moreover, had to cruise in groups to avoid being caught singly by the big raiders. Nevertheless, the pocket battleships, with these precautions scrupulously followed, were unable to accomplish all that had been feared from them.

President Roosevelt, we recall, had worked for the repeal of the Neutrality legislation from the beginning of the war—quite in contrast to President Wilson's injunction of 1914 to the nation to be "neutral in thought as well as in action." A considerable part of Congress had hung back hoping to avoid the complications that had drawn us into war in 1812 and in 1917, but early in November it passed the revisions we have already noted in that law, and thus changed the nation's relationship to those dangerous sea lanes. News of the *Flint's* seizure influenced that regulation by which vessels flying the American flag were definitely barred from the combat zone, as defined by the President. At first this zone included the British Isles and the western coast of the Continent from Bergen, Norway, to the Franco-Spanish frontier. Later, the Mediterranean and, temporarily, the Red Sea were prohibited.

This step, along with the continued ban against Americans traveling on belligerent ships, certainly helped in keeping the nation out of trouble. Not a single ship flying the American flag was sunk during the first year it was in force; and the one that was then destroyed struck a mine off Australia. Not for eighteen months was one sunk by a submarine; and only four had gone to the bottom when the war-zone provisions were repealed. In contrast, in the previous war, when there was a much smaller registered merchant marine, the United States had lost eight vessels during the first two years. To evade the restrictions, some of the American vessels were transferred, as we shall see, to other flags or to safer routes. Lisbon became our chief contact point with Europe during the two years of war-zone restrictions.

Meanwhile, the airways were giving a new safety for transatlantic passenger and mail traffic. Hundreds clogged the waiting lists for passage on the Pan American planes between Lisbon and New York. The demand for the westbound flight was naturally very heavy with the many refugees struggling to get out of Europe. Until our entry into the war, slower and cheaper passage was possible by the American Export liners which early in the war used the Mediterranean ports and were later restricted to Lisbon. Refugees often arrived in those earlier war years after nightmare crossings in foul, over-crowded Spanish steamers, but all who could afford the cost or get accommodations used the clippers. And their security from raiders or U-boats made the transatlantic crossing a much simpler matter than it was in our earlier wars.

While the passenger space in the planes was limited, tens of thousands were paying thirty cents a half ounce to have their mail carried by this fast and safe method. Within two years, 30 per cent of the European mail came by air, with each plane frequently carrying a ton. Among other advantages, this air mail in the beginning avoided the censorship of the British blockade. This immunity did not last long; Pan American quickly arranged a stop at Bermuda, where the censors could legitimately overhaul the mail.

Although as the war continued much military equipment of a pretty heavy sort began to be transported overseas by plane in increasing quantities, ordinary bulky cargoes still generally traveled in the holds or on the decks of freighters. Consequently, even while its own ships were denied access to the war zone, the United States maintained its keen interest in the safe crossings of the British, Norwegian, and other freighters bearing its cargoes.

By the beginning of 1940, that situation seemed fairly well in hand—the *Deutschland* and the magnetic mines to the contrary notwithstanding. The British announced that less than one ship in 750 had been lost out of convoy. In March, the sinkings dropped to about 100,000 tons, about half of what they had been in the first six months. And that was moderate even by the standards of the first war; although it equaled the four-year total of shipping destroyed by Confederate raiders in the Civil War.

The insurance underwriters reflected the general maritime optimism. The New York war-risk rates to west-coast Britain dropped from 6 per cent in December to 3½ per cent early in February. On April 3, the rates reached the lowest general average for the first three years of that war, when the quotations for belligerent trade with outer Scandinavia fell to 3 per cent. Americans were even allowed to trade with northern Norway, which was still outside the banned war zone; and the rate there was 2 per cent.[1]

That Scandinavian reduction was ironic. Six days later, the Germans suddenly swept into Denmark and Norway. Anxious hours followed for the John Street underwriters, for they had insured four millions in gold on an American vessel about to

[1] See p. 246.

sail from a Norwegian port! Two other Norway-bound American freighters on the high seas were ordered to turn around and begin to steam slowly toward New York, while developments were watched. The low rates were, naturally, withdrawn at once, and instead there appeared the danger sign, "Rates quoted only upon application."

The bright maritime outlook of March was black as night by mid-June; the incredible had happened to British sea power. With amazing speed the German blitzkrieg had overrun Denmark and Norway in April, Holland and Belgium in May, and France in early June. And, jeopardizing Mediterranean control, Italy was openly an Axis partner, Mussolini having been "sent in at the last minute to win his letter." The whole western coast of the Continent from the North Cape to the Spanish frontier was under German control—and the peril to general trade was extended to the Mediterranean.

These startlingly sudden changes meant new threats to America's "main line" to England, in various ways that had never imperiled it before, even in 1917. No longer did the U-boats have to operate from their own bases far inside the North Sea. Instead they had their free choice of lairs all along the coast from Norway to the Bay of Biscay. They could even operate from French ports just across the Channel. So, too, could the enemy planes; and aside from their grim opportunity to bomb England, they could blast shipping in its ports and threaten vessels several hundred miles out to sea. German warships, moreover, might now lie in wait in Norwegian or French ports to slip out against the Atlantic shuttle without having to pass the Royal Navy at Scapa Flow or the Straits of Dover. Entries in *Jane's Fighting Ships* indicate that in the terrible week of Dunkerque a German squadron, including the battleships *Scharnhorst* and *Gneisenau*, demolished a British convoy off the Norwegian coast, sinking several of the attendant warships.

Nor was that all. Destroyers, most valuable of antisubmarine weapons, had suddenly become more precious than capital ships

—and at the very moment that England was desperately short of them. During the latter part of World War I, Britain and its allies had 781 of these valuable vessels; during the early part of World War II, Britain and France together had about 250 available for use. But now few of these were left for Britain's hour of need. With most of the French fleet out of the war, and with the loss of a dozen or so destroyers in the "miracle of Dunkerque," along with some sixty more too damaged for immediate use at sea, the Royal Navy was in a bad way. By late summer, it was reported that only sixty destroyers were left for present use in home waters.

The convoy system lost its previous effectiveness and became very sketchy because of this breakdown in destroyer protection. England tried the substitution of seaplanes for a few hundred miles out to sea, but beyond mid-Atlantic these could not fly without refueling, and the convoys had to fend for themselves. The toll of sinkings rose rapidly. The 533,000-ton total for June was presumably swelled by the Dunkerque losses, which included one big Cunarder sunk by a bomb down her stack, and scores of lesser vessels; but the monthly totals for the next five months, with no Dunkerque as an excuse, remained around 400,000 tons, which was four times what they had been in March.

The United States came to the rescue in September with some of its two hundred over-age destroyers. These had been completed around or after the end of the previous war and had been lying idle for years, gaudy in their red-lead paint, at Philadelphia Navy Yard and elsewhere. Many of these old four-stackers were already out of rotten row and on the job again in the neutrality patrol, which the American Republics were already keeping in their own waters. Now, like the fleets of old emergency freighters, these veterans were to prove a godsend in keeping the seas safe for America's cargoes. In exchange for eight western Atlantic colonial bases from Newfoundland down to Guiana, the United States presented England with fifty of these, the first eight arriving at Halifax within a week to take up their strenuous convoy and patrol duties. That was the first of "neutral" America's efforts to protect that most vital of the highways of the seas.

But these fifty destroyers were not enough to restore relative security. To be sure, the sinkings did fall almost down to 300,000 tons in the winter months, only to mount again to 489,-000 in March, to 581,000 in April, and to 461,000 in May. Although these were still less than the tonnage loss of 881,000 tons in April, 1917, it was fully as gloomy a record, because this crisis was longer-protracted than that sharp one, and the total drain on shipping naturally proved greater. The war-risk rate to the west coast of England in July, 1940, had jumped to 10 per cent, which was about the 1917 average; and there it stayed for more than a year.

Meanwhile, the Gibraltar approach to the Mediterranean was almost completely shut to pro-British shipping, except for occasional convoys under heavy naval escort which fought their way through to beleaguered Malta. Everything else had to take the long, time-consuming route around the Cape. By early 1941, it was possible to approach the eastern Mediterranean by way of Suez, at war-risk rates of 15 to 20 per cent, but that passage was cut off when the Germans invaded Greece in April. The heaviest loss yet sustained by the New York underwriters was a three-million-dollar cargo of Turkish tobacco in a Greek steamer bombed at Peiraeus.

Spring also brought the worst surface threat thus far to the North Atlantic route. It was not a 10,000-ton pocket battleship this time, but the mighty *Bismarck*, suspected of being even mightier than her advertised 35,000 tons, reputedly unsinkable, and probably the most powerful warship afloat. The R.A.F., which tried to keep constant check on the German warships, suddenly found her missing from her Norwegian base. Such a ship could undoubtedly batter any convoy escort into submission and demolish the merchantmen. An American revenue cutter spotted her at last in the cold waters between Greenland and Iceland. The Royal Navy was quickly on the scene, but its greatest ship, the 42,000-ton *Hood*, went down when one shell from the *Bismarck* exploded her magazine; the powerful new 35,000-ton *Prince of Wales* withdrew badly mauled; and the *Bismarck* and her consort went their way.

Rarely has the North Atlantic been more perilous than with the *Bismarck* at large. The British summoned everything they had for the chase, and four hundred miles from the French coast, a flying boat spotted the *Bismarck* and called on the pack. British bombers had cut down her speed with aerial torpedoes, and British warships pounded her tough hull until her guns were silenced. A torpedo from a cruiser gave her the *coup de grâce* and sent her to the bottom. The British—and the neutral Americans too—breathed more freely. But she had a sister ship, the *Tirpitz,* almost ready for sea.

Neutrality was wearing thin by the spring of 1941. The situation on the seas was drawing the United States steadily closer to war. Hitler had declared in January,

> Whoever believes he will be able to help England must definitely know one thing: every ship, whether with or without convoy, that comes before our torpedo tubes will be torpedoed.

The answer was lease-lend, we recall, and President Roosevelt's frequently reiterated determination to "deliver the goods." The old principle of "freedom of the seas" had by now been radically curtailed from its wide scope in Jefferson's or even in Wilson's day. No longer did we seek the right to trade freely with everyone in wartime; all we tried to do was to enjoin one belligerent from interfering with our shipments of out-and-out contraband to the other.

With March, came the announcement of a protectorate over Greenland, already long occupied. May, saw the first American ship sunk by a U-boat, down in the South Atlantic. In July, American troops were sent to Iceland, which the British had taken into "protective custody" after the Germans had invaded Denmark. The United States Navy took on the job of the western Atlantic sea lanes and began to patrol outside its own waters.

This permitted the British to concentrate on the final dangerous stretch between Iceland and Ireland.

Evidently, by summer, the Germans found that home stretch to be too hot for comfort. By now, the British had some three hundred escort vessels, including destroyers and small, quickly built corvettes. The big American-built flying boats, now used by the British, had a cruising radius of several thousand miles, which made it possible to extend protection far out to sea. Smaller planes of the R.A.F.'s Coastal Command and the Royal Navy's Fleet Air Arm maintained incessant vigil in the waters just west of the British Isles. Not only were they on the alert for raiders and U-boats, but they were prepared to drive off any enemy planes that might be scouting for potential victims for those U-boats and raiders.

The Germans, finding that their old hunting grounds were no longer what they used to be, created a new danger zone between Greenland and Iceland. That was where the Americans got their first big crop of "incidents" in the late summer and early fall of 1941. At first, the neutral American warships simply acted as an "informational patrol" in those waters, spotting the presence of the enemy but calling up British warships or planes to do the actual fighting. That moderate concession to neutrality was abandoned in early September, a week after a U-boat tried to torpedo the American destroyer *Greer,* carrying mail from Portland to Iceland.

We were in the war on the Atlantic at last—although in a somewhat informal manner. Closely following the precedent of the "undeclared war" of 1798, President Roosevelt issued "shoot-on-sight" orders to the navy. No information was given about the number of U-boats attacked or sunk by American destroyers; but the newspapers that autumn told how the Germans were doing some shooting at sight on their own. In October, a torpedo ripped into the side of the destroyer *Kearney,* killing ten men. No destroyer was expected to survive such a blow, but the *Kearney* was a new ship, much stronger than the old "tin cans," and she managed to limp to port for repairs. An old four-stacker, the *Reuben James,* fared less fortunately a few weeks later; an almost identical torpedo wound sent her quickly to the bottom with more than half of her officers and crew.

Although merchantmen under the Stars and Stripes were not allowed on the dangerous Atlantic crossing, that did not prevent newspaper headlines from reporting sinkings of "U. S.-owned Ships," when four seized Danish freighters, operated by the United States Maritime Commission but flying the flag of Panama, were torpedoed near Iceland. Early in September, a naval vessel picked up a raft with three half-frozen survivors of the first of those victims, the *Sessa,* torpedoed in August. They had buried three of their companions at sea and twenty-one others had perished in the sinking.

The American public, reading with dismay of the sudden crop of attacks on their destroyers and Panamanian freighters, did not realize that the thoroughgoing precautions of the new elaborate convoy system, that we have already noted, were restoring safety to the Atlantic shuttle. After July, moreover, the British stopped publishing the statistics of monthly sinkings; that gave the impression that matters were growing worse for Atlantic shipping. Actually the situation was constantly improving. In November, Prime Minister Churchill announced that the sinkings from July through October had been only 180,000 tons a month on the average—which was what they had been in the relatively comfortable early period of the war—whereas they had averaged 500,000 tons a month in the previous four-month period. After more than a year at 10 per cent, the war-risk rate reflected this by dropping to 7½ per cent to west-coast Britain.

The British were further heartened by the repeal of the Neutrality Act restrictions, which had kept American vessels out of the war zone and had kept them from being armed. Grave warnings were sounded that removal of the restrictions would soon find us involved in a two-ocean war Thus was the Neutrality Act of 1935 gradually whittled away. American citizens, however, were still denied permission to sail on belligerent vessels. Naval guns were soon being hoisted onto the sterns of freighters,

but scarcely one of them had a chance to try her new liberty
in the war zone before neutrality was over.

On December 7, Japan attacked at Pearl Harbor; four days
later, Germany and Italy declared war upon the United States.
The predicted two-ocean war had come; but our projected two-
ocean navy was still far from reality.

The situation on the seas, which had been so favorable during
the summer and autumn, suddenly went bad. The "undeclared
war," in which the United States Navy had taken over the
western end of the Atlantic run, had definitely helped to reduce
the sinkings. But now, as an out-and-out belligerent, we found
the enemy trying to distract our warships from the cold Iceland
waters where they had been doing so well. Before we had been
in the war six weeks, enemy submarines were actually sinking
American vessels within sight of both the Atlantic and Pacific
coasts.

The Japanese submarines on the West Coast, as we shall see
later, were but a flash in the pan in those early days of our war,
but the Germans were in top form. Those who anticipated simply a repetition of the previous hit-and-run forays in the western Atlantic were quickly disillusioned. In the course of the five
months of the 1918 raiding, only at one brief period were as
many as three U-boats operating simultaneously, whereas 1942
would see several dozen or so steadily on the station, including,
perhaps, some Italians. The 1918 victims included only thirty
seagoing steamships, most of them fairly small, as compared with
about five hundred in the first nine months of the 1942 campaign. The earlier visits had simply provided a series of spectacular scares; the new ones seriously disorganized shipping in
American waters.

The U-boats concentrated at first upon the tanker fleet. Such
an objective brought the war close home to millions of Americans in short order. The tankers, most important of the constant procession of vessels up and down the Atlantic coast,
were the only remaining flourishing branch of our once-busy

coastwise shipping. These attacks helped to deprive eastern motorists of their "gas" and householders of their fuel oil, but those were minor considerations to the Germans. Their interest was the destruction of the type of vessel needed all over the world by the United Nations for cargoes of high strategic significance; and, moreover, tankers were relatively more difficult to replace than ordinary freighters.

In normal times, more than three hundred of these big "oil cans," some carrying heavy crude or fuel oil and others inflammable gasoline, were engaged in this coastwise trade. A tanker's average capacity was equal to some 450 railroad tank cars; and delivery by this method cost but a fraction of the rail haul. During the war period, they were not only supplying domestic needs, but also, to conserve shipping, were bringing large quantities to New York to be shipped overseas to England and elsewhere in foreign tankers. Two-fifths of all the nation's oil consumption was concentrated in that eastern seaboard; and 95 per cent of the supply came in tankers, mostly from ports along the Gulf, with a little from the Caribbean fields. The big tankers rounded Florida to eleven major ports, from Jacksonville, Florida, to Portland, Maine. Lesser tankers distributed the oil to the smaller ports, while interior points were served by tank cars or pipe lines. Two trips a month from the Gulf to "north of Hatteras" was the usual tanker progress; the average ship, it was reported, could keep some 100,000 automobiles supplied with "gas."

On January 14, 1942, five weeks after Pearl Harbor, a torpedo crashed in the night into the side of the big Norwegian-Panamanian tanker *Norness,* some sixty miles from the eastern end of Long Island. The attack was on. With no time to fire their 3-inch gun, the crew rushed to the lifeboats, while two more torpedoes finished the ship. Naval planes sighted the freezing survivors shortly after dawn, and the Coast Guard rescued them. Five days later, two torpedoes ripped the big tanker *Allan Jackson* in two. The thirteen survivors of the thirty-five-man crew horrified the nation upon their landing at Norfolk with their tale of men burning to death on deck and screaming as the life-boat pulled away, unable to get to them through the flames. A month later, eighteen survived from the *Pan-Massachusetts* by struggling through burning seas to a rescuing vessel, some of them looking "as if they had been roasted over an open grill." It was the same grim story from the *India Arrow*, while only two survived when the big *R. P. Resor* blazed for hours in full sight of horror-stricken crowds at Asbury Park on the Jersey coast, for no boat could get anywhere near that inferno of flames.

Submarine warfare had imposed new and intense suffering upon many of its victims, but none of the tortures equaled the agony of being caught by an ignited gasoline cargo, with blazing seas often cutting off the last hope of rescue. These men expected to brave danger to get vital supplies across the seas, but not to supply home motorists with their usual conveniences. Nor could the United Nations afford the loss of those essential vessels on that perilous coastal run. Their need was growing daily for every tanker afloat to carry oil to distant points, cut off from their usual supply by Japanese advances in the Far East. The tanker sinkings, appallingly numerous during the first two months of 1942, gradually grew less. This resulted partly from increased protections and precautions, but more from the actual removal of those precious ships from that dangerous service. Millions of motorists in the eastern states soon felt the impact of the U-boat raiding when they were placed on radically short gasoline rations in May. Unlike rubber, which was being cut off in the Orient, oil was for the time being abundant in the United States, but the Texas wells were a long, long way from the eastern seaboard, which had to bear the full brunt of the situation while alternatives were being discussed. As the summer advanced, the possible loss of Russia's oil fields threatened new burdens upon our tankers.

Just as the tanker sinkings fell off in late winter, so too did operations within sight of the Jersey boardwalks. That, however, did not mean a slackening of U-boat activity—far from it. The submarines simply spread out in their quest for victims, operating in more remote waters, and taking freighters or liners if tankers were no longer to be had. Several times within a year they shifted their main hunting grounds when the Anglo-American defenses grew too effective. The danger zone had moved successively from the waters just west of Britain to the seas south of Iceland, and then to the middle section of our coast between New York and Hatteras. The less protected sections of the western Atlantic caught it next—Canadian waters; our southern coast; the Gulf of Mexico; and, above all, the Caribbean, where bottleneck entrances had been scenes of maritime violence for centuries. In late summer, the submarines seemed to be moving into the South Atlantic, to the old raiding grounds off Brazil.

The full seriousness of the situation slowly dawned upon the Americans. By mid-March, our navy ceased to reveal the names and tonnage of the victims. Day after day, however, it disclosed circumstantial stories of the fate of some "large British passenger ship," "medium-sized American cargo ship," or "small Norwegian freighter." This information was limited to sinkings in the western Atlantic alone, aside from what might be happening on the Arctic run to Russia, in the Mediterranean or Middle East, in Far Eastern waters, or elsewhere on the seas. The local total, however, was bad enough, and what was more, it grew steadily worse. From mid-January to the end of February, the announced western Atlantic sinkings averaged about one a day; in March and April, two a day; and in May, three a day instead of the hoped-for falling off. By mid-June, the total passed three hundred; in late July came news of the four hundredth. Then such news slowed down. By late September, the announced total was 481; when the whole story is out, the score will doubtless be higher and those figures may be too incomplete to be taken seriously. Meanwhile, our shipyards were finally overtaking the sinkings, delivering in those nine months 460 steamships, averaging considerably greater tonnage than the vessels reported lost.

There was a certain grim sameness to most of those stories gathered from survivors who had drifted for days or even for weeks in lifeboats, but the tales were never identical. By no means did all survive; thousands were reported killed or missing by September. Some were killed below deck by the explosion; some were caught by a spray of machine-gun bullets even after they were in the lifeboats; some perished from thirst or unattended wounds in the long days adrift, or went mad and jumped overboard. One little girl was found in the arms of her dead mother; in another boat from that same liner, the injured doctor helped to bring a baby into the world. Sometimes the victims fought back; one freighter tried to ram the U-boat which had given her a mortal wound. More than one gun crew stuck to its post, while the water lapped over the deck, trying to pump shells into the aggressor. Though some submarine commanders showed a callous brutality, others offered rum, cigarettes, and sailing directions to the boatloads of survivors. One gave clothing to a naked sailor, while another seaman received surgical attention aboard the U-boat for his wounds.

On the whole, the submarines stuck to the business of sinking without the melodramatic stunting of the 1918 pioneers. There were, however, a few exceptions. The Caribbean terror started with a shelling of the oil establishments on the Dutch island of Aruba just off the Venezuelan coast. Later, a U-boat sank a United Fruit liner in a Costa Rican port. A few mines were apparently laid, but not many. A coastguardman, on his lonely night patrol of a foggy Long Island beach, stumbled upon some Germans landing from a U-boat; investigation revealed a cache of explosives, and a group of trained saboteurs with ambitiously destructive plans were rounded up. At the same time, the F.B.I. caught a similar group landed from a submarine on the Florida coast. Suspicions that the U-boats received supplies without having to return home were confirmed when a keen-eyed aviator's observations led to the arrest in British Honduras of the renegade "King of Belize" whose Caribbean schooners were furnishing oil. He had also learned through his connection with Panama dancehall girls details about sailings and destinations of merchantmen.

Naturally, the Americans began to wonder why our navy did not do something about all this. It had ships enough to have given adequate protection in home waters, but they had more important duties elsewhere. The destroyers, cruisers and battleships were keeping the North Atlantic "main line" so safe that one huge convoy after another was delivering a big A.E.F. intact in northern Ireland. They were giving less complete but highly valuable protection on the perilous North Cape run where, as we shall see, the huge *Tirpitz* and other big warships, along with planes and submarines, were threatening in flank that vital supply line to Russia. They were keeping open the still longer route across the Pacific to Australia, while Japanese operations elsewhere also called insistently for their presence. It would have served the Axis purpose well to have withdrawn many of the more important warships from those essential missions.

Home protection, therefore, would have to await a more adequate supply of smaller patrol boats and "blimps"; plenty were "on order," but for the moment the navy was caught short. It issued a few safety regulations to reduce the dangers of night attacks—coastal towns, for instance, were ordered to dim their lights so that ships would not be silhouetted as targets. Such force as was available was concentrated on the vital middle stretch where the attacks had started; that was why the Germans moved farther afield. By mid-May, the navy was providing regular convoy service along the coast. One never-to-be-forgotten sight came at the end of a long day on the Jersey coast during which the horizon, usually broken with a constant procession of passing shipping, had revealed nothing but one little tug with a lone barge. Then suddenly, from around Sea Girt appeared a long procession—sixteen gray ships in a row—tankers in the van, a few new cargo freighters, an old tramp or two, a passenger ship, a collier, and then more tankers bringing up the rear. Out in front were three little patrol boats, and overhead a "blimp" moved lazily up and down the column, its silver sides glistening in the late sun, ready to drop depth bombs should a submarine appear. Next morning, a similar convoy would move southward, and so it went day after day. That was why the Secretary of the Navy could remark in July that despite the continued heavy total of sinkings, not many had occurred of late within fifty miles of our coast. As more patrol boats became available, similar convoys were established in the Caribbean, but still the lone ships went down.

The official naval account of the 1918 U-boat raids ended with the remark, "There was no stampede on the Atlantic coast; no excitement; everything went on in the usual calm way." No stampede accompanied this later, heavier attack, but shipping routines were severely disrupted. The tanker traffic, as we saw, was radically reduced. Tank cars began to roll eastward; pipe-line connections were improvised; and barges were pressed into service, and new ones built, to utilize the protected inland waterway which runs along the whole coast from Texas to Cape Cod, except for Florida and New Jersey. The coal trade from Hampton Roads to New York and New England was likewise jeopardized; once more one saw the tows of barges which had been so popular years before. To relieve the congestion at New York, much of our Latin-American traffic was being diverted to New Orleans about the time the U-boats entered the Gulf; trade with the republics to the southward was badly disorganized. Meanwhile the western Atlantic sinkings were virtually nullifying our ambitious building program designed to relieve the desperate shipping shortage.

Those of us who had followed the war-risk insurance barometer whistled with amazement at the steady climb of the rates on these local runs. During most of the war, the underwriters had given 2000 to 1 odds for voyages along the coast, and 1000 to 1 for South America. By mid-July, the quotation from the Gulf to New York was 15 per cent, which was double the rate from San Francisco to Melbourne, and half again the rate to west-coast Britain. Between Norfolk and Boston, despite the navy's claims of safety, it cost that same 15 per cent to insure barges, 12½ per cent for steamships and 7½ per cent, the Australian rate, if vessels traveled by the protected inland waterway! Even when the Confederates had been raiding the coast in 1863, the rate was only 4 per cent, while 5 per cent was the short-lived maximum when the news first broke in 1918. To Rio, the rate was 20 per cent, the same as for the Red Sea or Persian Gulf. During the latter half of August, U-boat activities in the South Atlantic temporarily added an extra 5 per cent on those last three runs, already abnormally high.

The U-boats in the western Atlantic had put the New York underwriters in the red. Up to the end of 1941, they had received $85,252,000 in premiums and had paid $40,219,000 in losses, leaving a profit of $45,032,000. In the first five months of 1942, with premiums of $54,872,000 and losses of $101,358,000, their deficit of $46,486,000 more than wiped out the former profits, leaving them well over a million dollars in arrears. Most of those losses had been sustained in insuring hulls by the month in home waters, hitherto regarded as so safe. The underwriters soon left hull insurance to the government and boosted their cargo rates to the highest levels yet seen in the two wars.

By the late summer of 1942, the Secretary of the Navy, the First Lord of Admiralty, and Prime Minister Churchill were all commenting on the improved situation. Even Admiral Doenitz, the German submarine chief, added his testimony to that effect. "In spite of heavy losses in warlike operations, such as Russian and Malta convoys," sinkings were falling off rapidly, and it began to look as if new construction was overtaking them. The increased protection in American waters was the main cause for congratulation. Out of two thousand ships convoyed in three months, only five were lost. The record on the "main line" to England was almost identical, only eight out of 2,400. What was more, the destruction of U-boats was heavier than at any previous time in the war, for patrol boats were increasing steadily in number and the R.A.F. was bombing the assembly plants and yards where new subs were being fashioned. It was comforting to know that the spring crisis had been relieved, but men recalled that there had been similar optimism in March, 1940, and in November, 1941, just before new storms broke. Secretary Knox hinted at possible new dangers: "The minute you make it tough for the German U-boats along our coasts and off the British Isles, they hunt new areas—the high seas far from land."

Now and then one sees a little gray freighter, loaded deep and with a few planes aboard as deck cargo, stand out to sea for some unknown destination. As she ventures out onto the dangerous sea lanes, one watches her sturdy progress down the harbor with a tribute to the men brave enough to sail her and a hope that she will escape the lurking perils. The underwriters may be quoting pretty short odds on her safe arrival, but at least they are better than even. Whatever those risks may be, Axis shipping definitely faces far graver difficulties. Its communications with Norway and North Africa receive constant punishment, but it manages to sneak a "trickle" of traffic between Germany and Japan by way of Cape Horn. One can imagine, though, how any private insurance office would react if asked to underwrite a German ship from Hamburg to Buenos Aires or an Italian vessel from Genoa to Rio.

Chapter X

Distant Sea Lanes

ALTHOUGH THE NORTH ATLANTIC SHUTTLE LOOMED PREDOMINANT in the two World Wars, American vessels and cargoes found plenty of maritime adventure on other more distant routes, from the Arctic to the South Seas. Not only that, but events in some of those faraway seas permanently affected American shipping. Our vessels took over many routes during wartime dislocations of trade and altered them to suit American purposes.

War on all those routes assumed a different form from conditions on the "main line." Instead of the constant grueling battle of U-boat against convoy, brief periods of dramatic raiding broke long stretches of comparative serenity. The commercial contrast was equally great. Whereas the normal imports and exports of the trade with western Europe gave way to an abnormal eastbound rush of war materials, the intercourse with the other continents, until mid-1941, saw a more regular interchange of commodities. As for the efforts to supply Russia by the Arctic, Pacific, and Indian Oceans, they created special problems of their own. As the second war progressed, the situation changed with the spread of the fighting; and the cargoes on distant routes assumed greater strategic importance as the armies and navies shifted their major theaters of action away from western Europe.

The routes from our East Coast ports by way of the Cape of Good Hope and the Panama Canal grew in importance in each war, not only for through traffic to the Far East, but also for offshoots of that trade branching off toward ports in other regions. By an odd coincidence of geography, there was little to choose between the two routes in distance. A vessel from New York to Singapore, for instance, traveled 14,290 miles if she went by way of the Cape of Good Hope, and only 130 miles farther if she sailed in the opposite direction through the Canal and across the Pacific. The Cape run also tapped the increased commercial possibilities of the eastern South American ports, as well as those of Africa. As soon as Suez became dangerous in wartime, that route was used to reach Egypt and the Persian Gulf. The new Panama route—the canal was opened in 1914—started from our East Coast down through the Caribbean, and then once a ship was through the canal, offered vastly better contact than ever before with Peru, Chile, New Zealand, and Australia.

Of the other three sea routes to the Orient, the Suez short cut through the Mediterranean soon became unsafe for general use in both wars. The direct transpacific run from San Francisco, Seattle, and other West Coast ports had normal, steady business until accelerated by lease-lend and A.E.F. supplies in World War II. The stormy old Cape Horn passage was still occasionally used by sailing vessels whose cargoes were not valuable enough to warrant Canal tolls. Except for the Arctic routes to Russia, the rest of the seven seas did not matter much; enemy raiders and American traders would find their best picking along those better traveled lines, especially by Cape and Canal.

The enemy lost no time in striking. Those remote seas were the main scene of raiding during the first six months of the first war when the North Atlantic was still safe. German cruisers, regular or converted, played hide-and-seek with the Royal Navy. They sank numbers of British freighters, some of which were carrying cargoes to or from American ports. The surface raiders were the chief source of danger at the time. Altogether they sank 203,000 tons of British shipping in 1914, as compared with 35,000 tons sunk by mines and not quite 3,000 by submarines. The war-risk rates on belligerent shipping assumed a "cruiser pattern," radically different from the later part of the war but almost identical with the days of the *Alabama*. In late September, the premiums on those distant runs stood briefly at the identical

7½ per cent which they had been in June, 1863, when Confederate raiding was in its heyday.

The Germans had only eight regular cruisers at large outside of European waters when the war started; the Allies feared that many of their fast liners might also be armed for commerce destruction. Actually only two had any real measure of success in those distant regions. To oppose those ten vessels, Britain had many times that number, but they had to be spread out pretty thin over the eighteen thousand miles of sea essential to the Empire's communications.

These rival warships were playing the old game of sea raiding as practiced fifty years before when Semmes was hunting Yankee clippers—and Union cruisers were hunting Semmes. The Germans had studied the Confederate raider's memoirs carefully. They revisited some of his old haunts, and, with the usual painstaking German thoroughness, improved upon the coaling system that had given him so much trouble. But the British cruisers had one advantage over the Union warships that had so often lost the scent because of stale information. The wireless now was able to spread the alarm and make easier the final roundup. Even wireless, however, was not able immediately to strip away all the mysteries of the German whereabouts; and the Admiralty put in a good many anxious days. So too did the insurance underwriters and the ships at sea during those six months. The Germans, also well aware that the damage inflicted by cruiser warfare was not limited to actual sinkings, hoped to paralyze a considerable part of the British merchant marine in port.

That actually happened; but, to the German disappointment, for only a few brief periods. Rumors of imaginary German raiders kept shipping tied up briefly, we recall, in our Atlantic ports, but on the West Coast there was the very real presence of the cruiser *Leipzig*. She was stronger than any British or Canadian naval forces in the neighborhood, and that fact kept two dozen British freighters in port at San Francisco, and others elsewhere along the coast.

The *Leipzig* soon disappeared, which in a way was yet more nerve-racking. It was correctly suspected that she had gone to join Admiral Count von Spee; and no one knew where he was. He had slipped out of the German base in China with part of his Asiatic squadron just before the war started, and had simply vanished from sight for weeks. Early in November, grim news for England told the world of Admiral Spee's whereabouts. A British admiral with the entire 1,650 men of two cruisers had gone to the bottom after a brief unequal fight with Spee's squadron off Coronel on the Chilean coast. Hopelessly outmatched, the British did not have a chance. Silhouetted against the setting sun, they were helpless targets; only two Germans were even wounded.

By that time, shipping on both sides of South America was in real danger. The west-coast traffic was light, but if Spee should come around into the South Atlantic, he could threaten a major part of Britain's meat supply—not only the beef from the Plata, but also the New Zealand mutton cargoes traveling by way of Cape Horn. During November, fear held many British vessels at Buenos Aires as well as at other ports, for a squadron of the size of Spee's could snap up freighters by the score. A big British battle cruiser rushed across the Atlantic to lie in wait for the Germans if they tried to use the Panama Canal, while two others hurried south to block the approach by the Straits of Magellan or around Cape Horn. Spee stumbled upon the latter pair by chance as they lay coaling at the Falkland Islands accompanied by several ordinary cruisers. He fled to sea, but was overtaken. Hopelessly outclassed in his turn, Spee signaled his squadron, "It is my wish and belief that you will conduct yourselves with a gallantry equal to that of Admiral Cradock and his men off Coronel." Fighting stubbornly, Count Spee and 2,100 men of four of his cruisers went down, five weeks after his victory at Coronel. The fifth cruiser was finally tracked down off the bleak coast of southern Chile.

Although that powerful squadron had thrown a bad scare into naval and shipping circles, the damage actually done to merchantmen was far less than that inflicted by the other five German ships that were operating singly. Most spectacular of those was the *Emden*. In two months of wild raiding in the Indian Ocean, she inflicted eleven million dollars' worth of damage on shipping. She sank sixteen steamships, besides setting oil tanks afire at Madras and destroying two light Allied warships in a bold attack on Penang. Indirectly she accomplished much more damage: the fear she inspired paralyzed shipping at Calcutta and other ports. Perishable cargoes clogged the docks, and ships lay at anchor, not daring to put to sea. An Australian cruiser put an end to her formidable career early in November. But that stoppage of the Indian shipping bothered the United States very slightly. The *Emden,* moreover, released one British steamer bound from Calcutta for New York because her cargo was American-owned. Nor was the United States much affected by the brief and sterile career of the *Königsberg,* which was soon bottled up in an East African river.

It was a different story with the three others which operated in the old Confederate hunting ground in the South Atlantic. The cruiser *Karlsruhe* had sunk seventeen vessels—worth, with their cargoes, some five million dollars—when a mysterious magazine explosion blew her up off Barbados. The *Kronprinz Wilhelm* had been a liner that deliberately left New York at the very moment in August when the *Cecelie* and others were fleeing toward such havens. She took on an extraordinary amount of coal and ship's stores, and with a suspicious, huge, wooden case on her bow, had slipped out past Sandy Hook. She transferred part of her extra supplies to the *Karlsruhe* at sea, receiving guns in return, and as a naval auxiliary cruiser herself, turned to commerce raiding. Another converted liner at the same job was the *Prinz Eitel Friedrich,* which had left China to join Admiral Spee. She later managed to remain unmolested on the Chilean coast—talking to herself by wireless to fool the British—while he went to his death in the Atlantic.

Between them, the three ships sank some forty vessels in the South Atlantic alone. At least seven of their victims were bound to or from American ports. The news of the sinking of the *Indian Prince* from Brazil caused the price of rubber to jump two cents a pound on the New York market. A big refrigerator liner carrying beef from the Argentine, a ship loaded with nitrates and silver ore from Chile, two coal cargoes from Norfolk for Rio, and a tramp with mixed freight for South American ports shared a like fate. Above all, the *Prinz Eitel Friedrich* sank the first American ship of that war off Brazil late in January.

Coming north from Cape Horn, she met several big sailing vessels, including the four-masted Maine ship *William P. Frye,* built and owned by the Sewalls of Bath. She was bound from Seattle to Queenstown with a $300,000 cargo of wheat. At first, the Germans decided merely to shovel her grain into the sea to keep it from the British and let the schooner proceed without her cargo. This turned out to be a slower and more tedious task than they had expected, and the decision was made to sink her after all. And one more lively diplomatic controversy was begun.

In the spring, the *Eitel Friedrich,* and a month later the *Kronprinz Wilhelm,* put into Hampton Roads in need of supplies and repairs. The result was their internment and the end of the first crop of German raiders. When they put to sea again, they had become the United States auxiliary cruisers *De Kalb* and *Von Steuben.* Three other raiders, the *Moewe,* the *Wolf,* and the *Seeadler,* would later play lone but menacing roles on various distant routes; but they did not revive the terror of those early weeks when Spee was at large, the *Emden* was raising havoc in the Indian Ocean, and one freighter after another was being caught off South America.

The 7½ per cent panic war-risk rates of September, 1914, for belligerent shipping on distant runs had dropped to amazingly low levels by the spring of 1915 when the last of the early raiders had left the seas.[1] Cargo in a British ship could be insured from New York to the Far East by the Cape of Good Hope or even

[1] See p. 244.

the soon-to-be-dangerous Suez route at odds of around 200 to 1 for safely avoiding war risks. The Pacific crossing from the East Coast by Panama was rated twice as safe. By summer, the direct transpacific route was covered at 1000 to 1 even under a belligerent flag. American vessels could go almost anywhere outside European waters at that bargain rate—to the Orient by any of the four routes or anywhere around Latin America. For three months in mid-1916 the Pacific crossings or South American runs stood at 2000 to 1 for shipping under the Stars and Stripes. Shippers, it was remarked, would not have even bothered with war-risk insurance on the Pacific had not the banks insisted on the formality of such coverage. For the whole of the first World War when Japan was an ally (and even for the second World War until after Pearl Harbor), the Pacific rates averaged less than 2 per cent for belligerent shipping and considerably less than 1 per cent for American vessels while still neutral. The same was true of the run to Rio. War risks, obviously, were not based on distance.

This happy situation presented several remarkable openings to American importers, exporters, and shipowners which they were not slow to capitalize. Had we had more ships, we could have taken even greater advantage of them. It was the United States' golden opportunity for the development of direct trade to its own shores. With England distracted and Germany out of the commercial picture, we could increase our trade directly with South America, Africa, Asia, and islands of the South Pacific; and so could be the source of much that they had formerly received from Europe.

The resultant shifting of sea lanes in our favor was to have permanent importance. The strain of war broke up the artificial network built by the British so that they could collect toll from a considerable portion of the world's commerce as it passed briefly over the docks of London. That city was the entrepôt of much of the world's trade, until toppled from that position by our profitable use of wartime dislocations of commerce. The

British lines of freighters had provided regular service to almost every worth-while port in the world. The cargoes that they brought from distant seas were broken up at London and shipped off, along with England's domestic offerings, in many other directions. There was good money in that system; shipping earnings, insurance premiums, port expenses, commissions, discounts, and the like, ran into substantial totals for British pocketbooks.

It mattered not that cargoes often had to travel thousands of extra miles to reach their destinations. As long as a considerable part of those cargoes had been produced by British capital transplanted overseas, it was the British who could pretty well decide by what routes they would travel. They had proved apt pupils of the Dutch, who had demonstrated at Amsterdam in earlier days the rich possibilities of the entrepôt game. The Germans had developed some competition at Hamburg and Bremen before the war, but England's re-export business had jumped from a third of a billion dollars in 1900 to a full half billion in 1910. This was almost exactly equal to its huge exports of Lancashire cotton goods.

Regular line service under the American flag was extremely scanty to foreign ports outside the Caribbean. Between that lack of liners and the British entrepôt system, the United States in 1914 was receiving most of its Far Eastern rubber and tin, Australian and South African wool, Indian and Ceylon tea, as well as much else from the far corners of the world, by way of the port of London. Even bulky Honduras mahogany generally crossed the Atlantic twice to reach our ports. Our own exports also were apt to follow the same roundabout route and thus reach their destinations via London. Unless one had cargo enough to warrant the chartering of a whole ship, it was often easier to trade with the Argentine and Chile by way of London than to wait for the chance sailing of some tramp.

The U-boats, in their operations around the British Isles, did more to break up that London entrepôt and shift the American sea lanes than anything else. By 1917, it was sheer folly, whatever the inducement, to send a cargo twice through the danger zone when it could travel safely on other routes thousands of miles away from the perils of war. At times, when 20 to 25 per cent was the rate for a cargo from Singapore to New York by way of England, it could go for a hundredth of that by the Cape of Good Hope or the Panama Canal. Less directly, the submarines further hastened the shift of sea lanes by creating a serious shipping shortage. Ships were too precious to be placed in jeopardy even if insurers were ready to stand the huge difference in costs. Their carrying capacity was too much needed to allow it to be tied up needlessly for those extended trips of extra thousands of miles. By 1917, the shortage was forcing England to withdraw much of its shipping from distant commercial runs for emergency service in the war zone.

Another factor was the opening of the Panama Canal in August, 1914, two weeks after the war started. Unquestionably, war or no war, the new canal would have done something to shift the sea lanes even in normal times, for it brought our East Coast much closer to the ports of the west coast of South America, as well as to ports across the Pacific. Its effect cannot be entirely disentangled from the general war conditions, for the shift of sea routes did not become extreme until the U-boats really went into unrestricted action in 1917.

The Americans were not slow in appreciating the new trade opportunities opened to them. The commercial journals and the official publications of the Department of Commerce were full of the roseate prospects all through the war. New steamship lines to the Argentine and Australia were urged; so too was the need for shoes in Brazil and New Zealand, of colored cloth in Burma, and of lumber in South Africa. So the story went, week after week, month after month. In 1939, a similar situation would find us with ships enough to take the advantage, but in 1914 and even in 1917, our merchant marine was too small; and freight rates were terrific, even on the sailing vessels that were pressed into service by the hundreds.

Yet even with that handicap, American traders and shipowners did pretty well. Our trade with South America, Africa, Asia, and the Pacific islands showed a threefold increase between the last year of peace and the fourth year of the war. Direct imports, representing in part the breakdown of the London entrepôt, rose from 470 to 1,615 millions; while direct exports, reflecting to some extent the emergency markets for American wares, jumped from 350 to 950 millions.

Strange to say, the shipping that carried that trade actually fell off slightly. The number of vessels arriving from those regions dropped from 2,529 to 2,392, and their net tonnage from 6,416,000 to 5,177,000. There was, however, a marked shift in the flags they flew. American steamships increased from 84 to 472, and Yankee "windjammers" from 149 to 393. Our biggest steamship gain was in the South American trade, where the number rose from 26 to 350, while our sailing vessels increased from 51 to 167, on the longer routes to Africa and to the South Seas.

The wool trade was one of the striking examples of the breakup of the London entrepôt. In the last year of peace, one-third of all the wool imported into the United States was brought from England, but little of it had been grown there. Instead, it came to London from the Argentine, South Africa, Australia, and New Zealand. Four years later, only one-three hundredths of our wool imports were from England. We now got our wool direct from the countries that produced it, with no roundabout delays by way of the entrepôt. The direct imports from the Argentine had jumped from 30 to 161 millions, and from South Africa a hundredfold, to 55 millions. The shipments from Australia and New Zealand rose from 27 millions to 66 in the first year of the war and hit 174 in the second, only to fall away sharply after freight rates became too stiff on that long haul.

The century-old scramble to "sell South America" had never found the United States in a better position to forge ahead. The Caribbean situation was fairly well in hand, but the Argentine was always a tough customer. It lay about as far distant from New York as from England or Germany; and those nations wanted its meat and wheat. Even when the United States did sell automobiles and typewriters there or buy wool in return, they had both too often traveled by way of London. Now the direct trade down to Buenos Aires rose fourfold, while the number of American vessels so employed jumped from three to sixty-three.

In the first war, as in the next, the Latin-American trade was in a privileged class by itself. Even when the acute shipping shortages in 1917-18, as again in 1941-42, meant that private trading was pretty well crowded off the other routes to make room for urgent government services, political considerations dictated exceptions for the Latin Republics. It was highly desirable to preserve their good will, and we showed a co-operative eagerness to keep them supplied with the manufactures and coal they needed, to the annoyance of the British who foresaw difficulty in recovering those former markets after the war.

Africa, Australia, and New Zealand together did not produce quite as heavy a trade increase as the Argentine did alone, but again imports were diverted from the London entrepôt, and those outlying regions began to look to us directly for many of their general needs. Not particularly important from the commercial standpoint, those distant runs were unusual from a maritime point of view.

The "windjammers" which took over a considerable part of that distant traffic were the only American vessels caught by the later German raiders; the earlier crop had only found one, the *Frye*, it will be recalled. Trouble descended in the middle of 1917 from Count von Luckner's white-winged *Seeadler*, which had come around Cape Horn, and the converted freighter *Wolf*, approaching from Good Hope. For the only time in their spectacular, solitary wanderings, they were raiding in the same vicinity. Almost on the equator, northeast of New Zealand, Luckner caught three American four-masters in a month; by that time we were in the war and they were fair game. With his usual courtesy, he took everyone aboard the *Seeadler* before sinking the schooners and entertained them royally. One captain's lady intrigued the jovial count as she did not seem to be the usual type. He was not long left to wonder, for the captain nervously begged him not to publish her rescue—lest his real wife hear of it.

Meanwhile, closer to New Zealand waters where he was laying mines, Captain Nerger in the *Wolf* sank two more Yankee four-masters and an old former whaling bark which, loaded with benzine for Sydney, made a brilliant blaze as she disintegrated under shellfire. This unfortunate bark was one of the first to be sighted by a seaplane from a raider. The eighth and last American victim of the German surface raiders was the steel bark *John W. Kirby,* "a fine picture as she sailed before the great rollers coming from the southwest of the Cape." In her hold were 270 Ford cars, which would have fetched two thousand dollars apiece had they been landed in Natal; instead, she met the *Wolf,* on the way back to Germany, and the cars went to the bottom when time bombs shattered her steel hull.

More significant than all the other shiftings of sea lanes was the bringing of rubber and tin direct from Singapore and the Dutch East Indies. The number of direct arrivals jumped from five to seventy-eight, but in contrast to the African and South Seas trade, all those vessels were steamships, and only two were American. Imports from Singapore alone rose from 24 to 150 million dollars, but almost none of our exports were taken in exchange. The effect on the London entrepôt was sharp, for those precious cargoes were becoming on the eve of the war one of its main sources of profit.

The millions of Americans who were babying their tires in 1942 could appreciate and sharply regret the significance of the double shift in rubber that was taking place in those war years. Before that, most of the world's rubber came from the wild trees of Brazil, but an enterprising Englishman around 1890 smuggled thousands of shoots out of that country to take to London, whence they were transplanted in Malaya, the Dutch Indies, and other regions in the Far East. In 1900, those new "plantations" produced only four tons of rubber, against 26,750 tons from Brazil. In 1913, the Far Eastern output first overtook the Brazilian. The new supply was cheaper, of better quality, and could expand to meet the increased demands of the rapidly rising use of automobiles. By 1918, the Far East produced a quarter of a billion tons to Brazil's 30,000, and by 1934, the latter had dropped to 9,000 tons. This was less than 1 per cent of the billion-ton output of the distant plantations.

It was bad enough for the United States to have the control of that remote supply fall into the hands of an Anglo-Dutch monopoly; but it was worse on the eve of war in 1914, when it looked as if we were going to pay the additional cost of receiving it by way of the London entrepôt. The movement had already started in that direction, when at that time we received 35 per cent of our rubber by that roundabout route from England, with another 35 per cent from Brazil, and only 11 per cent direct from the Far East. Thanks to the shifting of the sea lanes through war conditions, we were able at least to get our rubber direct, even if we became more dependent on that distant source. By 1918, 82 per cent of our supply came straight from the Far East, and by 1939, only one ton of rubber in 2,500 was brought by way of London.

Tin was a somewhat different story, for although that trade also shifted to the more direct transpacific route, even in 1939 one-sixth of it passed over the English docks on the way to our shores.

This wartime shifting of the sea lanes was a "war baby" that lived to grow to husky manhood. In many cases the change proved lasting. Other commodities were not emancipated from the London entrepôt as fully as rubber, but many of the old roundabout routings had been too obviously unnatural and awkward to be resumed after the war. Also, the postwar years found the United States well supplied with merchantmen from its emergency shipbuilding program. It subsidized freight lines on many of those distant runs which enabled its shippers to enjoy the advantage of direct contact. The increased investment of American capital in these distant producing regions further helped preserve the change. Whereas on the eve of World War

I barely 30 per cent of our direct imports came from South America, Africa, Asia, and Oceania, 1939 found their share had jumped to 48 per cent. Direct exports, as a whole, had meanwhile risen from 14 to 34 per cent. The new contact with Asia produced most of that shift, but at the same time exports to South America had nearly doubled. The Africa rise was sharp but on a modest scale, while Oceania had pretty much reverted to its old level. At the same time, Britain's re-exports to the United States proved conclusively that the trade routes had shifted at the expense of the London entrepôt. Those re-exports fell from 150 million to 41 million dollars; the latter was little more than the value of the Scotch whisky shipped over here.

Most of the cargoes on those distant runs contained nothing more deadly than the Fords sunk off South Africa. Munitions, however, made up many of the 560 or so shipments which the United States sent to Russia by roundabout ways during the war. It was no easy job to reach Russia by sea, for nature had been very stingy in the matter of ports. All were either blocked for months with ice or else were cut off from the high seas by narrow bottlenecks, easily closed by an enemy. In normal times, American vessels used St. Petersburg, Riga, and other Baltic ports, now barred by the Germans; or Odessa and other Black Sea ports, now useless because of the Turks. That left, at the outset, only two remote and highly unsatisfactory alternatives—Vladivostok and Archangel.

The sea lanes to Vladivostok were safe enough in this war—with the Japanese on the Allied side—and it had the advantage, rare in Russia's ports, of being upon the open sea, even though Japan lay athwart its communications. It was decidedly undesirable for emergency munitions trade, however, largely because of the length of the haul. It was an extremely slow process to ship munitions halfway around the world to reach the Eastern Front in Europe. The lengthy Pacific crossing, which tied up vital tonnage for discouragingly long periods, was not the only delay; after cargoes reached Vladivostok, they faced the equally long and slow rail haul across Siberia and Russia proper on the Trans-Siberian.

The Vladivostok trade was distinctly an artificial war boom. It rose from almost nothing at all in 1913 to a peak in 1916 and 1917, when the exports to this port topped in value the totals to Africa, Australia, and New Zealand combined. By 1918, they had dropped away almost to nothing because of the Red Revolution. Some 360 ships went from the United States to Vladivostok during the war—and that was almost twice as many as took the Arctic alternative. The transpacific cargoes, however, were only worth half as much as those that went by the Arctic.

The Archangel run was the most desolate of all our wartime sea lanes. If things went right, it was a quicker route, but the shipping men hated it. Branching off from the Atlantic "main line," on which it naturally faced all the hazards of the danger zone, it led into the region of the midnight sun. It went up past the North Cape, along the dreary Murman Coast, and down into the White Sea, which was frozen many months each year. From Archangel, an inadequate little narrow-gauge line afforded a rail route far shorter than the Trans-Siberian. But ice interfered for months each year. Even when a Canadian icebreaker tried to keep the approaches open in spring and fall the floating ice cakes were hard on hulls. Marine risks, consequently, as distinct from war-risk rates, averaged 10 per cent; and that was higher than to any other port. One war winter the icebreaker broke down, and dozens of vessels, sorely needed in service, were imprisoned for long months.

Later in the war, the Allies, who wanted their precious ships back again for fresh cargoes as soon as possible, helped Russia to develop a little fishing village into the port of Murmansk. This was on the open Arctic, midway between the North Cape and the White Sea. Not only did the ice there not hinder the coming and going of ships all through the winter, but several hundred miles of sailing were saved by its closer position to the sources of supply.

Most of the two hundred vessels, which cleared from American ports for those Arctic approaches to Russia, went through without mishap. Of the three "windjammers" among them, all came to grief. One was the future *Seeadler;* the other two were sunk by German-sown mines at the entrance to the White Sea.

On the distant seas, as upon the North Atlantic, World War II found American shipping conditions growing infinitely more serious as the conflict progressed. The German surface raiders, despite initial expectations, did even less damage at the start than they had done in 1914; but the shift of Japan from Britain's side to the Axis brought disaster after disaster to the hitherto placid Pacific picture and changed it completely. Munitions and strategic war materials gradually replaced the old commercial activities both on the Cape and the Canal routes, and made them of far more essential significance than in the previous war.

The incredibly long sea lanes for the supply lines of this war became a factor of far-reaching significance and the key to many of the almost insoluble difficulties facing the United Nations. The three thousand miles of the North Atlantic shuttle had looked to most people in 1917 as being far too long a sea journey for the transportation and servicing of more than a small expeditionary force; yet the army sent across was one of two million men. In this second war, that transatlantic voyage actually appeared to be short when it was compared with the new lanes that often shifted in mileage with the progress of the war. It was, roughly, almost 9,000 miles across the Pacific to Australia, 5,000 miles to Murmansk, and over 14,000 miles from New York around the Cape to the Persian Gulf or to Suez. As we must realize, such long hauls inevitably meant far fewer trips a year for each vessel; and tied up much more tonnage than the old Atlantic "main line" at a time when ships were becoming increasingly precious with each day's news of enemy submarines at work.

Rumors were afloat before the war started that Germany was planning a cruiser warfare which would make the old exploits of the *Emden* look pale in comparison. Those expectations were based in particular upon the pocket battleships, relatively much more powerful than anything Germany had on the distant seas in the last war. Actually, their performance at the start was less impressive than even that of some of the converted merchantmen in that previous conflict. While the *Deutschland,* as we saw, was loose in the North Atlantic, her sister ships, the *Admiral Graf Spee* and the *Admiral Scheer,* were cruising far to the southward. They were apparently embarrassed in their operations by the hazard of revealing their positions; and their roll of victims was relatively small. The Allies successfully met the situation by working their ships in groups to "gang up" on the big super-cruisers.

The *Spee* had only nine freighters to her credit, when she was crippled in a daring attack by three British cruisers off the River Plate in December, 1939. Just a quarter of a century before, the admiral for whom she was named had gone down fighting in those same South Atlantic waters; but this time the Germans found a different way out. The battered *Spee* sought neutral refuge at Montevideo; and when her time was up there, her crew scuttled and set her afire in the shallow estuary of the Plate. They were interned at Buenos Aires, where her captain put a bullet into his brain.

Even in the initial scare, the war-risk quotations on the distant sea lanes had risen only half as high as the panic level of September, 1914, except on the Suez run which was affected by Mediterranean uncertainties. By the beginning of 1940, the original 3 and 4 per cent quotations had been generally cut in half for belligerent ships, while American vessels could traverse most of the remote runs for 1 per cent or less.

One of the main reasons for establishing a separate insurance center at New York, independent of London control, was to give American vessels preferential rates over belligerent and even other neutral competitors. Apparently this was having its effect late in 1940, when the rate from Singapore to New York by Panama stood at ¾ of 1 per cent for American vessels, 1 per cent for other neutrals, and 1½ per cent for belligerent British vessels.

Complaints came from British and Dutch shipping agents that

"American ships are leaving fully loaded, whereas British shippers are begging for cargo and the Dutch are not in a much better position." New York rubber importers, they insisted, were offering one-eighth of a cent a pound premium if space could be secured in American bottoms. All this was a far cry from the autumn of 1863, when a score of big Yankee clippers were found stranded at Singapore, unable to secure return cargoes because of the high war-risk rates resulting from the panic created by Semmes and his raiders. Of the 51,000 tons of rubber shipped from Singapore in September, 1940, nearly 34,000 had gone in American vessels. The remainder had been divided fairly equally among the British, Dutch, Japanese, and Norwegians.

The shipowners, who had protested when the Neutrality Act of November, 1939, had barred them from the war zone, soon found themselves making more money than ever on those long safe runs, while their British competitors were reluctantly having to withdraw their vessels for more perilous service nearer home. Those profits, as well as the low war-risk premiums, caused a greater participation of American shipping in those lucrative long hauls than occuerd in the last war. This time lack of vessels did not hamper us in that rich business either; for we had plenty, which were more efficient than the old schooners and barks, to throw into the gap. Scores of sturdy freighters of the earlier war period, together with a few fine new Maritime Commission ships, were soon operating on routes long exploited by the British. One freighter, the *City of Rayville,* became America's first casualty of the war when she accidentally struck a mine off the Australian coast in November, 1940, six months before the first "submarining." The rest, however, for the time being finished their voyages in safety.

As before, American direct commerce with South America, Africa, Asia, and Oceania boomed. For the first nine months of the various years (figures were not published after September, 1941), our imports from those regions rose from 662 million dollars in 1938 to 755 in 1939, 1,101 in 1940, and 1,503 in 1941. Exports likewise jumped in that period from 759 to 1,150 millions.

Part of those figures represented the shipments of munitions to the war zones and the bringing back of strategic materials, about which we began to feel alarm. The North Atlantic no longer had a monopoly of this abnormal war business; those emergency cargoes were beginning to crowd ordinary commerce from the distant runs as well. With tonnage growing increasingly scarce by 1942 and with the government in full control of all ships and cargoes, scant if any room was left for "business as usual." General mixed cargoes became increasingly rare, except in the South American trade, where our Good Neighbor policy again required exceptions to keep the Republics in good humor. Elsewhere, materials of war had clear and full right of way.

Lease-lend munitions found their first major outlet on the Cape run around Africa to the Red Sea, where they could be used by the British in their desert fighting back and forth across the sands of Libya. Our offerings took that route to avoid passing through the North Atlantic danger zone. In April, 1941, the President removed this Red Sea region from the war zone prohibited to American shipping, on the ground that the recent British victories had removed its dangers. Ironically, the war-risk rates thither went up sharply four days later, because a renewed German attack brought shipping within bombing range.

Nevertheless many American freighters were hastily assembled to carry tanks and other munitions in enormous quantities to that region. By September this steady stream of vessels, often under convoy, were reportedly reaching the Red Sea at the rate of one a day. One twenty-six-ship convoy alone had landed more than five hundred light tanks. Some 95 per cent of the lease-lend munitions, so one heard, were traveling by the Cape route at that time. The American vessels were not permitted to complete the voyage through the Suez Canal to Alexandria, as that was "war zone," but their anchorage at Port Suez or Port Sudan was to prove close enough for German air attacks.

The Germans were ready to cope with this new supply line, and struck on the South Atlantic before the regular munitions ships got under way. In April, a raider shelled and sank the semineutral Egyptian steamship *Zamzam*. Her passengers included an uncongenial group of American missionaries, college student ambulance drivers, and tobacco buyers. They were put aboard a German steamer that managed to slip through the British blockade to a port in occupied France.

In May came the first U-boat sinking of an American vessel, six months after the loss of the *City of Rayville* from a mine. The *Robin Moor* was carrying passengers and one of those increasingly rare general cargoes to various African ports when she was halted in those waters by a submarine with a "laughing cow" painted on her side. The ship's manifests were carefully scrutinized by the Germans. It was a most innocent-appearing cargo, whose hundreds of items filled three newspaper columns of small type—Post Toasties, Maxwell House Coffee, candy, peanut butter, toys, adding machines, cotton aprons, brassières, salvarsan, golf clubs, and so on ad infinitum. The U-boat captain was apparently as puzzled as the raider who had sunk the *William P. Frye* in those same waters. The final decision, however, was the same in both cases; on the ground that the cargo included "contraband" steel rails, the *Robin Moor* was sunk after her passengers and crew had put off in lifeboats hundreds of miles from the nearest land. The boats separated after five days, eventually to be picked up by two freighters, one of which was headed for Brazil and the other for South Africa. It was nearly a month before the United States learned the news from the survivors landed at Brazil. President Roosevelt denounced the act as "piracy by an international highwayman" and the State Department presented to Germany a claim for nearly three million dollars for the loss of ship and cargo; the Germans rejected it.

American indignation and protests had less justification in the sinking of the *Steel Seafarer* in the Gulf of Suez in September. One of those munitions freighters that had been heading around the Cape since May, she was loaded with 5,700 tons of military supplies from New York for the British. Several other freighters had been attacked from the air in that vicinity, but none had been sunk until that night when the *Steel Seafarer* received a mortal wound from a plane, presumably German, that swooped low across her bow. The crew of the unarmed ship rushed to the boats and got clear just in time, for she quickly rolled over on her starboard side to sink. This was only the beginning. Late that same month, a big Standard Oil tanker under Panamanian colors was sunk in the South Atlantic. Some weeks after that the American freighter *Lehigh,* proceeding in ballast from Spain to Sierra Leone for ore, was torpedoed without warning and went down off the coast of Africa. Later in the year, two British cruisers each sank a German surface raider in the South Atlantic to improve the situation somewhat.

Occasional sinkings, however, did not succeed in slowing up the steady flow of materials to the Red Sea. By November, the repeal of the "war zone" restrictions enabled American vessels to proceed on through the Suez Canal to Alexandria or Port Said—while the war-risk rates reflected the ebb and flow of battle. "General Grant" tanks and many other types of American-built equipment went to that desert front.

Late in 1941, Pan American Airways extended its service to this region by undertaking the ferrying of bombers, in addition to regular mail-passenger flights, to the Near East. This ten-thousand-mile route hopped from the bulge of Brazil to the African bulge at Liberia and thence crossed the Dark Continent overland to Egypt. Later, our army further expanded this service, a considerable amount of the less bulky material either being flown all the way, or carried by ship to the west coast of Africa and thence flown across to save time and tonnage.

Meanwhile another important flow of lease-lend munitions was heading for the Persian Gulf, over on the far side of Arabia. This was a new effort to solve the ever thorny problem of maritime access to Russia. It had not been possible in the last war, of course, because the Turkish alliance with the Germans blocked it. Now Russia's desperate needs in the autumn of 1941 pointed to this remote alternative. The Vladivostok route seemed jeopardized by the growing hostility of Japan; and the perennial disadvantages of the Archangel run were increased by the constant danger of German attack on land and sea. This Persian Gulf route had plenty of serious handicaps of its own, and would only be chosen as a last resort. Its length which was more than double the transpacific voyage to Vladivostok was one of its worst features, and, like Vladivostok, the ports were an exceptionally long rail haul from the war fronts.

It was bad enough to tie up shipping on that time-consuming run; it would be worse if, once arrived, the vessels had to lie around for weeks to unload. Basra, the only port on the gulf with modern equipment, was inadequate to handle the flood of traffic. So with characteristic American energy a whole new port was "dug out of the mud" and motor roads were built to connect it with other ports. Luckily Iran had recently completed a railroad running southward to the Persian Gulf. British and American railroad men, with rolling stock from home, put it in good working condition. Just as they were doing over at their new base in Eretria for the Egyptian supplies, the Americans sent out technicians to assemble the planes, trucks, and other equipment. Altogether, this work doubled and almost trebled the flow of supplies for Russia in the course of a few months.

Since adequate return cargoes were lacking both at Suez and here in the Persian Gulf, some returning freighters on their homeward voyage around the Cape stopped in lower Africa to pick up ladings of strategic materials needed in the United States. Others moved on to India or to ports in the Far East for similar cargoes, and then continued around the world to reach their East Coast home ports by way of Panama. Before long, however, Japanese advances closed that alternate way home.

Being farther away from possible enemy bombings, the Persian Gulf route was regarded as safer than the Suez traffic. On the eve of Pearl Harbor, the rate on cargo in belligerent ships between New York and Port Suez was 7½ per cent; the lower Red Sea ports, 5 per cent; the Persian Gulf, by the Cape, 2½ per cent; and the Persian Gulf by Panama, 1¾ per cent. By July, 1942, that final route was out, and the danger of Japanese raids in the Indian Ocean combined with the German advance in

Egypt to increase the jeopardy to all these supply lines. At that time, rates for the Cape route to the Persian Gulf and Red Sea ports stood at 20 per cent, to Alexandria and Port Said at 25 per cent, and Port Suez at midway between. In late August, the various rates all rose 5 per cent briefly and then returned to the July level.

Those returning freighters from the Middle East became involved in the ominous threat of Japanese interference long hanging over the Pacific sea lanes. Gone were the old days when the Japanese Navy had joined the British in hunting German raiders on eastern seas. By September, 1940, with Britain's fortunes at their lowest ebb, Japan formally allied itself with the Axis and secured a partial foothold in Indo-China from Vichy France. Although Japan remained a neutral like ourselves for more than a year longer, the clash of interests was ever obvious.

Among the various factors complicating the Pacific scene was the none-too-successful Japanese invasion of China, which had been actively resumed in 1937. Since neither had formally declared war, the United States had a loophole under the Neutrality Act to join England in furnishing munitions to China. With the Chinese seaports in Japanese hands, these supplies had to travel a long way around to Rangoon in Burma, and thence by rail up past Mandalay to Lashio, where reckless truck drivers picked them up for the tortuous ride through wild mountains on the Burma Road into China. In the general effort to appease the Japanese, England agreed in July, 1940, to send no war materials over that vital artery for three months.

Japan and the United States each began to think of laying in a reserve stock pile of essential strategic materials while the Pacific sea lanes were still open to them. The ironic feature of this business was that we furnished to Japan, a potential enemy, the gasoline and scrap iron it needed for war. At the same time, the selfish business interests of our future allies—the British and the Dutch, who would soon be clamoring for our aid—appeared to have blocked our getting all the rubber we sought from their distant plantations.

Our officials at Washington guessed wrong in both cases. The tanker loads of aviation gasoline and the eight million tons of scrap iron at least represented a hopeful effort to keep Japan quiet by paying blackmail. At it turned out, some of that iron was later dug out of the shrapnel wounds of American soldiers, at the very moment when our own war production was threatened by a shortage of scrap. There was not even that excuse for the bungling of the rubber situation. Whereas Japan had started to get its gasoline and scrap as early as 1936, it was not until the middle of 1940 that Washington took measures to lay in a heavy reserve supply of rubber, tin, and other strategic materials from the Far East.

This was virtually the first time since the Revolution that we were seriously concerned over wartime imports. As soon as Congress gave its authorization, the Reconstruction Finance Corporation formed the Rubber Reserve Corporation and the Metals Reserve Corporation to purchase more than a half billion dollars' worth of those materials on government account. Extra American vessels were placed on the Far Eastern runs to carry those additional supplies; and a steady stream of heavily laden freighters under various flags began to make their way toward America by the Cape or transpacific routes. But it proved to be too late for adequate stock piles to be gathered, and with the outbreak of hostilities with Japan, it was only too evident that the nation was sadly lacking several all-important commodities.

Rubber was the most conspicuous failure, as any American motorist would testify, for he was denied new tires even before the U-boats off the Atlantic coast cut down the gasoline supply. Imports of rubber, in spite of stock-pile efforts, had jumped only 145 per cent between 1938 and 1941. The government had planned to purchase 150,000 tons in 1940; it actually received only 58,000. The Secretary of Commerce placed the blame upon the Anglo-Dutch cartel, claiming that it had curbed the supply, apparently fearing that a big reserve in the United States might depress the prices of their precious product; they retorted that the failure was not their fault but lack of foresight in Washington. Recriminations passed to and fro also over the fact that the government had not taken adequate measures to develop quantity production of synthetic rubber in time. Pearl Harbor apparently had found us with little more than a year's normal supply on hand—and a fire in an old fire trap of a Fall River factory had destroyed part of that. And war needs would take all that meager stock pile and much more. The background of the rubber failure remained pretty much of a mystery in 1942, although the Baruch report at last clarified the current situation.

The need for quinine seems to have been overlooked for a while. At a time when American soldiers were being sent into many tropical regions, where the drug would be an absolute necessity, this was a serious matter. Java's entire supply was ordered for the United States; but according to report the order left Washington the day before that island fell to the Japanese.

The shutting of the Burma Road to appease Japan threatened the stock of Chinese tungsten for hardening steel, and antimony for storage batteries, but an alternative outlet was Haipong, Indo-China. In September, 1940, the *Birmingham City* brought 3,800 tons of tungsten and 1,000 of antimony, said to have been the largest quantity ever shipped in one cargo. Other ships were bringing more on that sixty-day run, when, long before they could arrive, the Japs cut off that contact with China. Luckily the Burma Road was again reopened, and until the war moved into that region the shipping was diverted to Rangoon.

As for the other Far Eastern supplies, tin shipments had been accelerated twice as fast as rubber shipments. Yet the reserve was inadequate. Less than a year's supply of Manila hemp was on hand. Outside of the strategic field, the closing of the Far Eastern sea lanes would find the United States temporarily better stocked with tea, spices, and tapioca.

Tension had measurably increased by the late summer of 1941, with Indo-China under Japanese military control, and with Eng-

land and the United States jointly warning Japan to keep its
hands off Thailand. We cut off imports from Japan, thereby
precipitating a scramble for silk stockings; and at long last,
stopped the shipments of scrap iron and gasoline across the Pacific to Japanese ports.

By that time, tankers were carrying gasoline to another transpacific destination—the old access point to Russia—Vladivostok.
Several cargoes of high octane aviation fuel were hurried to the
Russians, but there was keen anxiety for fear Japan might pre-
cipitate an "incident" by seizing them as they passed through
its waters. The big American ships, however, were able to deliver their cargoes and return safely. Even the outbreak of war
with Japan did not cause the destruction of any of these cargoes.
One large tanker was in the dangerous Sea of Okhotsk en route
to Vladivostok, but she turned around and managed to get home
unharmed.

The closing of the Pacific route threw added burdens on the
other Russian supply lines to Archangel, Murmansk, and the
Persian Gulf. The increasingly desperate needs of the Russian
front called for as much use as possible of those shorter, northern
sea lanes in particular. The Murmansk route at this time had to
await the freeing of its rail supply line from enemy pressure, but
this was eventually accomplished. In October, New Yorkers were
intrigued by pictures of four women in the crew of an old Russian freighter loading aviation gasoline for Archangel. Later in
the fall, a slip in censorship revealed that Boston was to be the
jumping-off place for many more cargoes in that direction. With
their hulls braced to withstand the ice cakes in the White Sea,
freighters from American ports began to move regularly through
channels kept open by the Atlantic patrol to Archangel.

With autumn, too, came rumors of German raiders at work
in the Pacific, where they were presumably getting their supplies
through the Japanese. American underwriters lost two million
dollars when a Dutch liner was sunk in that ocean. A large Norwegian motor freighter, loaded with rubber and tin from Singapore, Batavia, and Surabaya, did not reach Panama and was pre-

sumably lost. Later in the fall, the Australian cruiser *Sydney,*
close to the spot where her predecessor of the same name had
put an end to the *Emden's* career, had a fatal accidental encounter. In her normal routine check-up on all vessels, she stopped a
big freighter flying neutral colors. Suddenly the freighter, which
turned out to be the disguised German raider *Steiermark,* fired
a shot that smashed the cruiser's fire control. The *Sydney's* guns
sank the raider, but at high cost, for she herself went off ablaze
and was never heard from again.

Despite all that, the war-risk rates remained at an optimistically low level. Up to October 23, cargo in an American vessel
could be insured between Singapore and New York by way of
Panama for ¾ of 1 per cent; on that day it moved up to 1¼ per
cent; and three days before Pearl Harbor, had only reached the
still very moderate level of 1¾. By way of the Cape, the rates
were only a trifle higher, and to Australia they were yet lower.
Even the rates on belligerent vessels were exceedingly moderate.
In spite of a few anxious hours in John Street insurance offices
when valuable cargoes, such as one of seven million dollars,
were on dangerous seas, very few losses were incurred; and millions had been paid in premiums on the rich rubber and tin
shipments.

That optimism was not entirely unwarranted, for the merchant
marine escaped far more lightly than the navy from that yellow
surprise attack on the Sunday morning of December 7. While
our Pacific fleet was being critically crippled at Pearl Harbor,
the navy later reported that only one American merchantman,
the liner *President Harrison,* had fallen to the Japanese in their
initial sweep. She was off the China coast laden with rubber and
tin and did not have a chance to escape. Probably one cause of
this meager toll was the extreme caution with which merchantmen had been moving in those waters for some time; and there
were rumors that they had been having convoy service. Even the
vulnerable "clippers" of the transpacific air routes managed to
get home, thanks to forehanded planning and resourceful
handling.

For the time being, waters nearer home were more dangerous than the distant reaches of the Pacific. Four days after Pearl Harbor, a Japanese submarine off Hawaii fired two dozen shells at the Matson liner, *Lahaina,* and although half the shots missed her the rest were enough to sink her. Her crew made land "weak but otherwise in good condition after drifting, rowing and sailing for ten days through heavy winds and waves." The next week saw the sinking of two more American steamships on the Hawaiian run.

Next, the Japanese submarines moved right up to the Pacific coast of the United States itself in the week before Christmas. One torpedoed the big tanker *Emidio,* so close to the northern coast of California that her wreck drifted into the breakers. Two days later another tanker, the *Montebello,* was sent to the bottom by a submarine, which machine-gunned the crew as they struggled to pull away in their lifeboats. Then, astonished crowds on shore watched with amazement an enemy submarine, boldly cruising on the surface, torpedo a big lumber steamer; but she escaped sinking. Later, a coastal oil field just above Santa Barbara was shelled but scarcely damaged. Neither in numbers nor in skill did those Japanese submarines measure up to the German ones. Before long, with the air force at work, rumors of dead Japs washed up on the California beaches replaced those of more sinkings along that coast.

Meanwhile, conditions in the Southwest Pacific were growing daily more critically serious. The Japs, as Churchill aptly phrased it, were "making hell while the sun shines." Freighters still rushed through those seas in a despairing effort to get planes and other war materials to threatened Singapore, Java, and Rangoon, and to bring back, before it was too late, the increasingly precious rubber and tin. War-risk rates jumped to 10 per cent; and then in February came the ominous news that "in view of the increased seriousness of the situation in the Far East," the New York underwriters would no longer quote public rates for ports east of Calcutta.

With the fall of Singapore and Rangoon a month later and Java soon thereafter, those sources of vital supplies were lost to the United States. American officials in Australia chartered ships to carry supplies to the beleaguered American forces on Bataan, but only one in three arrived. A submarine fared better, taking antiaircraft shells to Corregidor and carrying away "ton upon ton" of gold and other valuables.

Planes, too, played an important part in transport and rescue work when the surface of the seas became too dangerous. One plane of the Air Corps Ferrying Command flew a diplomat from Miami to the Middle East by way of Africa, proceeded on to Australia, and then shuttled around between Rangoon, Surabaya, Calcutta, and other points in the East. In the first six months of war it had "traveled 125,000 miles . . . carried nearly every British and American general in the Far East, evacuated about one hundred civilians from Java and rescued two loads of men from the Philippines." A far cry, indeed, from the days when our diplomats were playing hide-and-seek with the Royal Navy on the North Atlantic.

By April, the Japanese had carried the war into the Indian Ocean. One returning captain reported that their cruisers had sunk more than twenty ships in a single convoy. That news doubtless explained the highest war-risk rate yet quoted in either war—30 per cent from New York to or from Calcutta, Madras, and Colombo, all of which were threatened. There was danger that the Japanese might move westward against the Red Sea-Persian Gulf supply line, and that Vichy France might give them the use of Madagascar which lay athwart that route. The British forestalled that move by occupying the island; one Jap sub appeared there, but the constant stream of freighters continued to come and go. In May, one of the greatest convoys in history, including some of the world's best-known liners, arrived safely in India with powerful reinforcements.

Australia was the one exception in that spring epidemic of high war rates. A cargo could be insured from San Francisco to Melbourne for the same 6 per cent charged in April for the coastal run from New Orleans to New York; by July, the Australian rate was only half the 15 per cent charged on that much shorter route. That was one answer to the question on every American's lips: "What is our navy doing in the Pacific?" Raids on the Caroline and Marshall Islands and other possible Japanese lurking posts helped to remove threats along that vulnerable, wearisomely long nine-thousand-mile line. Big troop convoys arrived safely in Australia, as well as groups of supply ships.

But that security was purchased at a heavy price to the merchant marine. It was now tied down by heavy duties on a route that was so extended that only three or four round trips a year were possible; and every ton of it was needed elsewhere. Even oil, once abundantly available in those Eastern seas, was lost to American ships and forces; it now had to be carried over that lengthy run from the United States, an almost intolerable burden on the overworked tankers.

Pacific shipping was just becoming adjusted to its new conditions of lost ports and new convoy routes by the spring of 1942, when the Latin-American situation suddenly went bad. With the U-boats moving southward to the Caribbean and the Gulf, the heavy sinkings thoroughly disorganized things for a while. New complications arose later when the enemy went into action off Brazil. Some of the results had strategic implications; the Canal Zone could be supplied from the Pacific side, but our island bases, including those newly acquired from England, had to be serviced through the dangerous waters. Bauxite and other ores, too, had to be brought from those areas.

Even more widespread were the commercial repercussions. Special considerations had kept alive the swapping of exports and imports with the Latin lands even during the severe tonnage shortage of 1917-18, we recall, and 1940-41, but now it was a different matter when those waters became one of the prime danger zones. Our supply of sugar and coffee was threatened; there were criticisms for a while that bananas continued to arrive here with shipping scarce, but before long so few came in that emergency bunches had to be flown around the country by plane for sick children. After the raid on Curacao and Aruba, the supply of oil from the Venezuelan wells dwindled away, throwing an added burden on ours. Meanwhile, the Latin Americans were suffering from a lack of our manufactures, upon which they had become dependent after the German, British, and Japanese sources were cut off. This drove the cost of living sky-high, particularly in Venezuela, where soap, for instance, sold at a dollar a cake. We attempted to relieve the economic distress of some of the republics by buying large stocks of their offerings, providing them immediately with funds, but delaying delivery until the sea lanes should become safer.

The U-boat raids, meanwhile, were driving some of the republics into the war on our side. Panama and a few other little Caribbean states followed us immediately into the conflict, but the larger countries held off, most of them contenting themselves with severing diplomatic relations. The U-boat victims, however, were not limited to British, Norwegian, American, and Panamanian vessels; howling mobs in some of the bigger Latin-American cities attacked German establishments when news arrived that some of their own vessels had been sunk. Mexico thus went into the war in late spring and Brazil in late summer, after five of the latter's vessels had gone down off its coast. The Argentine, however, remained the most "offish" of the southern republics. Though some of its vessels were sunk, it preferred to follow our earlier Neutrality Act example and bar its shipping from the war zone which the Germans proclaimed along our eastern coast in June.

The new danger zone produced a new sea route. Shipping from Buenos Aires and Montevideo no longer traveled up the perilous east coast; instead it went by way of the Straits of Magellan and the Pacific to our West Coast ports. The difference in mileage was not as great as it would seem at first glance, and the war-risk insurance was only 7½ per cent instead of the 20 or 25 per cent charged for the Atlantic alternative.

By that spring, also, Russian counterattacks made that front appear to be the most urgent spot for all possible munitions supplies. The Russians had pushed back the enemy enough, by this time, so that the route to Murmansk, shorter and more convenient than the one to Archangel, could again be utilized. Convoy after convoy, whose numbers and size remained a well-kept secret, journeyed thither, so that the Russians might be strengthened as much as was feasible to withstand the dreaded German offensive. Returning convoy crews told about being dive-bombed day after day by the German planes on those bleak seas, despite their antiaircraft guns spitting back strongly in return. U-boats and smaller surface warships joined the attack on the convoys in flank. One sailor, just back from Murmansk, was obviously not speaking of the climate when he called that run "just about the hottest thing on the seven seas," and when he referred to the North Atlantic crossing as mere child's play in comparison. Now and then a few freighters were sunk; even a cruiser or destroyer of the escort sometimes fell victim to those continuous attacks. As for Murmansk itself, it was ripped by German bombs steadily—by one account "every hour, on the hour." But its men and women kept on doggedly unloading cargoes, though the morgues ran ankle deep in blood. How many of the precious cargoes still pushed through to Murmansk or Archangel remained a well-guarded secret.

And not the least of the hazards was the ever-present fear that the *Tirpitz* and some of her consorts might suddenly dash into those northern waters for a thoroughgoing destruction of convoys. That dread haunted the Admiralty and the Navy Department, and made that route more than ever a constant nightmare to the hard-pressed sailors of the convoys. Early in July, that long-dreaded major raid struck. According to Berlin its planes and U-boats attacked the most powerfully protected convoy in history to sink thirty-two out of thirty-eight freighters. Moscow retorted that the *Tirpitz* herself had been torpedoed by a Russian submarine and sent limping home with her escorts. Censorship clouds the true details of that raided convoy, but there was no adequate denial of the German claims, such as came in September when another convoy was destroyed in German propaganda.

Such dangers brought into the picture another new sea lane— a fantastically strange and remote one, "across the top of the world." That Arctic route appeared to have been vigorously developed by the Russians during the thirties, with a fleet of a hundred tough vessels in "icebreaker convoys" during the summer months. Their particular objectives were the Arctic ports at the mouths of the large Siberian rivers, whence small steamers could carry wares into the interior, even to connections with the Trans-Siberian road. It was only six thousand miles by that Arctic seaway from Seattle to Archangel and only a fraction of that distance to the Siberian river ports. Another advantage was its remoteness from enemy interference, unless the Japs in the Aleutians might in time come within bombing range. As the captain of one of those Soviet icebreakers said upon his arrival at Seattle some weeks before our entry into the war, "You see, the ice is our friend. We can hide in the ice, if nothing else. There isn't a warship commander who would dare follow us in."

Naturally even this difficult route seemed to have possibilities as the North Cape runs grew more precarious, while the Persian Gulf route was faced with the triple threat of German raiders in the South Atlantic, the Japanese in the Indian Ocean, and the German armies advancing toward the Caucasus and the Caspian.

Thus the summer of 1942 found American merchantmen facing ever-perilous hazards and new complications on those distant seas. The current Axis strategy, according to a German admiral, was for the Germans to sink our tonnage in the Atlantic and for the Japs to scatter its efforts in the Pacific. It became a far cry from the comfortable days of 1918 when vessels "on our side" could pick up all the rubber and tin they needed at will and bring them home to augment our war effort—with friendly cooperation from the Japanese and scarcely a worry over interference from the Germans. It was a long way, too, from those days of the other war, when the difficult approaches to Russia were not as dangerous and, with the Soviet revolution, ceased to matter.

Chapter XI

The Race for Tonnage

TRYING TO MAKE SIX OR EIGHT THOUSAND SEAGOING SHIPS DO THE work of treble their number was one of the gravest, if not the gravest, problems facing the United States and England in the two World Wars. In both conflicts, Germany could strike by land and could sustain itself after a fashion without controlling the sea lanes; but the Allied side absolutely had to have cargo space and plenty of it. Allied strategy still depended upon the supply of ships despite the increasing utilization of planes, and so too did the food, the fuel, and the other basic wants of England and its European partners. Rarely were there ships enough, and all too often their lack threatened disaster in one theater of war or another.

The frantic call for ships and ever more ships returned the American flag to the seas. From almost scratch in 1914, the emergency shipbuilding of the first war revived our merchant marine in unprecedented volume by the early twenties, while the veterans of that boom were the nucleus for vaster numbers in the ambitious shipping program of the second. Yet this huge shipbuilding could not do the job alone, because of our slow start in the first war and various other factors in the second. As a result, a tremendous amount of foreign shipping had to be utilized in order to deliver our munitions, foodstuffs, and soldiers where they were needed.

Barely one vessel in nineteen that entered our ports from Europe between mid-1914 and mid-1918 flew the Stars and Stripes— only 1,131 out of 21,604. Even including arrivals from South America, Asia, Africa, and the South Seas, only about one ship in eight—3,989 out of 30,880—was American. The British led with 14,000, and the Norwegian score was almost identical with our own. In order thereafter came Italian, Dutch, Danish, Japanese, French, Swedish, Russian, and Greek vessels, and so on into the lesser merchant marines. On the tonnage basis, the American share was even less, with barely one-tenth in the trade with the other continents, while the British had more than half.

In World War II, our expanded merchant marine took over a larger proportion of the trade on distant runs; but nonetheless a substantial amount of foreign tonnage was engaged in our overseas commerce. This was especially true of the first two years, when American-flag shipping was rigidly barred by the Neutrality Act from the war zones. In 1940, only 1,550 out of the 6,714 vessels arriving from the other continents flew the American flag. From South America, Africa, and Oceania, the American proportion was almost half; from Asia, 286 out of 1,268; and from Europe, 172 out of 2,850. Most extreme, only one of the 1,495 incoming ships from war-zone Britain flew our flag!

This dependence upon foreign merchant marines explains why we have to consider the whole matter of world shipping, since everything available was gradually pooled for the common good in each war. With the race to assemble vessels faster than they were being sunk by the enemy, any sort of shipping, belligerent or neutral included, was fair game. The neutrals, to be sure, had to be cajoled or coerced into co-operation, but England and its allies could requisition at once their own merchantmen upon entry into war and could use any enemy ships they could catch. Besides these three sources, ambitious shipbuilding programs helped to replace the thousands of vessels sent to the bottom. In this desperate race, the man in the street was able to follow day by day the death of old ships and the birth of new ones. The three nations which bore the brunt of these contributions to the Allied pools of shipping were England with its huge ready-made merchant fleet, Norway with its useful tramps and tankers, and the United States with its eventual mass production of new vessels.

An equally urgent but less spectacular problem was the struggle to keep that assembled tonnage operating at its maximum

capacity. Hazards of war were by no means the only causes for
the reduction of the carrying power of shipping. We have already
seen how lengthened sea lanes, especially in World War II, and
the delays inherent in the convoy system sometimes did far more
damage to carrying capacity than did enemy sinkings; so too did
tie-ups at congested and undeveloped ports. At the same time,
the elimination of nonessential cargoes in the maximum utilization of tonnage space, and the efficient readjustment of hauls
often made more cargo space available than did even new
launchings. Rapid repairs, too, were necessary if ships were to
keep moving.

Only a few thousand seagoing steamships at the most were
at any time available for all those many Allied purposes. The
published shipping statistics give a very misleading sense of security on that subject, for they were cluttered with "small fry"
that made impressive totals but were of little if any use on the
long ocean hauls. Even when the tens of thousands of small vessels under a hundred gross tons were omitted, the totals remain
large, with the merchant marines of the world containing in 1914
some 30,836 vessels of 49 million gross tons; in 1939 the number
was almost the same at 29,673, but their tonnage had risen to
68 million. But for general seagoing service, only the larger
steamships really mattered; the arbitrary "seagoing" minimum
was 1,600 gross tons (about 1,000 net or 2,500 dead weight); in
1939, it sometimes raised to 2,000 gross tons. Except for relatively short voyages, such as England's North Sea and Channel
crossings, or our Cuban trade, ships had to be at least that size.
On that basis, the leading national fleets of seagoing merchant
ships, at the start of the two wars, lined up as follows:

JULY 1, 1914 (1,600 TON MINIMUM)

	SHIPS	THOUSAND GROSS TONS
World Total	8,445	35,145
British	4,174	18,197
German	743	3,799

	SHIPS	THOUSAND GROSS TONS
U. S.*	513	2,216
French	357	1,602
Japanese	429	1,496
Italian	355	1,310
Dutch	263	1,285
Norwegian	323	1,087

DECEMBER 31, 1939 (2,000 TON MINIMUM)

	SHIPS	THOUSAND GROSS TONS
World Total	9,161	51,998
British	2,529	16,321
U. S.*	1,296	7,881
Japanese	873	4,574
Norwegian	698	3,947
German	579	3,353
Italian	505	2,921
Dutch	405	2,453
French	414	2,383

* Not including the Great Lakes.

Even with those restrictions the figures still imply more vessels than were available for the vital war services, especially in the case of our 1914 shipping. The relative usefulness of the types of ships represented in those totals was another side of the picture. Many vessels were too specialized to be of general use for the varied cargo needs. Most practicable of all were the medium-sized freighters, or "dry cargo ships." Whereas many of the liners were specially designed for their particular runs, those tramps were built for general utility purposes. Moving seasonal cargoes and filling in other gaps in the world's shipping needs, they had to be versatile enough to carry wheat, sugar, lumber, iron, coal, or whatever else came to hand in their wanderings. Such adaptability made them doubly precious in wartime. Many a nation would gladly have swapped a big passenger liner for six or eight freighters of the same or even less tonnage. Tankers, of course, were valuable in their specialized function. Of the 9,161 ships in 1939, 6,403 were "dry cargo" freighters, 1,556 were tankers, and 1,202 were passenger or passenger-cargo liners. In 1914, the proportion of tankers had been much lower.

With the largest group of those seagoing vessels flying its red ensign, the British merchant marine was the great backlog of the Allied shipping effort in both wars. A considerable proportion, moreover, consisted of the highly useful general freighters, more of which were serving as tramps in World War I than in World War II. Britain's Continental allies proved more of a liability than an asset as far as shipping was concerned. France and Italy had merchant fleets of moderate size and quality, but they were insufficient to meet their own needs for coal, food and other wartime necessities. Russia's shipping ranked still lower in quantity and quality. Japan's growing merchant marine made the most of its opportunities in the Pacific in the first war, but did not do much to relieve the Atlantic "main line." Japan and Italy both extended their tramp fleets rapidly between the wars, while England's was falling off. The German merchant marine, England's closest runner-up in 1914, was soon swept from the seas as such, but many of its skillfully built units, particularly in the first war, were added to the Allied side by capture in port or on the high seas.

Most useful, on the whole, were the northern neutrals. They retained that status throughout the first World War and in the second, until invaded in the spring of 1940. After that, as we shall see, they were in a peculiar situation, but most of them still remained available. Most indispensable were the Scandinavians, especially the Norwegians. With only a modest commerce of their own, they had developed into common carriers for the world. Their hundreds of little tramps, frequently dingy but usually ably handled, prowled around the world's sea lanes and often for years did not revisit their home ports. The Netherlands had a very respectable fleet of good, well-run ships, many of which found constant employment in the rich, long haul from their East Indian islands, until they fell to Japan in 1942. The shipping of the southern European neutrals was of lower quality, and they proved less serviceable. By World War II, several Latin-American nations developed sizable merchant fleets, some legitimate, others definitely "phony."

Naturally, the relationship of neutral merchantmen to the Allied war efforts differed from that of the belligerent. Less preoccupied by national needs, neutral shipping was more free "to go places," but their services could not be directly commandeered. As long as the Allied fleets kept the sea lanes relatively safe, they flocked to take advantage of the high charter rates. But with rising danger on the seas, they sometimes forsook the war zones, where they were needed, for safer routes. The Germans were well aware of this, we recall, as a factor in their U-boat campaigns.

The British, however, were in a position to bring pressure upon many neutrals; and they did not hesitate to do so in both wars. Except in North America and the Far East, the British had pretty much of a monopoly of fuel bunkering and a strong hold upon repair facilities. A vessel that would not "play ball" was denied those necessities without which she was helpless far from home waters. Marine insurance could also be witheld because of the key position of London in that business. England also had the upper hand in the dependence of some of the neutrals for their home supply of coal and other imports and so could bring pressure upon their governments. The unrestricted submarine campaign of 1917 brought the matter to a head. As the Germans had hoped, many of the neutral shipowners refused to risk their vessels in the danger zone. The British used the extreme tactics of refusing permission for a neutral to leave their ports until another ship under the same flag should arrive. The United States, once it became a belligerent, resorted to some of these same forms of pressure to secure neutral co-operation. Similar practices, under somewhat different circumstances, were repeated by both England and the United States in World War II.

Unlike those foreign merchant marines which were fairly similar in the two wars, American shipping was in a class by itself. The meager handful of seagoing vessels flying our flag in 1914 was a far cry from the imposing aggregation in 1939; but one would never guess this from the total tonnage figures. These gave not the slightest intimation of the shortage in seagoing vessels. Only by thumbing through the official list of *Merchant Vessels of the United States* for 1914 and breaking down the figures can one appreciate that lack. Part of the difficulty lay in the fact that American vessels were highly specialized. Unlike the "Scowegian" ships, which were largely versatile tramps, relatively few American ones were fit for carrying general cargoes on the high seas, although they were useful enough in their own spheres.

At first glance we had an impressive merchant marine, with eight million tons of documented shipping in 1914. Leaving out the smallest vessels, the United States was virtually tied with Germany for second place in vessels of 100 gross tons or more, with 3,173 of them totaling 5,300,000 tons. Even in the exclusive, supposedly seagoing category of those over 1,600 gross tons (including the Philippine but not the Great Lakes shipping), we had 513 vessels of 2,126,000 tons—and that was more than the Scandinavian total in that class.

But even that 1,600-ton limit was no sure gauge, for big Fall River liners could never navigate Good Hope, nor would the capacious steamers of the Hudson River Day Line attempt the stormy North Atlantic. Scores of old wooden steamers and side-wheelers had to be written off also. So, too, did ferries, excursion boats, and the like, which were far less useful than the 123 sailing vessels of 1,600 tons or more. With all that stripped away, the net results were pretty meager. In our whole seagoing merchant marine, in fact, only twenty-three oceangoing vessels were as large as the "Liberty Ships" that were turned out by the hundreds in 1942!

The accompanying table has been mined out of the official lists to indicate at a glance the significant contrasts in the groups of vessels that made up our seagoing merchant marine on the

PRINCIPAL GROUPS OF SEAGOING U.S. STEAMSHIPS, 1914 AND 1939

Compiled from Merchant Vessels of the United States. Excludes all vessels under 1,600 gross tons, sailing vessels, Great Lakes shipping, and vessels obviously not seagoing. Certain lines engaged in both "coastal" and foreign trade are included in the field of major activity. The 1914 list includes all groups over 15,000 gross tons; the 1939 list, for considerations of space, omits the numerous groups under 25,000 gross tons. Abbreviations: i-c = inter-coastal; I.M.M. = International Mercantile Marine; Mar. Com. = Maritime Commission.

JUNE 30, 1914

	No.	M Gross Tons
PROTECTED "COASTAL"		
American-Hawaiian S.S. Co. (i-c, Hawaii)	26	177
Southern Pacific-Morgan (E. Coast-Gulf)	24	119
Clyde S. S. Co. (E. Coast)	20	58
Merchants & Miners (E. Coast)	21	53
Mallory S. S. Co. (E. Coast)	13	46
Ocean S. S. Co., Savannah Line (E. Coast)	9	43
Eastern S. S. Co. (E. Coast)	13	43
New York & Porto Rico S. S. Co.	12	38
Matson Navigation Co. (W. Coast-Hawaii)	9	38
Pacific Coast Co. (W. Coast-Alaska)	11	37
Luckenbach S. S. Co. (i-c)	11	36
Alaska S. S. Co. (W. Coast-Alaska)	9	25
A. H. Bull S. S. Co. (Puerto Rico & W. I.)	9	25
Atlantic & Pacific S. S. Co. (i-c)	4	24
Old Dominion S.S. Co. (E. Coast)	6	21
Coastwise Transp. Co. (E. Coast-coal)	5	20
New England Coal & Coke (E. Coast-coal)	4	20

JUNE 30, 1939

	No.	M Gross Tons	Building of the 1939 Fleet — To 1916	1917-21	1922-39
PROTECTED "COASTAL"					
Matson Navigation Co. (W. Coast-Hawaii)	45	275	3	40	5
American-Hawaiian S.S. Co. (i-c, Hawaii)	39	232	13	26	
Luckenbach S. S. Co. (i-c)	21	130	4	17	
Agwi-Porto Rico-Clyde-Mallory (cf. 1914)	27	117	14	6	7
A. H. Bull & Co. (Puerto Rico & W. I.)	25	94	9	14	2
Koppers Coal Co. (E. Coast)	17	86	7	10	
Calmar S. S. Corp. (i-c)	14	82	1	13	
Merchants & Miners (E. Coast)	22	80	5	12	5
Alaska S. S. Co. (W. Coast-Alaska)	19	73	8	9	2
Southern Pacific (E. Coast-Gulf)	13	68	5	5	3
Eastern S. S. Lines (E. Coast, Maritimes)	15	60	1	3	11
Portland-California S. S. Co. (W. Coast)	16	52		16	
McCormick S. S. Co. (i-c)	12	49		12	
Swayne & Hoyt-Gulf Pacific (W. Coast-Gulf)	9	43		9	
Wyerhauser S. S. Co. (i-c)	6	42		6	
Argonaut Line (i-c)	6	37		6	2
Ocean S. S. Co.-Savannah Line (E. Coast)	6	33	4		
States Shipping Co. (j-c)	6	33		6	
Pacific S. S. Lines (W. Coast-Alaska)	8	32	5	3	
Pocahontas S. S. Co. (E. Coast, coal)	8	31	5	3	
Coastwise Transp. Co. (E. Coast, coal)	6	26	5	1	
TANKERS					
Standard Oil of N. J. ("Esso")	73	597	7	50	16
Standard Oil of N. Y. ("Socony-Vacuum")	40	309	6	26	8
Gulf Oil Corp.	27	204	1	14	12
Texas Co.	27	185	3	19	5
Tide Water Associated Oil Co.	19	126		12	7
Standard Oil of California	16	121	4	10	2
Atlantic Refining Co.	18	105	1	10	4
Cities Service Oil Co.	14	103	1	13	
Union Oil Co.	11	77	1	8	2

eve of each war. The names and relative sizes of some familiar lines may help to give a more realistic impression than mere tonnage totals. The routes they served, moreover, show how restricted was the 1914 setup compared with the world-spanning network of a quarter of a century later. The protected "coastal" runs pretty much monopolized the picture in 1914, whereas that group was overshadowed by regular foreign services in 1939. Finally, the ages of the latter fleet show graphically the effect of the five feverish years of building at the end of the first war.

A misleading element in our maritime statistics is the technical use of the words "foreign" and "domestic," which pervert the value of the general figures unless used with caution. Crossing the narrow, fresh-water Detroit or Niagara rivers constitutes a foreign voyage. On the other hand, the rough trip from New York to New Orleans, from Portland, Maine, to Portland, Oregon, or even to our "noncontiguous territories" of Hawaii, Alaska, and Puerto Rico comes under the head of domestic shipping.

Because all that "domestic" commerce was barred by law to other flags, the vessels in our 1914 merchant marine best fitted for overseas duties were, ironically enough, those engaged in our protected "coastal" trade. Most useful of all were the capacious and fairly modern freighters of the American-Hawaiian Line, which in pre-Canal days operated on both oceans with a connecting rail line across Mexico. Of its twenty-six ships, seventeen served the government eventually on the ferry service to France; but they put in some very lucrative tramp charter trading before that. So too did the intercoastal freighters of the Luckenbach Line, some of them primitive ex-British tramps thirty years old. Several vessels of both those groups were torpedoed. Some of the other lines on the longer coastal runs and in service to the outlying territories had useful freighters or passenger-cargo ships, but childhood recollections raise questions concerning the seagoing qualities of some of the coastal steamers that creaked up and down the eastern coast—and a few were omitted from the table on that account.

On our strictly "foreign" runs, half-hearted subsidies had not been by 1914 the effective stimulus of the absolute coastal protection. Only six moderate-sized liners served the transatlantic route and two were a quarter of a century old. The Pacific Mail was about to abandon its half-century of service to the Far East; and the Great Northern contributed its lone 20,000-ton *Minnesota,* our largest merchantman. The Ward Line ran some good steamers to Cuba, but those of the Red D Line to Venezuela were small and old. Not much help would be had from those foreign runs, which left many major shipping lanes untouched.

No sooner was war declared in Europe in the summer of 1914 than Congress let down the bars to foreign-built vessels. Shipowners had failed to take advantage of similar partial permission in the recent Panama Canal Act, but now in less than a year more than a half a million tons flocked to American registry to avoid belligerent requisitioning and high war-risk rates. Among these ships were some excellent American-owned vessels employed under foreign flags because building and operating costs had been cheaper. In particular, the United Fruit transferred more than twenty of its "Great White Fleet" from British registry, and the Standard Oil did likewise with some tankers. In addition, many over-age vessels were purchased by the Americans, an exact reverse of 1940 when the British were busily buying second-hand old ships from the United States. The first three American ships sunk by mines and the first two lost through U-boat activity were all ex-British freighters.

Sinkings were less responsible for the early shipping shortage than those endless problems (which we have noted previously)— curtailed cargo space through military demands, lengthened sea routes, and congested ports. In fact, up to mid-1916, losses by sinkings had been pretty well matched by launchings and seizures. By the middle of that year, however, about a fifth of all available seagoing steamers had been withdrawn from commercial work, including many that had been carrying American cargoes. Some 1,600 ships were being used by the British for military or naval purposes, either of their own or to supplement those of their allies. We are aware of the tremendous burdens imposed by the longer sea lanes of World War II, but some cargo space was wasted in this way in the earlier war. To be sure, England could service the main theater of action on the Western Front with vessels too small for the high seas, but the Gallipoli campaign in 1915 needlessly wasted much tonnage, and later other far-away expeditions proved burdensome. Then, too, shifts in the nature of the traffic tied up much cargo space, such as the necessity for England to use cane sugar from Java or the Caribbean instead of beet sugar from near-by Germany. An enormous amount of cargo space went to waste, also, with that war-swollen, one-way eastbound traffic across the North Atlantic. Of the 21,604 vessels that returned to our ports from Europe between mid-1914 and mid-1918, 13,255 arrived in ballast.

Measuring miles was only half the story. It was possible for a five-thousand-mile voyage with good port handling at each end to tie up cargo space for less time than a three-thousand-mile voyage where the ships might lie idle for weeks awaiting a chance to load or unload. The time needed to plod across several thousand miles of salt water could be predicted with some accuracy, but not the time likely to be consumed in port. At best, unloading and reloading of cargo ships usually needed from three to five days, but too often a ship's carrying capacity was wasted for four or five weeks—enough to cross the Atlantic and back. England's foremost shipping authority called war-port congestion at some periods more harmful than sinkings. Many ports lacked adequate docking facilities for the rush of war orders. The longshoremen, moreover, were often decreased in number by the demands of military service. Above all, it was difficult to work out an adjustment between railroads and shipping in order to keep freight moving freely.

In World War I, the French ports were the worst bottlenecks, with imports swelled to three times their normal value. French genius was never at its best in the realm of synchronizing freight

trains and tramps. In England, the hazards of the London approaches forced shipping to west-coast ports, which were less well
adapted for handling general cargoes. Archangel was but one of
several nightmares scattered about the world; and the port of
New York was by no means the least.

New York was suddenly clinching its title as the world's busi-
est seaport after running neck and neck for first place with London, Liverpool, and Hamburg. Virtually half of the American
exports and imports and the lion's share of the passenger liner
traffic passed along its crowded docks. The peculiar configuration
of Manhattan with most of the railroads arriving on the far side
of the Hudson added to the difficulties. With the British and
Allied purchasing commissions ordering their supplies "F.O.B.
New York," sellers all over the nation naturally rushed their
goods there to get their pay quickly, regardless of whether cargo
space was ready. Largely because of the overseas congestion in
France, the ships were not there.

As a result warehouses were jammed and freight cars were
backed up far into the hinterland. One railroad reported that
every siding on its route was filled with freight cars headed for
New York. When a ship did arrive, everything had to be thrown
off schedule in a wild scramble to locate what it was supposed to
carry. Gradually the railroads imposed embargoes, holding back
freight until shipping was ready; and matters improved for a
while. But strikes, combined with the coldest weather in a gen-
eration, held up the coal supply in the critical winter of 1917-18,
and the congestion became worse than ever. Scores of vessels—
at one time some 150 of them—were held in port until lighters
could fight their way through the ice-choked harbor to fill their
bunkers. Some thirty thousand freight cars were tied up in this
area; to release some of them, their contents were dumped on the
Jersey marshes. One munitions order was canceled on the ground
that the material had become obsolete during its long wait. Dray-
men had to wait in line, sometimes whole days, and then not be
near the piers. Those conditions resulted in the postwar creation

of the Port of New York Authority, which was to do much to relieve the worst problems of port congestion in the next war.

Even before 1917, such inroads into carrying capacity had been causing shipping shortages, as the high freight rates demonstrated. But with the unrestricted U-boat activity, the situation turned desperate. Even after those sinkings had been checked, however, the shortage remained grave because of the reduced carrying capacity of anywhere from 20 to 40 per cent as a result of the convoy system. Under such circumstances, commerce was no longer allowed to go its own course. All the Allied nations soon tightened their control over their merchant marines, their imports, and their exports. The United States Shipping Board, established in 1916, around the same time as the British Ministry of Shipping, did not get under way until we entered the war. Eventually we shall find an Allied shipping control adjusting the shipping of the various nations to the needs of each. But that was not the case in those months while the United States was still a neutral.

Before considering our belligerent experiences in the two wars, it seems best to turn to our neutral months of the second war. An acute shortage of cargo space developed much earlier in that neutral period. Although the two wars followed much the same cycles, the shipping problem came to the fore within the first ten months of the second conflict, instead of after a "quiet" interval of about thirty months as in the earlier war. The merchant tonnage available to England and her friends totaled about the same in 1939 as in 1914, but the average ships measured about five thousand tons instead of three thousand. The outbreak of war in Europe, however, found the United States this time with a far larger seagoing merchant marine. Although most of it was obsolescent, an intelligent plan for replacement was in operation. This time the sinkings meant a heavier steady drain, but the new shipbuilding program became effective more quickly. Worst of all for shipping problems was that radical lengthening of the vital sea lanes about which we have heard so often.

Our first important shipping experience in the war was that self-denying extension of the Neutrality Act of November, 1939, to bar ships under the American flag from the war zone. As we know, it provoked an angry clamor from shipowners, seamen, and chambers of commerce much in the vein of that aroused by Embargo and Nonintercourse. It was pointed out that some eighty American vessels, with crews totaling some five thousand, would be thrown out of employment.

Whereas the start of the last war saw the United States attracting much foreign shipping to its flag, this time the Neutrality Act caused the transferring of many American vessels to other flags so that they might participate in the profits of the "main line." The Administration, not being enthusiastic about the new war-zone restrictions, was ready to co-operate in efforts to circumvent them. This situation gave a tremendous boom to one of the strangest merchant marines of modern times.

The merchant marine of Panama suddenly expanded into the sixth largest in the world; and this in spite of the fact that the little Republic built and used only a few small vessels itself. During the Napoleonic Wars, it will be recalled, the few merchant ships of some tiny North German states had almost overnight increased a hundredfold through transfers of registry from belligerent flags. In Panama, those bastard neutrals had a twentieth-century counterpart. The uses of the Panamanian flag were first discovered in 1922 when two big American passenger ships were transferred to that flag in order to be able to serve liquor during prohibition. Panama, fully realizing the chance for easy profit, passed a law in 1925 facilitating such transfers merely for a small tonnage fee and without requiring a change in ownership.

Even before the war this practice was well developed. Numerous American vessels took advantage of this opportunity to avoid the rigid American regulations regarding the pay, accommodations, and citizenship of crews and officers; of periodic inspections; safety devices, and the like. On such a transferred ship, foreign mariners could be used and need be paid only half the American rates. The American owner could still retain full title to the ship, merely setting up a dummy corporation in Panama. Such a ship did not have to visit Panama for the transfer; Panamanian consuls in any part of the world could make all the arrangements for provisional transfers. The United States was not alone in using this convenience; by 1932, Norwegian, Greek, Yugoslav, Dutch, Danish, and other shipowners began to follow suit, in some cases to avoid governmental requisitioning in case of war. Panama became a sort of international clearinghouse for shipping, where vessels could be shifted in and out with a minimum of red tape.

American shipowners immediately perceived that here was a way in which American-owned vessels could reap the profits of war-zone trade—in spite of the Neutrality Act and without endangering American crews or involving the flag in unpleasant incidents. Transfers had to be approved by the Maritime Commission, to be sure, but it proved to be broad-minded in that matter. Many vessels went directly from American registry, some 140 of 750,000 gross tons in two years. When the United States took over German, Italian, and Danish vessels, with title in the Maritime Commission, they too were transferred to Panamanian registry, where they could employ foreign officers and crews in a quantity forbidden on American ships.

The anomalous status of "our seagoing stepchild" was indicated in a table of war-risk rates, which quoted separate terms for belligerent, American, and other neutral shipping. A footnote pointed out that vessels of Panamanian registry were classed as belligerent, unless owned in the United States, and that former German, Italian, and Danish vessels were rated belligerent unless operated by the Maritime Commission. An embarrassing coincidence occurred in the autumn of 1941 when the president of Panama refused to permit the arming of merchantmen; within a week a revolution drove him into exile and his successor permitted the mounting of guns. All in all, one may well imagine a submarine commander scratching his head in puzzled ignorance of the particular status of some vessel flying that versatile and all-embracing flag.

Panama was not the only objective in this "flight from the flag." The United States Lines, operating eight ships to the European war zone, transferred them to Belgian registry, but through mortgages and other devices retained most of the property rights and profits. It had sought first the usual Panamanian registry but that action, attempted immediately upon the establishment of the war-zone restrictions, smelled too strongly, at that moment, of law evasion. The line also tried a Norwegian transfer unsuccessfully. As it turned out, most of their vessels were sunk within the coming year; but they were well insured.

Except for the loss of carrying power inherent in the immediate adoption of the convoy system, no serious strain on tonnage developed in the first nine or ten months of the war. In fact the spread of German power in Europe really improved, instead of damaging, the British shipping situation. Most of Norway's valuable merchantmen were not "at home" when the Germans seized their nation. The "government in exile" established in England requisitioned all this tonnage, which had not fallen into German hands, and placed it at British disposal. It included a large number of valuable tankers that carried almost half of England's oil supply. The same situation held for the Dutch shipping and the smaller Belgian merchant marine, and thus a more immediate control was effected than in the last war. Similar arrangements the following year also brought much of the Greek and Yugoslav shipping under British control. Denmark's ships were not so available because its king and government remained at home under German domination, but many of them were seized. Except for some "Free French" vessels, much of France's merchant marine was withdrawn from British use, as was naturally that of the other ally of the last war, Italy, when it joined the enemy. This was not so bad a loss as it might have been from the shipping standpoint, for, we recall, those allies in the last war had been a drain on shipping resources as they required more tonnage than they gave.

In the months after Dunkerque, however, other aspects of those German successes suddenly produced a grave shipping shortage which long remained acute. Sinkings mounted after that initial period of comparative quiet; and England's shipyards, battered by raids, could not furnish the needed replacements as they had in the last war. At the same time, with the disappearance of the Western Front and with the major theaters of war pushed farther away, there were no longer any places to use small Channel vessels for the transportation of men and supplies. The simultaneous closing of the Mediterranean to traffic necessitated the long Good Hope route for the Libyan campaign supplies, and that obviously tied up shipping for long periods and delayed delivery either from England or the United States.

Port delays, too, were again in the picture, although New York was able to do its job more efficiently this time. The railroads had a co-ordinator of traffic who managed to prevent many wasted days in port by synchronizing a steady flow of materials with shipping movements. Only after we entered the war did the congestion threat become serious in our own ports.

Overseas, however, conditions were worse than they had been in World War I, between the loss of European ports of entry and the merciless bombing of British seaports. Full details of the latter were drastically censored, but the punishment of Bristol and Plymouth was terrific and the London docks came in for their share. The burden fell heavily upon Liverpool and Glasgow, and they, too, were crippled by raids. In order to repair ships, the British towed a floating dry dock from port to port. Egypt and other more or less out-of-the-way places were not altogether free from bombing either; besides, they were not equipped to cope with the great influx of supplies which came with a rush when military operations moved in those directions. Even before we entered the war, Americans were making plans to improve port facilities and land transportation connections in the Red Sea and Persian Gulf regions to speed up the "turnaround" of shipping, while the Maritime Commission sent "trouble shooters" to the critical remote ports to keep things moving.

With the growing acuteness of the shortage, the 1914 situation was reversed, and the United States began to sell some of the second-hand vessels in its laid-up fleets to the British. Scores of old veterans of World War I's emergency building program came into their own at last. Slow, perhaps, they were, but they could plod along at convoy speed and carry the needed freight, just as the old destroyers of their same era aided the war effort when transferred to the British. Before long, however, the British came after new ships, and at the end of 1940 contracted for sixty freighters. These were to be the forerunners of the "ugly ducklings," soon to be built in enormous numbers by the Maritime Commission.

Thus in both wars our period of neutrality found us becoming increasingly involved through the emergencies of the sea lanes. In each case, a tremendous building of new merchantmen accompanied our war effort. In the first war, the building boom followed our entry into the conflict, and in the second, as we shall see, it was already well launched before the fatal Sunday morning of the Japanese attack on Pearl Harbor.

In April, 1917, our declaration of war was to make us for the time being just about as much of a liability to the British shipping worries as France, Italy, and Russia had been. And, we recall, April, 1917, was the blackest month of the U-boat sinkings anyway. Not only did we find ourselves unable to help Britain, but we could not meet even our own shipping requirements, particularly after the decision was made to send troops to the Western Front.

Through the Shipping Board and its subsidiary, the Emergency Fleet Corporation, the government struggled through the spring and summer to assemble every bit of available shipping. All steel freighters and all adequate steel passenger steamers over the minimum size (2,500 dead-weight tons, about equivalent to

1,600 gross tons) were made liable to requisition. Thanks to the purchase of foreign shipping and to new construction, the number of these had increased since 1914. The biggest single windfall was the seizure of scores of German and other belligerent vessels interned in American ports. These included many fine ocean liners, primarily the huge 54,000-ton *Vaterland* (renamed *Leviathan*). The Germans smashed cylinders and otherwise sabotaged machinery in those vessels, but naval welding put them all back in order within six months. Those liners looked out for troop transport, but the cargo-ship problem remained. A half a million tons or so of Dutch shipping were seized on the convenient old angary principle, that in time of stress a nation might make use of any shipping lying in its ports. A much larger amount of other neutral tonnage was secured, partly through copying the British methods of bunker control and partly through the lever of food agreements with hungry nations. The Danes proved cautious and insisted that most of their tonnage be kept out of the danger zone, but others were unable to be as particular. Yet all those vessels still left us badly shorthanded.

As a result the old "windjammers" came into their own for what seemed to be one last chance at profit and usefulness. Shipping men still look back with wistful longing to those rich returns. Like the farmers and munitions makers, prosperity, reminiscent of the lush neutral days of 1793-1812, was theirs. Already the lucky owners of seagoing steamships had been "sitting pretty." The dividends of the American-Hawaiian Line, for example, jumped from 10 per cent in 1915 to 405 per cent in 1917. (Between 1939 and 1941, they rose only from 1½ to 5 per cent.) But with the governmental requisitioning of steamships, the sailing vessels now offered the big rewards.

The United States had a much larger proportion of these than did England, including 123 that exceeded the 1,600 gross ton limit. About a quarter of these vessels were square-riggers in the grain trade, chiefly hailing from San Francisco. The rest were East Coast schooners, most of which had been busy in the coal trade, until, just before the war, barges and steam colliers had begun to replace them. Naturally these sailing vessels were often slow—one laden with Bataan mahogany took nine months from Manila to New York—and their war-risk and marine-insurance rates were higher than for steam vessels. Nevertheless, they could carry the all-essential cargoes. The majority were used for trade with South America, Africa, and the South Seas. Some sailed for France, but they were too vulnerable as U-boat targets. Even a few new ones were built under the impetus of the attractive freight rates. The four-masted 1,100-ton *Nancy Hanks,* Maine-built in 1917, received a $270,000 charter for a voyage to Africa and the return. That paid her full cost of construction, as well as the expenses of the voyage. On the day she first sailed from port, her fortunate shareholders received 100 per cent of their invest-ment back in dividend checks!

Still there was by no means enough tonnage, and under those emergency conditions the United States embarked upon its huge shipbuilding program. Designed as a war measure to replace the hulls shattered by U-boats, relatively few of the new fleet had left the ways before the Armistice. Nevertheless, they completely transformed the American seagoing merchant marine. The United States entered the war without enough vessels to meet more than a fraction of its needs, but after peace came, the nation had more seagoing freighters than it could use.

Had the first war dragged on into 1919, the emergency fleet might well have been hailed as one of the causes of victory; as it was, it suggested to many a futile orgy of spending. In fact, it was not until the U-boats once again went to work that those ships really came into their own in the next war.

The program was born in the summer of 1917, when sinkings were still running at more than half a million tons a month and the expeditionary force was being prepared. The plan called for freighters by the hundreds and as soon as possible. The govern-ment commandeered all steel vessels in the yards at the time, whether under construction or fitting out, and these numbered some 431 of many different types. The British were inclined to be annoyed, since they had placed heavy orders in American yards. Plans were made for thousands of new freighters of more or less standardized types to be built on government account. Contracts were placed for 2,851 steamships, of which 1,741 were steel, 1,017 wooden, 50 composite steel and wood, and 43 concrete.

From the quantitative standpoint it was a noteworthy achievement, as "the greatest shipbuilding feat in history" to that time. Its leaders could, and did, point with pride to the building ways which increased from 215 to 1,284; to the workers, whose numbers jumped from 50,000 to 350,000; and to what then seemed remarkable speed.

Some sour aspects came to light, however. The cost was some three billions, which was far more than was necessary. The chief abuse lay in the cost-plus contracts, by which the builder received for his overhead and profit a generous percentage of all money spent for labor and materials. Such contracts were in many cases too tempting for human nature to resist, and the costs went sky-high from many a padded account. Numerous contractors without previous shipbuilding experience operated on a shoestring and "cleaned up" handsomely from those cost-plus contracts.

The shipyard workers profited too. From many aspects, it was "nice work if you could get it." Often hard and sometimes hazardous, it was, nevertheless, in many respects preferable to compulsory military service; at any rate, it paid better. Wages soared far beyond what inexperienced or even experienced artisans had ever received before. The cost-plus contracts tempted some builders to hire scores more extra hands than were needed, since by those contract terms a percentage of every additional wage dollar went into the contractor's pocket. Among the numerous shipyard stories that floated around in that war, and were even heard about yards here and there in the second conflict, was the tale of the man hired at substantial wages and told to go in and walk around until he should be informed that he was needed. And usually in those stories there was the second man, whom he found following him about and who, when confronted, admitted to being his "helper." Labor disputes, too, caused many serious delays, but there were, of course, many workers who took an honest pride in a job well done.

Many of the emergency ships did not work out well. This was particularly true of the wooden, composite, and concrete vessels. The composite ships were found to be too difficult and costly to build, while the concrete craft, the pet idea of one senator, accomplished little.

The question of whether or not to use wood precipitated a row that almost blew the top off the Shipping Board at the outset. Avowedly only considered because of the emergency, wood was advocated on the grounds of a steel shortage and of the already congested state of the steel shipyards from naval or commercial orders. It was urged that many wooden-vessel yards and trained workers were going to waste; that small vessels averaging little more than 2,000 gross tons could be turned out in a hurry; and that it did not matter how long they lasted. They would, so it was argued, worry the enemy, and in that period of heavy sinkings, one trip apiece to France would justify their building.

Actually, the two hundred or so that were finished left a pretty sorry record. Some were awash almost before they left port. One, which sank in the Pacific, left the grim memory of a starving boat crew driven to the extremity of eating their dead shipmates. With the Armistice, construction stopped on most of them, and many a gaunt, unfinished frame lay for years on its rotting way until perhaps sawn up for firewood.

The steel ships, on the other hand, were on the whole a success. Steel proved to be less scarce than at first reported and their production went ahead on a large scale. The unique feature was prefabrication. Instead of having the whole ship built at a shore-front yard, much of the material was prepared in hundreds of plants scattered about the country. The assembling was then done at the yard by noisy riveting at top speed. Production was facilitated in many new ways—the plates, for example, came with the rivet holes already punched, some million holes for each ship.

Nearly 450 were built on the Great Lakes, but these averaged only about 2,500 gross tons, since they had to be small enough to get through the locks of the Welland Canal. At least two of this class, all named for various lakes, went down in overseas service. Many more were constructed on the Pacific coast. These were larger ships, generally ranging between five and six thousand gross tons. The great center, however, was the Delaware River.

Most conspicuous of all the yards was Hog Island, a huge plant dug out of the river mud just below Philadelphia at government expense, and operated by a private corporation. Along two miles of swampy river front, it had fifty building ways and twenty-eight fitting slips for completing the launched hulls. Some 35,000 men were employed here at its peak, and its prefabricated material was brought from dozens of plants from as far distant as Kansas City, St. Paul, and Montreal, to be riveted into position. All but 12 of the 122 ships turned out were of its celebrated Class A type of freighters, measuring about 5,000 gross tons, almost double the size of the average submarine victim of that war. These Hog-Islanders were far from beautiful, but unlike some of their jerry-built contemporaries which "spat rivets all over the seven seas," they proved tough. Designed to eliminate curves for greater speed in building, they were wall-sided, flat-bottomed, blunt-bowed, and square-sterned. Durable and satisfactory products of honest workmanship, they became the backbone of the new merchant marine. Hog Island's first product, launched in August, 1918, six months after her keel was laid, was the *Quistconk*, still in active service when the next war started. So, too, were our first two submarine victims of the second conflict, the *Robin Moor* and the *Lehigh*, as well as many other Hog-Islanders, while an undue number of Pacific shipyard products swung idly in the laid-up fleets.

The new vessels, however, did not come along fast enough to carry more than a fraction of the supplies needed by the two million men being transported to France. Much shipping had to be diverted from other important services for that huge job. The various Allied governments gradually had to assume complete control over all cargoes, as well as over all vessels under their respective flags. Going even beyond that, they eventually pooled their resources and set up international shipping control groups to estimate the relative value of conflicting needs and claims and to establish priorities for troops, munitions, food, or fuel for various destinations. Such decisions were often difficult and tremendously important, with the hunger of one nation sometimes balanced against the security of a remote outpost or the success of a distant campaign. Undoubtedly some of that diversion of shipping meant hardships, such as less food for the British and less coal for New England, but the Allied Shipping Council by its rigid economies managed to meet the most essential demands. Everything was done to get maximum service from the ships in use, with constant conflict for priorities between food and munitions authorities. Nonessential imports were curtailed or eliminated along with other economies of every sort. Montreal grain ships, for example, carried oil in their double bottoms and horses or mules on deck.

Expert planning went into the loading of those precious freighters long before the goods reached the docks. It was found, for instance, that completed artillery shells took up less space than their component raw materials, but that crated planes needed nine times as much space as their unassembled parts, and trench mortars more than twelve times as much. General Pershing estimated that the munitions agreement, by which our allies co-operated with these packing details, saved more than two million dead-weight tons of cargo space—and that was more than was then available. In explosives alone the saving was reckoned at 75 per cent in cargo space.

To speed up the "turnaround," conditions at New York were improved and the port facilities of Brest and St. Nazaire were modernized. Completed locomotives were carried over to expedite the latter work. As a result, the "turnaround" for freighters, which had sometimes exceeded 100 days, making barely three trips a year possible, was reduced to an average of 75 days, including slow convoy crossings and time in port. Liner-transports with their greater speed in crossing and with quick embarkation and disembarkation of troops, were often over and back in three weeks or so. To shorten runs, which also meant quickened "turnaround," Britain used Cuban instead of Javanese sugar, for example, and substituted North American for Australian wheat. British liners from distant routes appeared on the Atlantic. And so the saving of cargo space continued, while the emergency ships were still on the ways.

The war ended—with our huge projected building just getting under way. Of the 1,741 steel emergency ships contracted for, not one was launched in 1917. By the Armistice in November, 1918, only 107 steel, 67 wooden, and 4 composite vessels had been finished. There was talk of stopping the building, but the pressure of builders, making profits, and of laborers, earning big pay, was too strong. Contracts for 941 were canceled, to be sure, but much of the construction continued. Not only were partly completed ships finished, but keels were laid for more than a third of the Shipping Board's fleet after the Armistice was signed. Almost four years after our entry into the war, the last ship was launched in late February, 1921.

America had returned to the seas with a vengeance. In 1920, the nation's registered shipping reached its all-time peak of 9,924,000 gross tons, almost ten times what it had been in 1914. For the first time since 1863, half of the tonnage entering American ports from foreign countries flew the Stars and Stripes. All that tardy tonnage was more than the merchant marine could absorb. The surplus became as serious as the deficit had been! For a while after the war, the business of feeding Europe, and bringing home the army and its stores, kept many vessels well employed; but then the tide began to ebb.

Seagoing vessels became a drug on the market. Many Hog-Islanders and others of the better ships, to be sure, were operated with government subsidization on strategic trade routes to many parts of the world, while the new tankers were proving highly useful. But hundreds of others were held in less esteem. Some of the new steel ships, which had cost two hundred dollars a ton to build, were sold for as little as five dollars a ton. Ford bought 149 of the lake-built steamers for about eight dollars a ton to be broken up for scrap. Nearly two hundred more emergency freighters were laid up at anchor in rusting, desolate groups that swung with the tide year in and year out along the coasts. Half of them would still be there when the next war started.

The day was rapidly approaching, however, when the universal obsolescence of our shipping would find us in a new war-shipping shortage almost as serious as the old one. The Hog-Islanders and their contemporaries were all growing old together and were rapidly approaching in the late nineteen thirties their twenty-year mark. Many remained seaworthy, however, and many were still making money for their owners on those routes, which had been opened to American shipping during the past war. They were, nevertheless, being outclassed by newer, faster, and more economical vessels in foreign merchant marines. As for new American vessels, the fifteen years between 1922 and 1937 saw the launching of exactly two steel seagoing cargo ships.

In 1936, after long years of a vacillating shipping policy, Congress replaced the Shipping Board with the Maritime Commission, which at once undertook a thoroughgoing economic survey of the nation's shipping needs. It decided that a reasonable number of good ships were needed for the commerce of thirty or forty key runs and also to serve military or naval purposes in case of war. In 1937, the policy was begun of building fifty new ships a year for the next ten years, in three major standard classes of C-1 cargo ships of about 6,800 gross tons and fourteen knots speed; C-2 cargo ships of 7,500 to 8,000 tons and about sixteen knots; and larger C-3 cargo-passenger ships modified to meet specific needs and capable of sixteen and a half knots. These new "replacement" ships, equipped with turbines of latest design, cost about two to three million dollars each and were to be built under Maritime Commission supervision but operated by private companies. The government, moreover, made up the difference between American and average foreign costs in building and operation, as well as for any special features designed to fit the vessels for war service. A tanker program was also initiated by the Commission, as well as the construction of a medium-sized liner capable of use for military or naval purposes.

The outbreak of the second war changed these plans from moderate replacement to a far greater emergency program than the previous one. That past performance was to be greatly overshadowed by the new expansion of the merchant marine. The replacement scheme was retained, and was stepped up to four hundred ships a year instead of fifty as originally planned, so that fast auxiliaries would be available for the fighting services and first-rate ships would be on hand for postwar trade. In addition, emergency freighters were needed as quickly as possible to meet the crying need for tonnage. They were turned out, in fact, with more speed than seemed possible at first. The two hundred emergency ships planned in January, 1941, gradually expanded by September, 1942, into a program of sixteen hundred.

The new emergency ships were all built on a single standard design, similar to those sixty freighters ordered by the British in 1940. This was an improvement over the previous war, when vessels of various patterns and sizes were turned out by different yards. The "Liberty Ships," or EC-2's as they were officially termed, measured about 3,400 tons net, 7,200 tons gross, 10,500 tons dead weight (the figure popularized by the Maritime Commission), and 14,200 tons displacement. They were thus almost 50 per cent larger than the Hog-Islander in size and carrying capacity. Their hulls were similar to the C-2 ships, but their eleven-knot speed was about five knots slower. To avoid a bottleneck in engines, they were given reciprocating engines instead of the new turbines, which were being required in large quantities for the navy and the better ships. With those poorer engines, they would be badly handicapped in postwar trade, but for the duration they could go fast enough for a convoy. When, back in their blueprint stage, the President remarked that they were "not what a shiplover could admire," they were dubbed "ugly ducklings," but they scarcely deserved that slighting nickname. Their tapering bows, cruiser sterns, sheer lines, and sleek sides made them almost beautiful in comparison with the square bluntness of the previous emergency crop.

The most distinctive departures in construction were the use of welding and of increasing preassembling. Welding, instead of riveting the plates together, produced a smoother hull and simplified the labor supply. The preassembling carried the prefabrication of the last war much farther. Then punched plates, produced elsewhere, had to be riveted on the ways, but now a whole bow section or a bulkhead could be assembled in another part of the plant, and hoisted into place intact.

That was why more ships were built on fewer ways, and why they were built faster. Except for a few fast stunts, the builders of the last war averaged ten to twelve months between laying the keel and delivering a completed steel freighter. Hog Island's fastest job had taken more than seven months, about 235 days. Its average was around 330 days; launching records, of course, were quicker than final delivery. The Maritime Commission anticipated that, once its yards were well under way, "Liberty Ships" could be completed in 105 days; but actual performance was much faster. The average for August, 1942, was just under eighty-three days, with many yards delivering in two months; and in September the average dropped to seventy days. Meanwhile, Henry J. Kaiser's Portland, Oregon, yard launched the *Pierre S. DuPont* in August in twenty-four days and delivered her seven days later. He announced his next goal to be eighteen days; but within a month the *Joseph N. Teal* came off the ways of this same yard in *ten* days and was delivered in another four!

This time, honors went to the Pacific coast in general, and in particular to the several yards of Kaiser, who had built the great Boulder, Bonneville, and Grand Coulee dams, but had never before tried shipbuilding. When amazement was expressed that he had outstripped the experienced East Coast builders, one of the Maritime Commissioners explained the essential difference between this standardized construction and the tailor-made work on regular vessels: "In the West they are used to moving a mass of material. When they jumped into this building of ships it was just like building any other structure. . . . It is not a real shipbuilding job. It is a mass production job of collecting materials."

The emergency construction was carried on in yards of moderate size. Shipping concentration in this war meant the control of numerous such yards by single corporations, such as the Bethlehem Steel and the Todd Shipbuilding companies. The one project to rival Hog Island in magnitude was a two-hundred-ship contract with Andrew J. Higgins, a New Orleans builder of efficient small craft for the navy. He planned a huge plant where ships were to be slowly moved toward the sea on a vast assembly line. After the yard construction was well under way, the Maritime Commission canceled the contract, stating that the supply of steel and other materials was insufficient even for the yards already in operation. Each "Liberty Ship" required some three thousand tons of steel, and supplies did not appear to have been distributed evenly among the yards. For his part, Higgins accused the Commission of favoring the established shipbuilding concerns.

According to the Maritime Commission, the worst features of the previous emergency shipbuilding were to be avoided. In the actual construction of the ships, the cost-plus contracts of World War I were to be replaced by a bonus to yield about 6 per cent profit to the builder. Another type of contract was cost plus a fixed fee in which the contractor received the fee and the government paid the costs. Here and there, however, in side contracts for yard facilities, the unscrupulous appeared to be finding their way to the more abundant life much in the manner of the last war. A lucrative practice was for the facilities contractor to set up subcontractors of his own, and then to milk away from every conceivable angle. The President's comment that this war would produce no new millionaires was already seemingly being disproved in some defense areas before we had been at war six months. There will be plenty to tell when the public interest no longer calls for silence. At any rate, the "Liberty Ships" seemed to be far better vessels than their predecessors, and their cost of some $1,800,000 (including around $100,000 bonus) was about equal to the cost of five hours of W.P.A. at its 1939 rate!

As for the labor situation, time will show how it compared with conditions in the last war. Early in 1942, a member of the Maritime Commission remarked vigorously: "Too damn much loafing in shipyards all over the country. Too much agitation by labor agitators and capital agitators. Too much disturbance placed in the minds of workers by a few of their leaders." By summer, accelerated production led him to modify his opinion. Pay was once again very high; and it was still popular work.

While it was good to be in the shipbuilding game, it was bad to be in its way, as evicted homeowners could testify in more than one seaboard community. At times, such sacrifice seemed essential to the war effort; at others it appeared unnecessary. One seaport, where a Maritime Commission yard lagged and its local representation seemed unfortunate, was sadly defaced by the weird grades and curves of a rail spur winding through dooryards and gardens—outside of some roller-coasters, one of the crookedest stretches of track in the East. The rejection of a satisfactory alternate route was based on the need for speed, but persistent stories of waste and inefficiency were current about this yard, while one near by made a good record with similar supply facilities.

On the whole, however, the ships came off the ways in more gratifying fashion than in the other emergency. Once the yards were in operation, the tempo increased. By the end of 1941, launchings averaged one a day; by mid-1942, they reached two a day; and by late September, the rate was three a day. Yet greater output was expected, so that the goal of 2,300 seagoing ships, totaling 24,000,000 dead-weight tons might be far exceeded before the end of 1943—if steel enough could be found. About 1,600 of those projected vessels were "Liberty Ships," the rest tankers and fast C-ships of the replacement program. In addition, the Commission planned some seven hundred tugs, barges, and other smaller vessels, in some of which wood and concrete, that was rejected wisely in this war for the seagoing vessels, could be used. A novel type of small gasoline-driven freighters with automobile engines and with its propeller underneath, known as the "Sea Otter," was proposed but not adopted. Nor was this tremendous program of new merchantmen the only burden imposed on the nation's yards. They were rushing our "two-ocean navy" to completion two years ahead of schedule, along with the less spectacular but very essential task of repairing or converting some fifty-five hundred ships a year.

This time, too, the shipbuilding program began to produce results in time to relieve the war emergency far more than in 1917-18. The *Patrick Henry,* first of the "Liberty Ships," was launched at Baltimore on September 27, 1941; by mid-March of 1942 she had safely delivered a ten-thousand-ton cargo of war materials in Egypt. Some of the heavy bombs dropped upon Japanese warships in the Coral Sea battle in May, 1942, had been carried out to Australia in vessels whose keels had been laid since Pearl Harbor six months before.

It would have been no use to turn out ships if men could not be found willing and able to man them. It took courage of the sternest type to venture out in a merchantman on those dangerous seas, but except perhaps for a brief interval in the tanker terror, crews were never lacking, while the government set up schools to train the additional thousands of officers and seamen needed for the ever expanding fleet. Even the army, often sensitive on the matter of stipend, paid tribute to the merchant seamen; a soldier, guarding a stretch of beach, looked out at a passing freighter and remarked, "There goes *one* crowd whose high pay we don't begrudge." Torpedoed sailors returned to sea again and again to help carry essential cargoes, but the National

Maritime Union protested that it was bad for morale to expect men to risk their lives carrying "beer, bananas, and ballast."

Never before in either war had there been such a desperate need of shipping—barely enough to meet present needs, even with the exercise of utmost economy. Various factors made the situation worse than in 1917-18, as we know, both in the length of the new essential sea routes and in many other respects. The actual transporting of troops was not the prime problem, for the big passenger liners were little good for much else; but the plans of strategists came up against the stone wall of finding freighters enough to keep the troops supplied once they were landed beyond the seas.

The army authorities on "logistics" reckoned that the steady services of two dead-weight tons of shipping had been needed to keep a soldier supplied in France in 1918. A soldier in 1942, however, because of the bulkier implements of mechanized warfare, would need seven or eight dead-weight tons in western Europe, and perhaps double that amount in more distant theaters of war. Multiplied by the million or two soldiers needed for a full-dress expeditionary force, the immensity of the problem became apparent. A 50 per cent increase of the 1942 tonnage was estimated to be needed for carrying on large-scale operations in western Europe and the Middle East; another 50 per cent was required to supply two million men in the Orient. In the rapidly accelerating work of the American shipyards lay the hope of such a surplus—if they kept ahead of the U-boats.

The quest for more tonnage led back into the past, with sailing vessels once more called into action and forward into the future with an increased demand for cargo planes. Old "windjammers," which had been anchored outside the three-mile limit as gambling resorts, began to arrive at Cape Town with honest cargoes. Small schooners were pressed into service in the Caribbean trade, with tentative plans to build more. Other old schooners were converted into barges to serve, along with the new barges, in the coastal and Caribbean trade. At the same time, Kaiser caught the popular imagination by proposing to convert some of the shipyards for the construction of flying boats to carry cargo by air. His proposal received some rough treatment in Washington before he was finally authorized to go ahead with a very few.

Meanwhile, every ton of shipping already afloat had to be used to its maximum carrying capacity. With the Maritime Commission engrossed in building ships, its other functions were transferred to the new War Shipping Administration, but this was under the same chairmanship. Again, as in 1917-18, the government exercised its requisitioning power by gaining control of all our shipping, chartering much of it at moderate rates. Exports and imports were rigidly regulated; private cargoes became increasingly scarce as the transportation of lease-lend goods and our own military supplies consumed most of the space in vessels not already drawn off for direct service with the army or navy. Shippers, finding cargo space more and more difficult to secure, began to send their wares by parcel post, until the government shut down on that. Even the favored trade with Latin America suffered, as we have seen, when the U-boats went to work in the Caribbean and the South Atlantic.

Ingenuity was exercised in efforts to save cargo space. In exchange for lease-lend, it was agreed that the recipients would furnish supplies wherever possible for our overseas expeditions. England and the United States pooled their war resources toward that same end. We were to specialize, for instance, in bombers that could be flown across the sea, while the British would concentrate on the smaller planes that would have to travel by ship. It was to save space that material was shipped in a more or less knocked-down condition to the remote assembly plants established, as we saw, in Eretria, the Persian Gulf, and elsewhere, where American mechanics could assemble it. Tremendous space saving was possible in new methods of shipping food. Water, which makes up so large a part of vegetables, eggs, and milk, could be eliminated by dehydration, which cut the bulk down to a very small fraction; a shipment of twenty-seven million pounds of potatoes, for instance, would normally require 125,000 dead-weight tons of shipping space; after dehydration, 15,000 tons were enough. Fresh meat, instead of having to go in special refrigerator ships in whole sides, was boned and rolled into compact packages that could be filled into the nooks and crannies between tanks and other heavy equipment, and the whole space chilled with dry ice. The same amount of meat that, in whole sides would have filled ten ships, would not quite fill four ships when boned and rolled and could be carried in a single ship when dehydrated and compressed. The army found that by eliminating packing cases for clothing and other equipment, it could save about 10 per cent in space, while soldiers' mail was microfilmed, so that one mail sack could do the work of many.

To speed up the "turnaround," the Army and other branches of government attacked the old bogey of port congestion which once more threatened New York. Exports were rerouted to the outports, while inland depots were built to prevent war supplies from clogging the docks. After special courses under stevedores, officers and men were sent to handle unloading at distant ports. As at St. Nazaire in 1918, it once again proved economical to ship locomotives and other rolling stock to the Persian Gulf and elsewhere. Such methods cut a ship's time in port to a minimum.

Yet with all that, the shortage remained acute. The authorities of the United Nations debated the relative shipping needs for Russia, China, Britain, the Middle East, Australia, and lesser far-flung regions, while plans for a second front stalled on the shipping problem. And with more insistence was heard the popular clamor for cargo planes, as the experts and officials haggled.

Chapter XII
Towards Victory on the Sea Lanes

On the sea lanes, a quarter century ago, the merchant vessels were struggling against heavy odds to deliver their vital supplies. The first edition of this book went to press in September 1942—the end of the third year of what was to be a six-year war. Allied fortunes were at low ebb. The Germans were at the Volga and far across Africa into Egypt. The Japanese Navy was pounding at the Solomons and their army was at the gates of India. But by mid-November, President Roosevelt declared: "It would seem that the turning point of the war has now been reached." The Japanese Navy in the Solomons was already losing its offensive power, and in Russia and Egypt the turning point was thorough and dramatic. The United States and Britain, moreover, were starting their first major offensive in Northwest Africa.

While most fronts were beginning to justify guarded optimism, the Allied supply situation faced continued jeopardy on the seas. Samuel Eliot Morison called the period from July 1942 to April 1943 "Ten Months' Incessant Battle." The threat to Britain's food supply and to world contacts in general posed major maritime problems for the United States. Those submarines on the North Atlantic were not the only threat to Allied shipping, though they were the gravest, for those stormy three thousand miles were the virtual lifeline of the British Empire. The enemy attacks on Allied shipping were spreading to the South Atlantic, the Mediterranean, the Indian Ocean, and the Pacific. The instruments of enemy attack included not only U-boats but also aircraft, mines, warship raiders, merchant raiders, and motor torpedo boats (E-boats).

When the Allied statesmen and military-naval leaders met at Casablanca early in 1943 to decide "what next?" they agreed that "the defeat of the U-boat must remain a first charge on the resources of the United Nations" (Allies). But for several months thereafter they were not sure those resources would be enough. It still looked as if the "Battle of the Atlantic" might bring victory to Germany. Even the doughty Winston Churchill later wrote "The only thing that frightened me during the war was the U-boat peril."

Admiral Karl Doenitz, who headed the U-boat activities and eventually the whole German Navy, was primarily waging a "tonnage war." His main objective was to sink ships, without too much concern over what they were carrying or where they were going. He was well aware that if enough supply ships were lost, Britain, at least, would be unable to continue the war.

Right up to April 1943, it looked as though Doenitz's strategy might be going to be successful. Since July 1942, 989 Allied ships had been sunk, and of these 646 were on that most essential supply route, the North Atlantic. Its most perilous stretch was the mid-ocean area to which the land-based planes from Britain, Canada, or Iceland could not reach. That "Black Pit" or "Greenland Air Gap" saw the principal encounters between the German "wolf packs" and the convoys for which they lay in wait. During the month of November, 1942, the total Allied losses rose to 807,000 tons (134 vessels). This was short of the shocking 881,000 tons sunk in April, 1917, the month of the United States' entry into World War I, but it was one of the four times in the two wars that a monthly total ran that high. Major U-boat attacks in March, 1943, sank 85 Allied ships in twenty days. Of that paralyzing destruction, Morison wrote:

> So many escorts were under repair that the group organization was in danger of disintegrating. So many U-boats were out (an average of 116 operating daily in the North Atlantic) that evasive routine was futile; a convoy avoided one concentration of wolf-packs only to fall in with another. The enemy never came so near to disrupting communications between the New World and the Old as in the first twenty days of March 1943. Clearly we could not go on losing ships and men at that rate. When convoy after convoy came in with six to a dozen ships missing, the morale of seamen who had to make the next voyage was impaired.

Then came a startling reversal in the grim warfare on the supply lanes. March was to be the last month of the enemy's wholesale destruction. Both the Germans and the Allies, of course, had been keeping close watch on the statistics of the fluctuation, spread, and impact of that struggle, upon which even ultimate victory might depend. Now those statistics were swiftly confirming the new situation. In contrast to those disastrous figures of the 10 months since July, 1942 (989 sinkings, with 686 in the North Atlantic), the following 10 months, from May, 1943 showed the overall total of Allied losses dropping to a total of 359 ships. Of these, only 90 were in the now less hazardous North Atlantic! Conversely, the German record, now no longer tinged with hopes of victory, was closely linked to that change. In those first ten months, only 59 U-boats had been lost, but the numbers jumped to 219 in the following ten months.

In this spectacular drop in Allied sinkings and the increased toll of U-boats, various elements had been responsible. The United States and Britain had worked together and would continue to do so in joint operation. The credit for success belongs to each of them in different ways. The British had the longer and heavier share of the gruelling patrol and convoy work so vividly pictured in Nicholas Monserrat's *The Cruel Sea*; they sank more submarines than did the Americans; and their merchant seamen suffered far heavier casualties. But in the spring of 1943, probably the most important contribution consisted of the new developments in several fields, largely by the United States. In particular, there was a very effective combination of antisubmarine warfare (ASW) tactics and devices.

The new "hunter-killer" tactics were probably the most potent element in the new Allied successes. These utilized in particular two new types of vessels as well as several original scientific devices. The ships, the Destroyer Escort (DE) and the Escort Carrier (CVE) differed from their prototypes, the Destroyer (DD) and Carrier (CV) mainly in their lessened speed. The latter had never been used in connection with convoys as the DDs had been. In the new tactics, the planes of the Escort Carriers could cover the convoys all the way across the Atlantic, unlike the land-based air-craft from Britain, Canada, or Iceland. The Escort planes did not stay with the 10-knot convoys but swept the seas through which a convoy would pass. The particular purpose was to catch U-boats on the surface. Until nuclear craft began to appear a decade later, the submarine was essentially a surface vessel, which now and then could submerge to avoid detection. Its electric batteries were able to keep it submerged for only a relatively limited time before it had to surface to replenish them. When the scouting planes sighted a surfaced submarine—unless they could bomb it themselves—they directed the attendant destroyers or escorts where to go in for the kill. The latter, if not in position to depth-bomb the submarine, would try to keep track of it until it would have to surface.

An example of the typical "hunter-killer tactics" has been de-scribed by Rear Admiral Daniel V. Gallery, whose Task Group 23 was based around the CVE *Guadalcanal* early in 1944:

> We prowled through our assigned area with the carrier 3,000 yards behind a bent screen of five destroyer escorts, using our airplanes to scour the ocean for about one hundred miles on each side of our base course and 160 miles ahead. With four turkeys (planes) you could, during a four hour flight, cover an area of roughly 20,000 square miles. In round numbers, this is one-third the area of the New England states. . . .
>
> Aircraft can't find a submerged U-boat . . . Our destroyers could find them submerged with their sonar gear, but the maximum range at which we could get an echo off a sub was about 2,000 yards. Even with five destroyers sweeping a path ahead of us all day long we only searched 3,600 square miles with sonar—about three percent of the area the planes covered.

While on that duty, his Task Group performed the unique feat of boarding and capturing the *U-505*, and then brought it home to be an exhibit in a Chicago park.

The Destroyer Escort was needed badly not only in those "hunter-killer tactics" but also for regular convoy duty. The regular de-

THE "RACE FOR TONNAGE:" SINKINGS VS. NEW CONSTRUCTION, 1942-45

(Thousand gross tons; number of ships in parentheses) For 1939-41, see p. 247)

	Ships Built U.S.	Total Allied Losses	Sinking: By Areas — No. Atl.	So. Atl.	Med.	Ind. O.	Paci-fic	U-Boats Built	U-Boats Lost	War Risk Insurance — G.B. West	Australia Via Pan.	Australia Direct
1942												
Jan.	131 (16)	419 (106)	290	—	6	46	71	(20)	(3)	7.50	10.00	10.00
Feb.	206 (28)	679 (154)	431	—	19	38	181	(18)	(2)	..	6.00	6.00
Mar.	194 (26)	834 (273)	549	13	19	68	183	(19)	(6)	..	9.00	..
Apr.	267 (36)	674 (132)	445	48	12	153	16	(23)	(3)	10.00	12.00	..
May	416 (56)	705 (151)	635	9	21	22	31	(20)	(4)	..	..	..
June	504 (67)	834 (173)	626	26	59	90	31	(23)	(3)	..	..	7.50
July	524 (71)	618 (128)	503	23	..	47	1	(18)	(11)	..	..	..
Aug.	499 (68)	661 (123)	508	35	110	..	..	(20)	(9)	..	20.00	..
Sept.	604 (89)	567 (114)	475	57	1	30	13	(17)	(10)	..	25.00	..
Oct.	599 (84)	637 (101)	412	148	..	63	..	(23)	(16)	..	17.50	..
Nov.	691 (94)	807 (134)	515	58	102	131	13	(17)	(13)	..	..	..
Dec.	776 (124)	348 (73)	271	43	5	28	—	(26)	(5)	..	12.50	6.00
1943												
Jan.	647 (106)	261 (50)	188	16	47	15	9	(18)	(6)	..	..	..
Feb.	792 (132)	403 (73)	293	21	52	62	19	(19)	(19)	..	..	..
Mar.	1,005 (140)	693 (120)	477	61	86	43	6	(23)	(15)	..	..	..
Apr.	1,076 (159)	344 (64)	245	7	13	28	35	(23)	(15)	..	..	..
May	1,174 (179)	299 (58)	165	40	32	67	33	(22)	(4)	..	..	..
June	1,119 (167)	123 (38)	18	11	24	97	1	(25)	(17)	..	..	5.00
July	1,125 (165)	365 (36)	124	64	80	46	..	(26)	(37)	6.20	10.00	4.22
Aug.	1,177 (172)	119 (25)	10	15	43	39	4	(21)	(25)	..	7.22	..
Sept.	1,116 (167)	156 (29)	43	10	52	25	9	(21)	(10)	4.00	5.00	4.00
Oct.	1,117 (167)	139 (29)	56	4	45	29	7	(26)	(26)	..	..	..
Nov.	1,169 (169)	144 (29)	36	4	67	31	6	(25)	(20)	..	4.00	..
Dec.	1,466 (219)	168 (31)	53	—	83	..	..	(28)	(8)	3.00	..	3.00
1944												
Jan.	908 (131)	130 (26)	43	..	31	56	..	(21)	(15)	..	..	..
Feb.	959 (148)	116 (23)	16	..	36	64	..	(19)	(20)	2.50	..	2.50
Mar.	1,113 (163)	157 (25)	36	4	40	75	..	(23)	(25)	2.00	3.00	2.00
Apr.	1,156 (161)	82 (13)	34	13	34	..	..	(20)	(21)	..	..	..
May	1,115 (162)	27 (5)	..	17	10	..	..	(19)	(22)	..	..	..
June	1,034 (154)	104 (26)	79	3	2	19	..	(15)	(25)	1.50	2.50	..
July	931 (113)	178 (17)	34	14	..	30	..	(15)	(25)	1.25	2.00	..
Aug.	855 (124)	118 (23)	60	..	1	57	..	(20)	(32)	..	1.50	1.50
Sept.	927 (127)	44 (8)	37	..	1	5	7	(12)	(18)	..	..	1.00
Oct.	1,043 (168)	11 (4)	1	..	2	..	7	(17)	(12)	1.00	..	..
Nov.	1,144 (159)	37 (9)	16	..	2	..	..	(22)	(7)	.75	1.25	..
Dec.	1,073 (156)	134 (26)	91	..	1	14	43	(30)	(13)	..	..	..
1945												
Jan.	927 (121)	82 (18)	75	..	..	..	7	(29)	(12)	..	..	..
Feb.	945 (125)	95 (26)	80	7	..	7	..	(25)	(22)	..	..	..
Mar.	921 (128)	111 (27)	107	3	..	..	..	(25)	(26)	..	..	..
Apr.	756 (103)	104 (22)	81	..	..	..	22	(7)	(56)	..	..	..
May	791 (113)	17 (4)	9	..	..	..	7	(1)	(36)	.50	.87	.75

SUMMARY

	SHIPS BUILT U.S.	TOTAL ALLIED SINKINGS	NORTH ATLANTIC (INCL. G.B.)	SOUTH ATLANTIC	MEDITER-RANEAN	INDIAN OCEAN	PACIFIC OCEAN
1939	242 (28)	755 (221)	705 (212)	49 (8)	—	1 (1)	—
1940	449 (54)	3991 (1059)	3599 (999)	55 (6)	64 (13)	173 (24)	99 (15)
1941	804 (103)	4328 (1299)	3161 (846)	133 (29)	501 (158)	73 (20)	458 (246)
1942	5411 (760)	7799 (1664)	5686 (1097)	464 (75)	365 (73)	724 (205)	550 (214)
1943	13024 (1949)	3220 (997)	2006 (309)	258 (43)	635 (137)	486 (82)	132 (76)
1944	12257 (1786)	1045 (205)	453 (108)	52 (9)	159 (30)	322 (50)	57 (8)
1945	7732 (1097)	438 (105)	356 (92)	10 (2)	14 (2)	8 (3)	48 (6)
TOTAL	39919 (5777)	21570 (5150)	15688 (3663)	1024 (174)	1740 (413)	1789 (385)	1347 (315)

CAUSES OF SINKINGS

	SUBMARINES	AIRCRAFT	MINES	WARSHIP RAIDER	MERCHANT RAIDER	"E-BOATS"	UNKNOWN & OTHER
1939	421 (114)	2 (10)	262 (78)	61 (15)	—	47 (23)	7 (4)
1940	2186 (471)	580 (192)	509 (201)	96 (17)	366 (54)	58 (29)	203 (101)
1941	2171 (432)	1017 (371)	230 (111)	201 (40)	226 (44)	71 (23)	421 (272)
1942	6266 (1160)	700 (146)	104 (51)	130 (31)	194 (30)	15 (6)	323 (223)
1943	2586 (463)	424 (76)	108 (37)	7 (1)	41 (5)	26 (13)	43 (10)
1944	773 (132)	120 (19)	95 (28)	—	—	10 (5)	21 (12)
1945	281 (56)	44 (6)	93 (28)	—	—	—	8 (10)
TOTAL	14687 (2828)	2889 (820)	1406 (534)	498 (104)	829 (133)	229 (99)	1029 (632)

Adapted from the following sources: U.S. Shipbuilding, G. J. Fischer, Statistical Summary of Shipbuilding under the U.S. Maritime Commission during World War II, p. 40; sinkings from S. W. Roskill, The War at Sea, II, p. 486; III, pt. 1, p. 389; III, pt. 2, p. 479 (totals differ slightly in Morison); submarines built and lost, S. E. Morison, History of U.S. Naval Operations in World War II, X, p. 366; war risk insurance rates compiled from cargo rates established by the American Cargo War Risk Reinsurance Exchange, in New York Journal of Commerce.

stroyers' expensive equipment for their high speed of 33 knots was wasted in convoy duty, even had there been enough of them to go around. Their faster mobility, moreover, was essential to operations elsewhere. Convoys averaged barely 10 knots. To the uninitiated, the DE looked little different from the DD. But the DE made less of a demand upon critical materials and precious construction hours; it could be built more quickly; and with its lower speed was far cheaper, at about $5,500,000, than the wartime DD at about $8,000,000. Yet the DE was nearly as large, and its 20-knots were sufficient for chasing submarines away from the slow convoys and keeping up with the CVE in the "hunter-killer" group. It could, moreover, stand the gruelling work of the North Atlantic, for which the old 110-foot subchaser and the newer 175 patrol craft were too small.

Unfortunately there was shameful delay in producing DEs, which can be laid at the doors of the Navy's policy advisers in Naval Operations and the General Board. For years there had been a vague realization of the need for some sort of escort vessel, cheaper than the fast destroyer, yet tough enough to stand Atlantic gales. But now with ships being sunk by the hundred out in the Atlantic, the masterminds of the Navy, moved by considerations of perfectionism and economy, turned down one proposal after another. Later Admiral King was to say angrily that they were "bickering about details of displacement, speed, and armament, and behaving as if time were of no consequence." Action finally came through Captain (later Vice-Admiral) Edward L. Cochrane, a naval constructor, who would become the head of the Navy's whole construction program. He designed the DE; and the General Board turned it down. Thereupon he pulled enough wires to have the British request a hundred of them. With a strong push from Under Secretary James Forrestal, Cochrane's bold action ultimately led to the first of the DEs in February, 1943. In 1940, the Navy had only 225 DDs, but by the end of the war, there were 373, and 365 DEs in addition.

Whereas the Destroyer Escort represented in general both a type and function long in use, the function of the Escort Carrier was the new concept of giving continuing air protection to convoys. This made it of prime importance in the "hunter-killer" tactics of the antisubmarine warfare, particularly in the deadly "Greenland Air Gap." The British had already been experimenting with converted vessels, and now the United States followed a similar course with the Escort Carriers. Known popularly as the "baby flattop" or the "jeep carrier", the CVE was a far cry from the big CVs of the *Essex* class, which were developing an important new role in the Pacific warfare. The CVE measured some 7,880 tons to the 27,000 of the *Essex*; carried only 28 planes to 103 on the *Essex*; and its speed was 17 knots as against 33. The big ships, needed for the new "fast carrier task forces" in the Pacific, simply could not be spared for Atlantic antisubmarine work.

In 1940, one lone CVE, the *Long Island*, was launched, but not until the summer and fall of 1942 did these new "jeep carriers" begin to join the fleet in force. Four of them had been converted from four-year old tankers and appeared in August and September. They were followed closely, also from the Seattle-Tacoma Yard, by the *Bogue*, *Card*, and *Core*, which were to be the first CVEs in American action in the North Atlantic. The planes of the early Escort Carriers were the Avengers and Wildcats.

In the meantime, scientists had been rushing to complete some valuable new devices in connection with antisubmarine warfare. Probably the most significant was the small microwave radar for search planes. At any rate, Hitler and Admiral Doenitz blamed it for the sudden reversal in their U-boat successes in the spring of 1943. Radar itself was almost a complete novelty when the war started and it had taken a while to overcome the initial skepticism. Besides, the early plane radar equipment had given off certain emanations, which the Germans had ingeniously been able to detect, giving their submarines the chance to evade aerial searchers. But that new ten centimeter (4-inch) microwave radar did not betray its presence and the unsuspecting surfaced submarine had little chance to escape the search plane swooping down through the clouds.

While that microwave was aiding the CVE planes, further developments of sonar or asdic, as the British called it, enabled surface vessels, DD or DE, to follow the movements of submerged U-boats, but not, of course, over as wide a range as the search planes.

A further device, already in use, but in process of being improved, was the shore-based High-frequency Direction-finder (nicknamed Huff-Duff). This was able to plot the bearings from distant submarines. Then daily from Washington and London warnings went out to the convoy commanders of the presence of enemy U-boats in their vicinity. The Germans, too, maintained remote control over their submarine movements. Admiral Doenitz could even take over the direction of a wolf-pack attack from his headquarters in a chateau at Lorient in France. So much depended in this war on the efficiency of scientific devices, that the competition was close and strenuous in the laboratories of both Germany and the Allies. When the Germans, for instance, invented an acoustic torpedo that would track down the sound of a ship's propeller, the Allies quickly countered with the "Fix", strips of metal towed behind a ship so noisily that the enemy torpedo would be attracted to them and not to the propeller.

The new "hunter-killer" tactics and the searching devices were to be most effective against the U-boats from the Germans' first encounter with them, when their "wolf packs" were raiding what seemed to be easy convoy targets in the "Greenland Air Gap". This action on May 5, 1943, called "the climax of the Battle of the Atlantic", proved the tide had turned against the Germans. The CVEs were not yet at hand, but the combination of the new radar and the "Huff Duff" enabled seven convoy escorts, aided by the arrival of two Antisubmarine Support Groups, to drive off an attack of 15 U-boats which had threatened to annihilate that convoy. Before the month was out, 41 U-boats had been sunk.

With such North Atlantic losses, Admiral Doenitz decided to change his scene of operations to safer waters. This was not the first time he had done so. Back in 1942, it will be recalled, when the Allied coastal convoys had checked the sinkings off the American east coast, he had shifted his attack with deadly effect to the Gulf of Mexico, the Caribbean, and eventually to the Trinidad-

Brazil area. (See Chapter XI, pp. 267ff.) That was why the war risk insurance rates from New York to Australia via the Panama Canal in August 1942 reached the abnormal height of 25%, when the rates were only 7½% from San Francisco to Australia direct.

The safer waters to which Doenitz now set his course were southward to the vicinity of the Azores. But he found even there he was outmaneuvered. As one authority put it: "for rapidity of tactical innovations, operations during the next three months by groups centered on the escort carriers *Bogue*, *Card*, *Core*, and *Santee* in support of Central Atlantic convoys are virtually unsurpassed in naval history."

The British, too, with their similar devices, were running up a heavy score. Their largest killing came in the Bay of Biscay through which the Germans had to make their way to the open sea. They caught some U-boats there in May 1943, and then got nine more in the "Big Bay Slaughter" in late July. Altogether in the war, the British sank about twice as many U-boats as the Americans.

With even the Azores too hot, Doenitz moved his offensive still farther afield to the Mediterranean and the Indian Ocean. But vessels on those sea lanes, too, were no longer easy prey. His triumphant raiding of Allied shipping was coming to an end. The statistics of the comparative sinkings on each side were now increasingly gloomy for Germany. While the sinkings of Allied vessels in the North Atlantic in the second half of 1943 dropped from 1,386,000 to 323,000 tons, those in the Mediterranean rose from 257,000 to 377,000 tons and in the Indian Ocean rose slightly from 257,000 to 269,000. By 1944, however, the sinkings of U-boats had increased so sharply that Doenitz even considered calling in all his U-boats, but he knew Hitler would not stand any such admission of defeat.

Just as it took courage of the highest order for Allied merchant seamen to venture out into the Atlantic in the earlier years of the war, it now took similar stamina in the later years for German submarine officers and crews to face the "hunter-killers". The statistics show that in the sinkings of merchantmen more than half aboard (53.7%) survived, but when a U-boat was lost, only rarely were there any survivors. Altogether, the rival seaborne forces were about equally deadly. It has been estimated that about 30,000 British and American merchant officers and seamen and about 30,000 German submarine officers and seamen lost their lives.

In World War I, the problems of seaborne supply of military-naval operations, it will be recalled (see Chapter XI), had not weighed heavily upon the United States Navy or upon American shipping authorities. The Navy's role had been largely one of safeguarding the movement of troops and supplies across the Atlantic, a task which they had performed with remarkable effectiveness. The shipping authorities likewise were not overburdened because there were relatively few American ships suitable for the purpose. The Hog Islanders came along too slowly to be of much use and most of the troops and supplies moved in British or other foreign bottoms. The Army, to be sure, had had some practice in transporting and supplying the two million men of its American Expeditionary Force, but its task was eased by the well-appointed maritime bases in England and France, particularly at Brest.

Logistics were to be a very different story in World War II. There would be extensive operations in both the Atlantic and Pacific, and the Navy this time would have to conduct some very ambitious campaigns of its own. It is naturally good strategy to keep the enemy away from one's own shores, but the corollary to that is that a tremendous amount of shipping is necessary to support distant operations. In the eighteenth century, warlike material was not too bulky, but with the modern developments of the mid-twentieth century, that had entirely changed. If one has seen, for example, a single packaged five-inch shell and realizes how many thousand are shot away in an hour in even a moderate operation, or if one visualizes the cubic space required for the transport of trucks and tanks, some of the colossal new demands upon shipping may be appreciated.

Also, the distance at which the fighting of World War II had to be waged meant an extra heavy demand. According to Admiral Nimitz, the Commander-in-Chief in the Pacific, more time was spent fighting distance than in fighting the Japanese. Another delaying factor was the slowness of the "turnaround," the shipping term for the time it takes to carry a cargo out, to unload, and to get back for another load. In the Atlantic, this was not too bad, provided that the ports were not too crowded or damaged by bombing. But out in the Pacific, these transatlantic figures had to be more than doubled. Against the 3,000-miles to Europe, it was more than 6,000 miles from San Francisco to Melbourne and pretty much of that distance to the outer islands. By the time the United States entered the war, moreover, there was scarcely a port on the continent of Europe or in the far Pacific, except Australia and New Zealand, which was not in enemy hands, or else wholly undeveloped. To offset that lack of facilities, a transport was sometimes kept on hand as a sort of floating warehouse. This practice was one that had to be curbed since it detained the vessel from use elsewhere.

Another difficulty was that "logistics" was almost an unknown subject to the Navy. The Army had had some experience in World War I, but the Navy lacked both experience and an open mind, for its fighting men had always regarded the supply function as something beneath them. The lips of the early line officers were apt to curl when they uttered the word "paymaster".

Now faced with supporting extensive and expensive operations thousands of miles away, they rose to the emergency in magnificent fashion. Two outstanding techniques that might well be called "secret weapons" were of utmost importance in the war, particularly in the Pacific. One of these, "Magic", was the Navy's ability to decipher the codes of intercepted Japanese despatches, including those with the plans for the Pearl Harbor attack. The other, in the logistics field, was developed a few years before the war. In the old days, especially after the introduction of steam, the Navy had been tied down to its bases for fuel, supplies, and repairs. At the Washington Naval Conference (1921-22) Japan, reckoning that a fleet could not operate at more than 1,500 miles from its base, had secured the agreement of the Americans and British to fortify no bases closer to Japan than Pearl Harbor and Singapore. Each of these was more than twice the 1,500 miles distance from Japan.

Between the wars, the United States began to meet that problem by developing the practice of fueling at sea. This would have been an extremely difficult and backbreaking problem in the days of coal, but experiments showed that an oiler (as the Navy called its own tankers) could travel alongside one or two warships and re-plenish their oil through a pipeline. The process took expert ship handling, of course, which the Navy could furnish in quantity. It was of inestimable value with the dearth of Pacific bases and the distances.

With the coming of war after Pearl Harbor, the Navy began to appreciate the neglected subject of logistics, and to meet its prob-lems with the usual effective Navy versatility. At that time, it was caught with a scant supply of tankers and freighters, for the pro-jected North African landings were absorbing a large amount of the available tonnage. This was particularly felt in the Solomons opera-tions, which had to be improvised on a shoestring. This shortage had its effect on tactical developments for a while. Admiral Ghormley at Noumea had to do what he could with increasing demands and short supply.

Even that early in the fall of 1942, the United States was begin-ning to realize the difference between the Atlantic and Pacific war theatres so far as submarines were involved. For some reason, for which the United States should be grateful, Japan failed to utilize the commerce-destruction potential of its submarines. In the first weeks of the war only, Japan's submarines had shown some activity off the West Coast; but that was all. Thereafter, American shipping was relatively unmolested. Had Japan sent occasional wolf-packs into the sea route between the West Coast and Hawaii, and then on into outer areas, it would have made the American logistical problems far more difficult.

Instead, the Japanese submarines were used to pick off American warships, including some important ones. But aside from that, Japan wasted them in supplying the garrisons on Truk and other islands. Japan was apparently unaware that they were not going to be attacked, but left to "wither on the vine." Except for the initial months of the Japanese spread of power, their sinkings of merchant vessels were negligible. From February 1942 to the end of the war, only 53 Allied ships were sunk in the whole Pacific. By thus being able to obviate rigid, slow convoys, the American logistical problem was greatly lessened.

At the same time, the American submarines, mines, and planes were doing to the Japanese freighters and tankers what the Germans had been trying to do to Allied shipping in the Atlantic.

ALLIED AND JAPANESE MERCHANT SHIPPING SUNK IN THE PACIFIC
(Thousand Gross Tons)

	Allied Shipping	Japanese Shipping
1942	550	1,065
1943	132	1,820
1944	57	3,892
1945	48	1,782
	789	8,560

Japan had 6.0 million tons of merchant shipping at the time of Pearl Harbor; at the end of the war, this had been cut to 1.4 million; new construction had amounted to only 3.2 million. Like Britain an island kingdom, Japan was exceptionally vulnerable to having its water-borne supplies sunk by its enemies. In fact, in 1945 the American naval authorities urged—but in vain—that the projected invasion, with its very heavy potential casualties, or the drastic use of an atomic bomb were unnecessary because the submarine-air attacks were already rendering Japan impotent.

The tide of war shifted in the Pacific after the Navy had beaten off the Japanese in the Solomons. Its new strategy was to work out its approach to Japan from island to island across the Pacific. General MacArthur, at the same time, would be "climbing the ladder" northward from Australia. In this "island-hopping," some were taken over by the Navy, and others deemed a lesser threat to its progress were by-passed. That plan confused the enemy and caused them at times to waste supplies and arms on the wrong islands. The "island-hopping" led to the policy of advance bases, preferably in safe atolls.

The lack of regular port facilities faced the Navy as one of its most serious problems, as it began its "island-hopping" advance across the Pacific. There were no adequate ready-made ports beyond the great base at Pearl Harbor until New Zealand and Australia. Consequently, the Navy showed real ingenuity in its development of successive improvised bases as it moved westward. In many cases these advance bases were located on coral atolls, which had space enough to accommodate large numbers of ships, and had entrances narrow enough to give protection against possible enemy submarine attack. So it was that places few people had ever heard of before the war—Bora Bora, Funafuti, Kwajalein, Manus, and Majuro—were eventually providing services rivalling those of a regular navy yard or base at home. These bases received and stored for distribution the cargo items—"beans, bullets, and black oil"— brought out from America generally in normal merchant shipping. These supplies were transferred to naval vessels that would carry them to the fleet at sea. In addition, these bases were able to carry on fairly complicated repair work. Thus a combatant vessel would not have to waste time in having to go back to Pearl Harbor or the West Coast yards.

With those advance bases in operation, shipping in the Pacific fell into two not very clear-cut categories. Ordinary Liberty Ships, tankers, and other merchantmen could safely bring out the needed supplies from the West Coast or from the East Coast through the Panama Canal. For the most part, these merchant ships had been allocated for the specific purpose by the War Shipping Administration. (See Chapter XI, p. 340.) They would be returned to the latter for possible reallocation for other duties. They were wholly under civilian control and their crews were under the control of the American maritime unions, which were determined to preserve their new rights. There was a sour episode when, with marines ashore in dire need for the cargo aboard ship, the crew stopped unloading and quit work at four in the afternoon—according to their union rules. Word of that almost led to the Navy's putting all merchant crews into uniform and under naval discipline, but prominent Labor leader Sidney Hillman helped to prevent that extreme action through his White House influence.

In order to carry the material beyond those new bases to the fleet the Navy took over a large number of vessels of merchant type, commissioning them and manning them with naval officers and crews. They were designated with the conventional "A" for auxiliary. Closest to the normal merchant marine status were the cargo transports (AKs). These differed little from the usual Liberty Ship, except that they now sported a crew some three times the size of their original 45. Likewise, some of the liners taken over were designated as transports (APs). But these vessels seldom were close to the shooting.

For actual work at close range two further types, the attack transports (AKA and APA), were developed. The second "A" stood for attack. These were designed for "combat loading," which meant that a ship's cargo destined for a combat zone would be punctiliously arranged, so that what was needed first was located where it could be unloaded first, and so on. This orderly packing was something that merchant liners, serving several ports, had long practiced. The military importance of "combat loading" was shown early in World War I by the disastrous blundering of the British in the Gallipoli-Dardenelles campaign. Their transports arrived with cargoes so badly jumbled that an artillery battery might find its guns far down in the hold of one ship, its caissons in another, its ammunition in a third, and its horses in a fourth. With no docking facilities at the scene, the ships had to cross the Mediterranean to Egypt and spend weeks sorting and repacking. Planned as a surprise attack on the Gallipoli peninsula, all elements of surprise were lost between the delays and enemy spy activity. When the eventual attack came, the reinforced defenses inflicted terrific losses on the landing forces. The AKA was a cargo ship and the APA carried troops, landing craft, and such equipment as might be needed first.

Among other merchant types commissioned in the Navy were the "oilers" (AO), tankers that were equipped for fueling at sea, and smaller gasoline tankers (AOG); the ammunition ships (AE), likewise equipped for transferring munitions at sea, as were the Store ships (AF) also. These were regular full-time commissioned ships in the Navy, commanded and manned by Navy men. Most numerous of those categories were the 227 APA's, followed by 123 AP's, 114 AK's, 108 AKA's, 92 AO's, 62 AOG's, 40 AF's, and 18 AE's. The Army had wanted similar allocation of merchantmen for its own use, but the War Shipping Administration insisted on granting ships only for a specific operation, after which they returned to WSA for reallocation.

In addition to those primarily merchant types, the Navy also carried some cargo in their landing craft. Designed primarily for getting men and material onto a hostile shore without regular port facilities, some of the larger ones, which could cross the ocean under their own power, could be used for long hauls. This was particularly true of the roomy LST (Landing Ship, Tank) which often carried many other cargo items beside tanks.

For the Navy's operations across the Atlantic, the situation was somewhat different from that with the Pacific's coral atolls. Once an area was seized from the enemy, whether it was North Africa, Italy, or Normandy, it did not take long for the Allies to put conventional, well-equipped seaports back into shape. For the initial landings, obviously, these facilities aided the enemy in fighting off the Allied attacks. Britain's ports were available still, though overcrowded and in some cases badly damaged. As comparatively nearby "jumping-off" places they were a definite asset.

The most elaborate procedure was needed in the build-up for the Normandy landings in the spring of 1944. For more than a year, men and military supplies had been pouring into England; and this called for a huge amount of tonnage, both naval and merchant shipping. The demand for vessels started with the transportation in January 1942 of 4,000 Army and Air Force troops and 411 tons of military cargo. It rose to 241,000 men and 2,179,000 tons by the end of that first year of American participation in the war. By the end of 1943, it had increased to 918,000 men and 7,943,000 tons; and by May, 1944, the month of the Normandy invasion, 1,071,000 men and 14,050,000 tons. Unlike the Pacific situation, these had had to be brought across the sub-infested Atlantic, still dangerous before mid-1943; but instead of Kwajalein and Majuro atolls, their destinations were British ports with normal landing

facilities available despite bombing damage and delaying congestion. This transportation of men and supplies was primarily an
Army (then including Air) problem. The Navy's one function
was to protect their crossing, which it accomplished with a perfect
safety record, as it had done in its similar job in World War I.

For the eventual actual invasion across the Channel to the
Normandy beaches, landing craft rather than conventional vessels
had the task. Artificial harbors had been secretly placed just before
D-Day at the landing beaches, with old ships and other barriers
sunk to give shelter to the invading landing craft. The huge gasoline needs were met by Operation Pluto (Pipeline-under-the-
Ocean).

With the endless demands upon the merchant marine from all
the widely spread operations between the belligerents, it was the
War Shipping Administration that was empowered to determine
and administer priorities among the many rival claimants. As already noted, it had been set up two months after Pearl Harbor with
plenary authority over almost all American seagoing merchant
shipping, with direction of where the vessels should be used and
what cargoes they should carry. In view of the vociferous claims of
the Army's service chief, it was given strong leadership. Its titular
head, Admiral Emory S. Land, a salty naval constructor, also headed
the Maritime Commission. The latter absorbed much of his time
with its remarkable building program and the actual burden of
War Shipping Administration guidance fell upon its Deputy Di-
rector, Lewis A. Douglas, later ambassador to Britain. Both were
able and forceful men and, also very important, both had the ear
of President Roosevelt.

At the highest level of WSA operation came the relations with
projected naval and military operations because of the tremendous
amount of shipping which they required. That availability of shipping became one of the main considerations in determining what
campaigns could be undertaken. At the Casablanca conference in
January 1943, "shipping, including landing craft and escort vessels,
became a major part in the choice between a series of operations
in France, Sicily, Burma, the Pacific." Incidentally, War Shipping

was not invited to the conference—the Army and Navy leaders didn't want to bother with a civilian organization and they showed a lack of grasp of the shipping situation. Thereafter WSA was usually represented by Douglas or someone else who knew the answers and could speak with authority on the logistical possibilities of a proposal. At times special demands for shipping led WSA to reshuffle existing commitments. Early in 1943, for instance, the British, who wanted support for a proposed campaign in Burma

> "presented requests for material that amounted to 263,000 tons of military cargo and 267,000 tons of civilian supplies, and for American shipping to make 113 trips from either the United States or the United Kingdom to India. . . . As a start, twenty additional ships were allocated to sail to India during April, squeezed out of those originally assigned for Panama, Hawaii, the South and Southwest Pacific, and military lend-lease services to Australia and the Middle East. Turn-around time was computed at two and a half times that to the original destinations for these ships, thus meaning a drain equivalent to fifty cargo ships from the pool of shipping available to support other military operations."

In the field of civilian shipping, the War Shipping Administration had worked out an elaborate system of controls. Compared with the situation in World War I, this was rendered practicable as a result of the subsidized fleets which had developed on the essential trade routes. In addition to their large number of vessels, the lines had acquired a "know-how" in ship operation and also had made commercial contacts in most of the important ports in the world. For actual operations, WSA depended upon those private shipping houses. This was of mutual value. The government had the services of the men with the best pertinent experience and the companies were able to keep their shoreside organizations intact, even though the government had taken all their ships.

For the ships actually owned by it, the War Shipping Organization developed the "General Agency Agreement." Each ship was assigned to a particular firm for "husbanding"—that is, management. The firm's marine division would select the officers and attend to the crews, maintenance, and supplying of the vessels, as it did with its own ships in peacetime. Overseas, the company's agents would perform similar services in foreign ports.

At the same time, those same shipping firms entered into a different plan in regard to cargo, which was all under WSA control. A company's traffic division handled the "Berth Sub-agent Agreement" which was linked with a particular overseas region, preferably with the one with which it already had commercial contacts. Thus, Moore, McCormack, whose Scantic Line had had trade with Russia, was to handle all cargo arrangements for the dangerous Murmansk run. Likewise the berth traffic for South and East Africa was to be in charge of the three lines with previous trade relations there—American South African, Robin, and Lykes Lines. Only occasionally did firms handle their own vessels; more and more, they were dealing with the new Liberty Ships as they came off the ways in rapid succession.

In addition to those arrangements, for which the companies received an adequate management fee, the War Shipping Administration sent its own representatives to oversee American shipping and cargo conditions in various foreign ports. The men selected not only knew shipping but could also speak the language. For Murmansk, however, a man could not be found who knew both shipping and Russian. Consequently two men were sent to meet the dual need, but one of them was lost in a convoy attack. The other, unable to function alone, had to console himself with vodka at Murmansk until a replacement arrived.

Priorities were also necessary, of course, in this non-military cargo field. Overriding all other commitments was the agreement to keep Britain fed and provided with steel and other necessities despite the U-boats. There were other nations in need of basic necessities, both in the British Commonwealth and elsewhere among the Allies. The general policy was to do for them what was possible. A sharp scrutiny was kept, however, on all individual shipments and they were carefully examined to be certain just how essential they were.

In various distant regions, cargoes from the United States were beginning to replace material previously brought from other countries. For example, its share of Australia's imports jumped from 13% in 1938 to 48% in 1953; in New Zealand, the rise was from 12% to 36%; and in Brazil, from 30% to 61%. One exception was the Argentine, where British ships went regularly for meat. In Africa, "South of Sahara," American exports more than trebled during the war and went on to still higher levels afterwards.

In the spring of 1943, as the Battle of the Atlantic was reaching its dramatic turning point, the tremendous American shipbuilding program was outstripping the sinkings. It had gone ahead briefly in September, 1942; relapsed in October and November; and then went into a steadily increasing ascendancy. In December, 1943, the shipyards hit an all-time high of 219 ships totalling 1,466,000 gross tons; sinkings in that month were only 31 ships at 168,000 tons. There was no longer concern about keeping Britain supplied with food and other essential imports, although the roomy new ships would all be needed for the mighty 1944 offensives in Normandy and the Far Pacific. Altogether, the Maritime Commission produced 5,777 ships, totalling nearly 40 million gross tons (56 million deadweight).

At the same time, American shipyards were turning out the largest crop of warships in history. Naval tonnage was too diversified to provide comparable statistics, but so far as cost went, the merchant shipping produced in Admiral Land's Maritime Commission program cost 13 billion dollars, while the naval building, under Admiral Cochrane, came to 18 billions, not counting ordnance. Both were regular naval constructors, picked from the top of the class at Annapolis. The more sophisticated and exacting naval construction required the use of the principal regular yards, whereas the merchant vessels had to be put together in improvised new yards. So far as the story of the sea lanes was concerned, the two programs were not entirely distinct, for the destroyer escorts and escort carriers were needed to protect the merchant convoys, while the LSTs and some other landing craft played their part in the final delivery of cargo on hostile shores.

Of all the new merchant shipping, the Liberty Ships (see Chapter XI) had the most significant role. There were 2,708 of them, totalling 29 million deadweight or 19 million gross tons. This was half of the Maritime Commission program. They might be slow, with their 11-knot speed, but their bulky holds met the need for carrying vast amounts of cargo overseas.

As the critical demand for tonnage gradually relaxed, Land and others began to think about the postwar needs of the merchant marine. It was obvious that those slow Libertys would be at a disadvantage in peacetime competition. That led to the Victory Ship, similar in size to the Liberty but equipped with turbines that would give a speed of 16½ knots, almost half again as fast as the Libertys. There was long disputing over the proper type of propulsion, but the first vessel was delivered in February, 1944 and by the end of the war, 414 Victory cargo ships and 117 Victory transports had been built.

With the same concern for the postwar situation, Admiral Land kept up the construction of the regular program C-ships—more tailor-made and expensive than even the Victorys but which would be highly useful in equipping the American lines after the war—altogether, 541 of them were built, chiefly C-2's and C-3's.

In addition to the cargo ships, the Maritime Commission also included some uniform types of tankers, particularly the "T-2." They would become the standard by which postwar tankers would be compared. At the time, their 16,765-ton size and 125,000 barrel capacity was considered a generous size. Twenty years later, however, tankers would have reached more than five times that size—and the ultimate size was not in sight.

CHARACTERISTICS OF PRINCIPAL WARTIME MERCHANT TYPES

(Figures approximate, often varying slightly from ship to ship)

| | TONNAGE | | | | | | | |
	DEAD-WEIGHT	GROSS	NET	LENGTH	BEAM	HORSE-POWER	SPEED KNOTS	COST MILLION $
World War I "Hog Islander"	8,500	5,100	3,100	390	54	2,500	10½	1.7
World War II *Emergency*								
EC-2 "Liberty"	10,400	7,200	4,400	441	56	2,500	11	1.8
VC-2 "Victory"	10,700	7,600	4,500	455	62	8,500	16½	2.5
Standard Types								
C-2	8,800	6,100	4,600	459	63	6,000	15½	2.7
C-3	12,500	8,000	5,700	490	69	8,500	16½	3.6
Tankers								
T-2	16,750	10,700	6,100	523	68	6,000	14½	2.7

Altogether the Maritime Commission program produced three times as many ships as the World War I Shipping Board emergency program, and four times as much tonnage. It also, as mentioned earlier, avoided some of the worst pitfalls of that initial experiment in emergency shipbuilding; its speed of construction was infinitely faster; and its vessels were completed in time to be of invaluable service on all the major wartime routes.

In May, 1945 on the eve of the German surrender (VE Day—Victory in Europe) and three months before the Japanese gave up (VJ Day—Victory over Japan) the increased safety of the sea lanes was being reflected in the war risk insurance quotations. (See Table A.) To the west coast of Britain, they had fallen to 50 cents (per $100.00) from a maximum of ten dollars, and to Australia from New York via Panama to 87 cents from 25 dollars. There were, to be sure, some last minute sinkings. The collier *Black Point* was torpedoed and sunk off southern New England the day before the German surrender. It was characteristic in the Pacific that the final major victim of Japanese submarine attack was not a merchantman but the heavy cruiser *Indianapolis*. She was sunk with a loss of nearly 900 lives. She had just brought across the Pacific to the Marianas the atomic bomb that would be dropped on Hiroshima.

Those two ships were the last to be sunk in open war in this story of America's experience with troubled sea lanes. But with the Russian Navy in recent years rapidly growing in size and aggressiveness, while the British Navy dwindles away, there is no telling how long that fortunate situation may last. Yet in the two Asian major encounters since World War II—Korea in the early 1950s and Vietnam in the mid-1960s—the United States has enjoyed that attribute of command of the sea, the ability to "come and go as one pleases—and to keep the enemy from doing likewise."

Bibliography

To LIST THE THOUSANDS OF WORKS BEARING ON THIS MANY-SIDED SUB-
ject would require a small book in itself. Even to cite all the books
and articles drawn upon in the preparation of this volume would
carry the length beyond reasonable bounds. This bibliography, therefore, will start with a few of the titles that will be most useful in
giving the general reader a background of the broader aspects of
maritime development. It will then indicate the writings most immediately pertinent to the problem in each period, deliberately omitting many valuable general works and sources of illustrative matter.

Newspapers from the various seaport cities have been the most
valuable original sources from the Revolution to the present; particularly useful is the New York *Journal of Commerce* with its invaluable quotations of war-risk rates for the two World Wars. Official
statistical collections, particularly the annual report on *Commerce
and Navigation of the United States,* have been analyzed in detail.
Numerous manuscript records of insurance rates have been consulted
in various repositories, especially the policy files of the Boston Marine
Insurance Company at the Massachusetts Historical Society. The
"Disaster Books" of the Atlantic Mutual Insurance Company contain
colorful accounts of many wartime sinkings. A wealth of detail is
to be found in the New York Public Library's extensive collection
of printed briefs of cases of American vessels tried before the Lords
Commissioners of Appeal in Prize Causes and in Congressional
records of the French Spoliation Claims.

GENERAL

Atherly-Jones, L. A. *Commerce in War* (1907).
Baldwin, H. W. *What the Citizen Should Know about the Navy*
 (1941).
Brodie, B. *Sea Power in the Machine Age* (1941).

Chapelle, H. I. *The History of American Sailing Ships* (1935).
——. *History of the American Sailing Navy* (1949).
Columbia University, Council for Research in the Social Sciences, *Neutrality, its History, Economics and Law*, 4 vols. (1935-36).
Davis, G. T. *A Navy Second to None: the Development of American Policy* (1940).
Emeny, B. *The Strategy of Raw Materials* (1936).
Hutchins, J. G. B. *The American Maritime Industries and Public Policy, 1789-1914* (1941).
Landström, B. *The Ship, an Illustrated History* (1961).
Livermore, S. A. *United States Merchant Shipping Policies and Politics* (1966).
McFee, W. *Watch Below* (1940) (Life in tramp streamers).
Mahan, A. T. *The Influence of Sea Power upon History, 1660-1783* (1890).
Pratt, F. *The Navy, a History* (1938).
Potter, E. B. and Nimitz, C. W. *Sea Power: A Naval History* (1960).
Russell, Sir H. *Sea Shepherds: Wardens of our Food Flocks,* (1941) Convoy system.
Rutter, O. *Red Ensign, a History of Convoy* (1942).
Savage, C. *Policy of the United States toward Maritime Commerce in War*, 2 vols. (1934-36).
Sprout, H. and M. *The Rise of American Naval Power, 1776-1918* (1939).
Villiers, A. ed. *Men, Ships and the Sea* (1962).
Wright, C. and Fayle, C. E. *A History of Lloyd's* (1928).

THE AMERICAN REVOLUTION

Albion, R. G. *Forests and Sea Power, the Timber Problem of the Royal Navy, 1652-1862* (1926, 1965).
Allen, G. W. *A Naval History of the American Revolution*, 2 vols. (1913, 1962).
Brebner, J. B. *The Neutral Yankees of Nova Scotia* (1927).
Clark, W. B. *Lambert Wickes, Sea Trader and Diplomat* (1932).
——. *Ben Franklin's Privateers* (1956).
East, R. A. *Business Enterprise in the American Revolutionary Era* (1938).

Essex Institute, *American Vessels Captured by the British During the Revolution and War of 1812: the Records of the Vice-Admiralty Court at Halifax, N. S.* (1911) (Also in *Essex Inst. Hist. Coll.,* XLV-XLVII).

Gillingham, E. E. *Marine Insurance in Philadelphia, 1721-1800* (1933).

Haldane-Robertson, L. "Some Philadelphia Ships Captured at Jamaica during the Revolution," *American Neptune,* II, 203-08 (1942).

Jameson, J. F. "St. Eustatius in the American Revolution," *Am. Hist. Rev.* VIII, 683-708 (1903).

Kite, E. S. *Beaumarchais and the War of American Independence,* 2 vols. (1918).

Mackesy, P. *The War for America, 1775-1783* (1964).

Martin, G. "Commercial Relations between Nantes and the American Colonies during the War of Independence," *Jour. Econ. & Business Hist.* IV, 812-29 (1932).

Morison, S. E. *John Paul Jones, a Sailor's Biography* (1959).

New York Historical Society Collection. *The Deane Papers, 1774-1790* (1887-90).

Paullin, C. O. *The Navy of the American Revolution: Its Policy and Administration* (1906).

Stephenson, O. W. "The Supply of Gunpowder in 1776," *Am. Hist. Rev.* XXX, 271-81 (1925).

VanTyne, C. H. "French Aid before the Alliance," *ibid.* XXXI, 20-40 (1925).

United States, Naval History Division, *Naval Documents of the American Revolution* (15 vols.), (1964—).

1793-1815

Albion, R. G. "Maritime Adventures of New York in the Napoleonic Era," in *Essays in Modern English History in Honor of Wilbur Cortez Abbott* (1941).

Allen, G. W. *Our Navy in the War with France* (1909, 1967).

Bemis, S. F. *Jay's Treaty, a Study in Commerce and Diplomacy* (1923).

Clauder, A. C. *American Commerce as Affected by the Wars of the French Revolution and Napoleon* (1932).

(Cobb, E.) *Elijah Cobb, 1768-1848, a Cape Cod Skipper,* ed. R. D. Paine (1925).

Coggeshall, G. *Voyages to Various Parts of the World,* (1851ff).

Cranwell, J. P. and Crane, W. B. *Men of Marque: a History of Private Armed Vessels out of Baltimore during the War of 1812* (1940).

Essex Institute, *American Vessels Captured . . .* see previous section.

Forester, C. S. *The Age of Fighting Sail: The Story of the Naval War of 1812* (1956).

Galpin, W. F. "The American Grain Trade to the Spanish Peninsula, 1810-1814," *Am. Hist. Rev.* XXVIII, 22-44 (1922).

——. "The American Grain Trade under the Embargo of 1808," *Jour. of Econ. and Business Hist.* II, 71-100 (1929).

Harrington, V. D. "New York and the Embargo of 1807," *N.Y. State Hist. Assn. Journal,* VIII (1927).

Heaton, H. "Non-Importation, 1806-1812," *Jour. Econ. Hist.* I, 178-98 (1941).

Jennings, W. W. *The American Embargo,* 1807-09 (1921).

Luke, M. H. *The Port of New York, 1800-1810: The Foreign Trade and Business Community* (1953).

Mahan, A. T. *Sea Power in its Relations to the War of 1812,* 2 vols. (1905).

Moore, J. B. *International Ajudications, Ancient and Modern,* Modern Series IV-V (1931-33).

Morison, S. E. *The Maritime History of Massachusetts, 1783-1860* (1921).

Mullins, J. E. "The Liverpool Packet," *Dalhousie Rev.,* XIV, 193-202 (1934).

(Napier, H. E.) *New England Blockaded in 1814; the Journal of Henry Edward Napier, Lieutenant in H.M.S. Nymphe,* ed. W. M. Whitehill (1939).

Olson, M. *The Economics of Wartime Shortage,* (1963).

Picking, S. *Sea Fight off Monhegan: Enterprise and Boxer* (1941).

Pratt, F. *Preble's Boys,* (1950).

Reindehl, J. H. *The Impact of the French Revolution and Napoleon upon the United States as revealed by the Fortunes of the Crowninshield Family of Salem* (1953).

Rubin, L. I. *New York State and the Long Embargo* (1961).

Smelser, M. *The Congress Founds the Navy, 1787-1798* (1959).

Snider, C. H. J. *Under the Red Jack; Privateers of the Maritime Provinces of Canada in the War of 1812* (1928).

Stephens, J. *War in Disguise; or the Frauds of the Neutral Flags* (1805).

United States Office of Naval Records and Library, *Naval Documents related to the Quasi-War between the United States and France,* ed. D. W. Knox, 7 vols. (1935-38).

Zimmerman, J. F. *Impressment of American Seamen* (1925).

PIRATES

Allen G. W. *Our Navy and the Barbary Corsairs* (1905, 1965).

——. *Our Navy and the West Indian Pirates* (1929).

Bradlee, F. B. C. *Piracy in the West Indies and its Suppression* (1923). (Also in Essex Institute Hist. Coll., LVIII-1922).

Cathcart, J. L. *The Captives,* comp. by J. B. Newkirk (1899).

Goodrich, C. F. *Our Navy and the West Indian Pirates, a Documentary History* (1917). (Also in U.S. Naval Inst. Proc. XLII-XLIII, 1916-17).

United States Office of Naval Records and Library, *Naval Documents related to the United States Wars with the Barbary Powers,* ed. D. W. Knox, 7 vols. (1934-45).

Wright, L. B. *First Americans in Africa . . . 1799-1805* (1945).

THE CIVIL WAR

Anderson, B. *By Sea and River: The Naval History of the Civil War,* (1962).

Balch, T. W. *The Alabama Arbitration* (1900).

Boykin, E. C. *Ghost Ship of the Confederacy* (1957). Semmes-*Alabama.*

——. *Sea Devil of the Confederacy* (1959). Maffitt-*Florida.*

Bradlee, F. B. C. *Blockade Running during the Civil War* (1925).

Briggs, H. W. *Doctrine of the Continuous Voyage* (1926).

Chamber of Commerce of the State of New York, *Annual Reports* (1861-65).

Cranwell, J. P. *Spoilers of the Sea* (1941).

Dalzell, G. W. *The Flight from the Flag; the Continuing Effect of the Civil War upon the American Carrying Trade* (1940).

Ginzberg, E. "Economics of British Neutrality during the American Civil War," *Agricultural Hist.,* X, 147-56 (1936).

Hackett, F. W. *The Geneva Award Acts* (1882).

Jones, V. C. *The Civil War at Sea,* 3 vols. (1961-62).

Morgan, M. *Dixie Raider: The Saga of the C.S.S. Shenandoah* (1948).

Ousley, F. L., Jr. *The C.S.S. Florida: Her Building and Operations* (1965).

Robinson, W. M. *The Confederate Privateers* (1928).

Robinton, M. R. *Introduction to the Papers of the New York Prize Court* (1945).

Semmes, R. *Memoirs of Service Afloat* (1869).

United States Department of State, *Correspondence concerning Claims against Great Britain,* 7 vols. (1871). Details of individual victims in vol. VII.

——. *Papers relating to the Treaty of Washington,* 6 vols. (1872-75).

United States Naval History Division, *Civil War Naval Chronology, 1861-1865,* 5 vols. (1962-66).

United States Office of Naval War Records, *Official Records of the Union and Confederate Navies in the War of the Rebellion,* 30 vols. (1894-1922).

West, R. S. *Mr. Lincoln's Navy* (1957).

WORLD WAR I, 1914-1918

Alexander, R. *The Cruise of the Raider Wolf* (1939).

Bailey, T. A. "The Sinking of the Lusitania" *Am. Hist. Rev.* XLI, 54-73 (1935).

Baldwin, H. W. *World War I: an Outline History* (1962).

Beveridge, Sir W. *The British Food Control* (1928).

Consett, M. W. P. *The Triumph of Unarmed Forces* (1923) Neutral leakage.

Cornford, L. C. *The Merchant Seaman in War* (1918).

Cranwell, J. P. *Spoilers of the Sea* (1941).

Crowell, B. and Wilson, R. F. *The Armies of Industry. . . . Our Nation's Manufacture of Munitions for a World in Arms, 1917-1918,* 2 vols. (1921).

——. *The Road to France. . . . The Transportation of Troops and Supplies,* 2 vols. (1921).

Fayle, C. E. *Seaborne Trade (Official History)*, 3 vols. (1920-24).
——. *The War and the Shipping Industry* (1927).
Gleaves, A. *A History of the Transport Service: Adventures and Experiences of U.S. Transports and Cruisers in the World War* (1921).
Grant, R. M. U-Boats Destroyed . . . 1917-1918 (1964).
Hoehling, A. A. *The Last Voyage of the Lusitania* (1956).
Hurd, A. S. *The Merchant Navy (Official History)*, 3 vols. (1921-29).
Hurley, E. N. *The Bridge to France* (1927).
James, H. J. *German Subs in Yankee Waters: First World War* (1940).
Jellicoe, Earl *The Submarine Peril; the Admiralty Policy in 1917* (1934).
Lyddon, W. G. *British War Missions to the United States, 1914-1918* (1938).
Mattox, W. C. *Building the Emergency Fleet; a Historical Narrative of the Problems and Achievements of the United States Shipping Board Emergency Fleet Corporation* (1920).
May, E. M. *The War and American Isolation, 1914-1917* (1959).
Ousley, F. L. Jr. *The Economics of Wartime Shortage* (1963).
Salter, Sir J. A. *Allied Shipping Control* (1921).
Sims, W. S. *The Victory at Sea* (1920).
Smith, D. H. and Betters, P. V. *The United States Shipping Board; its History, Activities and Organization* (1931).
Thomas, L. J. *Count Luckner, the Sea Devil* (1927).
United States Navy Department, Historical Section, *American Ship Casualties* (1923).
——. Office of Naval Records and Library, *German Submarine Activities on the Atlantic Coast of the U.S. and Canada* (1920).

WORLD WAR II, 1939-45

Albion, R. G., Connery, R. H. and Pope, J. B. *Forrestal and the Navy* (1962).
Ballantine, D. S. *U.S. Naval Logistics in the Second World War* (1947).
Behrens, C. B. A. *Merchant Shipping and the Demands of War* (1955).

Campbell, Sir I. and Macintyre, D. *The Kola Run: A Record of Arctic Convoys, 1941-1945* (1958).

Carter, W. R. *Beans, Bullets and Black Oil: The Story of Fleet Logistics in the Pacific in World War II* (1953).

——. and Duvall, E. E. *Ships, Salvage and Sinews of War: The Story of Fleet Logistics in the Atlantic and Mediterranean during World War II* (1954).

Chalmers, W. S. *Max Horton and the Western Approaches: A Biography of Admiral Sir Max Kennedy Horton* (1954).

Churchill, Sir W. S. *The Second World War*, 6 vols. (1948-53).

Conn S. and Fairchild, B. *The Framework of Hemisphere Defense* (1960). *Guarding the U.S. and its Outposts* (1964).

Creighton, W. K. *Convoy Commodore* (1956).

Doenitz, K. *Memoirs* (1959).

Eccles, H. E. *Logistics in the National Defense* (1959).

Farago, L. *The Tenth Fleet* (1963).

Fischer, G. J. et al, *Statistical Summary of Shipbuilding under the U.S. Maritime Commission during World War II* (1949).

Gallery, D. V. *Twenty Million Tons under the Sea* (1956). (U-505 in 1967 paperback ed.)

Gretton, D. W. *Convoy Escort Commander* (1964).

Hall, H. D. *North Atlantic Supply* (1955).

Land, E. S. *Winning the War With Ships* (1958).

Lane, F. C. et al, *Ships for Victory: A History of Shipbuilding under the U.S. Maritime Commission in World War II* (1951).

Leighton, R. C. and Coakley, R. W. *Global Logistics in World War II* (1955).

Lockwood, C. A. *Sink 'em All: Submarine Warfare in the Pacific* (1951).

Macintyre, D. *The Battle of the Atlantic* (1961).

Morison, S. E. *History of U.S. Naval Operations in World War II*, 15 vols. (1947-62).

——. *The Two Ocean War: A Short History of the U.S. Navy in the Second World War* (1963).

Poolman, K. *The Battle of Sixty North* (1958).

Riesenberg, F. Jr. *Sea War: The Story of the U.S. Merchant Marine in World War II* (1956).

Roscoe, T. *U.S. Destroyer Operations in World War II* (1953).

——. *U.S. Submarine Operations in World War II* (1949).

Roskill, S. W. *The War at Sea,* 3 vols. in 4 (1956-61).

——. *The Secret Capture* (1959).

Ryan, C. *The Longest Day,* (1959). The Normandy landings.

Standard Oil Co. of New Jersey, *Ships of the Esso Fleet in World War II* (1946).

United States, Navy Dept. Bureau of Yards & Docks, *Building the Navy's Bases in World War II,* 2 vols. (1947).

Woodward, D. *The Secret Raiders: The Story of the German Armed Raiders in the Second World War* (1955).

Index